Jonnette Watson Hamilton

ADR — 1-5, 13-17, 18, 23-4 27-8
38, 71, 77, 82, 14 117+ 126
210+, 277+, 306+

CT - 16-17

Eg. -70

Rural electr 140+, 307+

Jennifer 316-17

GLOBAL PRESCRIPTIONS

GLOBAL PRESCRIPTIONS

The Production, Exportation, and
Importation of a New Legal Orthodoxy

Edited by
Yves Dezalay
and
Bryant G. Garth

Ann Arbor

The University of Michigan Press

2005   2004   2003   2002   4   3   2   1

A CIP catalog record for this book is available from the British Library.

Library of Congress Cataloging-in-Publication Data

Global prescriptions : the production, exportation, and importation of
     a new legal orthodoxy / edited by Yves Dezalay and Bryant G.
     Garth.
        p.   cm.
     Includes bibliographical references and index.
     ISBN 0-472-11235-X (cloth : acid-free paper)
     1. Law reform.   2. Legal polycentricity.   3. Comparative Law.
   4. Globalization.   5. Law and economic development.   I. Dezalay, Yves,
   1945–   II. Garth, Bryant G.
     K236 .G59   2002
     340'.2—dc21   2001006440

Contents

Introduction   1
Bryant G. Garth and Yves Dezalay

Breaking Out: The Proliferation of Actors in the
International System   12
Anne-Marie Slaughter

Transnational Advocacy Networks and the Social
Construction of Legal Rules   37
Kathryn Sikkink

Modern Law as a Secularized and Global Model:
Implications for the Sociology of Law   65
Elizabeth Heger Boyle and John W. Meyer

What Institutional Regimes for the Era
of Internationalization?   96
Robert Boyer

Between Liberalism and Neoliberalism:
Law's Dilemma in Latin America   139
Jeremy Adelman and Miguel Angel Centeno

Legal Education and the Reproduction of the Elite
in Japan   162
Setsuo Miyazawa with Hiroshi Otsuka

Cultural Elements in the Practice of Law in Mexico:
Informal Networks in a Formal System   209
Larissa Adler Lomnitz and Rodrigo Salazar

The Discovery of Law: Political Consequences in
the Argentine Case   249
Catalina Smulovitz

Hybrid(ity) Rules: Creating Local Law in a
Globalized World   276
   Heinz Klug

Legitimating the New Legal Orthodoxy   306
   Yves Dezalay and Bryant G. Garth

Contributors   335

Index   337

INTRODUCTION

Bryant G. Garth and Yves Dezalay

The rule of law has become a new rallying cry for global missionaries. "Money doctors" selling competing economic expertises continue to be very active on the global plane (Drake 1994), but the 1990s have also witnessed a tremendous growth in "rule doctors" armed with their own competing prescriptions for legal reforms and new legal institutions at the national and transnational levels. The activities of multinational law firms spreading U.S.-style corporate law; constitution writers making new constitutions for newly democratic states; NGOs concerned with protecting the environment, attacking violence against women, and guaranteeing basic human rights; reformers active in legal education and in the judiciaries; and now a new group of fighters against corruption have all begun to gain the attention of academics from inside and outside the law. The World Bank[1] and other major institutions concerned with economic development, such as the Inter-American Development Bank, the Asian Development Bank (Metzger 1997), and the European Bank of Reconstruction and Development, have begun to hire more lawyers and social scientists to build their programs aimed to strengthen the rule of law (see Carothers 1996, 1998, 1999; Dezalay and Garth 2002; Hammergren 1998; McClymont and Golub 2000; Pistor and Wellons 1998; Quigley 1997; Rose 1998).[2]

This is not the first time that we have seen the ascendancy of law among the recipes for state transformation—termed *modernization* in the 1960s and 1970s. The "law and development" movement of that period was a similar effort to export a set of institutions and practices supposed to build the rule of law. The efforts to change the position of law, however, were not very successful at the time. The promised reforms in legal education and legal research—the centerpieces of the efforts—did not take place. Law schools continued to be dominated by part-time professors active in politics, litigation, the judiciary, business, or elsewhere, and legal education continued to be primarily a passive and nonstimulating experience designed more for making contacts than for gaining a deep knowledge of legal technologies. The "failure" of this wave of law and development, as a result, was quite quickly conceded (Gardner 1980; Trubek and Galanter 1974) and built into the conventional wisdom of developmental assistance. The effort to export U.S. models of law failed.

Today, however, national and multilateral agencies are investing much more in the rule of law than they did in the earlier period. There is a greater consensus in favor of this developmental strategy among policymakers and within the academic disciplines that study development. The consensus is furthered by the activities of policymakers in the south who studied law in the United States as part of the first law and development movement, and by numerous individuals from the south who now deem a U.S. degree indispensable for a career in politics, the law, business, or the academy. There are even strong signs of a parallel consensus among both critics and supporters of globalization. While the disagreements are profound between different sides, it is instructive that many of the prominent critics of the World Trade Organization and the World Bank tend to couch their criticisms in terms of procedural changes and expanded opportunities for legal representation of unrepresented groups. Within the World Bank, for example, reformers have pushed for more transparency and a kind of legalized accountability through Inspection Panels "to give those who feel they have been harmed by the Bank a chance to hold the Bank accountable to its own operational policies" (O'Brien, Goetz, Sholte, and Williams 2000: 31).

So far the rule of law industry cannot claim too many successes in the latest campaign. Thomas Carothers, perhaps the leading commentator on the rule of law, notes in his recent book that "the projects have fallen far short of their goals" (1999: 170).[3] Similarly, the Lawyers Committee for Human Rights is turning out one report after another on the limitations of projects promoting judicial reform (e.g., Lawyers Committee for Human Rights 2000). It is difficult to account for these disappointing assessments. The explanations so far proffered by the advocates of reform include the lack of political will within the target countries, the power of entrenched interests, and pervasive corruption (Carothers 1999: 165–77; Hammergren 1998: 270–80). Others suggest the need for more participation by local and global NGOs (Lawyers

Committee for Human Rights 1996). These criticisms and suggestions appear to be supported by many within the World Bank who have participated in these efforts (World Bank 1998). There is a search for "best practices" that will avoid the mistakes of the past, but the momentum for reform continues unabated.

This volume starts with the proposition that, while the demand for the services of experts on the rule of law is increasing, the academic tools for understanding these activities remain relatively undeveloped. We therefore aim to take stock of these academic tools and suggest some approaches for future research. Our primary focus will not be the highly practical one of trying to determine what works and does not work in projects to promote legal institutional reform. For reasons that will become apparent, we are skeptical about efforts at this point to determine the best technologies to achieve desired reforms. We are convinced that it is necessary to go well beyond legal institutions and reforms to understand the position of law and how it is changing. We need to build tools for research that will place legal reform and legal reformers in their broader social context.

The organization of this volume has both a theoretical and a practical justification. The four essays following this introduction suggest different ways to characterize and understand the new orthodoxy that is emerging. The approaches come from law, political science, sociology, and economics. Anne-Marie Slaughter, an international law scholar, seeks to develop a new model for international law that goes beyond the traditional focus on states as the basic actors and creators of law. She highlights the "disaggregated state" and the role of new actors "above, below, beside, and within the state." These actors, she suggests, form networks capable of producing a "transnational consensus on specific rules and approaches." This consensus moves "soft law" into firm principles of international law that focus on various levels of enforcement as well— "primarily among courts and administrative agencies." International environmental law and human rights law exemplify the kind of law produced by these networks—including networks of Supreme Court judges who gather together, exchange ideas, and promote preferred approaches. National actors operating on the international scene therefore help to promote a new emphasis on the law and on particular legal approaches. Slaughter suggests, therefore, that international law scholars must take these actors into account in trying to explain the emergence of new kinds of norms and approaches central to international law.

Kathryn Sikkink, from political science, provides a similar explanation for "the social construction of the rule of law." She focuses on transnational advocacy networks and their role in the creation of norms—which then can transform national behavior. The networks mobilize on behalf of norms and also on behalf of enforcement measures—which leads to a process of legalization. Sikkink thus highlights the importance of law in these transnational political processes that potentially transform national states. At the same time, however, she warns that "hidden power asymmetries" can lead to some problems in these processes, that the strategy of legalization tends to favor some groups over others, and that there are political limits to the processes of legalization. Nevertheless, she highlights the positive impacts that have come from these advocacy networks in developing the issue of violence against women and protecting human rights more generally.

From a sociological perspective, Elizabeth Heger Boyle and John Meyer explore the "global diffusion of the nation-state form (including the modern legal system)" as a feature of global processes of rationalization and universalization. They suggest that this diffusion is not explained by any specific advantages or disadvantages of these forms in particular places. Rather, "they diffuse in ways that have not been predicted by theories that view them as dependent on local or national boundaries of sovereignty." The explanation, they suggest, is that "states maintain their legitimacy through their responsiveness to perceived universal principles. National laws become an important symbol of the acceptance of these perceived principles." Law steps into the shoes of religion in an earlier era.

Robert Boyer, a French economist, examines the same phenomenon from a more critical perspective. He focuses attention on the institutions of regulation—which can be seen as representing a broad conception of the state—and their importance in the future of production. Providing a counterpoint to the previous essays, Boyer highlights the differences in modes of regulation, emphasizing the importance of resisting the importation of institutions that could clash with embedded approaches that allow economies to prosper in particular settings. Too much of a commitment to market forces—put another way, too much investment in a U.S. model—cannot be expected to produce the institutions necessary for other economies to operate effectively.

The four essays described above have brought into focus the international pressures to bolster the position of law as a key authority for legitimating the state and the economy. Anne-Marie Slaughter—an international lawyer—sees a new and emerging international legal community developing norms that will transform the way states are governed. Kathryn Sikkink, from political science, emphasizes the power of transnational advocacy networks and the way that power is translated into legal approaches and laws. Boyle and Meyer take a very different approach, which focuses on the sociology of institutional legitimation and diffusion, but they end up in a similar place. They see long-term trends that lead almost inexorably to importation from the United States and Europe. Countries outside the West rely on approaches developed in key Western countries to provide credibility and legitimacy to their governments both locally and in global arenas. Boyer is skeptical about the consequences of this process, but he does not dispute the trend.

The next part of the book moves from a focus on the construction and exportation of a new legal orthodoxy to the impact of the imported expertises and institutions in particular settings. As suggested above, there has to date been relatively little success in importing institutions supposed to strengthen the core of the law. Commentators have seen little change, for example, in the commitment of faculties of law to the development of new legal technologies oriented toward the United States. The same story is true about efforts to build judiciaries independent from governmental and political party pressures and capable of playing a more pronounced role in regulating the state and the economy. That is not to say, however, that there is no impact from these and other efforts to transform the states of the south in line with the ortho doxies coming from the north.

The impacts differ according to the countries, the expertises, and the positions of the importers and exporters (Dezalay and Garth 2002). As we have documented elsewhere with respect to Argentina, Brazil, Chile, and Mexico, the structures of power in Brazil and Chile have made them more successful in transforming institutions related to both law and economics. We have also shown that economics has been relatively more successful than law and that business law has been more successful than public interest law. In all these places, however, legal education and the judiciaries have been relatively slow to move. Unlike economics, which is a relatively new state expertise, the core institutions of the law have been closely implicated with the state and with the leading families that comprise the state elite. It is easier to generate new institutions outside state power than to refocus long-standing institutional structures with deeply embedded patterns of practices.

The next essay in this volume raises this problem with the rule of law generally in Latin America. Jeremy Adelman, a historian, and Miguel Angel Centeno, a sociologist, combine their disciplines to examine why countries in the region have been unable to combine liberal economics and democratic politics, and they suggest that one of the problems is the position of law. They are skeptical, however, about the impact that the new emphasis internationally on the rule of law will have. In their words:

> The internationalization of the rule of law is not a solution to this dilemma. Our argument is that the precondition for any salutary effect of the internationalization of the rule of law is its nationalization. Lacking a set of institutions to convey the idea and its practice that "ruled and rulers obey the same rules," internationalization threatens to aggravate the uneven national development of the rule of law. Internationalization of law assumes that the rule of the state and its principles have been absorbed by civil society. In Latin America, where state authority was barely consolidated, legal transnationalism can only perpetuate the problems it claims to solve.

Internationally generated imports succeed only where the local situation allows them to be nationalized—made part of indigenous structures and practices. Local histories determine what can be assimilated into local settings and how what is assimilated will affect long-standing local practices.

The essay on legal education and the reproduction of the elite in Japan, written by Setsuo Miyazawa and Hiroshi Otsuka, tells the history of legal education and its role in Japanese governance. The essay well-illustrates some of the pressures for change, including those generated by the authors, but it emphasizes a story of continuity in the bureaucracy, business, the judiciary, and legal education. In all the cases, the connection between law graduates, especially those from the University of Tokyo, and the governing elites in Japan is highlighted. According to Miyazawa and Otsuka:

> It is quite evident that law graduates are hired by the bureaucracy neither as professional lawyers nor for their legal expertise. Ever since the College of Law of Tokyo Imperial University was desig-

nated as the central institution to train future elite bureaucrats, law faculties have been the most competitive departments in nearly all universities. Law graduates are hired essentially because they are considered to be more intelligent than students from other departments. Legal education, particularly that at the University of Tokyo, is playing a decisive role in the reproduction of the elite in Japanese bureaucracy. This does not mean, however, that legal education per se is directly related to the reproduction of the elite. Legal education of elite bureaucrats has not contributed, for instance, to the advancement of the rule of law in Japan.

The authors refer to evidence of change—pressures to increase the number of individuals who can pass the bar examination, reform of administrative procedures, the potential enactment of a "freedom of information" act. Some other consequences include a relative decline in the movement of elite bureaucrats into the management of leading businesses. But the overall theme is resistance to the reform and the ideal of reform promoted in the United States and elsewhere.

The essay on Mexico authored by Larissa Adler Lomnitz and Rodrigo Salazar takes a similar approach, although it highlights the impact of internationalization on the legal profession in Mexico. The focus is on the relative importance of social relations and technical law, with internationalization putting a greater premium on technical law. The consequences can be profound within the state and in the legal profession.

> The introduction of neoliberal policies in the 1980s, the country's admittance into the international market, and the shrinking of the state apparatus have had a clear effect on the educated middle classes and on the previously protected family enterprises. A new group of technocrats (known as the *técnicos*) has appeared and taken command of elite positions within the state apparatus. At the same time, the state apparatus has closed its doors to the traditional middle-level professionals. This has created a division between these traditional practitioners (trained in national universities . . .) and the new "globalized-transnationalized" group, which stands for firms that have teamed up with financial institutions of foreign investors.

At the same time, however, internationalization has transformed the way that the system of informal personal relations operates, but the system itself has been maintained for the most part. To quote Lomnitz and Salazar:

> The new elite bases its practice on strict knowledge of the law and imported technical knowledge of economics and business administration. The traditional lawyers, on the other hand, base their practice not only on their knowledge of Mexican law, but also on informal means, complementing their skills with the traditional administration of social relations. In both cases, a combination of technical formal knowledge and skills regarding the upkeep and use of social relations is needed, but in different proportions. Moreover, the formal knowledge of each group is of a different nature: one based on the internal constitution of Mexico, the other on international practices. Finally, their social networks are based on different social class relations.

Similarly, no one would argue that the major public law school, the National University of Mexico, has changed substantially, or that the courts occupy a different position or are substantially improved. There is change, but it is built on existing patterns.

Catalina Smulovitz focuses her study on the Argentine judiciary, which played a central role at the time of the trial of the Argentine generals in the mid-1980s. She highlights the disappointing aftermath of the trials and the inability of the judiciary to live up to the new expectations. At the same time, however, she notes the pressures that have been generated locally and internationally for a new role. In her summary, she concludes:

> The politicization of the judiciary that can be observed in the Argentine case can also be explained through domestic and general reasons. On the one hand, the recent conversion of the judiciary into a strategic space for decision making in the local political game has transformed it into a valuable arena and has led, therefore, to open and visible partisan political struggles to control it. On the other hand, and in spite of the more scandalous features that have tarnished the politicization of the judiciary in Argentina, recent analyses of court actions have stressed the impact of external polit-

ical variables on judicial decisions. . . . Therefore, although specific local factors explain the particular dynamic of the Argentine case, its development is not foreign to the global process of the judicialization of politics.

The potential new position is consistent with the new importance of legal discourse in political legitimation, but it is also consistent with the long-standing, almost violent political contestation in Argentina (Dezalay and Garth 2002). The courts have become more important actors in this contestation, but there is still relatively little evidence of legal autonomy.

The essay by Heinz Klug on constitution making in the new South Africa concentrates on the international factors and pressures that affected these highly contested national processes. He highlights the importance of international legitimacy and credibility both in the way that private property was protected in the constitution and also in how both national and international factors led to a much greater role for the Supreme Court. As in the contribution by Smulovitz, the ways that international factors relate to existing structures of power are not discussed in detail, but the results in a few key institutions reveal the impacts and the importance of international legitimacy for change at the national level.

The final essay of the book, written by the editors, focuses on the process that generates this potential new legal orthodoxy and the theoretical tools used to study it. It uses the disciplinary approaches seen in this book to suggest the ways that scholars participate in the production of the new orthodoxy. It also highlights the particular way that the law is used and legitimated as part of this process, and it develops a theoretical approach that can complement the other approaches to help understand both the processes and the scholarly role in facilitating them.

NOTES

1. According to a report of the Lawyers Committee for International Human Rights, the World Bank and the Inter-American Development Bank initiated or approved loans totaling over $300 million for judicial reform projects in some twenty-five countries in the five years leading to 1997 (Armstrong, cited in Messick 1997).

2. As Carothers states, "One cannot get through a foreign policy debate these days without someone proposing the rule of law as a solution to the world's troubles" (1998: 95).

3. Juan Méndez agrees: "The judiciaries, and those who lead them, have been particularly resistant to change" (1999: 223).

REFERENCES

Carothers, Thomas. 1996. *Assessing democracy assistance: The case of Romania.* Washington, D.C.: Carnegie Endowment for International Peace.
————. 1998. The rule of law revival. *Foreign Affairs 77,* no. 2: 96–106.
————. 1999. *Aiding democracy abroad: The learning curve.* Washington, D.C.: Carnegie Endowment for International Peace.
Dezalay, Yves, and Bryant G. Garth. 1996. *Dealing in virtue: International commercial arbitration and the construction of an international legal order.* Chicago: University of Chicago Press.
————. 2002. *Global palace wars: Lawyers, economists, and the contest to transform Latin American states.* Chicago: University of Chicago Press.
Drake, Paul, ed. 1994. *Money doctors, foreign debts, and economic reforms in Latin America from the 1890s to the present.* Wilmington, Del.: Jaguar Books.
Gardner, James. 1980. *Legal imperialism: American lawyers and foreign aid in Latin America.* Madison: University of Wisconsin Press.
Hammergren, Linn. 1998. *The politics of justice and justice reform in Latin America: The Peruvian case in comparative perspective.* Boulder: Westview.
Keck, Margaret, and Kathryn Sikkink. 1998. *Activists beyond borders: Advocacy networks in international politics.* Ithaca: Cornell University Press.
Lawyers Committee for Human Rights/Venezuela Program for Human Rights Education and Action. 1996. *Halfway to reform: The World Bank and the Venezuelan justice system.* New York: Lawyers Committee for Human Rights.
Lawyers Committee for Human Rights. 2000. *Building on quicksand: The collapse of the World Bank's judicial reform project in Peru.* New York: Lawyers Committee for Human Rights.
McClymont, Mary, and Stephen Golub, eds. 2000. *Many roads to justice: The law related work of Ford Foundation grantees around the world.* New York: Ford Foundation.
Méndez, Juan. 1999. Institutional reform, including access to justice. In Juan E. Méndez, Guillermo O'Donnell, and Paulo Sérgio Pinheiro, eds., *The (un)rule of law and the underprivileged in Latin America.* Notre Dame: University of Notre Dame Press.

Messick, Richard. 1997. *Judicial reform: A survey of the issues.* Washington, D.C.: World Bank draft.

Metzger, Barry. 1997. Law and development: An essential dimension of government. *Proceedings of seminar in Fukuoka, Japan on Governance: Promoting sound development management,* May 1997, http://www.asiandevbank.org /law/proceedings/1997/governance/governance.htm.

O'Brien, Robert, Anne Marie Goetz, Jan Aart Sholte, and Marc Williams. 2000. *Contesting global governance: Multilateral economic institutions and global social movements.* Cambridge: Cambridge University Press.

Pistor, Katharina, and Philip A. Wellons. 1998. *The role of law and legal institutions in Asian economic development, 1960–1995. Final comparative report. Revised Text.* Prepared for the Asian Development Bank, March.

Quigley, Kevin. 1997. *For democracy's sake: Foundations and democracy assistance in central Europe.* Washington, D.C.: Woodrow Wilson Center Press.

Rose, Carol V. 1998. The 'new' law and development movement in the post–Cold War era: A Vietnam case study. *Law and Society Review* 32:93–140.

Sarat, Austin, and Stuart Scheingold, eds. 1998. *Cause lawyering: Political commitments and professional responsibilities.* New York: Oxford University Press.

Trubek, David, and Marc Galanter. 1974. Scholars in self-estrangement: Some reflections on the crisis in law and development studies in the United States. *Wisconsin Law Review* 1974: 1062–1102.

World Bank. 1998. *Seminar on judicial reform: Lessons from experience.* May 12. Washington, D.C.: World Bank.

Breaking Out: The Proliferation of Actors in the International System

Anne-Marie Slaughter

Anne-Marie Slaughter, a professor of international law at Harvard, examines how international law is changing to accommodate transformations in the global political economy. International law classically applied only to sovereign states and assumed the states were essentially monolithic. In contrast, she observes, the international scene is now populated by proliferating actors and legal norms that cannot be captured by classic international law. Law is no longer the product only of the acts of the sovereign states, but rather of an increasing number of actors. In particular, states themselves are disaggregating into their component parts—courts, regulatory agencies, legislatures, and chief executives—all of whom are taking their place alongside nongovernmental organizations, corporate entities, and actors in the international legal order. Examples now even include supreme courts of different nations exchanging ideas and opinions on constitutional and human rights issues.

This new perspective—quite different from earlier interpretations of the global political economy—can be used both as description and as prescription. As prescription, it serves as a model of how the system ought to operate. The model puts law as the key discourse for legitimating the system and provides for a set of legitimate actors who can produce the law.

Introduction

The central phenomenon transforming both public and private international law in the 1990s is the proliferation of actors in the international system above, below, beside, and within the state. Public international law has witnessed a resurgence of international and supranational organizations as actors in their own right, together with a veritable explosion of nongovernmental organizations (NGOs) advancing their own causes by pushing, challenging, and monitoring states and seeking recognition as autonomous international actors. Parts of states have also joined the fray, from regional, provincial, and even local governments to regulatory agencies, courts, and legislative committees, all interacting with their foreign counterparts in ways that challenge our very conception of the state.

On the private side, multinational corporations, now reborn as transnational corporations (TNCs), bestride a global economy in which state borders are virtually invisible to capital flows and less and less of a barrier to commerce. Globalization seems a virtually inexorable force, which states can accommodate, perhaps regulate, but not stop. The emergence of global economic law has swept away traditional distinctions between public and private international law (many of which have been dissolving for many decades), given rise to customized international dispute resolution systems that coexist with both national and supranational tribunals, and highlighted a new generation of soft law produced, or at least voluntarily adopted, by TNCs themselves.

This proliferation of international actors has both caused and accompanied debates about the decline of the nation-state as a basic organizing unit of domestic and international life. Few developments could be more important for the social construction of international legal rules than a change in the relevant "actors" doing the construction, actors who are themselves constructed both as entities and agents (Meyer and Jepperson 1997). The elemental assumption that states are the sole sources and subjects of international legal rules dictates the scope and content of those rules. To take only one example, international legal rules governing the use of force flow from the state-to-state paradigm of cross-border aggression. The result is Art. 2(4) of the UN Charter, requiring states to "refrain from the use of force in their international relations." In an international legal system in which the rule makers were the individuals—civilians and soldiers alike—directly affected by violence organized for the purpose of defending, splitting, creating, or reshaping a state, the rules would likely look quite different. Obligations might devolve on all leaders of armies, militias, armed bands, or irregular forces, requiring them to use force in any dispute only as a last resort and in conformity with basic guarantees of human rights.

Before abandoning the state and embracing the search for its replacement(s), however, it is important to realize that we have been here before. The 1970s witnessed a flourishing literature on transnational and transgovernmental actors in political science; the age of transnational law dawned a decade earlier in 1958. The same debates about the excessive state-centrism of the analytical frameworks employed by international law and international relations, about allegedly declining state power, about the relationship of transnational actors to the state and to international organizations, and about the nature and strength of transnational society were fully aired. Indeed, Charles Kindleberger announced in 1969 that "the nation-state is just about through as a economic unit" (1969: 207).

So why now again? Is the proliferation of international actors in the 1970s and again in the 1990s simply a function of an unusually (and temporarily) benign security climate created either by a bipolar or unipolar state system? Or was the resurgence of apparent state primacy in the 1980s a temporary reversion that cannot obscure a larger and longer-term trend toward a new global architecture that could take decades or even centuries to achieve?

Such questions will ultimately collapse into deeper assumptions and assertions about the cyclical or teleological nature of history—a debate that far exceeds the scope of this essay. Within a far more limited frame, however, it is instructive to canvass possible reasons for the apparent revival of transnationalism and transgovernmentalism through the 1990s until the present, at least before September 11. A range of factors present themselves: technological, geopolitical, intellectual, and social. Some of these factors bear directly on the social empowerment of actors charged with "making" international rules by shining a spotlight on different areas of international life and interpreting the practices and principles revealed. To the extent that these factors prove to have causal significance, predictions about the social construction of legal rules in the international realm will depend on domestic social trends in powerful countries.

As important as the actors constructing legal rules, however, is the conceptual framework within which that process takes place. The concept of a paradigm shift is overused and consequently disfavored, but what is required in international law is nothing less than a basic rethinking of what "the state" is. The vocabulary of "substate," "suprastate," "nonstate," even "infrastate" actors betrays an inability to escape some ur-conception of a unitary entity in which sovereignty resides, an entity that is actor, unit, building block, network node, or black box in various conceptualizations of the "world" or the "international system." Substitute "government" for "state," meaning executive, administrative, legislative and judicial institutions, and individuals for state "leaders" and "policymakers," and a whole host of new problems and prospects for international politics, economics, and society results. The "state" can no longer be demonized or dramatized as an impersonal force for good or evil. It is as near or far, as competent or bumbling, as transparent or opaque, as are domestically elected, appointed, or imposed government officials. This is a completely obvious point, once made, but the social construction of "the state" as the fundamental actor in international life has proven extraordinarily difficult to dislodge.

Section I briefly describes the perceived explosion of nonstate, substate, suprastate, and infrastate actors in the international system and their impact on public and private international law. Section II presents an overview of earlier literature on transnationalism and transgovernmentalism. In a spirit of sociological self-reflection, section III then offers a discussion of the analysis presented in section I, canvassing a range of possible reasons for the resurgence of these themes in the 1990s, both as the result of empirical differences among the phenomena observed and the interests and incentives of the observers. Section IV concludes with a discussion of the prospects for genuinely breaking the frame of actor-analysis in the international system and global society.

I.   Sharing the Stage: The Nation-State and a Host of New International Actors

The state is out of fashion, or at least out of focus. The 1990s are the age of "the new medievalism," a back-to-the-future model of the twenty-first century. The term was originally coined by Hedley Bull (1977), who described "a secular reincarnation of the system of overlapping . . . authority" characteristic of pre-Westphalian Europe.[1] The 1990s version emphasizes not only the devolution of state power upward to supranational institutions and downward to regional or local governments, but also sideways to a fast-growing array of nonstate actors, both civic and corporate (Mathews 1996; Kobrin 1998). In response, however, the state

itself is changing, disaggregating into its component judicial, administrative, executive, and legislative institutions and thus itself becoming a
multifaceted or perhaps even hydra-headed actor on the international
scene.[2]

A.   Nonstate Actors

1.   NGOs

NGOs exert increasing influence on the making and implementing of
international law in a wide range of issue areas, from human rights and
humanitarian law to environmental law to trade and labor law (Clark
1995; Spiro 1995; Bramble and Porter 1995; Rubinton 1992; Tracy 1994;
Sikkink 1993; Charnovitz 1996; Shell 1996; Grossman and Bradlow 1993;
Strange 1994). They participate in international negotiations, implement international missions, and drive international litigation. They
link up with one another in "transnational issue networks" (Keck and
Sikkink 1995, 1997), creating a "global operating system" that can compensate for state incompetence in many areas (Lipschutz 1992). More
fundamentally, they may be challenging states' hold on their citizens, by
creating "new commonalities of identity that cut across national borders" (Spiro 1995: 45). Their proliferation lies at the root of the "power
shift" away from the nation-state documented by Jessica Mathews
(1996).

The legal implications of the growth of NGOs are only beginning to
be felt. They are making a mockery of the old-fashioned and always
highly stylized image of states as the only or at least the principal actors
in the international system. NGOs seek increasingly formal status in
international organizations and as recognized subjects of international
law. They want litigation rights before international and supranational
tribunals. Further, as Maria Garner (1991) argues, they may require their
own international organizations to coordinate their activities. As they
grow increasingly important and assertive, they pose troubling issues of
accountability either to states or citizens (Spiro 1995: 51–54).

2.   TNCs

On the private side, Peter Drucker argues that multinational corporations are giving way to transnational corporations. Whereas a multinational corporation is a national company with foreign subsidiaries that
replicate the structure and production of the parent, a transnational

corporation produces for a global market through specialized facilities located all over the world (1997: 168). Fittingly enough, the law governing these entities is transnational law, pioneered by Philip Jessup in 1956 and recently defined by Joel Trachtman as "the integrated body of domestic and international law that regulates both private persons and states, competition in both the market for private goods and the market for public goods" (1996: 35).[3] Trachtman argues that the entire discipline of international law has actually been redefined as transnational law (35; see also Koh 1996, 1997, 1998).

TNCs also generate their own law. In addition to a proliferation of voluntary corporate codes of conduct, regulating industries from software to telecommunications to credit cards, they also benefit from and hence often push for uniform standards through organizations such as the International Standards Organization (Roht-Arriaza 1995a, 1995b).[4] They can similarly design their own dispute resolution systems through the use of international commercial arbitration, choosing a site of arbitration and the law governing the dispute (Dezalay and Garth 1996). The generation of such options contributes to a fundamental decoupling of law from either physical territory or a particular polity, in ways that may foreshadow the growing portability of national law in a transnational society (Choi and Guzman 1998).

B. Suprastate and Substate Actors

The new medievalist image owes a great deal to the conceptual fashioning of an alternative international architecture in which individuals become increasingly conscious of multiple identities as members of local, national, regional, and global communities and are prepared to answer to multiple overlapping regulatory authorities empowered by these different communities (see Franck 1996; Kobrin 1998). The leading model of this new architecture is purportedly the European Union, in which an individual can define herself as a Barcelonan, a Catalan, a Spaniard, a Mediterranean, and a European. The Spanish state, in turn, has ceded some of its functions down to Catalonia and others up to Brussels.

Other examples include growing regional consciousness in areas such as the Pacific Northwest in the United States and Canada; the increasing foreign affairs activity of the states of the United States, not only on trade issues but also concerning traditional national security concerns (Shuman 1986–87, 1991), the visions of many Quebecois of a sovereign Quebec participating in North American regional affairs through NAFTA, and the revitalization of regional organizations from Latin America to Africa to East Asia. In many ways the growth of sub- and suprastate actors depends on one another, as the two ends of a channel of communication and authority that bypasses the nation-state.

C. Infrastate Actors: Government Networks

The proliferation of actors above, below, and beside the state is sup-posed to spell the death, or at least the serious decline, of state power (Ohmae 1995; Wriston 1993; Schmidt 1995), not only because the state can no longer police its borders, but more fundamentally because the information technology revolution means that networks are displacing hierarchies as the organizational form of the future (Mathews 1996). Yet governments, it is argued, are hopelessly hierarchical. They are thus consigned to imminent obsolescence in a globally networked world.

A closer look at the nature of recent state activity, however, reveals that governments are disaggregating into their component institutions and forming transgovernmental coalitions. The same institutions that make and execute laws and regulations and resolve disputes in domes-tic affairs are increasingly performing the same functions in interna-tional affairs. Moreover, they are interacting with their foreign counter-parts to perform these functions, transnationally as well as nationally, or simply to improve their performance nationally (Slaughter 1997, 2000b, 2000c; Risse-Kappen 1995a; Picciotto 1997).

The result is government networks. Global rule of law norms are increasingly being constructed through transgovernmental legal rela-tions, primarily among courts and administrative agencies. National courts are participating in transgovernmental judicial networks to an ever greater degree, both informally and through regional judicial orga-nizations such as the Organization of the Supreme Courts of the Amer-icas. On the administrative side, central bankers, securities commis-sioners, antitrust officials, environmental regulators, and trade officials are working actively with their foreign counterparts to create transgov-ernmental regulatory networks and organizations designed to imple-ment common solutions to domestic problems that have spilled over national borders. These networks and organizations are prime sites for competition over national legal rules and frameworks for defining and addressing these problems. They are also sites for interaction between members of international institutions—courts and regulatory institutions—and domestic officials.

These networks produce a tremendous cross-fertilization of ideas and the gradual evolution of a transnational consensus on specific rules and approaches that can then be formally implemented as international treaties and/or national statutes. In addition, these transgovernmental networks offer considerable opportunities for the socialization of national judges and regulators as members of "rule of law communities" (Helfer and Slaughter 1997: 366–70; Slaughter 2000c), through the transmission and reinforcement of metanorms such as judicial independence, regulatory transparency, and public participation.

The emergence of government networks has potentially enormous implications for the social construction of international legal rules. The addition of infrastate actors to the above roster of actors holds out the prospect of supplanting rather than merely supplementing the state, although without abandoning the coercive core at the heart of state power. The result could be deep changes in the rule-initiation, rule-making, and rule-enforcement processes in the international system, through the transformation of the basic architecture of that system itself.

II.   Transnationalism Redux

A.   Previous Proliferation of Nonstate and Substate Actors

The widening of the conceptual or analytical lenses used to examine the international system may be a cyclical phenomenon. The decades since 1945 have witnessed at least one previous round of "transnationalism," from the late 1950s to the late 1970s. In a slim volume published in 1956, Philip Jessup defined "transnational law" as "all law which regulates actions or events that transcend national frontiers. Both public and private international law are included, as are other rules which do not wholly fit into such standard categories" (2).[5] Henry Steiner and Detlev Vagts later translated this concept into a casebook, collecting materials designed to bridge the gap between the domestic and international legal worlds (1976: xv–xvi).[6]

"Transnational" was designed to dissolve the reified distinctions between public and private law and domestic and international law, expanding the traditional sphere of public international law—the law governing interstate relations—to include the rules governing the myriad private and public-private transactions accompanying the rapid expansion of global trade and investment and the accompanying emergence of multinational corporations. By focusing on relations "across" borders by the full range of actors within them, rather than relations "between" monolithic spheres, transnationalism shifted attention away from the sources and defining features of different types of law and toward efforts to frame and regulate a world in which borders were no longer barriers. It also, not coincidentally, allowed international lawyers to move away from the increasingly static and apparently irrelevant field of global government in an era defined and dominated by great power rivalry and stalemate and to reinvent themselves as pragmatic contributors to a growing global economy.

Political scientists embraced transnational relations somewhat later, in the late 1960s and 1970s, acknowledging the plethora of nontraditional actors in the international system and trying to relate them both to states and international organizations. The theoretical debate initially focused on whether to define transnationalism in terms of the identity of the actors or the nature of the activity. In an influential edited volume, *Transnational Relations and World Politics,* Robert Keohane and Joseph Nye defined transnational relations as "contacts, coalitions, and interactions across state boundaries that are not controlled by the central foreign policy organs of government" (1972: xi).[7] Samuel Huntington responded to this idea, arguing that the definition of transnational relations should focus not on the actors involved in the process, but rather on the activity itself. He viewed transnationalism as a peculiarly American mode of expansion, based on "freedom to operate" rather than "power to control" (1973: 344).

A related issue concerned the role of "substate" or governmental actors in transnational relations. Huntington's view of the character of transnationalism included both public and private organizations as well as governmental and nongovernmental actors as participants in the "transnational revolution" (337).[8] Keohane and Nye instead distinguished between "transnational" and "transgovernmental" relations, defining "transgovernmental interactions" as interactions between governmental subunits across state boundaries, as opposed to traditional "interstate" relations in which "actors are behaving in roles specified or reasonably implied by the formal foreign policy structure of the state" (1972: 383). These government units could be expected to act relatively autonomously from higher authority in international politics.[9] Keohane and Nye concluded: "Transgovernmental applies when we relax the realist assumption that states act coherently as units; transnational applies when we relax the assumption that states are the only units" (1977: 24–25).[10]

This distinction is linked to yet a third area of debate: how to integrate transnational relations into the traditional framework of interstate or international relations. Keohane and Nye, following Stanley Hoffmann, saw transnational relations as occurring "outside" state-to-state relations, developing as a separate path of communication between nongovernmental actors.[11] In this view, transnational relations challenge traditional state-centric analysis by augmenting the number and identity of actors in the international system, but do not alter the basic framework of interstate cooperation and conflict.[12] For others, however, the impetus to define and chronicle transnational relations was the perceived need to break out of the traditional framework, rejecting not only state centrism but also the sharp divide between international and domestic affairs. Theorists such as Karl Kaiser and James Rosenau argued that the emerging complexity of world politics required a new analytical framework, one that included elements of local, national, and international systems, permitted a focus on various actors acting across boundaries beyond state control, and accommodated a view of policymakers as acting against "state" interest (Kaiser 1971: 792–94; Rosenau 1966: 73–74; 1969).

If transnationalism posed a challenge to state-centric thinking, it also led analysts to question their conception of the state itself and of the long-term impact of transnational relations on state power. Transnational actors were alternately portrayed as slowly usurping the nation-state, coexisting with it, and acting as underlings who would ultimately strengthen it.[13] Keohane and Nye argued that whereas "transgovernmental" relations could transform traditional state-to-state communication by creating a multilevel interaction, "transnational" relations occurred outside the state. Karl Kaiser, on the other hand, identified three ways in which transnational relations would trigger responsive state action: (1) national reaction, in which a government will attempt to influence through intervention the part of the activity that takes place within the jurisdictional boundaries of the nation-state system; (2)

encapsulation, in which the creation of national policy completely controls behavior, thus cutting off all channels of transnational societal interaction; and (3) multinational regulation, which, on a permanent basis, coordinates policies with other affected governments and possibly makes use of international organizations (Kaiser 1971: 804–7; see also Kaiser 1972: 359).

A final issue addressed by many theorists in the 1970s was the definition of a transnational society. Hoffmann used the term to describe a "society" within a nation operating on a separate level from that of the state (1970: 402). Kaiser picked up on this definition of a "society" operating across state boundaries, arguing that transnational politics presupposes the existence of such a society (1971: 801). Transnational society was also viewed as an overarching concept that encompassed the emergence of world communication, emerging as part of an impressive achievement of growth in technology, communication, trade, and investment (Mendershausen 1969).[14]

III.   Reinventing the Wheel?

The empirical observations and theoretical debates of the 1990s in both international law and international relations are in many ways little more than a recapitulation of the 1970s. Two questions thus arise: why again and why now? Has a particular academic fashion simply come around again? Have these actors been there all along and we are just noticing them again now? Or is the discipline actually responding to a new empirical trend, at least as a matter of relative level of activity? The answer, of course, is a bit of both, or rather a bit of all these factors. External empirical developments play a role, highlighting both the need for a reprise of 1970s scholarship and a new consideration of the ways in which the literature of the 1990s through the present differs from its predecessor. Equally important, however, are sociological factors flowing from the internal dynamics of both disciplines.

A.   External Factors

Underneath the proliferation of actors in the international system are the great tides of peace or war among major global powers. The first flowering of transnationalism and transgovernmentalism was during the major U.S./Soviet détente of the 1970s; the resurgence of the nation-state as the dominant actor in the international system coincided with renewed U.S./Soviet confrontation in the 1980s. It is thus not surprising that the post–cold war 1990s, in which the risk of major-power war seemed lower than at any time in the century, proved fertile ground for the flourishing of international actors lacking armies or even embassies.

The end of the cold war also led to the expansion of a community of liberal democracies that reaches across continents and cultures. Peace and liberal democracy are two of the preconditions for Keohane and Nye's conception of complex interdependence, which is additionally marked by "multiple channels of contact connect[ing] societies," multiple levels of communication among government units, and a collapse of any meaningful distinction between foreign and domestic affairs (1977: 25–27). Bruce Russett actually defined *transnationalism* in the 1990s as based on a claim that "individual autonomy and pluralism within democratic States foster the emergence of transnational linkages and institutions—among individuals, private groups, and governmental agencies" (1993: 26). Risse-Kappen also emphasizes this dimension of transnationalism, arguing that transnational relations should be expected to "flourish in alliances among democracies" because the separation of state and society characteristic of democratic systems renders democratic governments "less able to control the transnational activities of their systems" (1995a: 37; 1995b: 294; see also Hoffman 1970).

A third major factor is the information technology revolution, providing the capacity for transnational communication to actors as far-flung as Commander Marcos of the Zapatistas, human rights groups from Nigeria to China, and child labor activists in India and Pakistan. Globalization has been the work of many decades, but the emergence of electronic communication and now the Internet has dramatically expanded transnational networking opportunities for corporations, criminals, and civic associations of all kinds. In many cases governments have simply followed suit; in others, the rollback of the regulatory state has led government officials to form partnerships with private actors in ways that create new opportunities for transnational cooperation and communication.

Fourth, the 1990s were a decade of restructuring and reinventing government, both domestically and internationally. Widespread disillusionment with the United Nations resulted less from a perception of its paralysis due to political conflict than from a sense of generalized incompetence due to excessive bureaucratization and mismanagement. Many domestic governments engaged in major restructuring during the same period: privatizing, consolidating, rationalizing, and reducing their functions. In this context, ideas about both public-private partnerships and networks were likely to fall on particularly fertile ground.

Finally, the revolution of 1989 in Central and Eastern Europe and later in the Soviet Union itself spotlighted the crucial transformative role of groups operating in domestic civil society, groups that had somehow escaped the smothering embrace of the state and survived to undermine it. Religious, cultural, and political organizations thus emerged as crucial sites of resistance to a deformed or oppressive state, just as Robert Putnam was reminding both academics and policymakers of the critical role played by civic associations of all types in building and supporting a well-functioning and accountable state. Whereas much of the focus in the 1970s was on the potential threat posed by multinational corporations to national regulatory control and democratic decision making, as vividly documented in Raymond Vernon's *Sovereignty at Bay*, many of the nonstate actors prominent in the international system of the 1990s had much more positive associations. Indeed, it is striking that in international legal debates the proposals for integrating nonstate actors into international lawmaking processes and organizations focus almost exclusively on civic rather than corporate actors, a bias frequently built into the very definition of *NGO*.

B.   Internal Factors

Other differences between the academic and policy debates of the 1970s and the 1990s regarding the proliferation of actors in the international system are more easily traceable to changes within the disciplines of international law and international relations than to external developments. The line between internal and external, of course, is in many ways an artificial one, as the ways in which external phenomena are perceived and interpreted depend heavily on the identity and preconceptions of the perceivers. Nevertheless, at least for heuristic purposes, it is possible to identify distinct categories of psychological, institutional, and sociological factors that could both spur a revival of the debates of the 1970s and lend them new direction and animation.

The first factor relates to the changing face of both international law and international relations in terms of a new generation of scholars hired in the late 1980s and 1990s. Many of these scholars, including many women and minority candidates long excluded from the sacred precincts of national security studies, on the one hand, and from public international law, on the other, harbored strong criticisms of the dominion of state-centric analysis (Charlesworth 1993: 1; Kennedy 1988: 1). They saw it as reinforcing an obsession with guns, bombs, and the configuration of great powers on the political side and with the law governing the use of force, arms control, and traditional international organizations on the legal side. Issues of social and economic justice, the treatment of women, minorities, and indigenous peoples, and environmental and human rights concerns were all relegated to the margins. Conversely, an emphasis on actors other than the state challenged the hegemony of analytical frameworks, the focus of which was the special concerns of a limited group of government officials charged with the conduct of foreign policy, and instead opened the door to the study of a wide range of issues much more likely to be of concern to a host of nonstate actors.

A second and related factor intersects with the more general perception, outlined above, of groups and organizations operating in domestic civil society as sources of resistance and potential political transformation. This new generation of scholars may have been quicker to perceive the range of political and social interests not adequately represented in domestic decision-making processes and hence almost entirely excluded from international negotiations and rule making. This perception would have led not simply to a focus on the issues being championed by NGOs, but on the role of NGOs themselves as voices for individuals and groups excluded at many levels of governance. From this perspective, an emphasis on nonstate actors, as well as sub- and suprastate actors, is a kind of appeal to grassroots democracy in the international system. It also harnesses the potential for far-reaching social transformation, broad and deep enough to counterbalance the changes being wrought by economic globalization.

Finally, both international relations and international law have witnessed the substitution of economics-based rationalism for politics-based realism as the mainstream of the discipline. Many prominent international relations scholars are locked in a debate between rationalism and constructivism; in law generally, and increasingly in international law, it is law and economics versus various types of interpretivism, constructivism, and critical theory. In this context, a focus on

networks of nonstate actors resonates with conceptions of social movements built on epistemic communities, "principled issue-networks"
motivated by moral causes instead of material incentives (Sikkink 1993;
Keck and Sikkink 1997). It offers a conception not only of the world, but
of human action, that is likely to seem intellectually and even spiritually
refreshing in the face of relentlessly rational calculation. Even networks
of governmental actors offer the possibility of shared communities
based on professional norms and values that may in some cases trump
narrower conceptions of national interest. These are associative qualities that are not inherent in the study of nonstate and infrastate actors,
but they may explain much of their appeal.

IV.   Really Rethinking the State

In the end, the question is whether actors other than the state are a constant in the international system, who periodically become more or less
prominent due to shifts in structural conditions such as great power war
or peace, or whether the second half of the twentieth century marks the
beginning of sea change from internationalism to globalism, a transformation of Westphalian proportions. No neat date will mark this transformation in the way 1648 purportedly marks the beginning of the
Westphalian state system, but the conditions of "absolute" territorial
sovereignty were similarly decades if not centuries in the making (Krasner 1992: 1). It may be impossible to know, but some of the differences
between the literature of the 1970s and the 1990s suggest a deepening
trend rather than a purely cyclical debate. More fundamentally, the preconditions now exist for a genuinely fundamental reconceptualization
of the state as an actor in the international system, in ways that could
provide an intermediate point between internationalism and globalism.

A.   Differences That Make a Difference?

The discussions of the 1990s arguably improve on the earlier literature
in a number of small ways, but two more significant differences stand
out. First is an increased emphasis on the relationship between the state
itself and actors other than the state. Alongside the often hyperbolic
rhetoric about the "end of the nation-state"—and even the more sober
insistence that an increase in power for nonstate actors necessarily spells
a decrease in state power—is a growing recognition that state and non-

state actors are necessarily interdependent. Risse-Kappen argues: "Rather than diminishing state control over outcomes, TNAs (transnational actors) seem to depend on a minimum of state capacity in the particular issue-area in order to be effective. TNAs need the state to have an impact" (Risse-Kappen 1995b: 294). The weaker the state domestically and internationally and the weaker international institutions, the less relevant are TNAs. Similarly, states need TNAs to achieve economic growth, to gain new policy-relevant ideas, to create international institutions, and to monitor regime compliance.

Second, the emphasis by Mathews and others on the critical importance of communications technology as a precondition for effective networking means that the debates of the 1990s addressed a profound revolution in organizational form that will create previously unimaginable options for the way in which government services are delivered and functions are performed. Judicial, regulatory, and even legislative networks may make it possible to decouple the making, administration, and enforcement of bodies of rules from any defined physical space or territorially defined population (Ruggie 1993). Transnational communities may be able to choose genuinely transnational government. Governmental institutions may be able to link up with both their subnational and supranational counterparts, creating vertical as well as horizontal networks in ways that ensure local or international surveillance of important domestic issues without requiring the devolution of primary decision making to the supranational or subnational level.

Focusing on the links between state and nonstate actors and on the technological possibilities for reinventing transnational as well as domestic government moves the debate beyond the increasingly false dichotomy of internationalism versus globalism. The critical question is no longer whether the state is being superseded, but rather how its functions and modes of exercising power are changing in an international system that combines international and global elements. That question, in turn, sets the stage for really rethinking the state itself, as a disaggregated rather than a unitary actor.

B.   Erasing the Line between the Domestic and the
International State

Decades of challenges and critiques notwithstanding, the state is remarkably difficult to dislodge not only as the primary actor in the international system, but also as a unitary actor. The language tells the tale. Even ardent transgovernmentalists refer to state institutions such as administrative agencies or government ministries not as *infra*-state actors but as *sub*-state actors. The "state" thus floats as a brooding omnipresence "above" the government. Government entities can somehow be "additional" actors, but they cannot actually constitute the state itself as an international actor. The result is that the increasing chorus of claims made on behalf of transnational, supranational, and even transgovernmental actors helps entrench a particular myth of the state itself.

The disaggregated state is a constellation of the government institutions performing executive, administrative, judicial, and legislative functions. Each of these institutions can and often does act quasi-autonomously in the international system, typically in relations with either their counterpart or coordinate branches of government abroad. "Quasi-autonomous" action is not meant to suggest that these institutions do not represent their national interest, only that they represent a particular conception of national interest that is shaped by their particular institutional/professional interests, values, and goals.

The disaggregated state is neither dismembered nor diffuse. It is not disaggregated into ever smaller parts, but only into the component institutions that perform familiar government functions. It is no more or less cohesive than domestic government. The point is simply that rather than speaking with many voices at home and one voice abroad, the state or government is the same in both spheres. At various times and in various situations it will still be necessary for a nation to speak with one voice. But the task for analysts, policymakers, and scholars will be to define precisely when, as the exception rather than the rule.

Disaggregating the state redefines the components of the international system in terms of common governance functions rather than reified units of power. The result is to create a different space for the making and enforcement of international rules. First is the shift in the rule makers themselves and the type of rules they make. If the participants in the rule-making process are not states but parts of states, then the form and ultimately the substance of the rules themselves are likely to change. Regulators working closely with one another across borders conclude memoranda of understanding rather than treaties or even executive agreements—memoranda that are informal, general, and flexible statements of the parameters for ongoing cooperation and conflict resolution. These understandings will coexist alongside more traditional international legal rules, whether conventional or customary, but are ultimately likely to circumscribe the areas in which more traditional rule-making is necessary.

Second is the improved opportunity for enforcement even of traditional international legal rules. The European Union model of partnership between national courts and a supranational tribunal can be expanded to other regional and even global tribunals (Helfer and Slaughter 1997). The key element of such partnerships, which can also be forged between supranational tribunals and other national government institutions such as parliaments and administrative agencies, is the harnessing of the coercive power of national governments in the service of international rules. States have, of course, long been subject to a general obligation to implement the international agreements they conclude, but the likelihood of such implementation has depended either on a further calculation of strategic advantage vis-à-vis other states or on the relative power of the executive versus the legislature. Disaggregated implementation offers the prospect of using international agreements as leverage or sources of advantage in internal struggles among different governmental institutions. The approach is particularly promising in the myriad regulatory areas in which the content of the rules involved directly overlaps or supersedes existing domestic law.

The third major implication of redefining the state in terms of its component government institutions is the potential for the creation and regulation of global communities without global government. Courts around the world, for instance, may constitute a "community of law."[15] The purpose of such a community might be to enforce a particular global or regional agreement; more generally, however, it might be simply to promote adherence to the core values embodied in a common, albeit broadly defined, conception of the rule of law. Similarly, national regulators and even legislators in any substantive area, from environmental protection to competition policy, could effectively constitute a common regulatory space by virtue of their repeated interaction, shared goals and values, and a deepening sense of obligation to one another to maintain and enforce rules applicable in their respective jurisdictions (Slaughter 2000a). Gentlemen's agreements among kings, prime ministers, and presidents, from the Concert of Europe to the G-7, can now extend well beyond heads of state and ripen into much more than temporary and shifting alliances.

These are distant visions. The exuberance and energy inherent in the possibility of designing a new international architecture based on new actors and new forms of organization will certainly dim in the face of practical problems and political battles. But the blueprint for that new system will not be drawn up at a successor conference to San Francisco, in which formal state delegations negotiated a new world government—complete with executive, legislature, and judiciary—with states as subjects. Such a constitutional moment will be superseded by myriad smaller plans and decisions of the entire panoply of suprastate, substate, nonstate, and infrastate actors.

The state will be left standing, but it will be a very different state. Its components will network up, down, and sideways with their functional counterparts wielding governmental authority at all levels of political organization. They will also interact with the same range of nonstate actors transnationally as they do domestically. They will engage in both conflict and cooperation. And they will gradually construct a very different body of international rules.

NOTES

1. Mark Movsesian (1996) documents the use of the term *neomedievalism* or *the new medievalism* by a number of other scholars (see Spiro 1995). Christoph Schreuer describes the international system as a "multilayered reality consisting of a variety of authoritative structures" (1993: 453), while Anne-Marie Slaughter describes and challenges "the new medievalism" as an alternative paradigm to liberal internationalism (1997: 183–84).

On the political science side, James Rosenau describes a tendency toward decentralization and away from centralization of the past—which includes both nation-statism and transnationalism (1990: 13; see also Barkin and Cronin 1994; Cerny 1995).

2. For example, I have described the "disaggregation of the state" and the resulting quasi-autonomous interaction of distinct government institutions in relations among liberal democracies: "The state is not disappearing; it is disaggregating into its separate, functionally distinct parts" (1995: 522–28; quote from 1997: 184). Renaud Dehousse remarked that "the conventional (unitary) vision of the state ignores the centrifugal effects of integration, which have led to a fragmentation of state structures and the emergence of functional networks among the institutions of governance in the various member states" (1997: 39), and likewise Sol Picciotto further commented that "officials whose powers and policies have been developed within the hierarchy of the national state have increasingly developed horizontal cross-border contacts with their counterparts in other states" (1997: 1038–39).

3. Joel Trachtman points out that alternative terms that have been used to describe the body of law he wishes to denote include "law of nations" (Janis 1991: 371) and "world law" (Berman 1995).

4. "The voluntary law of individuals and groups in transnational society" has also been described as the first level of "law among liberal states" (Slaughter 1995: 522).

5. In note 3 of the first chapter, Jessup cites Joseph Johnson as one of the originators of the term in an address of June 15, 1955, to the Harvard Foundation.

6. Steiner and Vagts built on Jessup's broad definition and focused on topics including aspects of national legal systems dealing with principles and procedures for decision making that have been specifically developed to regulate problems with some foreign element. The relevant participants in transnational activity include private individuals or firms; national courts, legislators, or treaty-makers; governmental instrumentalities; international officials; and regional and international organizations (1976: xvii).

7. Keohane and Nye identify a separate subset of "international interactions" as "the movement of tangible or intangible items across state boundaries when at least one actor is not an agent of a government or an intergovernmental organization" (1972: xii).

8. In Huntington's view, transnational organizations shared three basic characteristics: (1) they are large, hierarchical, centrally directed bureaucracies; (2) they perform a set of limited, specialized, somewhat technical functions; and (3) they perform functions across one or more international boundaries. Examples of such organizations range from aid missions to military bases to corporate investments (1973: 347).

9. Keohane and Nye included the increased communication between governmental agencies and the business carried on by separate departments with their counterpart bureaucracies abroad in their definition (1974: 41–42). By contrast, a meeting of heads of state at which new initiatives are taken was still the paradigm of the state-centric (interstate) model (1974: 43–44).

10. Transgovernmental interaction among central banks and finance ministers of industrialized countries was as significant in economic policy formation as intergovernmental interaction (Russell 1973).

11. Stanley Hoffmann locates transnational relations "outside" traditional, that is, interstate, world politics (1970: 401).

12. Keohane and Nye quote Arnold Wolfers: "The United Nations and its agencies, the European Coal and Steel Community, the Afro-Asian bloc, the Arab League, the Vatican, and a host of other nonstate entities are able on occasion to affect the course of international events. When this happens, these entities become actors in the international arena and competitors of the nation-state. Their ability to operate as international or transnational actors may be

traced to the fact that men identify themselves and their interests with corporate bodies other than the nation-state" (Keohane and Nye 1972 quoting Wolfers 1962: 377; see also Keohane and Nye 1974: 39–40; 1977: 33–34).

13. Huntington, for example, discussed the position of the "new globalists" who argued that the transnational organization stands to challenge the existence and effectiveness of the nation-state in the future (1973: 363). However, he asserted the contrary view that national governments may be strengthened by the presence of transnational organizations if they are able to control and dictate access (355–56). Similarly, Hoffmann contended that there would be no "superseding of the nation-state" at the global level, although there would be considerable development of international and regional institutions and pursuit of international policy (1970: 410). Keohane and Nye questioned the traditional notion of international organizations as existing "above" the state and argue that they could have their greatest impact in aligning their activities with subunits of governments (1974: 50–62; see also Keohane 1978: 931).

14. Raymond Vernon focused on the huge increase in international trade and connection between national economies—while warning of the danger of U.S. dominance in these emerging relationships (1972).

15. I have elsewhere defined a "community of law" as a web of relations among subnational and supranational legal actors capable of interacting directly with one another, in which the interaction is consistent with the incentives of individual participants and the participants are aware that they are operating in a nominally apolitical context (Helfer and Slaughter 1997: 368–69). A community of law could also arise solely among national courts interacting horizontally across borders in an effort to resolve common problems or promote common values.

REFERENCES

Barkin, J. Samuel, and Bruce Cronin. 1994. The state and the nation: Changing norms and the rules of sovereignty in international relations. *International Organization* 48:107–30.

Berman, Harold. 1995. The role of international law in the twenty-first century: World law. *Fordham International Law Journal* 18, no. 5: 1617–22.

Bramble, Barbara J., and Gareth Porter. 1995. Non-Governmental Organizations and the making of U.S. international environmental policy. *C990 ALI-ABA* 407.

Bull, Hedley. 1977. *The anarchical society.* New York: Columbia University Press.

Cerny, Philip G. 1995. Globalization and the changing logic of collective action. *International Organization* 49:595–625.

Charlesworth, Hilary. 1993. Alienating Oscar? Feminist analysis of international law. In D. G. Dallmeyer, ed., *Reconceiving reality: Women and international law.* Washington, D.C.: American Society of International Law.

Charnovitz, Steve. 1996. Participation of Nongovernmental Organizations in the World Trade Organization. *University of Pennsylvania Journal of International Economic Law* 17:331–57.

Choi, Stephen J., and Andrew T. Guzman. 1998. Portable reciprocity: Rethinking the international reach of securities regulation. *Southern California Law Review* 71:903.

Clark, Ann Marie. 1997. Non-Governmental Organizations and their influence on international society. *Journal of International Affairs* 48:507–25.

Dehousse, Renaud. 1996. European integration and the nation-state. In M. Rhodes, P. Heywood, and V. Wright, eds., *Developments in West European politics.* Basingstoke: Macmillan.

Dezalay, Yves, and Bryant Garth. 1996. *Dealing in virtue: International commercial arbitration and the construction of a transnational legal order.* Chicago: University of Chicago Press.

Drucker, Peter F. 1997. The global economy and the nation-state. *Foreign Affairs* 76, no. 5: 159–71.

Franck, Thomas M. 1996. Clan and superclan: Loyalty, identity and community in law and practice. *American Journal of International Law* 90:359–83.

Garner, Maria. 1991. Transnational alignment of nongovernmental organizations for global environmental action. *Vanderbilt Journal of Transnational Law* 23:1057–84.

Grossman, Claudio, and Daniel D. Bradlow. 1993. Are we being propelled towards a people-centered transnational legal order? *American University Journal of International Law and Policy* 9:1–25.

Helfer, Lawrence R., and Anne-Marie Slaughter. 1997. Toward a theory of effective supranational adjudication. *Yale Law Journal* 107:273–391.

Hoffmann, Stanley. 1970. International organization and the international system. *International Organization* 24:389–413.

Huntington, Samuel P. 1973. Transnational organizations in world politics. *World Politics* 25:333–68.

Janis, Mark W. 1991. International law? *Harvard International Law Journal* 32:363–72.

Jessup, Philip. 1956. *Transnational law.* New Haven: Yale University Press.

Kaiser, Karl. 1971. Transnational politics: Toward a theory of multinational politics. *International Organization* 25:790–817.

———. 1972. Transnational relations as a threat to the democratic process. In Robert O. Keohane and Joseph S. Nye, eds., *Transnational relations and world politics.* Cambridge: Harvard University Press.

Keck, Margaret, and Kathryn Sikkink. 1995. Transnational issue networks in international politics. Paper presented at the Nineteenth Conference of the Latin American Studies Association, September 28–30 (on file with author).

———. 1997. *Activists beyond borders: Advocacy networks in international politics.* Ithaca: Cornell University Press.

Kennedy, David. 1988. A new stream of international law scholarship. *Wisconsin International Law Journal* 7:1–49.

Keohane, Robert O. 1978. The international energy agency: State influence and transgovernmental politics. *International Organization* 32:930–51.

Keohane, Robert O., and Joseph S. Nye Jr. 1974. Transgovernmental relations and international organizations. *World Politics* 27:39–62.

———. 1977. *Power and interdependence: World politics in transition.* Boston: Little, Brown.

Keohane, Robert O., and Joseph S. Nye Jr., eds. 1972. *Transnational relations and world politics.* Cambridge: Harvard University Press.

Kindleberger, Charles P. 1969. *American business abroad.* New Haven: Yale University Press.

Kobrin, Stephen J. 1998. Back to the future: Neomedievalism and the post modern digital world economy. *Journal of International Affairs* 51, no. 2: 361–86.

Koh, Harold H. 1996. Transnational legal process. *Nebraska Law Review* 75:(8).

———. 1997. Why do nations obey international law? *Yale Law Journal* 106:2598.

———. 1998. Bringing international law home. *Houston Law Review* 35:623.

Krasner, Stephen D. 1992. Westphalia and all that. In Judith Goldstein and Robert Keohane, eds., *Ideas and foreign policy.* Ithaca: Cornell University Press.

Lipschutz, Ronnie. 1992. Reconstructing world politics: The emergence of global civil society. *Millennium* 21:389.

Mathews, Jessica Tuchman. 1996. Power shift. *Foreign Affairs* 76:50–66.

Mendershausen, Horst. 1969. Transnational society vs. state sovereignty. *Kyklos* 22:251.

Meyer, John W., and Ronald L. Jepperson. 2000. The 'actors' of modern society: The cultural construction of social agency. *Sociological Theory* 18:100.

Movsesian, Mark L. 1996. The persistent nation state and the foreign sovereign immunities act. *Cardozo Law Review* 18: 1083–1109.

Ohmae, Kenichi. 1995. *The end of the nation state: The rise of regional economies.* London: HarperCollins.

Picciotto, Sol. 1997. Networks in international economic integration: Fragmented states and the dilemmas of neo-liberalism. *Northwestern Journal of International Law and Business* 17:1014–1109.

Risse-Kappen, Thomas. 1995a. *Cooperation among democracies.* Princeton: Princeton University Press.

————. 1995b. Structures of governance and transnational relations: What have we learned? In Thomas Risse-Kappen, ed., *Bringing transnational relations back in: Non-state actors, domestic structures and international institutions.* Cambridge: Cambridge University Press.

Roht-Arriaza, Naomi. 1995a. Shifting the point of regulation: The international organization for standardization and global lawmaking on trade and the environment. *Ecology Law Quarterly* 22:479–539.

————. 1995b. Private voluntary standard setting, the international organization for standardization and international environmental lawmaking. *Yearbook of International Environmental Law* 6:107–63.

Rosenau, James N. 1966. Pre-theories and theories of foreign policy. In R. Barry Farrell, ed., *Approaches to comparative and international politics.* Evanston: Northwestern University Press.

————. 1990. *Turbulence in world politics: A theory of change and continuity.* Princeton: Princeton University Press.

Rosenau, James N., ed. 1969. *Linkage politics: Essays on the convergence of national and international systems.* New York: Free Press.

Rubinton, David Scott. 1992. Toward a recognition of the rights of non-states in international environmental law. *Pace Environmental Law Review* 9:475–94.

Ruggie, John Gerard. 1993. Territoriality and beyond: Problematizing modernity in international relations. *International Organization* 47:139–74.

Russell, Robert W. 1973. Transgovernmental interaction in the international monetary system 1960–1972. *International Organization* 27:431–64.

Russett, Bruce. 1993. *Grasping the democratic peace: Principles for a post–cold war world.* Princeton: Princeton University Press.

Schmidt, Vivien A. 1995. The new world order, incorporated: The rise of business and the decline of the nation-state. *Daedalus* 124:75.

Schreuer, Christoph. 1993. The waning of the sovereign state: Towards a new paradigm for international law? *European Journal of International Law* 4:447.

Shell, G. Richard. 1996. The trade stakeholders model and participation by nonstate parties in the World Trade Organization. *University of Pennsylvania Journal of International Economic Law* 17:359–81.

Shuman, Michael H. 1986–87. Dateline main street: Local foreign policies. *Foreign Policy* 65:154–74.

————. 1991. A separate peace movement: The role of participation. In M. H. Shuman and J. Sweig, eds., *Conditions of peace: An inquiry.* Washington, D.C.: Expro Press.

Sikkink, Kathryn. 1993. Human rights, principled issue-networks, and sovereignty in Latin America. *International Organization* 47:411–41.

Slaughter, Anne-Marie. 1995. International law in a world of liberal states. *European Journal of International Law* 6:503.

————. 1997. The real new world order. *Foreign Affairs* 76:183–97.

————. 2000a. Agencies on the loose? Holding government networks accountable. In George A. Bermann, Mathias Hergegen, and Peter Lindseth, eds.,
Transnational Regulatory Competition.

————. 2000b. Governing the global economy through government networks.
In Michael Byers, ed., *The role of law in international politics: Essays in international relations and international law.* London: Oxford University Press.

————. 2000c. Judicial globalization. *Virginia Journal of International Law.*

Spiro, Peter J. 1995. New global communities: Nongovernmental organizations
in international decision-making institutions. *Washington Quarterly*
18:45–56.

Steiner, Henry J., and Detlev F. Vagts, eds. 1976. *Transnational legal problems.*
2d ed. Mineola, N.Y.: Foundation Press.

Strange, Susan. 1994. Who governs? Networks of power in world society. *Hitotsubashi Journal of International Law and Politics* (special issue): 5–17.

Trachtman, Joel P. 1996. The international economic law revolution. *University
of Pennsylvania Journal of International Economic Law* 17:34.

Tracy, Christopher. 1994. The roots of influence: Nongovernmental organizations and the relationship between human rights and the environment.
Journal of International Law and Practice 3:21–46.

Vernon, Raymond. 1971. *Sovereignty at bay: The multinational spread of U.S.
enterprises.* New York: Basic Books.

————. 1972. Multinational business and national economic goals. In Robert
Keohane and Joseph Nye, eds., *Transnational relations and world politics.*
Cambridge: Harvard University Press.

Wolfers, Arnold. 1962. The actors in world politics. In *Discord and collaboration: Essays on international politics.* Baltimore: Johns Hopkins Press.

Wriston, Walter B. 1993. The twilight of sovereignty. *Fletcher Forum on World
Affairs* 117, no. 2: 117–30.

Transnational Advocacy Networks and the Social Construction of Legal Rules

Kathryn Sikkink

Kathryn Sikkink, a political scientist at the University of Minnesota, complements the perspective provided by Anne-Marie Slaughter by examining the increasingly important role of networks of nongovernmental organizations in producing international norms. Sikkink shows how NGOs and other kinds of international advocates form networks and develop strategies to challenge states in favor of new international norms—that may then ripen into law. Examples include international human rights and efforts to deter violence against women. Sikkink suggests the conditions that allow these advocacy networks to become successful in both building and enforcing international norms and some of the problems associated with this particular political strategy. The reliance on law, she suggests, may indeed succeed in empowering and legitimating the transnational networks that promote these norms.

She also has some caveats for this emerging approach. The power to influence international agendas is unevenly distributed. In addition, she points out, legal rules exclude as well as empower, and the processes of fighting for new rules can marginalize some groups while empowering others. Sikkink thus describes a process akin to that posited by Slaughter— geared to an international focus of a range of actors on developing and enforcing legal norms that will apply around the globe. As a political scientist, however, she raises more questions about how power will be distributed in this kind of global political economy.

Introduction

A burgeoning literature in political science argues that norms are becoming increasingly consequential in international relations and international organizations and that transnational nongovernmental actors are key instigators and promoters of new norms (Finnemore and Sikkink 1998; Risse-Kappen 1995; Smith 1997; Katzenstein 1996; Lipschutz 1992: 389–420; Wapner 1995: 311–40; Boli and Thomas 1999; Peterson 1992: 375–76; Thomas 2001; Nadelmann 1990: 479–526; Klotz 1995; Finnemore 1996; Crawford 1993: 37–61; Price 1998; Risse, Ropp, and Sikkink 1999; Khaghram, Riker, and Sikkink 2002). The insights from some of the norms literature in international relations has some interesting parallels with work in international law (Slaughter 1998). Other scholars suggest that there may be important similarities in the way norms work domestically and internationally (Sunstein 1997). What these literatures have not yet understood adequately is the relationship between transnational nongovernmental actors and international legal rules. Thus the purpose of this essay is to begin to delineate the processes through which transnational advocacy networks build and encourage the implementation of international law.

A transnational advocacy network includes those relevant actors working internationally on an issue who are bound together by shared values, a common discourse, and dense exchanges of information and services. Advocacy networks often reach beyond policy change to advocate and instigate changes in the institutional and normative basis upon which international interactions take place (Keck and Sikkink 1998). When they succeed, they are an important part of an explanation for changes in international law, but because they often work behind the scenes, their role may not always be recognized. Using the cases of transnational networks around human rights and violence against women, I will highlight the role of these networks in the creation of issues, agenda setting, and helping to build and enforce international norms, that is, in the social construction of the rule of law.[1]

In political science, the words *social construction* are sometimes used without much specification as to how, when, and why such social construction occurs, or what its limits are. It suggests a process that is quite abstract and that happens mainly at the level of discourse.[2] The social construction story of networks is a concrete and active story about groups who strive to re-create their world. Martha Finnemore and I call this process *strategic social construction*, in which actors strategize rationally to reconfigure preferences, identities, or social context (Finnemore and Sikkink 1998). The process of strategic social construction, however, takes place within constraints and limits, those of the material world as well as those of the imagination. When networks encounter the legal world, those limits also include the limits of law, a world with which not all nongovernmental organizations (NGOs) are intimately familiar. Networks differ with regard to their knowledge of and interest in law. Human rights networks have long involved international and domestic legal scholars, and law has been an essential component of human rights activism.[3] International women's activism has focused much less exclusively on legal rules, although women's networks are increasingly involved in the construction of legal rules on issues of violence against women (Basu 1995; Bunch and Reilly 1994).

In this essay, I discuss the diverse ways that network actors contribute to the social construction of legal rules. They help build legal norms by bringing new ideas and issues into policy debates, by serving as sources of information and testimony, and in some cases by actually drafting legal rules. Advocacy networks espousing norms also promote norm implementation by publicizing the existence of legal norms and documenting rule-breaking behavior. In some cases networks and NGOs facilitate international litigation, pressure target actors to adopt new policies and laws and to ratify treaties, and monitor compliance with international standards. Networks contribute to changing perceptions that both state and societal actors may have of their interests and their preferences, by helping to transform the discursive and legal world within which interests are formulated.

But there are significant limits and constraints to the changes that networks can provoke. Not all issues lend themselves equally, or easily, to the social construction of new legal rules. Powerful states block the construction of legal rules contrary to their perceived interests, and networks themselves are often permeated by informal or hidden power asymmetries that raise serious questions about their representative capabilities.

Networks and Nongovernmental Organizations (NGOs)

International and domestic nongovernmental organizations play a central role in all transnational advocacy networks. Although advocacy networks may also include social movements, foundations, and individuals in international organizations and governments, the NGO members of networks usually initiate actions and pressure more powerful actors to take positions.

Often the power that NGOs exercise is "hidden" because it is carried out informally or behind the scenes. This may lead observers to overlook or disregard the influence of NGOs. For example, in the United Nations, NGOs play a far greater role than is recognized by the terms of the category of "consultative status." As former secretary-general Boutros Boutros-Ghali recognized, nongovernmental organizations "are now considered full participants in international life" and are "a basic form of popular participation and representation in the present day world" (Weiss and Gordenker 1996: 18, 7). A UN study to prepare the ground for the 1996 guidelines governing consultative status recognized that NGO involvement in the decision-making systems and operational activities of the UN "far exceeded the original scope of these legal provisions," and "relationships have diversified well beyond the formal framework" (UN ECOSOC 1994: 12, 13). But the new guidelines did not significantly alter the formal framework for NGO participation. This situation symbolizes a broader paradox of the role of NGOs in international life: NGOs are increasingly involved in diverse international issues, and yet neither the formal structure of international institutions nor international relations theory has formally recognized this role.

There has been significant growth in transnational advocacy NGOs since 1953. This growth has occurred across all issues, but to varying degrees in different issue areas. Human rights has been a predominant focus of international nongovernmental social change organizations since the 1950s. There are five times as many organizations working primarily on human rights as there were in 1950, but proportionally human rights groups have remained roughly a quarter of all such groups. The same holds true for groups working on women's rights, which accounted for 9 percent of groups in 1953 and 1993. Transnational environmental organizations have grown most dramatically in absolute and relative terms, increasing from 1.8 percent of total groups in 1953 to 14.3 percent in 1993. The percentage share of groups devoted specifically to international law, however, has declined from 12.7 percent in 1953 to 4.1 percent in 1993 (Keck and Sikkink 1997: table 1, p. 11; Smith 1997). Compared with the post–World War II period when international law was promoted by NGOs devoted to the general cause of international law, advocacy today tends to be carried out by more issue-specific groups. This may be because the increasing diversity and complexity of international law means that few can follow or advocate general developments.

Networks and Norms

One of the main ways networks and NGOs influence international law is by promoting new international norms and working to ensure compliance with existing norms. Political scientists now define norms as a standard of appropriate behavior for actors with a given identity (Katzenstein 1996: 5; Finnemore 1996: 22; Klotz 1995). According to legal scholar Cass Sunstein, norms are defined as "attitudes of approval and disapproval, specifying what ought to be done and what ought not to be done" (1997: 39). Thus the primary difference between law and social norms is the consequence of violating them: if you break a law you risk criminal and civil punishment; if you break a norm you risk social sanctions, such as being shunned and ostracized (1997: 39; Rosen 1997: 172). While norms and law often serve to reinforce each other, in some cases, norms may influence behavior more effectively than law, even within a domestic setting where law is strong (Sunstein 1997; Lessig 1995; Rosen 1997).

This helps explain why understanding norms is so essential for international relations and international legal scholars. Because the international system is characterized by law and norms operating without direct punitive capacity, both international norms and law depend primarily upon social sanctions (rather than punishment) for implementation and effectiveness. It is thus imperative to understand the process through which these social norms function internationally. The processes through which legal scholars claim norms work domestically are quite consistent with the research done by norm scholars in international relations and sociology. For example, Cass Sunstein's concepts of norm "bandwagons" and "norm cascades" are similar to the processes of the rapid global diffusion of legal principles that John Meyer and Elizabeth Boyle discuss in their contribution to this volume (Sunstein 1997: 46–48). But what is still missing from these models is an understanding of the specific actors and mechanisms that contribute to building and implementing new norms.

How Do Advocacy Networks Contribute to Building Legal Norms?

Networks exercise influence on international norms in numerous ways. Martha Schweitz categorized NGO roles in the following way: (1) provide information; (2) lobby and advocate; (3) participate in dispute resolution in international tribunals; (4) implement policies and programs of intergovernmental institutions; (5) collaborate in policy-making; (6) engage in lawmaking; (7) hold intergovernmental institutions accountable for compliance with their own internal directives (Schweitz 1995: 418).[4] Of these various roles, providing information is by far the most important, although a significant portion of groups also lobby (indeed, providing information is often a form of lobbying), collaborate in policy-making or lawmaking, or assist in implementing policy.[5]

In some cases discussed below, members of advocacy networks literally help write international declarations and conventions or facilitate international litigation. Prior to such direct involvement, and perhaps more significant than their actual role in drafting legal rules, is the role of networks in helping to create issues, set agendas, and provide the information to help create awareness of a problem.

Agenda Setting: Naming, Framing, and Interpretation

Networks call attention to issues, or even "create issues" by using language that dramatizes and draws attention to their concerns. They often do this by reinterpreting an event or problem in such a way that it becomes amenable to legal action. Social movement theorists refer to this reinterpretation or renaming process as "framing" (Keck and Sikkink 1998: 2–3, 7).[6] Legal theory is very familiar with the world of framing and interpretation, but is more likely to argue for the primacy of law for creating the symbolic frameworks that condition the way citizens and officials interpret events.[7] Here I argue that the frames that later appear in the law often originate in groups in civil society. The construction of cognitive frames is an essential component of networks' political strategies, and when they are successful, the new frames *resonate* with broader public understandings and are adopted as new ways of talking about and understanding issues.

A good example of this kind of agenda setting through framing is the campaign against the practice of female genital mutilation. Before

1976, the widespread practice of female circumcision in many African and a few Asian and Middle Eastern countries was known outside these regions mainly among medical experts and anthropologists.[8] A controversial campaign initiated in 1974 by a network of women's and human rights organizations began to draw attention to these issues.

One way the campaign drew attention to the issue was to reframe it by renaming the problem. Previously the practice was referred to by more technical and neutral terms such as female circumcision, clitoridectomy, or infibulation. The campaign around female genital mutilation raised its salience, literally creating the issue as a matter of public international concern. By renaming the practice, the network broke the linkage with male circumcision (seen as a personal medical or cultural decision), implied a linkage with the more feared procedure of castration, and reframed the issue as one of violence against women. It thus resituated the problem as a human rights violation. The campaign contributed to laws against female genital mutilation in many countries, including France and the United Kingdom; the United Nations studied the problem and made a series of recommendations for eradicating certain traditional practices.[9]

New frames also create new conflicts. The initial campaign on female genital mutilation (FGM) had become an explosive topic for the women's movement by the Copenhagen conference in 1980. Some women and men from countries where such practices occurred argued that for Western feminists to criticize FGM was inappropriate and even a form of "cultural imperialism" and racism. Other African women's organizations recognized the problems associated with FGM, but wondered why it got so much more attention than other pressing problems of health and development.

In some senses, we can say that networks help create issues that did not exist before. The creation of issues and of awareness about problems in turn helps create a demand for legal rules to address these problems. One recent and clear example of issue creation is the case concerning violence against women. In the 1970s, the issue of violence against women was not on the agenda either of the women's movement or of international human rights groups. The main international treaty on women's rights, the Convention for the Elimination of All Forms of Discrimination against Women (the CEDAW Convention) that was drafted in the 1970s and adopted in 1979, does not mention violence against women. The thirty articles of this otherwise extremely comprehensive document establish detailed norms on matters of equality and opportunity. But they contain not a single mention of rape, domestic or sexual abuse, female genital mutilation, dowry death, or any other instance of violence against women.[10] In retrospect, it is a glaring absence.

In one sense, international women's networks literally created the issue of violence against women—they helped construct it as a problem. At first such a claim seems obviously false. No one created domestic abuse, or rape—it is all too real and common. But what networks did was create a category—violence against women—that didn't exist before. They used the term to encompass a range of violent practices in diverse locations, from household brutality to the practices of state security forces. Essentially, by using the concept "violence against women," the campaign unified a series of practices that until then were not understood to be connected.

What existed prior to the mid-1970s was not a category "violence against women" but separate activist campaigns on different practices—against rape and domestic battery in the United States and Europe, female genital mutilation in Africa, female sexual slavery in Europe and Asia, dowry death in India, and torture and rape of political prisoners in Latin America. It was neither obvious nor natural that one should think of female genital mutilation and domestic abuse as part of the same category. The category "violence against women" had to be constructed and popularized before people could think of these practices as the "same" in some basic way. And yet, activists cannot make just any category stick. This one caught on because in some way it made sense and captured the imagination. As the Latin American activist Susana Chiarotti, the founding coordinator of Indeso-Mujer, Rosario, Argentina, pointed out, "the violence theme is very evocative. No woman can help but feel it as her own. I don't think any one of us can say that she has never felt violence against her. It crosses all our lives" (quoted in Center for Women's Global Leadership 1993: 25). At the same time, the category served some key strategic purposes for activists trying to build a transnational campaign because it allowed them to attract allies and bridge cultural differences. This strategic focus forced transnational activists to search for a most basic common denominator—the belief in the importance of the protection of the bodily integrity of women and girls—that was central to liberalism and at the same time at the core of understandings of human dignity in many other cultures.

The campaign created a new category. When wife battering or rape in the United States, female genital mutilation in Africa, and dowry death in India were all classified as forms of violence against women, it helped women to interpret these as common situations and to seek similar root causes. But the new category also helped diffuse conflict within the women's movement because it pointed out that women everywhere were victims of violence, rather than singling out a particular practice like female genital mutilation for criticism. When female genital mutilation was resituated as one practice within a broader category of violence against women, it was diffused and legitimated as an issue. At that point, the issue was embraced by a wider number of groups, including and especially groups of African women.

The fundamental work of renaming, issue creation, and attention made possible the later work of the construction of legal rules. By 1994, the UN General Assembly had adopted a Declaration on the Elimination of Violence against Women, and the Organization of American States (OAS) adopted the Inter-American Convention on the Prevention, Punishment, and Eradication of Violence against Women.[11] The OAS convention includes stronger enforcement mechanisms than those of any existing convention on women's issues. It sets out a specific section on the duties of states, both to refrain from engaging in violence against women, and to prevent, investigate and impose penalties for violence against women in the public and private sphere. The Convention permits any person or group of persons, or any nongovernmental organization legally recognized in one or more states of the organization, to lodge petitions with the Inter-American Commission on Human Rights containing denunciations or complaints of violations of Article 7 of the Convention (the article listing the duties of the states) by a state party. The Convention was rapidly ratified by thirty member states of the OAS.

Providing Information and Testimony: Persuasion

One of the most important tactics that networks use is "information politics" or what human rights activists sometimes call the human rights methodology: "promoting change by reporting facts" (Thomas 1993: 83). Networks often provide information that would not otherwise be available in public debates. This information is central to the social construction of legal rules because legal remedies are seen as necessary and appropriate only after publics are convinced that a problem exists that needs to be addressed and that the problem is sufficiently widespread and intractable that it requires a legal solution. Human rights networks have been particularly effective in this regard, and legal scholars have been most attentive to this aspect of NGO influence (Weissbrodt 1984: 403–38; Wiseberg and Schoble 1979).

"Information flows in advocacy networks provide not only facts, but also *testimony*—stories told by people whose lives have been affected. Moreover, activists interpret facts and testimony: usually framing issues simply, in terms of right and wrong, because their purpose is to *persuade* people and stimulate them to act" (Keck and Sikkink 1997: 19). Persuasion is the mission of norm entrepreneurs: they seek to change the beliefs, positions, or courses of action of other players to reflect some new normative commitment.[12] Among individuals, persuasion is the process through which attitudes are formed and changed (Chaiken, Wood, and Eagly 1996). Most definitions of *persuasion* stress that it is a communicative process that happens through argument and the reception of messages which leads to changes in beliefs and preferences. In this sense, persuasion should be seen in contrast to coercion that is based on threats rather than communication. Both coercion and persuasion (or some combination of the two) can lead to normative change, but they rely on very different resources and methods and so must be distinguished analytically.

Nongovernmental actors rely on a variety of techniques to persuade, including appeals to emotion or affect, evoking symbols, as well as the use and extension of logical arguments. Although some authors privilege the role of logic in the extension of norms, much psychological research suggests that both affect and cognition operate synergistically to produce and change attitudes (Crawford 1993; Eagly and Chaiken 1993). Networks implicitly understand the necessity to link emotion and cognition in persuasion because they often evoke powerful symbols and use personal testimony together with factual information to dramatize and amplify their "information politics" so the dry facts are humanized. All of these efforts create the impression of a pressing human problem that needs to be addressed, which in turn helps create a demand for legal rules to help address this problem.

Drafting Legal Rules

In some cases, individuals in networks are directly involved in the actual drafting of legal rules. Process-tracing the origins of legal rules very often reveals key roles for specific individuals without whom attempts to build the norm might have failed. The Genocide Convention owed a singular debt to the work of a Polish lawyer, Raphael Lemkin, who coined the term *genocide* in 1944, helped promote the use of the term, and assisting in drafting and securing the passage of the genocide treaty.[13] Nadelmann has called such activists "transnational moral entrepreneurs" who engage in "moral proselytism" (1990).[14] This kind of norm entrepreneurship is not necessarily new, though it has become more frequent recently with the proliferation of international conventions. As early as 1923, Eglantyne Jebb, founder of the Save the Children Fund, wrote a "Declaration of the Rights of the Child" that was adopted by the fifth Assembly of the League of Nations in 1924. The 1924 Declaration is mentioned in the preamble to the 1989 Convention on the Rights of the Child, and some of its language and concerns are echoed in that document (Wilson 1967: 182–83, 224).

More commonly, however, activism to promote new norms of behavior is shared among a number of individuals in an NGO or an advocacy network (Boven 1990). For example, in 1945, the forty-two nongovernmental consultants to the U.S. delegation at the San Francisco Conference played a pivotal role in securing the inclusion of human rights language in the UN Charter, language that served as the basis for all further UN efforts in the human rights area. The initial U.S. drafts of the Charter contained no reference to human rights, while the proposals that emerged from the Big Four meeting at Dumbarton Oaks to prepare for the San Francisco conference contained only one reference to human rights (Robinson 1946: 17). Nongovernmental organizations representing churches, trade unions, ethnic groups, and peace movements, aided by the delegations of some of the smaller countries, "conducted a lobby in favor of human rights for which there is no parallel in the history of international relations, and which was largely responsible for the human rights provisions of the Charter" (Humphrey 1984: 13; Department of State 1946). In particular, NGOs urged four amendments to the Dumbarton Oaks Proposals that would further institutionalize and incorporate human rights concerns and language into the Charter. The most important of these amendments were the proposal to add the phrase "to promote respect for human rights and fundamental freedoms" to the first chapter outlining the basic purposes of the new organization and the specific provision calling on the Economic and Social Council to set up a human rights commission (Robins 1971: 218–19). These early NGO activists were aware of the importance of finding an institutional home for the human rights idea.

A member of the U.S. delegation later told the NGO consultants, "If you had been at Dumbarton Oaks where we struggled for weeks literally to get just the two words 'human rights and fundamental freedoms' somewhere into the proposals, you would realize what enormous progress has been made during the last six months. . . . it has largely resulted from the action of this group . . . which really changed history" (Robins 1971: 132).

But the contribution of NGOs and networks to the drafting of international human rights law did not end with the UN Charter. When John Humphrey, Director of the UN Division on Human Rights, wrote the "Secretariat Outline" (a draft bill of rights) for the Human Rights Commission to use in its deliberations, he used for models the score of drafts the secretariat had collected from law professors and legal and social NGOs.[15] Although the secretariat outline was modified significantly during the debates, the influences of these diverse nongovernmental sources are clearly seen in the final version of the Universal Declaration of Human Rights.[16]

Such a substantial role for networks and NGOs occurred with later human rights treaties as well. For example, Amnesty International has played a fundamental role in contributing to the development of international legal rules on torture, disappearances, and summary execution (Clark 2001). Amnesty's Campaign against Torture (in 1973) created the impetus behind the decision of governments to bring torture before the General Assembly, and Amnesty's legal staff contributed to the actual drafting of the wording of the Torture Convention (Clark 2001; Boven 1990: 213; Burgers and Danelius 1988: 13; Burgers 1992; Leary 1979).

The normative process is a circular one: transnational actors both help create some international norms and in turn are empowered by them (Thomas 2001). Once international legal rules and norms are in place, they empower and legitimate the transnational networks that promote them. But legal rules exclude as well as empower, and new rules can silence or marginalize some groups at the same time they empower others. Participation in the drafting of new international legal rules does tend to privilege certain types of NGO and network activists at the expense of others. For example, as women's organizations began to work on women's human rights, they increasingly needed to privilege international legal expertise. In 1997, women's rights NGOs participated in a working group drafting an optional protocol to the CEDAW Convention that would allow the submission of individual complaints of violations to the CEDAW Committee. The working group drafting the Optional Protocol was open to NGO observers, but one NGO, the International Women's Rights Action Watch (IWRAW), warned its members that NGOs who wished to participate should be "well prepared to follow the technical discussion. IWRAW's experience suggests that the most effective NGO participants with respect to the optional protocol are lawyers or those who have extensive experience in working with the wording of international legal instruments" (IWRAW 1997: 2). The newsletter then cites a recent law review article that provides a comprehensive review of the elements of the protocol for members to consult. Increasingly, more professional NGOs have staff with this kind of expertise, but it does limit the involvement of other, more grassroots organizations.

Transnational Advocacy Networks and Compliance with International Law

Building international norms is, in and of itself, insufficient, because many existing international norms are frequently violated. Thomas Franck has discussed the conditions under which countries are more likely to comply with international legal rules. Many of these conditions have to do with the qualities of the rules themselves (Franck 1992: 51, 56). Applying this framework, the prohibition against torture is the most embedded in international law. It has the oldest pedigree, the greatest determinacy, and possesses high magnitudes of coherence and adherence (McEntree 1996: 1–20).

Nevertheless, torture continues to be widely practiced in the world today. Clearly, the embeddedness of the legal rule and the qualities of the rule itself are insufficient to explain compliance with the rule. How can these widely accepted international and domestic legal norms be implemented? The absence of formal enforcement mechanisms for most international human rights law does not mean that such law is not enforced. Networks contribute to a range of informal actions that help ensure compliance with international law. These informal actions can be thought of as a way that states are socialized to new legal rules (Risse and Sikkink 1999).

Socialization involves the "induction of new members . . . into the ways of behavior that are preferred in a society" (Barnes, Carter, and Skidmore 1980: 35). International socialization thus implies the presence of an "international society" and is the process through which new members to that society are induced to change their behavior in accordance with international norms.[17] According to the international relations theorist Kenneth Waltz, socialization occurs through the emulation (of heroes), praise (for behavior that conforms to group norms), and ridicule (for deviation) (1979). In addition to the processes mentioned by Waltz—emulation, praise, and ridicule—socialization can also occur through learning, shaming, ostracism, and coercion. The point often overlooked is that socialization is not always a benign process, but can involve painful interactions.

The primary way that networks contribute to socialization is by publicizing behavior they deem inappropriate, using factual information or symbolic politics. A transnational human rights advocacy network promotes these socialization processes through adverse international publicity about a state's violations of human rights so that noncompliance leads to embarrassment or damages the state's reputation. Moreover, once a state's human rights misconduct has been exposed, more damaging bilateral or multilateral enforcement measures may follow. Such publicity, as well as focused network lobbying, may also activate bilateral foreign policies of other countries toward target states.

Publicizing the Existence of International Legal Norms

One first step toward ensuring compliance with international human rights norms has been informing citizens of the existence of these legal rules and their possibilities for redress. Some NGOs devote large amounts of time simply to publicizing the existence and the specific rules of international conventions. Women's groups such as the International Women's Rights Action Watch (IWRAW) have been especially active, for example, in publicizing the contents of the Convention on the Prevention of All Forms of Discrimination against Women (CEDAW Convention) and monitoring implementation of the convention. These NGOs also intervene in the reporting procedures for CEDAW. When government reports to the CEDAW Committee have been weak, groups help write counter reports to circulate among friendly government delegations. Women's groups have also worked to bring national women's NGOs from member countries to the Vienna CEDAW Committee meetings to hear and perhaps challenge their government's reports on the status of women in their country.[18]

These kinds of pressures have recently proven quite effective vis-à-vis Japan. After Japan ratified the CEDAW Convention ten years ago, it made some tentative efforts to comply by enacting a limited employment discrimination law. In 1995, after reviewing Japan's second and third periodic reports, the CEDAW Committee strongly criticized the Japanese government and suggested that it address the issue of indirect discrimination in the workplace. The committee's observations had been influenced by the information submitted by twelve Japanese NGOs to counter the government report. Encouraged by the CEDAW review, twenty-one women sued the giant Sumitomo conglomerate, claiming wage discrimination, failure to promote, and a company and government policy that violated the CEDAW Convention. The plaintiffs are receiving support from women's rights organization within Japan as well as international support from IWRAW and other women's rights groups (IWRAW 1997: 1–2).

Publicizing Rule-Breaking Behavior

If we assume that states (or individuals) sometimes break legal rules because they believe that nobody will ever know, then the simple collection and dissemination of information about rule breaking can have a dampening effect on violations. Torture survivors from all over the world report that torturers use a common refrain—"no one will ever know what happened to you. No one cares." This is both a psychological device to isolate and torment the individual and a statement that torturers believe that their actions are hidden or secret (Weschler 1990: 171–72, 238). A similar situation exists with problems of violence against women in the household. When women's rights organizations in India documented that large numbers of women who died in kitchen fires were not victims of household accidents but were being set on fire by their in-laws because of dissatisfaction with their dowries, the police began to investigate any case of a kitchen fire more closely. A few high-profile convictions of people for murder—the so-called dowry death—sent a message to other families that these actions could no longer be as easily hidden (Kumar 1995: 67). Once again, publicity and documentation in and of themselves may make a significant contribution to compliance with law.

Facilitating International Litigation

In the Americas, networks of NGOs have taken on the task of supporting international human rights litigation by bringing cases before the Inter-American Commission and Court. For example, Americas Watch represented the families of four victims of disappearance in Honduras before the Inter-American Court and obtained a landmark decision that is frequently cited as an important international law precedent (Mendez and Vivanco 1990: 507, 535).

In 1990 a network of human rights organizations throughout Latin America together with Americas Watch set up a new NGO specifically dedicated to the task of bringing human rights cases before the Inter-American human rights system. The new organization, the Center for Justice and International Law (CEJIL), has taken responsibility, in partnership with domestic human rights groups, for a large docket of cases before the Inter-American Commission (Mendez 1992: 5).

Aside from their legal expertise, one of the most important activities of NGOs involved in bringing cases before the commission and court had been to secure funding from foundations to enable the pursuit of the case. For example, in the important Honduras disappearance case, the Inter-American Court could not pay the expenses to bring witnesses to testify in Costa Rica. Americas Watch secured funding from the Ford Foundation and other foundations in order to pay airfares and per diems to bring witnesses before the court.

Another venue for the implementation of international human rights law has been the contribution of NGOs in bringing human rights cases in domestic courts in other countries. Courts in countries such as the United States, Spain, and Italy have condemned violations of international human rights norms and imposed penalties on rights-violating states or individuals. Once again, the plaintiffs often depend upon NGOs to help them prepare and present their cases.

In 1979 Jose Filartiga and his daughter Dolly, who then resided in the United States, filed a lawsuit against Américo Peña Irala who was also in the United States. They accused Peña Irala, former police inspector of Asunción, of kidnapping and torturing to death Filartiga's teenage son, Joelito, in 1976 in Paraguay. The Filartiga family was assisted by the Center for Constitutional Rights in New York in crafting a novel and convincing legal argument (Claude 1992). They invoked the Alien Tort Claims Act of 1786, which grants federal courts jurisdiction in "any civil action by an alien for a tort only, committed in violation of the law of nations or a treaty of the United States" (Burley 1989). The court's decision in the Filartiga case broke new ground because it held that in the 1970s the torturer now had a status in customary international law akin to that of the pirate and slave trader—"an enemy of all mankind."[19] Since the Filartiga decision, U.S. federal courts have adjudicated numerous cases involving human rights abuses in other countries under a variety of jurisdictional statutes (Lutz and Sikkink 2000). Courts in the United States and Europe have become mechanisms through which victims of violations of customary international human rights law norms have sought to vindicate their rights, but these cases reach U.S. and European courts because of the efforts of a network of human rights and legal activists and NGOs who prepare, support, and litigate the cases. Some of these have had a chilling effect on government, police, and military officials in repressive countries (Lutz and Sikkink 2001).

Convincing More Powerful Actors to Impose
Bilateral Sanctions to Enforce International Law

Aside from their ability to publicize rule breaking, NGOs have few tools available to convince states to comply with international human rights norms. They can use their information and influence, however, to lobby more powerful actors to apply bilateral sanctions to enforce international legal rules. In the early 1970s, the authors of U.S. human rights policy explicitly incorporated language from international human rights treaties into legislation requiring the United States to impose enforcement measures including sanctions on states that engage in a consistent pattern of gross violations of internationally recognized human rights (Fraser 1979).

Such language was rarely used, however, because policymakers were hesitant to accuse any country of engaging in a consistent pattern of gross violations of rights. With reports detailing extensive human rights abuses, human rights organizations such as Amnesty International brought the human rights situation in countries such as Uruguay, Argentina, and Chile to the attention of U.S. congressmen and thus contributed to country-specific cessation of military and economic aid. It is likely that these bilateral sanctions would not have been possible in the absence of the information and lobbying of human rights networks (Schoultz 1981: 84–85).

Networks have also targeted multilateral institutions to try to change their policies and to gain additional political leverage to influence change in target states. Environmental networks have successfully lobbied multilateral banks (especially the World Bank) to make their projects less environmentally destructive and to encourage them to use their influence to change state policies. These campaigns have brought together network activists from northern and southern countries to pressure for compliance (Keck 1995).

The Limits to and Asymmetries within the Process of Network Social Construction of Legal Rules

While the overall assessment of the contribution of networks to building and implementing legal rules has been positive, it is important to note the limitations and problems with these processes. Not all kinds of ideas lend themselves equally well to the process of the social construction of legal rules. Some scholars argue that norms that are clear and specific are more likely to be effective than norms that are ambiguous or complex, and that norms that have been around longer are more likely to be effective (Chayes and Chayes 1993; Legro 1997).

Claims about which substantive normative claims will be more influential in world politics have varied widely. Boli and Thomas argue that five principles are central to world culture: universalism, individualism, voluntaristic authority, rational progress, and world citizenship. By implication they suggest that norms underpinned by these principles will be more successful internationally (Boli and Thomas 1999). Thus we would not expect to find much support for norms that do not reflect these principles, such as, for example, collective economic or cultural rights. My colleague Margaret Keck and I have specified which norms are particularly effective transnationally and cross-culturally. These include norms involving (1) bodily integrity and prevention of bodily harm for vulnerable or "innocent" groups, especially when there is a short etiological chain between cause and effect; (2) legal equality of opportunity; and (3) issues that successfully invoke "adjacency" claims to already existing strong global norms (Keck and Sikkink 1997: 204–5). Norm entrepreneurs must speak to aspects of belief systems or life experiences that transcend a specific cultural or political context. Although notions of bodily harm are culturally interpreted, they also resonate with basic ideas of human dignity common to most cultures, because they respond to minimal criteria of commonality—human frailty.

Finally, divisions and imperfections within networks themselves limit the effectiveness of new legal rules. First, although most NGOs stress democracy and democratization, many are not themselves internally democratic. One dilemma with "democratizing" NGOs is that it is not always clear who should participate in decision making about leadership and policies—should NGOs be run by their staff, their boards, their volunteers, their members, those who provide funds, or those on whose behalf they organize? How might such systems of accountability be set up?

Second, the vast majority of NGOs originate in and are still based in the developed world. In 1993, 72 percent of the transnational advocacy NGOs still had their secretariats in Western Europe, the United States, or Canada. Even those international NGOs based in the developing world often depend on funding from foundations located in the wealthy countries.[20] Almost half of international human rights funding provided by U.S. foundations from 1973 to 1993 was provided by a single foundation—the Ford Foundation (Keck and Sikkink 1997: 99). Thus, another source of hidden power within transnational networks resides in the influence of foundations from wealthy countries who are part of these networks.

Because of the dominance of northern NGOs and foundations, the asymmetries within transnational networks have often been framed in north/south terms. As such the actions of networks may be seen as vehicles for "exporting" norms from the north to the south, or of cultural imperialism.[21] While this may be a useful starting place or shorthand for some of the internal divisions within transnational networks, it does not capture fully the complexity of such divisions and asymmetries. Margaret Keck and I have argued that networks, while plagued with asymmetries, are communicative structures and political spaces in which differently situated actors negotiate—formally or informally—the social, cultural, and political meanings of their joint enterprise (1997).[22] The campaign on violence against women illustrates this potential of networks because it picked up on issues that were not initially dominant strands in the mainstream national women's movement in the United States and Europe during the 1970s; concerns about rape and domestic abuse were more common in local women's groups and among more radical feminists in the United States. The movement to combat violence against women also has its roots in local action in other parts of the world. Locally based projects and coalitions in the Third World— such as GABRIELA in the Philippines, Mujeres por la Vida in Chile, and various women's groups in India and Bangladesh working on dowry death—had started to work on issues of violence in the mid- to late 1970s (Kumar 1995: 61, 65–66; Jahan 1995: 6). The way in which these various groups came together around the issue of violence illustrates that the process of the social construction of international law can be more than the "export" of practices from the developed world. Networks can be part of an interactive process by which people in far-flung places communicate and exchange beliefs, information, testimony, strategy, and sometimes services. In the process of exchange, they may influence and alter one other.

Nevertheless, many of the legal rules promoted by networks have both empowering and exclusionary effects. Although the examples in this essay have tended to focus on the empowering effect of international norms, there are also "silences," exclusions, or paradoxical effects of some international advocacy. Economic rights have not received the kind of attention that basic civil and political rights receive, although campaigns on infant health and child labor suggest that campaigns on economic rights are possible, at least if the "victims" fit the category of innocent or vulnerable children.

Some women's rights activists now admit that they jumped into the rights frame without fully thinking through the consequences for their movement.[23] What the human rights discourse implied was that if women's organizations were going to use international and regional human rights bodies and machinery, they would have to enhance their knowledge of international law. This requires privileging lawyers and legal expertise in a way that the movement had not previously done or desired to do. The wisdom of this approach is still being debated within the transnational network, and some activists are now trying to reframe violence against women as a health issue. They note that the human rights frame has been important for raising consciousness about the issue, but fear that it won't be as effective for prevention and treatment.

When measured against ideal visions of representation, democracy, accountability, and autonomy, most transnational NGOs fall short. Yet the appropriate standard against which to measure the representive capacities of NGOs is the existing degree of representation in international institutions and in the process of building international law. International institutions are imperfectly representative. In such a situation of highly imperfect representation, most efforts by NGOs and networks bring into international institutions and international law a greater diversity of viewpoints and information than would be available in international institutions devoid of their presence.

NOTES

1. This essay draws upon concepts developed in my book with Margaret Keck, *Activists beyond borders: Advocacy networks in international politics* (1998), and I want particularly to recognize my coauthor's contributions to the ideas presented here. This essay tries to build on discussions in that volume to address more systematically the specific issue of advocacy networks and the social construction of legal rules. I also want to recognize the contributions of three additional coauthors to my thoughts on these issues: Martha Finnemore, Ellen Lutz, and Thomas Risse.

2. Some legal scholars have been quite successful in linking theoretical constructs to rich empirical case studies of the social construction of legal rules. See, in particular, Yves Dezalay and Bryant G. Garth (1996) and David M. Trubek, Yves Dezalay, Ruth Buchanan, and John R. Davis (1994).

3. Jack Donnelly identifies challenging or altering state legal norms as one of the principal uses of human rights claims (1993: 20).

4. A simpler taxonomy of NGO roles divides them into two broad categories: (1) operational roles and (2) educational and advocacy roles. Operational roles involve all the multiple ways in which NGOs increasingly provide services and become project "subcontractors" for international institutions (Weiss and Gordenker 1996: 32).

5. A survey of the activities of 150 international human rights NGOs about their activities in 1995 found the following percentage of groups engaged in these international activities: "provided information to U.N. or other intergovernmental agency—92%; lobbied U.N. officials—70%; lobbied government delegations at the UN—65%; participation in the 1995 UN Human Rights Commission Meeting—62%; consulted with international agency official to plan international strategy—60%; developed international policy paper/draft resolution on human rights—56%; assisted intergovernmental agency to implement human rights policy—56%" (Smith, Pagnucco, and Lopez 1997: 8).

6. David Snow has called this strategic activity *frame alignment*—"by rendering events or occurrences meaningful, frames function to organize experience and guide action, whether individual or collective" (Snow, Rochford, Worden and Benford 1986: 464).

7. For example, McCann argues that law consists of "a complex repertoire of discursive strategies and symbolic frameworks that structure ongoing social intercourse and meaning making activity among citizens" (1994: 282).

8. Female genital mutilation is most widely practiced in Africa, where it is reported to exist in at least twenty-six countries. Between 85 and 114 million women in the world today are estimated to have experienced genital mutilation (World Bank 1993: 50).

9. For example, Leonard Kouba and Judith Muasher (1985) and Alison Slack (1988) address the issue of female circumcision generally. Elise Sochart talks about the British campaign in her 1988 article, while an example of the French campaign can be found in the November 23, 1993, *New York Times*. UN recommendations on the subject can be found in the Report of the "Working Group on Traditional Practices Affecting the Health of Women and Children" (1986), and Elizabeth Boyle and Sharon Preves (2000) have written about the emergence of national laws against female genital mutilation.

10. The only mention of the issues that today are categorized as violence against women is one article that calls on governments to suppress traffic in women and exploitation of prostitution (UN General Assembly 1981).

11. The convention was adopted at the 24th regular session of the General Assembly of the OAS on June 9, 1994, in Belém de Pará, Brazil.

12. This section draws on ideas from a coauthored work with Martha Finnemore, "International Norm Dynamics and Political Change" (1998).

13. The term *genocide* was first used by Raphael Lemkin (1944: 79). His efforts to promote the word and the treaty were reported in the October 20, 1946, *New York Times* (section 4, p. 13) and were also discussed by Leo Kuper (1985: 10) and William Korey (1989: 45–46).

14. Yves Dezalay and Bryant Garth apply the concept of the "moral entrepreneur" to the legal area in chapter 3 of *Dealing in Virtue* (1996: 33–62).

15. Some of the more important of these drafts were written by Hersch Lauterpacht and by a committee started by H. G. Wells and chaired by Viscount Sankey after a public debate conducted in Britain by the Daily Herald, the American Law Institute, the American Association for the United Nations, and the American Jewish Congress (Humphrey 1984: 31–32).

16. On this point I want to recognize the research assistance of Douglas Olsen, who prepared an article by article summary of the UDHR, "The Textual Origins of the Universal Declaration of Human Rights," which points to the influence of the Secretariat Draft as well as the declarations of scholars such as Professor Lauterpacht, and the influence of historical human rights declara-

tions within countries such as the U.S. Bill of Rights, the French Declaration of the Rights of Man and Citizen, and the Constitution of the USSR.

17. The idea of an international society was first developed by Hedley Bull. According to Bull, we live in an international society when, on the basis of common interests and values, states "conceive themselves to be bound by a common set of rules in their relations with one another and share in the working of common institutions" (1977: 13). Bull, however, conceived of international society as a society of states, while here I present a vision of international society in which nonstate actors are fundamental players.

18. Interview with Marsha Freeman, Minneapolis, Minnesota, March 1, 1996.

19. *Filártiga v. Pena-Irala*, 630 F.2d 876, 890 (2d Cir. 1980).

20. In their survey of international human rights NGOs, Smith, Pagnucco, and Lopez found that 60 percent of the NGOs received foundation grants to support their work, and 52 percent received grants from government or intergovernmental agencies (Smith, Pagnucco, and Lopez 1997: 22, 7).

21. Stephen Brill underscores this kind of perception: "The rule of law is on the march in the world. It is a product that America should be exporting, because we're the best at it. I say that proudly" (*Baltimore Sun*, May 23, 1994).

22. The idea of networks as political spaces developed in conversations between Margaret Keck and Elizabeth Umlas; for an application of this concept to domestic environmental NGO networks in Mexico, see Umlas 1996.

23. Interview with Lori Heise, Washington, D.C., September 27, 1995.

REFERENCES

Barnes, James, Marshall Carter, and Max Skidmore. 1980. *The world of politics.* New York: St. Martin's.

Basu, Amrita, ed. 1995. *The challenge of local feminisms: Women's movements in global perspective.* Boulder: Westview.

Boli, John, and George M. Thomas. 1999. INGOs and the organization of world culture. In John Boli and George Thomas, eds., *Constructing world culture: International non-governmental organizations since 1875*, 13–49. Stanford: Stanford University Press.

Boven, Theo van. 1990. The role of non-governmental organizations in international human rights standard setting: A prerequisite of democracy. *California Western International Law Review* 20:207–25.

Boyle, Elizabeth Heger, and Sharon Preves. 2000. National politics as international process: The case of anti-female-genital-cutting laws. *Law and Society Review* 34:703–37.

Bull, Hedley. 1977. *The anarchical society*. New York: Columbia University Press.

Bunch, Charlotte, and Niamh Reilly. 1994. *Demanding accountability: The global campaign and Vienna tribunal for women's human rights*. New York: United Nations Development Fund.

Burgers, J. Herman. 1992. The road to San Francisco: The revival of the human rights idea in the twentieth century. *Human Rights Quarterly* 14.

Burgers, J. Herman, and Hans Danelius. 1988. *The United Nations convention against torture: A handbook on the convention against torture and other cruel, inhuman, and degrading treatment or punishment*. Dordrecht: Martinus Nijhoff.

Burley, Anne-Marie. 1989. The alien tort statute and the judiciary act of 1789: A badge of honor. *American Journal of International Law* 83:461–93.

Center for Women's Global Leadership. 1993. *International campaign for women's human rights 1992–1993 report*. New Brunswick: Rutgers University.

Chaiken, Shelly, Wendy Wood, and Alice Eagly. 1996. Principles of persuasion. In E. T. Higgins and A. Kruglanski, eds., *Social psychology: Handbook of basic principles*. New York: Guilford.

Chayes, Abram, and Antonia Handler Chayes. 1993. On compliance. *International Organization* 47:175–205.

Clark, Ann Marie. 2001. *Diplomacy of conscience: Amnesty International and changing human rights norms*. Princeton: Princeton University Press.

Claude, Richard P. 1992. The case of Joelito Filártiga in the courts. In Richard Claude and Burns Weston, eds., *Human rights in the world community: Issues and action*. 2d ed. Philadelphia: University of Pennsylvania Press.

Crawford, Neta. 1993. Decolonization as an international norm: The evolution of practices, arguments, and beliefs. In Laura Reed and Carl Kaysen, eds., *Emerging norms of justified intervention*. Cambridge: American Academy of Arts and Sciences.

Department of State. 1946. *The United Nations conference on international organization, San Francisco, California April 25 to June 26, 1945: Selected documents*. Washington, D.C.: United States Government Printing Office.

Dezalay, Yves, and Bryant G. Garth. 1996. *Dealing in virtue: International commercial arbitration and the construction of a transnational legal order*. Chicago: University of Chicago Press.

Donnelly, Jack. 1993. *International human rights*. Boulder: Westview.

Eagly, Alice, and Shelly Chaiken. 1993. *The psychology of attitudes*. Fort Worth: Harcourt Brace Jovanovich.

Finnemore, Martha. 1996. *National interests in international society*. Ithaca: Cornell University Press.

Finnemore, Martha, and Kathryn Sikkink. 1998. International norm dynamics and political change. *International Organization* 52 (4): 887–913.

Franck, Thomas M. 1992. The emerging right to democratic governance. *American Journal of International Law* 86:46–91.

Fraser, Donald M. 1979. Congress's role in the making of international human rights policy. In Donald Kommers and Gilbert Loescher, eds., *Human rights and American foreign policy*. Notre Dame: University of Notre Dame Press.

Humphrey, John P. 1984. *Human rights and the United Nations: A great adventure*. Dobbs Ferry, N.Y.: Transnational.

IWRAW (International Women's Rights Action Watch). 1997. *The women's watch* 11:1 (June).

Jahan, Roushan. 1995. Men in seclusion, women in public: Rokeya's dream and women's struggles in Bangladesh. In Amrita Basu, ed., *The challenge of local feminisms: Women's movements in global perspective*. Boulder: Westview.

Katzenstein, Peter. 1996. *Cultural norms and national security*. Ithaca: Cornell University Press.

Keck, Margaret. 1995. Social equity and environmental politics in Brazil: Lessons from the rubber tappers of Acre. *Comparative Politics* (July 27).

Keck, Margaret, and Kathryn Sikkink. 1998. *Activists beyond borders: Advocacy networks in international politics*. Ithaca: Cornell University Press.

Khagram, Sanjeev, Jim Riker, and Kathryn Sikkink. 2002. *Restructuring world politics: Transnational social movements, networks, and norms*. Minneapolis: University of Minnesota Press.

Klotz, Audie. 1995. *Norms in international relations: The struggle against apartheid*. Ithaca: Cornell University Press.

Korey, William. 1989. Raphael Lemkin: The unofficial man. *Midstream* (June/July): 45–46.

Kouba, Leonard J., and Judith Muasher. 1985. Female circumcision in Africa: An overview. *African Studies Review* 28.

Kumar, Radha. 1995. From Chipko to Sati: The contemporary Indian women's movement. In Amrita Basu, ed., *The challenge of local feminisms*. Boulder: Westview.

Kuper, Leo. 1985. *The prevention of genocide*. New Haven: Yale University Press.

Leary, Virginia. 1979. A new role for non-governmental organizations in human rights: A case study of non-governmental participation in the development of norms against torture. In Antonio Cassese, ed., *UN law/fundamental rights: Two topics in international law*. Alphen aan den Rijn, Netherlands: Sijthoff and Noordhof.

Legro, Jeffrey. 1997. Which norms matter? Revisiting the failure of internationalism. *International Organization* 51:31–63.

Lemkin, Raphael. 1944. *Axis rule in occupied Europe*. New York: Carnegie Endowment for International Peace.

Lessig, Lawrence. 1995. The regulation of social meaning. *University of Chicago Law Review* 62, no. 3: 968–73.

Lipschutz, Ronnie. 1992. Reconstructing world politics: The emergence of global civil society. *Millennium* 21:389–420.

Lutz, Ellen, and Kathryn Sikkink. 2000. International human rights law and practice in Latin America. *International Organization* 54, no. 3: 633–59.

———. 2001. The justice cascade: The evolution and import of foreign human rights trials in Latin America. *Chicago Journal of International Law* 2, no. 1: 1–33.

McCann, Michael. 1994. *Rights at work: Pay equity reform and the politics of legal mobilization.* Chicago: University of Chicago Press.

McEntree, Andrew. 1996. Law and torture. In Duncan Forrest, ed., *A glimpse of hell: Reports on torture worldwide.* New York: New York University Press.

Mendez, Juan. 1992. New center seeks justice in the Americas. *Human Rights Watch: Quarterly Newsletter* (winter): 5.

Mendez, Juan E., and Jose Miguel Vivanco. 1990. Disappearances and the Inter-American court: Reflections on a litigation experience. *Hamline Law Review* 13: 507, 535.

Nadelmann, Ethan. 1990. Global prohibition regimes: The evolution of norms in international society. *International Organization* 44:479–526.

Peterson, M. J. 1992. Transnational activity, international society and world politics. *Millennium* 21, no. 3: 375–76.

Price, Richard. 1998. Reversing the gun sights: Transnational civil society targets land mines. *International Organization* 52, no. 3: 613.

Risse, Thomas, Stephen Ropp, and Kathryn Sikkink, eds. 1999. *The power of principles: International human rights norms and domestic change.* Cambridge: Cambridge University Press.

Risse, Thomas, and Kathryn Sikkink. 1999. Introduction. In Thomas Risse, Stephen Ropp, and Kathryn Sikkink, eds., *The power of principle: International human rights norms and domestic change.* Cambridge: Cambridge University Press.

Risse-Kappen, Thomas. 1995. Bringing transnational relations back in: An introduction. In Risse-Kappen, ed. *Bringing transnational relations back in: Non-state actors, domestic structures, and international institutions.* Cambridge: Cambridge University Press.

Robins, Dorothy B. 1971. *Experiment in democracy: The story of U.S. citizen organizations in forging the charter of the United Nations.* New York: Parkside.

Robinson, Jacob. 1946. *Human rights and fundamental freedoms in the charter of the United Nations.* New York: Institute of Jewish Affairs.

Rosen, Jeffrey. 1997. The social police: Following the law because you'd be too embarrassed not to. *New Yorker* Oct. 20–27: 170–81.

Schoultz, Lars. 1981. *Human rights and United States policy toward Latin America.* Princeton: Princeton University Press.

Schweitz, Martha L. 1995. NGO participation in international governance: The question of legitimacy. *Proceedings of the 89th Annual Meeting of the American Society of International Law.* April 5–8.

Slack, Alison T. 1988. Female circumcision: A critical appraisal. *Human Rights Quarterly* 10:437–86.

Slaughter, Anne-Marie. 1998. International law and international relations theory: A new generation of interdisciplinary scholarship. *American Journal of International Law* 92:367.

Smith, Jackie, et al., eds. 1997. *Transnational social movements and world politics: Solidarity beyond the state.* Syracuse: Syracuse University Press.

Smith, Jackie, Ron Pagnucco, and George Lopez. 1997. *Globalizing human rights: The work of transnational human rights NGOs in the 1990s: A report on a survey of international human rights organizations.* South Bend: Joan B. Kroc Institute for International Peace Studies.

Snow, David A., E. Burke Rochford, Steven K. Worden, and Robert D. Benford. 1986. Frame alignment processes, micromobilization, and movement participation. *American Sociological Review* 51:464.

Sochart, Elise A. 1988. Agenda setting, the role of groups and the legislative process: The prohibition of female circumcision in Britain. *Parliamentary Affairs* 41.

Sunstein, Cass. 1997a. *Free markets and social justice.* New York: Oxford University Press.

———. 1997b. Social norms and social roles. *Columbia Law Review* 96, no. 4: 903–68.

Thomas, Daniel C. 2001. *The Helsinki effect: International norms, human rights, and the demise of communism.* Princeton: Princeton University Press.

Thomas, Dorothy Q. 1993. Holding governments accountable by public pressure. In Joanna Kerr, ed., *Ours by right: Women's rights as human rights.* London: Zed Books.

Trubek, David M., Yves Dezalay, Ruth Buchanan, and John R. Davis. 1994. Global restructuring and the law: Studies in the internationalization of legal field and the creation of transnational arenas. *Case Western Reserve Law Review* 44:407–98.

Umlas, Elizabeth Dora. 1996. *Environmental non-governmental networks: The Mexican case in theory and practice.* Ph.D. dissertation, Yale University.

United Nations. 1986. *Report of the working group on traditional practices affecting the health of women and children.* U.N. Doc. E/CN.4/1986/42.

UN General Assembly. 1981. Convention on the elimination of all forms of discrimination against women, adopted and opened for signature, ratification, and accession by General Assembly resolution 34/180 of 18 December 1979. Entry into force: 3 September 1981.

UN ECOSOC (United Nations, Economic and Social Council). 1994. Open-ended working group on the review of arrangements for consultation with non-governmental organizations, General review of arrangements for consultations with non-governmental organizations: Report of the Secretary General, 26 May 1994.

Waltz, Kenneth. 1979. *Theory of international politics*. Reading, Mass.: Addison-Wesley.

Wapner, Paul. 1995. Politics beyond the state: Environmental activism and world civic culture. *World Politics* 47:311–40.

Weiss, Thomas, and Leon Gordenker. 1996. *NGOs, the UN, and global governance*. Boulder: Lynne Reinner.

Weissbrodt, David. 1984. The contribution of international nongovernmental organizations to the protection of human rights. Theodor Meron, ed., *Human rights in international law: Legal and policy issues*. Oxford: Clarendon.

Weschler, Lawrence. 1990. *A miracle, a universe: Settling accounts with torturers*. New York: Pantheon.

Wilson, Francesca M. 1967. *Rebel daughter of a country house: The life of Eglantyne Jebb, founder of the Save the Children Fund*. London: Allen and Unwin.

Wiseberg, Laurie S., and Harry M. Schoble. 1979. Monitoring human rights violations: The role of nongovernmental organizations. In Donald P. Sommers and Gilbert D. Loescher, eds., *Human rights and American foreign policy*. Notre Dame: University of Notre Dame Press.

World Bank. 1993. *World Bank development report 1993: Investing in health*. New York: Oxford University Press.

Modern Law as a Secularized and Global Model: Implications for the Sociology of Law

Elizabeth Heger Boyle and John W. Meyer

Elizabeth Heger Boyle, a lawyer and sociologist at the University of Minnesota, and John W. Meyer, a sociologist at Stanford, offer a theoretical account of why laws and legal forms flow rapidly around the world. Boyle and Meyer argue that the institutionalized context of the global system explains both the new global actors highlighted by Slaughter and Sikkink in the previous two chapters and the willingness of states to reform.

From Boyle and Meyer's institutionalist view, law and the sovereignty of the modern state, with which it is now linked, are constructed out of a common world cultural frame. Modern legal systems worldwide rest on universalistic and rationalistic assumptions about the natural and moral world outside of society. These historically rooted assumptions define appropriate national action, including legal reform. Boyle and Meyer thus highlight the peculiarity of sovereignty: sovereignty is a claim to autonomous decision power, but under exogenous universal principles and addressed to an exogenous and often universal audience.

To highlight the implications of their perspective, Boyle and Meyer contrast the development of national laws with mundane organizational rule-making less closely tied to the world cultural frame. The contrast illustrates how law might look today but for the guiding assumptions of the world system. While sharing a description of the expansion of (Western) law and approaches, which might be depicted as a potential new orthodoxy for the emerging world political economy, their explanation for the mechanisms that produce it differs from that found in other essays. Befitting their disciplinary grounding, they highlight the structures and processes rather than the agents of change.

The Enlightenment view of humanity, adopted by social scientists, places the rational, opportunistic individual at the center of the universe. The unique personality of this individual (charismatic, ambitious, passive) and his or her local milieu (resources, class standing, networks, ethnicity) create his or her unique identity and interests. Under the functional or consensus perspective, individuals trade in some of their "uniqueness" and "interests" to form institutions that benefit the collective. The legal system is one such institution. Individuals agree to abide by its laws and decisions to increase certainty in their lives and to protect themselves from the selfish interests of others. The legal system is used instrumentally to solve collective problems. Standing in opposition to the functional perspective, but sharing many of the same Enlightenment assumptions, is the conflict perspective. According to this perspective, because of the uniqueness of each individual, pursuits of interests and expressions of identity do not converge, but rather clash in a cacophony of conflict. Law is a coercive, repressive system linked to the winners of the conflict.

These perspectives often treat legal systems as irrelevant in the modern process of globalization (Sklair 1995). According to one popular perspective, "international law" develops simply to coordinate the global economy. After all, it is frequently pointed out, there really is no international legal system—national legal systems lack jurisdiction over the international realm. Others see law as more opaque and imagine the law and its authority to be the products of social functioning and the interests and powers involved (Black 1982).

Our perspective is different from these "realist" accounts. We propose that individuals do not construct legal systems (or other systems) to reflect inherent interests or identities. We propose that individuals *derive* their identities and interest from some perceived natural order and create legal systems to reflect these higher "Platonic ideals." We do not, here, advocate or subscribe to such ideals, but we see the modern state and legal system as being, in good part, organized around them. Like God in an earlier era, they become the center of action and interests in the modern world. From this perspective, finding the proper function for an international rule of law is problematic. Law is inherently neither functional nor repressive. Law is important for its linkage to perceived universal principles and as a source of identity for individuals and, importantly, nation-states.

For example, consider that legal rules, principles, standards, and ideas now flow very rapidly throughout world society: similar legal themes appear, in waves, on a very widespread basis. This is difficult to understand if we take only a realist and bottom-up view of the law as the product of local conflicts, powers, and interests: such processes would engender internationalization rather slowly from evolving interaction and interdependence. Internationalization is very easy to understand, however, if we add a more institutionalist view of the law—and the sovereignty of the modern state, with which it is now linked—constructed from a common and universalistic world cultural frame. In this essay, we develop such a view and show its implications.

The arguments of contemporary sociological institutionalism are useful here. Institutionalists stress (1) the dependence of contemporary rationalized organization on wider cultural environments, and (2) the rationalism, universalism, and now globalization of those environments (Meyer, Boli, and Thomas 1987; Meyer 1994; DiMaggio and Powell 1991). In these views, the modern nation-state system is governed by cultural assumptions derived from earlier religious principles. These cultural assumptions provide nation-states with clearly specifiable goals, such as obtaining "justice" through a "rule of law."

The purpose of this essay is not to criticize other explanations of law and the consequences that follow from their assumptions. Rather, its focus is to note some of the distinctive consequences for legal systems that follow from a more institutional and cultural perspective. Further, we do not intend to imply that laws and actions are always in conformity. On the contrary, because law reflects spiritual ideals, we do *not* expect a high degree of correspondence between law and action. This will be addressed later in the essay.

Background

It is generally understood that the historical sources of modern rationalized law and legal systems are ideas and assumptions about a religious or transcendental cosmos. Modern legal systems, now more or less worldwide, stem historically from the law and culture of the Catholic Church, which itself perpetuated recodified traditions from the Roman Empire (Berman 1993: 35–54; Anderson 1972). Other universalistic religious traditions could, under favorable circumstances, have generated worldwide legal arrangements of some sort, but in historical reality, the Western traditions, diffused through colonialism and military, political, and cultural hegemony, played this role.[1]

In the feudal world, no general sovereign existed who could or would create general law. God's will, embodied in the Church, governed, and the suggestion that humans as secular individuals could refine and generalize law was blasphemy. Jurists were bad Christians (David and Brierly 1985; see 1 Corinthians 6; cf. Greenhouse 1986). In the thirteenth century, law began to develop outside the Church, although still bound by its culture, Latin language, organization, and professionals (Berman 1993). With the legitimated development of the state (Strayer 1970) and its universities, and of urban life and commerce, some authority was acquired by civil and common law and a Thomistic celebration of reason. Reason, reflecting the myth of Rome, was universalistic, like divine law. Regional customary law, including "national" law, was scorned for giving no expression to universalistic justice (David and Brierly 1985: 2).

In the modern period, with the slow destruction of the authority of the Church and the triumph of the state, rulers—whether kings or legislators—became the creators and carriers of law. This trend was fueled by Western imperialism. The assumptions of universalism and rationality embedded in modern Western thought prompted the increasing globalization of the world system (Habermas 1984; Weber 1985), including the globalization of the nation-state form and the related universalistic legal system. Thus, legal systems are a constitutive element of that form of society known as the modern nation-state. The two arose concomitantly, each lending legitimacy to the other. National legal systems emerged more through the global system than through local organization.

Although law and legal systems are produced and changed by particular "societies," they carry sociocultural meanings and values about a larger natural and spiritual environment. Many modern lines of thought about the law also see it as rooted in notions of justice that transcend individual interests, as with traditions emphasizing "legal science," "natural law," and so on (Black and Coffee 1994; Nonet and Selznick 1978). We take seriously the idea that modern legal systems historically and currently rest on exogenous cultural assumptions. These assumptions shape both the content of laws and the particular organization and meaning of legal systems.

The modern system's pretenses, and much social scientific theory about the law, take the triumph of the state and its claims at face value.

The source of law's legitimacy has become so embedded, so taken for granted, that the supranational character of law is given little attention (David and Brierly 1985; Blankenburg 1994; Gaete 1991).[2] In its place arise pictures of the contemporary world as being "secularized," and the legal decisions of nation-states are seen as those of autonomous "actors" in history (Carter 1993). This is an important mistake. The rise of the state indeed essentially destroyed the organizational authority of the Church, but it did so, in our view, by absorbing, and thus becoming dependent upon, a secularized version of the wider culture carried by the Church. The processes are dialectic and continue throughout modern history. In claiming autonomy and sovereignty under various secularized principles of rationality and universality, both the nation-state and the law that is partially its creature intensify their dependence on these secularized principles.

Law and the Nation-State System

First, the expanded autonomy and sovereignty of the modern state were legitimated and supported by secularized (often scientized) versions of universal principles. So scholars (David and Brierly 1985), but also legislators and kings, justified their nominally autonomous authority in terms of principles of law that were universal in spirit and scope. One cannot read the great claims of the French or American (or later national, and still later socialist) revolutionaries, without seeing these highly dramatic justifications in terms of putatively universal principles. In recent years, the state has become central in universal declarations of human rights (Donnelly 1989; Shue 1980). The modern state and its purposes move center stage under the claimed cultural umbrella of formerly divine law, which has now become scientific and "natural" law (even today, there remain frequent direct references to spiritual forces). Sovereignty is a peculiar claim: it is a claim to autonomous decision-making power, but under exterior universal principles and addressed to an exogenous and often universal audience. The idea of sovereignty itself emanates not from each nation independently but from the *global* recognition of the nation-state form.

Second, law, with remarkable uniformity (Boli 1987), creates states both "defined" by and constituted from legally assumed "societies" (Bendix 1964; Marshall 1964). As the legitimate basis of their authority, modern states claim to be made up of constitutive elements beyond the legislator: "society" is discovered, and individuals appear as "citizens." Here again is a wholesale absorption of the earlier religious principles of equality in the eyes of God, now secularized and defined in terms of principles of scientific and natural law. The great mobilizing power of the modern nation-state (Tilly 1990), which is also a form of cultural dependence, is its claim and capacity to incorporate society and individuals within its structure. Society and citizenship are defined in terms of universalistic cultural rules, such as the scientific principles of social development, natural or scientific principles of individual rights, and later scientific or natural laws concerning the environment. Justice, defined in terms of universal principles, comes to be a constitutive function in this system.

These processes of building nations and societies continue, expand, and intensify in our own period. The long-term expansion of the nation-state model around the world (Strang 1990; Anderson 1991) and penetration of that model into more and more domains of social life (Thomas et al. 1987; Thomas 1987; Meyer et al. 1997) create a global arena in which standardized models of the nation-state are organized at the world level, understood to apply universally, and at least in form enacted by practically every nation-state. The expansion of the nation-state system extends and elaborates the rationalistic and universalistic culture upon which it depends. In the post–World War II period, global structuration occurs exponentially (Magnarella 1995), with explosions in central intergovernmental organizing (e.g., the United Nations system), and even greater expansions in global nongovernmental organizing (Boli and Thomas 1999; Otto 1996).

Global society has developed extremely elaborate conceptions of the collective purposes of the state in managing society (Meyer et al. 1997; Finnemore 1996). It contains comprehensive doctrines of economic, social, and political development, often with standardized measures of "success" (e.g., the GDP per capita, now gone worldwide). It embraces very elaborate visions of social and individual rights and justice (Ramirez and Meyer 1998), now including justice and equality across age, gender, sexual preference, ethnic, and racial lines (Berkovitch 1999; McNeely 1995; Dryzek 1996). In addition it now also includes elaborate and standardized conceptions of the proper relationship of societies to their natural ecosystemic environment (Frank 1998).

All this is phrased quite universally[3] and justified in terms of the scientific and natural law understanding of a universalized and rationalized cosmos. The result is the modern picture of the environment (Frank et al. 1999), society, and the individual (Frank, Meyer, and Miyahara 1995). The impact on typical nation-states is enormous. First, this universalism aids legitimation of the global spread and stability of these entities (Strang 1990; McNeely 1995). It also impacts formal structure—and often practice—in the widest variety of areas (Meyer 1994; Meyer et al. 1997; Donnelly 1989). Formal isomorphism around universalized principles is a dominant trend, despite the enormous practical variation among countries in resources or cultural traditions.

Thus, the modern nation-state is very much a creature of a theoretically imagined community (Anderson 1991), and the theoretical imagination is prominently a worldwide rationalistic and universalistic model of state, society, and the individual (Thomas 1987).

Impact on the Law and the Legal System

In two ways, as discussed above, the wider universalistic culture of modernity impacts the law. First, modern legal systems are rooted in the nominal sovereignty of the national state. But as we discuss above, this sovereignty principle is associated with dependence on the wider legitimating rationalistic culture. Thus legislators, lawyers, and judges are creatures of the nation-state organization (variably across national distinctions, such as the civil/common law one [Jepperson and Meyer 1991; Boyle 1998, 2000]). Even the most despotic dictators now claim to represent the interests of their nations' citizens. In playing these roles, however, they are also creatures of the wider culture in which the state is embedded and are dependent on its definitions and conceptions: the servants of the state are involved in the business of applying to their local polities the putatively universal and rational principles of science and natural law, and of the rational pursuit of progress and justice.[4]

Second, wider universalistic and rational principles apply not only to the state, but also to every aspect of the status of society, its functional groups and interests, and the individuals within it. Law and lawyers play an independent role. Professionalized, the lawyers and law have direct responsibilities to apply the overall rationalized and universalized principles to myriad particular situations, not all of which may be covered by the interests of a particular state. The law is above the particularities of the state and is to speak a wider universalistic truth. Liberal and/or common-law contexts emphasize this independence, and all democratic countries in the modern world, almost by definition, claim independent judiciaries. The law is thus dependent on wider truths, organized by scientists, social scientists, and professionalized knowledge of all sorts about nature, society and its interests, and individuals (Meyer 1987; Meyer et al. 1997). We note once again that these "truths" may or may not actually exist—the important point for this essay is that actors in the modern world operate *as if* they exist.

Implications of the Dependence of Modern Law on Globalized, Rationalized, and Universal Cultural Principles

An understanding of the "secularized religious" dependence of the law aids an understanding of modern legal systems. Law is at once derived from, and ostensible evidence of, general but powerful rules of nature. The connection to religious principles also illuminates the organization of the modern world-system around a central tenet—not God's will, but similar universal ideas embodied in sovereignty. Agency rather than predestination determines the future, "social" change exists and can be systematically analyzed, "neutrality" replaces doctrine. The modern system of sovereign nation-states, like God's will in an earlier time, encompasses reality and becomes the foundation for an explanation of the world.[5] Bringing attention to the necessarily imperfect correspondence between modern legal systems and the taken-for-granted beliefs in universal ideals helps make sense of issues raised in the sociology of law.

The closer a rule system is tied to ideas of universalism, the more, we argue, it will manifest the characteristics described below. Resource capacity is a competing explanation for conformity, but the effects of that variable are less clear. If a new human rights doctrine arises, a core country like Sweden is likely to learn of it early on and have many professionals who can translate the new doctrine into policy. On the other hand, those same resources could allow Sweden to resist or modify the new doctrine, an option unavailable to resource poor countries. Although having more resources enables core organizations to conform, having less resources simultaneously limits peripheral organizations' ability to resist or modify the operating frame. While resources undoubtedly play a role, links to the universal ideal frame seem more consistently and predictably important.

While the assumption and integration of universal principles is most profound at the international and nation-state levels, over time these ideals penetrate many other spheres. Business organizations adopt elaborate due process procedures (Edelman 1990), schools forbid corporal punishment, and even families come under increasing pressure to conform to universal standards. These latter spheres are subjected to the influence of universal principles later and more indirectly than nation-states. They maintain more discretion and more idiosyncrasies. Consequently, they make useful points of comparison with the exogenous focus of national legal systems. We loosely refer to entities in these spheres as *organizations.*

The contrast with mundane rule-making in the nonsovereign sphere or in countries with competing religious universals (e.g., some Islamic countries) illustrates the appearance of law within organizations that are less linked to exogenous universal principles or assumptions about sovereignty. To make operational the continuum of links to putative universal principles, one could consider the extent to which an organization's identity was connected to the sovereignty of the nation-state and to the international community. One could also consider organizational, associational, and professional ties. In the case of typical nation-states themselves, these cultural and associational linkages would, of course, be extremely high. Among nonsovereign organizations, state monopolies (e.g., schools) or organizations with major state regulation should be more linked to universal ideals than those that are local economically competitive organizations.

The global diffusion of the nation-state form (including the modern legal system) was facilitated by its universalism and rationalism. To summarize the implications of rule-system dependence on universal cultural principles, we propose the following three general themes:

1. The more closely an organization is tied to the global and putatively universalistic system, the more its rule system will participate in the diffusion and expansion of universal principles through (a) the adoption of laws and legal discourse consistent with international cultural accounts, (b) isomorphism, and (c) the extension of its jurisdiction into more areas of the organization.

2. The more closely an organization is tied to the global and putatively universalistic system, the more its rule system will engage
in the ritualized enactment of law through (a) greater ceremony
surrounding law, (b) decoupling of law and social reality, and
(c) elaborate restrictions on how to find the truth.

3. The more closely an organization is tied to the global and putatively universalistic system, the more its rule system will assume
the existence of an integrated and rationalized cosmos by (a)
adopting scientific methods of inquiry, (b) relying explicitly on
the idea of rationality, (c) decoupling abstract justice rules of the
system from concrete assessments of the justice of particular
outcomes, (d) seeking and attempting to maintain consistency,
and (e) expanding into new areas.

This section of the essay is organized around these three general themes.
We discuss each in turn.

1.   Diffusion and Expansion

The assumption, built into all modern legal systems, that the law reflects
universal principles produces a consequence that realist theories cannot
well explain. The organization of legal systems and the laws themselves
are remarkably similar around the world, in spite of much local cultural
and material variation. Further, these similarities cannot be attributed
entirely to Western imperialism, since they continued and in some ways
even increased in the decades following decolonization. Overarching
principles are prompting conformity, while local differences are creating small variations.

A.   *Exchange of Laws, Rules, and Legal Discourse*
Across nation-states, laws diffuse much more rapidly than theories
emphasizing local interests and culture would predict. They diffuse in
ways that have not been predicted by theories that view them as dependent on local or national boundaries of sovereignty. This can easily be
explained in terms of our arguments. States maintain their legitimacy
through their responsiveness to perceived universal principles. National
laws become an important symbol of the acceptance of these perceived
principles. So laws readily diffuse across state boundaries in the United
States (Walker 1969). Furthermore, they now rapidly diffuse around the

world, from national constitutions (Boli 1987) to legal policy (Strang and Meyer 1993; McNeely 1995) down into localized domains.

The content of the international ideals that diffuse has been discussed at length elsewhere (Meyer et al. 1997). In general, these ideals are consistent with Western notions of individual rights and progress. The more a nation-state is linked to the international system, the more its rules will follow these basic ideas. Rape laws provide a useful example. Highly universalistic legal systems make no distinction between categories of persons; all types of women and men can perpetrate and be the victims of rape. In contrast, weakly universalized systems have entirely different legal rules for different types of people. In some Islamic countries, Hudood (religious) laws apply to Muslim rapists, and civil laws apply to other rapists. Some legal systems lie between these two extremes, as in countries with only one legal system that applies to all persons, but that differentiates between different kinds of persons, for example, the rape of a prostitute versus the rape of other types of women (Frank 1998). Thus, the greater the linkage to the international system, the more laws' application and content will conform to Platonic ideals.

It is routine for legislators, law professors, and even courts to cite principles established in courts operating under an entirely different sovereignty: the cross-national citing of cases and decisions has increased dramatically in the current period (Robinson 1996; Strauss 1995; Rosenberg 1997). It is also true that the principles of international law (including international governmental and even nongovernmental organizations) routinely appear in legal decisions in particular countries, despite the extreme ambiguity of the sovereignty involved. In turn, international courts begin to perceive conformity across nation-states as evidence of universal principles. The European Court of Human Rights is a case in point (Harris, O'Boyle, and Warbrick 1995). Since its inception in 1955, over 25,000 claims have been filed with the court. Consensus among European nations has had a considerable impact on the decisions of the court. A state with a unique policy within the European community is particularly at risk of an adverse judgment[6] because European consensus is deemed to be inspired by a common universal law.

In all these cases, underlying assumptions of universalism make for the easy flow of legal rules across the boundaries of nominal sovereignty. The flows of legal rules seem most extreme when high general principles, such as those of human rights, the scientized environment, or national socioeconomic progress, are involved (Dezalay and Garth 1995). Fundamental principles, contrary to much theory, may flow more easily than less fundamental adaptations. This characterizes a world in which local structures are envisioned in terms of universal rules. It probably describes much better the world of the high culture of the law (Risse and Sikkink 1999), than that of practical or mundane organizations dealing with local issues based on local principles.

In the same way, the organizational system of the law permits the flow of participants and communication across sovereignty boundaries more readily than conventional theories might suppose. Legal cultures and discourse flow readily across state and national boundaries. U.S. legal research resources such as Lexis and Westlaw routinely include the codes and legal decisions of non-U.S. sovereigns. Law firms specializing in international law now flourish and hold prestigious positions within the legal community. Hiring lawyers from other countries becomes routine for law firms as well as corporations, and transnational legal practice guides appear with increasing frequency (Campbell 1982; Pritchard 1991). Legal culture and discourse assemble themselves easily in international governmental and nongovernmental organizational arenas (Boli and Thomas 1997). General legal expertise, it is assumed, moves beyond particular systems of law and training. Such beliefs assume that common underlying principles are involved.

On the other hand, at the localistic extreme, practical organizational rules set out in nonlegal situations flow slowly across organizational boundaries. These rules are geared to satisfying local clientele. Even within the same multinational corporation, corporate rules tend to vary from country to country.[7] The allocation of responsibilities to particular departments or occupations, the exact definitions of employee rights, and other rules such as these are expected to differ significantly from organization to organization. It is routine to assume that organizational cultures might naturally vary in different contexts; this becomes a problem only when the high legal culture intervenes.

B.   Isomorphism among Legal Systems
The ideas above imply something that is often observed in specific cases, but less often noted in general. Legal systems—supposedly linked to particular societies, but in our view reflective of much common cultural material—are often more similar than might be expected. Nation-states differ by ratios of 100 to 1 in resources per capita. In addition, they dif-

fer enormously in local cultural traditions. It is therefore surprising how similar their legal arrangements tend to be. The literature naturally emphasizes differences in property rules, family law, and the like, exaggerating what are often quite modest differences. It is more realistic to note how similar these systems are and how much they change in parallel. For instance, formal legal rules about human rights show a great deal of isomorphism and isomorphic change, despite enormous differences in practice and practical circumstances (McNeely 1995; Meyer et al. 1997; Risse and Sikkink 1999).

The intensification and expansion of world society and culture in the post–World War II framework, and the creation of many new nation-states highly dependent on this framework, have greatly increased world pressures for legal isomorphism. We could therefore expect to find increases in this dimension during the current period and more rapid rates of change toward isomorphism. We would also expect to find expansions in the number of domains (such as the environment or family law) in which rapid isomorphism occurs.

Prevailing theories of a more realist vein would suggest that legal isomorphism among countries is to be found particularly in social areas (such as the economy) with relatively high international interdependence. In contrast, our argument is that legal isomorphism obtains when great similarity of identity is perceived (Strang and Meyer 1993), and can explain rapid legal diffusion in areas with quite low interdependence: rationalized family law, human rights principles, many environmental domains, education, medicine, and the like. In fact, an extreme version of our argument would treat much societal interdependence as slowing down—not speeding up—diffusion and isomorphism, since it tends to create networks of differentiated and opposing interests and mobilization.

A striking feature of modern world legal development is its isomorphism precisely in domains with relatively low levels of exchange and interdependence. Family arrangements are viewed as a core cultural difference from place to place. One might expect that law and the state would allow wide latitude for variation in a sphere so central to the transmission of local culture. But when these systems are legalized, for example in terms of human rights, pressures for coherence and consistency rise, and consultants, advisers, and legal principles flow readily across national boundaries. Recent expansions of law to encompass issues formerly left to a parent's discretion (spanking, female circumcision, and so on) raise the issue of cultural autonomy, but come down strongly on the side of universal principles (Boyle and Preves 2000; Frank 1998). A "proper" family does not beat its children, and the state has an obligation to ensure that this is so; a "proper" family is the union of two individuals with equal rights to marital dissolution; and so on. From family planning to child rearing to divorce, the legally established meaning and "purpose" of the family have been surprisingly standardized around the world.

Other domains outside of international interdependence have also become the focus of laws consistent with the universalized ideas. Despite obvious geographic differences, the proper relationship of individuals to the environment has an assumed uniformity, and regulation looks very similar from one nation-state to the next. The role of women in society is another example. Recent articles have suggested that the state has not only negative obligations to refrain from abusing its citizens, but also a positive obligation to insure a more even distribution of power between men and women (Etienne 1995; Stetson 1995; Schuler 1992). Another example is military strategy, a key element of sovereign autonomy. Legal restraints on particular types of warfare, such as the use of chemical weapons or land mines, are often readily accepted throughout the international system (Price 1997). Theories of globalization based on local movements or interdependencies have a hard time explaining the pressure for uniformity in areas such as these. Nations, like Tocqueville's Americans, may be most similar at the points at which they most stress their uniqueness and autonomy.

C.   Expanding Jurisdiction of Legalized Rule Systems

Legal decision-making that is not based on the system of universal principles is the object of much suspicion. So myths about the importance of the universal ideals are maintained despite the diversity of local social organizations and cultures. The modern expansion of the nation-state into many more domains—family life, the environment, economic regulation, and so on—is accomplished through the extension of standardized legal rules. Alternatives, such as arrangements of hierarchical domination over, rather than penetration of, local segments, are undercut. This explains, in modern times, the increasing reach of the law into areas that previously were unregulated, including rule making in nonsovereign organizations. Belief in the correctness of universal principles mandates a concern that segmentation or indirect control will undermine sovereignty. Modern sovereignty seems to call not so much for organizational domination as for the legalized penetration of standardized rules. So relations between spouses, parents and children, employers and employees, buyers and sellers, or teachers and students are managed by ever-expanding direct legal application of general principles rather than simply by organizational domination.

Organizations that are linked to exogenous universal principles pick up this idea (or are required to) and, at least in appearance, subordinate themselves to such principles, acknowledging their lack of complete sovereignty. They often voluntarily attempt to link with the universal principles themselves and accept legalized controls. They also expand their subordinated rule-making authority into areas of the organization and into areas of employee lives. They formalize maternity leave and set up on-site day care, create proper grievance procedures and systems of employee rights, and incorporate the appropriate professionals (Meyer and Rowan 1977; DiMaggio and Powell 1983). The correctness of all this is taken for granted.

The dependence of modern states and legal systems on wider models, combined with the elaborated and universalistic character of these models, creates a situation in which the widest variety of social interests and social problems leads to expansions of legalization both in national societies and in the world as a whole. This is most striking in the peripheries of the world, where the availability of expanded general models leads both states and local interests to build elaborated rules and claims. Injustices and inefficiencies are seen that would otherwise be taken for granted. But the effects occur in core countries, too, and in the world as a whole: all sorts of interests, grievances, and problems lead both states and local actors to participate in the expansion of the system to cover, for instance, newly perceived environmental problems.

Thus, the widest variety of local interests and problems, in the modern context, can feed into the overall expansion of globalized legal arrangements as well as their penetration of local life.

2. Ritualized Enactment

As in all situations in which transcendent principles are at issue, the law is enacted and enforced in highly ceremonial ways (Meyer and Rowan 1977). While general ideas are broadly understood, the ability to translate reality into a legal framework is limited to specialists—lawyers and judges. We discuss three dimensions in which the legal system tends to be distinctive. It is difficult to explain these properties without resort to our arguments concerning the extent to which the law carries and depends on assumptions of higher values.

A.   Ceremony

Rule systems that are more closely tied to exogenous universal principles enact law in highly ceremonially constituted contexts. This maintains the special status of the law and suggests its separateness from, and superiority to, ordinary individual decision making. Legislators, judges, and even lawyers take special oaths and occupy prominent positions with distinctive rights and responsibilities. Courts are highly ceremonial places. Witnesses swear before God to tell the whole truth, and perjury is the most serious of transgressions. Just as sinners were central to but disassociated from Church rituals, so too the public is distanced from courtroom rituals. Legal proceedings are conducted on behalf of the public; the public is expected to contribute in certain limited respects (e.g., as jurors in common-law countries), but the heart of the courtroom is the area from which the ordinary public is barred. In this way courts are easily distinguished from the mundane society around them.

Further, within nation-states, lawyers generally make up a bounded and nominally unified profession, despite the diversity of their activities. Analogous to a priesthood, there are elaborate rituals of socialization, principles of professional unity, and extremely sharp designations of who is, and who is not, a lawyer. Learning the arcane rhetoric of law (*habeas corpus, replevin, appellee,* and so on) is an important aspect of becoming a lawyer (Sarat 1995). Stringent controls characterize entry into the legal profession—in the common-law world, through lawyers' voluntary associations; in the civil-law world, through controls exercised by the state (Abel 1988). Within the legal profession, those lawyers with the closest ties to universal principles of justice (e.g., constitutional law professors) or science (e.g., patent lawyers) are those with the highest prestige (Heinz and Laumann 1982; Abbott 1988). In modern nation-states, those who find or interpret the law have special insight into the universal principles and are clearly distinguishable from those who merely try to live according to the law.

Note how distinctive national legal systems are from protolegal rule making and enforcement in contexts where the high culture of modernity is less invoked. Typical organizations make mundane rules routinely. Examples might include decisions about subunit responsibilities and resources, detailed rules about travel allowances or office supplies, rearrangements of roles and their authority, the specification of particular office hours, or systems for handling complaints. Organizations can often create such rules rather casually through payroll employees, minor administrators, or committees, enact them without much ceremony (Zhou 1993), and enforce them in organizationally routine ways. Until recently, organizations did these things without much blessing from a symbolically unified and bounded legal profession (Dobbin et al. 1994), though legalization has now increased.[8] Rather, it was assumed that responsible people could interpret the rules without any special knowledge. Creating and changing routine rules did not legitimate or delegitimate management in a typical organization because management was not understood as trying to implement higher universal principles. As organizations become more dependent on exogenous ideals to maintain their legitimacy, they may begin to develop special predesignated spaces and procedures to deal with problems and "independent" departments (e.g., human resources departments) to deal with employees.

B. Decoupling between Law on the Books and Reality

Nation-states, because of their ostensible link to universal principles, also produce extreme decoupling of the law from practical social life (Meyer and Rowan 1977; Weick 1976; March and Olsen 1976). Law expresses and defines society in terms of the general principles on which it depends, and doing so makes it important to bound the law from mundane social reality. We are not suggesting that there is no relationship between law and action—both are influenced by the putatively universal principles. Because law is more a reflection than an instrument of these principles, however, it is unlikely to have great direct influence on much social action above and beyond the general effects of globalization.

Reality, practicality, and ease of use are emphatically not what the law is about. The law is about principle and the belief in some greater good, at least in part transcending any specific society or situation. Laws are as much invocations of perceived universal ideals and symbols of state legitimacy as they are routine concessions to various special-interest groups. This explains why national laws emerge for which practical society shows more ambivalence than enthusiastic support (e.g., right-to-strike laws, or laws giving rights to unpopular minorities). It also explains why legal systems have a profusion of symbolic, impractical rules (Gusfield 1986; Duster 1970), unenforced rules (Black 1972), and legal fictions (Fuller 1967).

The actual invocation of law is a dramatic step, infrequently taken, although the threat to invoke the law is omnipresent. Contracts are written but not used (Macaulay 1968), and elaborate criminal court procedures are created, but not employed to deal with the vast majority of discovered deviations (Kaplan and Skolnick 1982). Judges create legal fictions to maintain the immutability of the law long after social change has reduced the actual terms of the law to nonsense. This is difficult to explain from most theoretical points of view. Why would impracticable, unenforced rules be so common and so important? But the law survives and expands, in our view reflecting substantially different considerations than the practicability or wisdom of implementation.

From our point of view this decoupling is central to the national project. While decoupling characterizes all sorts of rationalized organization (Meyer and Scott 1992), decoupling occurs particularly in areas where corporate self-interest and extraorganizational legal requirements conflict (Meyer and Rowan 1977; Edelman 1992). In other words, decoupling occurs at precisely the point where the law intrudes.

The less a rule is linked explicitly or implicitly to ideals outside the organization, the less separation of "spirit" and "practice" is possible. If an office closes at 5 P.M. for no particular reason—just because—it is quite different from an office that closes at 5 P.M. as a requirement of state law. In the latter case, closing the office at 5:15 has numerous interpretations. Are the office employees being exploited? Are office clients at this particular location receiving an unfair advantage over clients who live across town? In our view, decoupling reflects, not the extreme practical difficulties faced by the law, but rather the extraordinarily important and universalized culture on which it depends and which it must reflect. We propose that organizations, like the nation-state and its legal system that are more tied to universalistic cultural accounts, will have less specific enforcement provisions and more unused, unenforced rules and procedures than more localized, mundane organizations.

The decoupled character of legal systems is sometimes (and rather reasonably) taken to be an indicator of their ineffectiveness and functional unimportance. This may be realistic in dealing with some traditional legal systems, but misses important points in approaching the modern one. The modern system is decoupled precisely because of the extent to which it is linked to universal models and standards, despite the limited and variable character of local social life. These universal ideas are available, not only to states and some lawyers, but to a wide variety of local interests and potential grievants as well. Despite the practical constraints and limitations of local circumstances, some wider perspectives are empowered by the expanded and universal character of the models. Local actors can look at their limited situations in terms of great rules about socioeconomic progress and social justice: mobilizing resources, and sometimes concrete resource networks, can be envisioned and are sometimes available. Thus, social interests and forces feed into the expansion and penetration of the wider models and lead to the creation of new variations in these models.

C. Restrictions on Determining Truth

Ritualization also appears in the legal obsession with "proper" evidence. Rule systems that imagine more links to universal principles tend to have elaborate restrictions on proof. In modern courts, the use of "tainted" evidence, regardless of its probity, is strictly limited. In general, individuals may only speak for themselves: if others try to speak for them, it is deemed hearsay. The introduction of evidence into the courtroom is surrounded by elaborate ceremony. Evidence is formally introduced, the chain of possession is carefully reconstructed, the judge determines admissibility, and only then is the evidence considered. Who can bring a claim and when that claim can be brought are also circumscribed. In general, individuals and organizations cannot bring claims for the common good, as that would belie the special access of the state to the universal principles.

Organizations outside the system of universal principles are more likely to consider pieces of information that come to their attention as they try to resolve issues. Any person presenting information may well be listened to; "relevance" has a broader scope, and evidence flows informally, perhaps through gossip. The ritualized enactment of universal principles occurs in organizations with more links to global cultural accounts through formal rule systems that limit evidence, claims, and the standing to bring claims.

3. The Assumption of an Integrated and Rational Cosmos

Modern legal systems rest on the idea that natural and social worlds occur in a unified and lawful context and that this context can be understood in an integrated way. The core of this integrated system is a belief in rationality. Many features of modern law can be understood in these terms.

A. The Scientific Progress of the Law

Modern national legal systems are more dependent on expanding scientific or scientized knowledge, including scientific methods, than the rule systems of nonsovereign organizations. Expert witnesses are commonly used in both legislation and court activity (Stryker 1994). Increasingly, expert witnesses include social scientists, for example, in the gender discrimination lawsuit brought by Ann Hopkins against the Price Waterhouse accounting firm in the 1980s, where Susan Fiske, a well-known social psychologist, figured prominently in the trial court's judgment (Hopkins 1996). Economics becomes the basis for numerous legal doctrines. Lawyers routinely hire jury experts and survey potential juries to predict outcomes. Criminal cases rest on the ability of the FBI crime laboratory to stick meticulously to its scientific mandate. Scientized knowledge about nature and the rational causal principles derived from its laws have an extraordinarily high standing. Legal systems that are tied to universal principles also tend to follow a scientific model. For example, Harvard Law School in 1870 adopted a "scientific" method for learning and understanding law that quickly spread to, and still exists in, the rest of the United States (Friedman 1985).

In more recent times, the world is frequently considered a "laboratory" wherein national laws become natural "experiments" (Black and Coffee 1994; Zimring and Hawkins 1973). Legal cases mimic the aura of scientific experiments, for example, when jurors undertake the rigorous testing of the null hypothesis of the defendant's innocence. Legal systems exalt science and rationality.

Scientific methods are less likely to be employed in the day-to-day operations of typical organizations that often make policy decisions on the basis of hunches and interests. Typical organizations are less likely to systematize the actions of employees, and more willing to let things drift. As universal and legalized principles in the current period penetrate nonsovereign organizations, the organizations are more likely to depend on the knowledge of professional and scientific consultants. They might employ scientists as in-house psychologists, economists, and the like. They might also enthusiastically recruit experts to systematize the way in which employees approach their work.

B. An Expanded and Invented Rationality

In the modern period, rational motivation replaces religious explanations for individual action. Typically, the existence and importance of this rationality is taken for granted. National legal systems constantly search for rational, or rational choice, explanations to underlie legal rules and decisions. Elaborate scientific and rationalistic analyses are sought to adjudicate issues around the "battered wife syndrome," "repressed memory syndrome," or issues of effective legal deterrence. Numerous legal scholars suggest or assume that crime occurs after individuals rationally weigh the costs and benefits of committing crimes. Crimes and criminals that do not fit the model well are either brought imaginatively into a rational frame or else minimized and rendered as unimportant to an understanding of crime generally. Elaborate literatures arise, and their conclusions are routinely cited in the courts and legislative hearings. Courts also regularly measure individuals according to "reasonable person" standards. Would a reasonable person rationally believe that his or her conduct could lead to great bodily harm or death? Could a reasonable person be misled by the conduct of the defendant? Just as all individuals at one time had access to God through penance and prayer, now all individuals are assumed to have access to "universal truth" through rational thought.

Note how much more casual all this is in nonlegal organizational rule-making. Although it is true that mundane organizational rules depend on such analyses, the urgency involved appears to be significantly lower. In business, personal preferences may figure prominently in the allocation of work, and personal contacts may form the basis of continued business with particular suppliers or clients. In families, expressiveness is the key, and rationality still seems out of place. Weighing the costs and benefits of each potential spouse when deciding who to marry seems inappropriate (and callous), for example.

C. Decoupling between the Justice of the System and the Justice of Particular Outcomes

Unfortunate outcomes are more easily explained as resorts to higher principles in rule systems linked to universal ideals. When a system is linked to justice as a universal principle, then the system does not need to justify every outcome it produces. Rather, these rule systems are legitimated by their linkage to universal justice. Thus, in the 1200s, death was perhaps an unfortunate side effect of determining whether a person was a witch. When suspected witches were tossed into water with stones tied to their feet, those who sank (and perhaps drowned) were deemed innocent; those who floated were deemed true witches and were burned at the stake. The witch trials emphasized "truth" over "justice": it was more important to know whether a person was a witch than to have a just outcome for the accused. Modern national legal systems are often equally unconcerned with particular outcomes, although the universal principle of sovereignty inverts the religious universals, emphasizing "justice" over "truth." Under the modern universal law, a dead body and a smoking gun may not be enough to convict a guilty person if the state did not follow the proper procedure in accusing him. In both the religious and sovereign systems, problematic outcomes are sometimes celebrated in the name of higher universal principles.

At the other end of the continuum, the practical effects of decisions are central to mundane organizational decision-making, even though ordinary organizations are increasingly subjected to institutional pressures for legalization (Meyer and Rowan 1977). Justice and truth are considered after assessing the impact of any outcome on the future of the organization. Complaints by disgruntled employees against the owner's son might be ignored or minimized regardless of their merit. Complaints by an important client are likely to be acted upon even if unfounded. Such inconsistency is rarely noted, but if it does come to the attention of management, organizational authorities "not wanting to stand on principle" might justify it as good business. Depending on the strength of an organization's ties to exogenous universal principles, its rule system may focus more on fair process than specific outcomes, and it may emphasize merit over lockstep or familial justifications for promotion and pay.

D.   The Search for Consistency

National legal systems assume the importance of ultimate consistency while more mundane organizational rule-making authorities may not. Inconsistency is seen as irrational, and extreme efforts are made to expunge it, in civil-law systems with detailed codes and internal coordinating committees (Blankenburg 1994), and in common-law systems with elaborately structured hierarchical courts (Damaška 1986). Inconsistent rules provide counterevidence to the idea that legal systems are based on universal principles, and thus they represent a serious threat to legitimacy. The emphasis on consistency by nation-states occurs both within, and increasingly across, jurisdictions. Legal doctrines of one country, for example, inheritance or rules of evidence, are assumed to exist in all others (Malinowski 1934). Much argumentation and citation is devoted to finding and rooting out inconsistency: if different courts, states, or now even countries have different conclusions on fundamental matters, something is wrong.

There are at least two strategies for dealing with perceived inconsistencies. The first response is to change inconsistent laws or overturn inconsistent cases on appeal. The second, and probably more prevalent response, is to "explain" the inconsistency. To a scientist this is the imposition of scope conditions; to a lawyer this is distinguishing cases or laws. Scholars seek to derive universal principles from diverse national laws (Frase 1990; Black and Coffee 1994; LoPucki and Triantis 1994). The ideal of consistency is one source of the extreme decoupling discussed earlier. Unenforced rules allow the legal system to avoid the head-on conflicts that might threaten "secular" religious assumptions about universality. Legal fictions are devised so that "the internal coherence of the new with the old is ensured, and thus the systematic unity of the whole law" (Savigny 1880).

This is all quite different in mundane organizational rule-making and enforcement. It is not surprising or troubling to discover that Corporation A gives ten weeks of unpaid maternity leave while Corporation B gives six weeks of paid maternity leave. It is easy to understand, and not an urgent problem, if one organization has different rules from another, and if the two rule systems are inconsistent. As putative universal principles increasingly penetrate organizations and become a source of legitimacy for corporate actions, however, consistency becomes more important to organizations. They develop elaborate job descriptions that ensure that any individual can take on a job without changing the fundamental character of the organization. They acquire external validation of their conformity to universal standards, such as ISO-9000 procedures (Mendel 1996). Formal advancement mechanisms ensure the consistent treatment of all employees (Sutton et al. 1994), and management techniques such as Taylorism or, more recently, McDonaldization (Ritzer 1993), maintain consistent decision-making procedures in numerous contexts.

E. The Drive to Expansion
The dependence of modern legal systems on universal models and standards linked to scientific and rationalistic analysis of a broader nature produces much pressure on, and opportunity for, expansion and glob-

alization. Legitimated social interests have many incentives to support their claims with expanded scientific and rationalistic analysis. They find new efficiency claims (e.g., with economic analysis) to support and stabilize themselves; new medical, social, and psychological analyses to empower justice claims; and new environmental analyses to support both individual and collective interests. On the other side, the elites of national states search for similar grounds with which to legitimate and stabilize their authority. The activities of all these parties operate to expand and further globalize the legal arrangements produced, providing an expansive dynamic for the whole system. We can imagine that a more closed world state system would find devices to block the processes of discovery and analysis involved: in the modern world, however, no central authority exists to block the spread in cultural knowledge and authority that expand and globalize legal arrangements.

Conclusion

One useful conception of modern legal systems is that they emerge to serve coordinating functions in increasingly complex and interdependent economies and polities. This is undoubtedly true, but focusing solely on this explanation misses important features of these systems that can better be explained in terms of their common historical and contemporary dependence on an evolving world cultural frame—originally religious and now secularized in terms of very general lawful principles about the physical world, the proper goals of state society, and the natural status of individuals and interests within society. Taken-for-granted principles define and regulate sovereignty, rationality, collective goals, along with individual rights, interests, and justice: these lead to the alignment of interests and actions under common legal principles.

This view can help explain many features of modern legal systems: their surprising isomorphism, even in domains with little interdependence; their ritualization and decoupling from practical reality; and their rationalism and chronic search for consistency. A legal world is produced with much more commonality—diffusion, isomorphism, and shared rationalism—than would result from more realist models of power and interest in growing interdependence.

This is a world that attempts to control dissension and resistance through the dynamic expansion of integrated and universalistic models justified by analyses of nature and rationality. Dissension and resistance, then, feed into expansion and globalization by locating new claims—for instance, for new rights, for socioeconomic development, or for environmental protection—within the models and the analyses of nature upon which they are based. Both the forces of control and the forces of resistance lead to the expansion of generalized and universalistic legalized frames. The system may be hegemonic—it certainly is Western in its notions of justice and progress—but it also enables an extraordinary range of both powerful and relatively powerless interests to take mobilized action, effecting both expansion and globalization.

NOTES

We wish to extend our appreciation to Bryant Garth and Yves Dezalay for organizing the New Challenges for the Rule of Law Conference. Special thanks to Gary Hamilton and Susan Silbey for their thoughtful critiques. We are also indebted to the following colleagues who provided feedback on earlier drafts of the work: Dan Cooperman, David Frank, Mayra Gómez, Jennifer Pierce, Sharon Preves, Francisco Ramirez, Joachim Savelsberg, Perry Seymour, the members of the University of Minnesota international relations colloquium, and the members of the Stanford University comparative sociology workshop. An earlier version of this essay appeared in *Soziale Welt* 49:213–32.

1. Many former colonies now maintain dual court systems, one system that applies "state law" and one system that applies "customary law." Even in these systems with their emphasis on autonomy, there is little doubt that "customary law" is influenced over time by "state law" (Sierra 1995).

2. Despite the "separate" national tracks along which legal systems developed over the last 200 years, the basic spirit and purpose of law continued to be tied to the "secular religious" principles of justice, sovereignty, and science. As law became increasingly central to the modern nationalist project, these exogenous forces extended first to the legal profession and currently to specific legal procedures (see, e.g., Frase 1990; Black and Coffee 1994).

3. Naturally, some countries resist pressure to conform to a notion of natural law, particularly outside the West, but even these countries engage in rationalizations based on Western ideas in the international realm (Crystal 1994).

4. The states that fail to follow these roles are the exceptions that prove the rule. For example, when Iraq challenged notions of sovereignty by occupying Kuwait, it was labeled a rule breaker and soundly condemned by the international community (Kahn 1992).

5. *Quod semper, quod ubique, quod ab omnibus creditum est* (The thing which has been believed always, everywhere, and by all) (Saint Vincent of Lirens, ca. 450).

6. See *Tyrer v. UK*, A 26 para 31 (1978).

7. For attitudinal data see Hofstede 1980.

8. Rules in areas that have been considered mundane historically are coming under increasing pressure to conform to external legal guidelines, for example, firing employees (Edelman et al. 1992).

REFERENCES

Abbott, Andrew. 1988. *The system of professions: An essay on the division of expert labor.* Chicago: University of Chicago Press.

Abel, Richard. 1988. Lawyers in the civil law world. In Richard L. Abel and Philip S. C. Lewis, eds., *Lawyers in society,* vol. 2, *The civil law world.* Berkeley: University of California Press.

Anderson, Benedict. 1972. *Java in a time of revolution: Occupation and resistance, 1944 to 1946.* Ithaca: Cornell University Press.

————. 1991. *Imagined communities: Reflections on the origin and spread of nationalism.* London: Verso.

Bendix, Reinhard. 1964. *Nation-building and citizenship: Studies of our changing social order.* New York: Wiley.

Berkovitch, Nitza. 1999. *From motherhood to citizenship: Women's rights and international organizations.* Baltimore: Johns Hopkins University Press.

Berman, Harold. 1993. *Faith and order: The reconciliation of law and religion.* Atlanta: Scholars Press.

Black, Bernard, and John Coffee Jr. 1994. Hail Britannia? Institutional investor behavior under limited regulation. *Michigan Law Review* 92:1997–2087.

Black, Donald. 1982. The boundaries of legal sociology. *Yale Law Journal* 81:1086–1100.

Blackenburg, Erhard. 1994. The infrastructure for avoiding civil litigation: Comparing cultures of legal behavior in the Netherlands and West Germany. *Law and Society Review* 28:789–808.

Boli, John. 1987. Human rights or state expansion? Cross-national definitions of constitutional rights, 1870–1970. In George Thomas, John W. Meyer, Francisco Ramirez, and John Boli, eds., *Institutional structure: Constituting state, society, and the individual.* London: Sage.

Boli, John, and George M. Thomas. 1999. Introduction. J. Boli and G. M. Thomas, eds., *Constructing world culture: International nongovernmental organizations since 1875,* 1–12. Stanford: Stanford University Press.

Boyle, Elizabeth Heger. 2000. Is law the rule? Using political frames to explain cross-national variation in legal activity. *Social Forces* 78:1195–1226.

———. 1998. Political frames and legal activity: The case of nuclear power in four countries. *Law and Society Review* 32:141–74.

Boyle, Elizabeth Heger, and Sharon Preves. 2000. National politics as international process: The case of anti-female-genital-cutting laws. *Law and Society Review* 34: 401–32.

Campbell, Dennis, ed. 1982. *Transnational legal practice: A survey of selected countries.* Boston: Kluwer.

Carter, Stephen L. 1993. *The culture of disbelief: How American law and politics trivialize religious devotion.* New York: Basic Books.

Crystal, Jill. 1994. The human rights movement in the Arab world. *Human Rights Quarterly* 16:435–54.

Damaška, Mirjan. 1986. *The faces of justice and state authority: A comparative approach to the legal process.* New Haven: Yale University Press.

David, René, and John Brierly. 1985. *Major legal systems in the world today: An introduction to the comparative study of law.* 3d ed. London: Stevens and Sons.

Dezalay, Yves, and Bryant Garth. 1995. Merchants of law as moral entrepreneurs: Constructing international justice from the competition for transnational business disputes. *Law and Society Review* 29:27–64.

DiMaggio, Paul J., and Walter W. Powell. 1983. The iron cage revisited: Institutional isomorphism and collective rationality in organizational fields. *American Sociological Review* 48:147–60.

———. 1991. Introduction. In Walter W. Powell and Paul J. DiMaggio, eds., *The new institutionalism in organizational analysis.* Chicago: University of Chicago Press.

Dobbin, Frank, John Sutton, W. Richard Scott, and John W. Meyer. 1994. Equal employment opportunity and the law: The construction of internal labor markets. *American Journal of Sociology* 99:396–427.

Donnelly, Jack. 1989. *Universal human rights in theory and practice.* Ithaca: Cornell University Press.

Dryzek, John S. 1996. *Democracy in capitalist times: Ideals, limits, and struggles.* New York: Oxford University Press.

Duster, Troy. 1970. *The legislation of morality: Law, drugs, and moral judgment.* New York: Free Press.

Edelman, Lauren. 1990. Legal environments and organizational governance: The expansion of due process in the American workplace. *American Journal of Sociology* 95:1401–40.

———. 1992. Legal ambiguity and symbolic structures: Organizational mediation of civil rights law. *American Journal of Sociology* 97:1531–76.

Edelman, Lauren, Steven Abraham, and Howard Erlanger. 1992. Professional construction of law: The inflated threat of wrongful discharge. *Law and Society Review* 26:47–84.

Etienne, Margaret. 1995. Addressing gender-based violence in an international context. *Harvard Women's Law Journal* 18:139–70.

Finnemore, Martha. 1996. *National interests in international society.* Ithaca: Cornell University Press.

Frank, David. 1998. *Sex and the state: Individualization, globalization, and the reconstitution of national policies, 1945–1995.* Grant proposal to the National Science Foundation, Harvard University.

Frank, David, Ann Hironaka, John W. Meyer, Evan Schofer, and Nancy Brandon Tuma. 1999. The rationalization and organization of nature in world culture. In John Boli and George Thomas, eds., *Constructing world culture: International non-governmental organizations since 1875.* Stanford: Stanford University Press.

Frank, David, John W. Meyer, and David Miyahara. 1995. The individualist polity and the presence of professionalized psychology: A cross-national study. *American Sociological Review* 60:360–77.

Frase, Richard. 1990. Comparative criminal justice as a guide to American law reform: How do the French do it, how can we find out, and why should we care? *California Law Review* 78:539–683.

Friedman, Lawrence M. 1985. *History of American law.* 2d ed. New York: Simon and Schuster.

Fuller, Lon. 1967. *Legal fiction.* Stanford: Stanford University Press.

Gaete, Rolando. 1991. Postmodernism and human rights: Some insidious questions. *Law and Critique* 2:149–70.

Greenhouse, Carol. 1986. *Praying for justice: Faith, order and community in an American town.* Ithaca: Cornell University Press.

Gusfield, Joseph. 1986. *Symbolic crusade: Status politics and the American temperance movement.* 2d ed. Urbana: University of Illinois Press.

Habermas, Jürgen. 1984. *The theory of communicative action,* vol. 1, *Reason and the rationalization of society,* trans. Thomas McCarthy. Boston: Beacon.

Harris, David J., Michael O'Boyle, and Colin Warbrick. 1995. *Law of the European Convention on Human Rights.* London: Butterworths.

Heinz, John P., and Edward O. Laumann. 1982. *Chicago lawyers: The social structure of the bar.* New York: Russell Sage Foundation.

Hofstede, Geert H. 1980. *Culture's consequences, international differences in work-related values.* Beverly Hills: Sage.

Hopkins, Ann Branigar. 1996. *So ordered: Making partner the hard way.* Amherst: University of Massachusetts Press.

Jepperson, Ronald, and John W. Meyer. 1991. The public order and the construction of formal organizations. In Walter W. Powell and Paul J. DiMaggio, eds., *The new institutionalism in organizational analysis*. Chicago: University of Chicago Press.

Kahn, Paul. 1992. Lessons for international law from the Gulf War. *Stanford Law Review* 45:425–41.

Kaplan, John, and Jerome Skolnick. 1982. *Criminal justice: Introductory cases and materials*. 3d ed. Mineola, N.Y: Foundation Press.

LoPucki, Lynn, and George Triantis. 1994. A systems approach to comparing U.S. and Canadian reorganization of financially distressed companies. *Harvard International Law Journal* 35:267– 343.

Macaulay, Stewart. 1963. Noncontractual relations in business: A preliminary study. *American Sociological Review* 28:55–67.

Magnarella, Paul. 1995. Universal jurisdiction and universal human rights: A global progression. *Journal of Third World Studies* 12:159–71.

Malinowski, Bronislaw. 1934. *Law and order in Polynesia: A study of primitive legal institutions*. New York: Harcourt, Brace.

March, James G., and Johan P. Olsen. 1976. *Ambiguity and choice in organizations*. Bergen, Norway: Universitetsforlaget.

Marshall, Thomas H. 1964. *Class, citizenship, and social development*. Garden City, N.Y.: Anchor.

McNeely, Constance L. 1995. *Constructing the nation-state: International organization and prescriptive action*. Westport, Conn.: Greenwood.

Mendel, Peter J. 1996. *The institutional development of global production: The case of the ISO 9000 international management standards*. Paper presented at the Conference on Standards and Society, Third Annual Meeting of the European Academy for Standardization, Stockholm, May.

Meyer, John W. 1994. Rationalized environments. In W. Richard Scott and John W. Meyer, eds., *Institutional environments and organizations*. Thousand Oaks, Calif.: Sage.

Meyer, John W., John Boli, and George M. Thomas. 1987. Ontology and rationalization in the western cultural account. In George M. Thomas, John W. Meyer, Francisco Ramirez, and John Boli, eds., *Institutional structure: Constituting state, society, and the individual*. London: Sage.

Meyer, John W., John Boli, George M. Thomas, and Francisco Ramirez. 1997. World society and the nation-state. *American Journal of Sociology* 103:144–81.

Meyer, John W., and Brian Rowan. 1977. Institutional organizations: Formal structure as myth and ceremony. *American Sociological Review* 83:340–63.

Meyer, John W., and W. Richard Scott, eds. 1992. *Organizational environments: Ritual and rationality*. Newbury Park, Calif.: Sage.

Nonet, Philippe, and Philip Selznick. 1978. *Law and society in transition: Toward responsive law*. New York: Octagon.

Otto, Dianne. 1996. Nongovernmental organizations in the United Nations system: The emerging role of international civil society. *Human Rights Quarterly* 18:107–41.

Price, Richard M. 1997. *The chemical weapons taboo.* Ithaca: Cornell University Press.

Pritchard, John. 1991. *Law firms in Europe: The guide to Europe's commercial law firms.* London: Legalease.

Ramirez, Francisco, and John W. Meyer. 1998. Dynamics of citizenship: Development and the political incorporation of women. In Connie McNeely, ed., *Public rights, public rules.* New York: Garland.

Risse, Thomas, and Kathryn Sikkink. 1999. The socialization of international human rights norms into domestic practices: Introduction. In Thomas Risse, Stephen C. Ropp, and Kathryn Sikkink, eds., *The power of human rights: International norms and domestic change.* Cambridge: Cambridge University Press.

Ritzer, George. 1993. *The McDonaldization of society: An investigation into the changing character of contemporary social life.* Thousand Oaks, Calif.: Pine Forge Press.

Robinson, Mary. 1996. Constitutional shifts in Europe and the US: Learning from each other. *Stanford Journal of International Law* 32:1–11.

Rosenberg, Gerald. 1997. *Do not go gently into that good right: The pernicious effects of first amendment jurisprudence on the high court of Australia.* Paper presented at the Law and Society Association Meetings, St. Louis, May.

Sarat, Austin. 1995. Prophecy of possibilities: Metaphorical explorations of postmodern legal subjectivity. *Law and Society Review* 29:615–30.

Savigny, Friedrich C. 1880. *System des Heutigen Romischen Rechts.* Edinburgh: T. and T. Clark.

Schuler, Margaret, ed. 1992. *Freedom from violence: Women's strategies from around the world.* New York: OEF International: UNIFEM WIDBOOKS.

Shue, Henry. 1980. *Basic rights: Subsistence, affluence, and US foreign policy.* Princeton: Princeton University Press.

Sierra, Maria Teresa. 1995. Indian rights and customary law in Mexico: A study of the *Nahuas* in the Sierra De Puebla. *Law and Society Review* 29:227–54.

Sklair, Leslie. 1995. *Sociology of the global system.* 2d ed. London: Prentice-Hall, Harvester Wheatsheaf.

Stetson, Dorothy Mcbride. 1995. Human rights for women: International compliance with a feminist standard. *Women and Politics* 15:71–95.

Strang, David. 1990. From dependency to sovereignty: An event history analysis of decolonization, 1870–1987. *American Sociological Review* 55:846–60.

Strang, David, and John W. Meyer. 1993. Institutional Conditions for Diffusion. *Theory and Society* 22:487–511.

Strauss, Andres J. 1995. Beyond national law: The neglected role of the international law of personal jurisdiction in domestic courts. *Harvard Journal of International Law* 36:373–424.

Strayer, Joseph R. 1970. *On the medieval origins of the modern state.* Princeton: Princeton University Press.

Stryker, Robin. 1994. Rules, resources, and legitimacy processes: Some implications for social conflict, order, and change. *American Journal of Sociology* 99:847–910.

Sutton, John, Frank Dobbin, W. Richard Scott, and John W. Meyer. 1994. The legalization of the workplace. *American Journal of Sociology* 99:944–71.

Thomas, George M. 1987. Revivalism, nation-building, and institutional change. In George M. Thomas, John W. Meyer, Francisco Ramirez, and John Boli, eds., *Institutional structure: Constituting state, society, and the individual.* London: Sage.

Thomas, George M., John W. Meyer, Francisco Ramirez, and John Boli, eds. 1987. *Institutional structure: Constituting state, society, and the individual.* London: Sage.

Tilly, Charles. 1990. *Coercion, capital, and European states, A.D. 990 to 1990.* Cambridge, Mass.: B. Blackwell.

Walker, Jack L. 1969. The diffusion of innovation among the American states. *American Political Science Review* 63:880–89.

Weber, Max. 1985 [1958]. *The Protestant ethic and the spirit of capitalism*, trans. Talcott Parsons. London: Unwin.

Weick, Karl. 1976. Educational organizations as loosely coupled systems. *Administrative Science Quarterly* 21:1–19.

Zhou, Xueguang. 1993. The dynamics of organizational rules. *American Journal of Sociology* 98:1134 66.

Zimring, Franklin E., and Gordon Hawkins. 1973. *Deterrence: The legal threat in crime control.* Chicago: University of Chicago Press.

What Institutional Regimes for the Era of Internationalization?

Robert Boyer

Robert Boyer, an economist at the Centre d'études prospectives d'économie mathématique appliqués à la planification (CEPREMAP) in Paris, provides an economic analysis of some of the trends that the previous essays highlight. Transformations in the international political economy, Boyer emphasizes, must take into account the complex institutional arrangements necessary to make state economies grow and survive. He suggests that the market cannot by itself generate institutions that will do the work essential to promote this economic growth. Indeed, the market erodes existing institutions such that "institutional arrangements presenting an alternative to the market are required in order to control the market's corrosive nature." Law is one of the key institutions providing this regulatory alternative to—and complement to—the market. How institutions are built and shaped, including the law and legal institutions, will therefore be essential in shaping our economic futures.

More than the prior essays, Boyer's emphasizes that "it is an extremely difficult task for social planners and societal elites to prepare blueprints for the institutional arrangements that will implement this type of delicate balance and to make a correct assessment of the impact of any radical departure from past institutional arrangements." He adds, "Where such an equilibrium does exist, . . . it is invariably the product of the path-dependent logic of the institutional history of a particular society." In other words, Boyer is very cautious about what institutions can be designed, and in particular whether U.S. models—built mainly on a reverence for the market and a very strong position for law and legal institutions—can be built in places with different histories and models of state and economy. The questions he raises go to a basic dilemma of globalization—whether what we characterize as a potential new legal orthodoxy—a new state orthodoxy with a special relationship between law and markets—can (or should) take root and thrive as the universal rules of the game.

Contemporary Institutional Change in Historical Perspective

Examined retrospectively, the interwar period and the post-1945 reconstruction shed light on the reasons for the surprising economic boom that took place after World War II. Many observers at the time attributed the troubles associated with the Great Depression to a combination of labor market rigidity, excessive state intervention, and a lack of competition in product markets (Rueff 1932). By contrast, present-day economic historians tend to argue that price and wage formations were far more competitive during the 1920s than the 1960s and 1970s. Indeed, the American and French economies were structurally unstable during the 1920s due to an excessive reliance on market mechanisms (Aglietta 1982; Boyer and Mistral 1982). Relatively few contemporaneous observers were convinced that markets had to be disciplined by public intervention (Weir and Skocpol 1985). On reflection, therefore, it appears that Karl Polanyi (1957) was right: an excess of markets leads to instability.

The advanced industrialized countries overcame the interwar economic collapse not by a blind obedience to the myth of market efficiency, but by controlling and regulating markets (Milward 1979; Vatter 1985). The primacy of politics after World War II provided for significant changes in monetary and credit control, industrial relations, public infrastructures, and education, and this restructuring of the basic institutional forms of modern economies was such that growth and cyclical patterns were altered: mild recessions replaced depressions. Chronic inflation did occur, although unprecedented increases in productivity were translated into a continuous rise in standard of living. Nevertheless, this does not represent a victory of pure market mechanisms. On the contrary, the success was a result of large corporations, unions, and of course numerous state agencies taming the market. (It was assumed that a similar "miracle" had taken place in some Asian countries until the summer of 1997.) This period of history demonstrates that markets are efficient not only when they are used and channeled according to clear political or social aims (Wade 1990), but also when they are contained and tamed by a variety of social and political institutions (White 1991).

The Double Embeddedness of the Fordist Regime

The containment of market forces played a positive role in the unprecedented increase in productivity and standard of living that occurred in advanced industrial societies. The French Ecole de la Régulation has argued that this process was far more important than merely an economic catch-up following the quasi-stagnation of the interwar period (Boyer 1989; Boyer and Saillard 1995). Between the end of World War II and the mid-1960s these three types of regulatory systems—at the global, national, and subnational regional levels—coalesced into a surprisingly coherent growth regime. For most advanced capitalist countries after World War II, a common process of institutional change took place. The disruptions associated with the end of the war promoted the implementation and diffusion of several institutional forms.

- The United States had the power to implement a new international regime, which complemented their diplomatic, military, economic, and technological hegemony. With the basic stability provided by Pax Americana, other countries were able to design and implement their own national regimes (Gilpin 1987; Keohane and Milner 1996; Kindleberger 1988; Calleo 1982).
- Governments developed genuine institutional forms overseeing the wage-labor nexus; oligopolistic competition under the supervision of the state; and welfare systems covering education, health, and retirement. Despite national variations in the specific forms of regulation and coordination, this system—in which a host of regulatory institutions are embedded at the central level of nation-states—has been called the politics of Fordism.
- Any social system of production has a spatial configuration that may give rise to regional variation. In other words, a country's social system of production is not necessarily homogeneous in spatial terms. In some cases after World War II, distinctive regional forms of coordination formed cohesive industrial districts, for

example in the Third Italy, the German Länder, and various regions of Japan (Sabel and Zeitlin 1985; Zeitlin 1990; Friedman 1988; Pyke and Sengenberger 1992; Pyke, Becattini, and Sengenberger 1991; Herrigel 1990). In other configurations, national institutional forms were projected onto regions or towns, as happened in France and to some extent the United Kingdom (Zeitlin 1994). Thus markets became embedded in the social and political institutions at both the regional and national levels of societies (Lazonick 1991).

Social systems of production are embedded both in specific national institutional forms and, where strong local traditions continue to exist, in regional orbits of trust (Herrigel 1990; Whitley and Hollingsworth 1996; Hollingsworth and Lindberg 1985). For example, the diffusion of mass production and consumption from the United States to Europe and Japan generated a genuine hybridization of national political bargaining and regional legacies in terms of productive systems. This helps to explain why, internationally, there are various forms of oligopolistic competition (Dumez and Jeunemaitre 1991), a large diversity of capital-labor relations (Boyer 1995), and of course differing forms of state intervention (André and Delorme 1980).

From Erosion to the Crisis of Previous Institutional Arrangements

The success of this mode of regulation set in motion three destabilizing mechanisms. In recent years these have led to a surge of such mechanisms, which in turn are dissolving many of the national and regional institutions in which market activity had previously been embedded.

1.   Initially, Pax Americana resolved the inherent instability of the interwar international regime. The Bretton Woods system was so efficient in rebuilding the European and Japanese industrial capabilities that the American trade surplus declined from being largely positive to significantly negative. Similarly, despite the diffusion of the politics of Fordism (Boyer 1990), in country after country emerging financial innovations increasingly undermined the legitimacy of strongly regulated national monetary and financial regimes. Various national economies entered into acute competition with one another, creating excess capacity and the likelihood of creeping protectionist wars, until

some threshold was reached during the 1970s. Thus, national systems of production that were initially quite independent became complementary, and then more and more competitive with one another at the international level.

2. Simultaneously, the growth regime of individual countries encountered increasing difficulties coping with labor discipline, investment efficiency, accelerating inflation, recurrent external disequilibria, emerging financial instabilities, and in some cases a loss of efficiency in Keynesian countercyclical policies. This created public deficits and a loss of confidence in the ability of national governments to monitor macroeconomic activity (O'Connor 1973; Calleo 1992). The result was that many institutional forms of regulation inherited from the post–World War II period were either challenged, eroded, or circumvented. The strategy of multinationals, the loss of strength among unions in many countries, and the political shift from Keynesian orthodoxy toward neoclassically inspired conservative policies increasingly challenged the idea that markets had to be tamed and contained.

3. Consequently, the spatial distribution of economic activity within national borders and across countries has changed. One example of crisis in the regional embeddedness of the postwar regulatory order has occurred in highly capital-intensive sectors, leading to economic decline in some regions with heavy specialization in automobiles, equipment goods, and mining. On the other hand, a transformation in the coordination of advanced capitalist economies has provided new opportunities for densely organized industrial districts, particularly those with a high degree of industrial manufacturing adaptability and, more important, flexibility. Thus, disruption of the postwar international regime has altered the spatial distribution of social systems of production (Pyke, Becattini, and Sengenberger 1991; Pyke and Sengenberger 1992).

Throughout the last two decades, these forces have been eroding the previous macroeconomic regularities and have thus had interrelated destabilizing effects. The demise of the postwar regulatory international system led to an intensification of competition among the various national systems of production and triggered some significant shifts in market share and ultimately in employment within and between countries. Governments have found that they could rely less and less on the conventional Keynesian policies that assumed relative national autonomy, both in terms of competition in existing national product markets and fiscal and monetary interventions. A new neoclassical economic theory began to emerge that provided the rationale for either a Keynesian or anti-Keynesian policy with the primary aim toward monetary stability, external competitiveness, and profit restoration. Many economic theorists now argue that public spending has little economic impact, given the full rationality of private agents, and that any economy operates near a Walrasian equilibrium (Sargent 1979; Lucas 1988). Thus, the erosion of post–World War II institutions precipitates a key question: what other economic institutions should replace the configuration of postwar regulatory regimes and Keynesian strategies?

Social Sciences and Institutional Change: Alternative Conceptions

One of the novelties of the contemporary world is the experience of considerable structural change in economies organized and institutionalized according to a network of interrelated arrangements and coordinated mechanisms. But do the social sciences provide any convenient interpretation or theory about the processes now taking place all around the world? Three main visions are competing to shape our understanding and guide economic policies. Market, tradition, and polity are the main factors that the literature focuses upon.

Self-Interest, Rationality, and the Market as a Selective Device

Transaction costs economics (Williamson 1985), as well as the new institutional economics based upon agency theory (Tirole 1988), have launched a renewed interest in the study of economic institutions (see also Furubotn and Richter 1991; North 1990; Eggertsson 1990). These perspectives are built upon two pillars: (1) the rationality principle governs the behavior of actors whatever the context and delivers predictable patterns; (2) markets organize competition between alternative strategies. According to this literature, rationality delivers the best policies: markets will favor the most appropriate behavior and thus deliver a convergence toward the perceived "one best way" of doing things. However, in the tradition of Herbert Simon (1983), let us suppose that in real economies, it is unlikely that the minds of company managers, consumers, workers, and bankers would be able to cope with the complexity and uncertainty of their economic interactions. In such circumstances, institutional arrangements other than market mechanisms must be involved in coordinating transactions between economic actors.

Neoclassical economists still maintain that a market system will select the most efficient solution to problems, whether it be the development of a new product, a technology, a type of contract, or even collective institutional arrangements. This argument is quite convincing where ordinary goods of a given quality are supplied and demanded by a large number of traders according to anonymous transactions. However, when the transactions concern labor, skills, or finance, in which the product involves very complex technology, many pitfalls tend to occur: markets then are quite likely to provide inefficient outcomes such as rationing, speculative bubbles, financial instability, social exclusion, and inequalities.

Polanyi states that the selection of institutional arrangements by an intense market mentality tends to be myopic and inefficient (1957). Given the indivisibility inherent in any institution, inefficient arrangements survive on the basis of their previous implementation. An intrinsically superior institution may suffer from its association with inadequate arrangements and be ruled out by market mechanisms. In contrast with general equilibrium theory, the Austrian school of economics actually recognizes that the market as a solution to problems may lead to dead ends, which then result in calls for some type of state intervention (Hayek 1976–82). Such a conclusion is infrequently emphasized, but is very important in the present context.

The theory of voluntaristic, rational self-building of institutions can be applied to an analysis of how social systems of production are constructed (see fig. 1). In terms of this theoretical perspective, organizational innovations derive from the rational calculus of individuals and firms that compare alternative solutions. The model assumes that any radical uncertainty can be removed by adequate insurance contracts and that each individual innovation can be disentangled from all the others in order to allow for a series of independent optimizing solutions. The model also assumes that the expansion of firms will be guided by competition for finance, labor, natural resources, or alternative organizational forms.

To be more specific, this kind of institutional regime would combine free trade, consumer sovereignty, optimal labor contracts with a

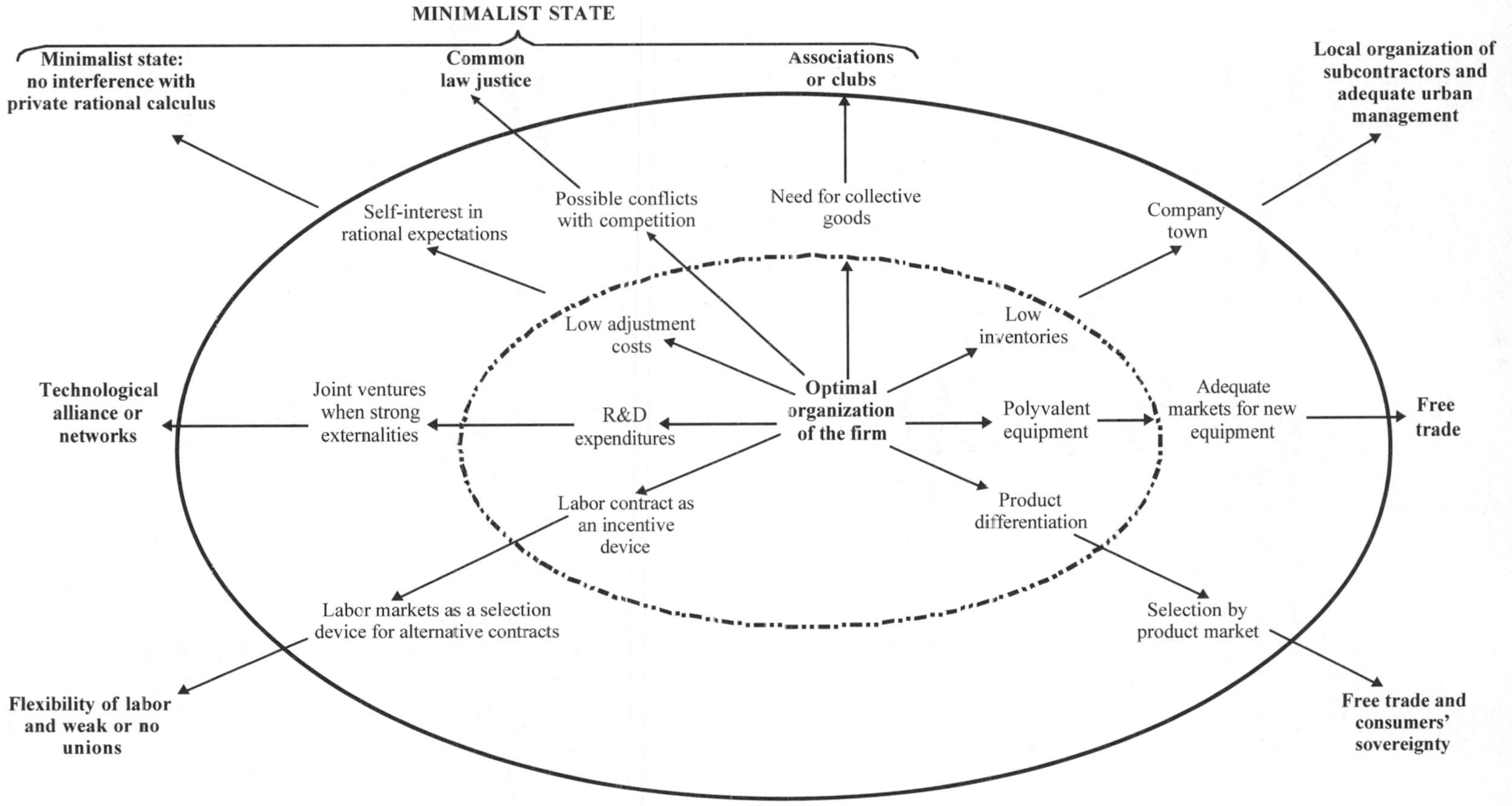

Fig. 1. The self-building of institutions

high degree of flexibility, technological alliances and networks designed to discover new technologies, a benevolent urban and regional environment, and a minimalist state, that would not interfere with private rational calculus by firms. In this model, the managers who submit to market competition eventually obtain the best institutional arrangements, whereas, for example, civil servants and governments tend to make numerous mistakes.

However, this type of social system of production is idealized and does not concur with basic historical evidence. Given the strong complementarities among technologies, markets, and localization tendencies, any institutional regime requires monitoring by extramarket mechanisms such as business ethics, rules of the game, business associations, and the state (Schneiberg and Hollingsworth 1990; Amable et al. 1997). It is true that business histories provide many examples of sectoral institutions built by expansion of the strategy of a single or limited number of large firms, which attempt to internalize their strategies (Chandler 1969, 1977, 1990). Nevertheless, at some point, external coordinating institutions are required: politicians to manage local political matters; an association of firms in order to establish industry standards, to foster product quality, and to set rules of fair competition; and a state in order to negotiate the opening of foreign markets and also to provide many of the functions that business associations may be unable to establish (Campbell, Hollingsworth, and Lindberg 1991; Schneiberg and Hollingsworth 1990).

Similarly, a high-wage, high-skill economy cannot simply be implemented at will by a single entrepreneur, however successful he might be in inventing new production methods. The Henry Ford experience of paying workers five dollars a day is a wonderful example that clearly indicates the limits of purely private strategies in building a new economic and social configuration (Raff 1988; Boyer and Orlean 1991). Basically, the real world does not behave as the normative proposals of a voluntaristic, "rational" theory for the construction of institutional regimes suggest; capitalism does not operate in this way.

Contrasted Regional Trajectories: Still a Strong Spatial Embeddedness

The vision of the supremacy of the market as a coordinating institution is becoming less relevant and should be compared to alternative conceptions of the mechanisms that might monitor the transformation of institutional forms. The embeddedness hypothesis (Granovetter 1985, 1992) argues that pre- (or non-) capitalist logics provide an essential ingredient for markets and capitalism to exist. Totally rational individuals would consistently break down previous institutional agreements if they were free to do so, whereas, for example, trust, reciprocity, and long-term strategies—prerequisites for a capitalist economy—require communities, associations, and/or networks for their existence and are sustained by families, community-like structures, and clans (North 1981; Polanyi 1957; Polanyi-Levitt 1990; Hollingsworth and Lindberg 1985). Opportunistic behavior cannot be completely avoided by optimal contracts, either within or without vertical hierarchies (Williamson 1985).

For institutional regimes whose production systems rely on forms of flexible specialization or mass production, this is particularly relevant. These systems require that firms be embedded in an institutional environment that will produce a high level of trust (Sabel 1992). Products that entail a high degree of technological complexity, rapid and unpredictable innovations, and unexpected variations in demand cannot be produced in a world coordinated purely by market relations. Rather, they can be produced only in a world that has institutional arrangements providing trust, risk sharing, tacit knowledge, and strategic information. The social system of production portrayed in figure 1 cannot provide the support for such production. The kind of institutional environment within which firms must be embedded in order to meet the prerequisites for complex technologies is depicted in figure 2.

This type of embeddedness is especially important for economic systems that display an alternative to the mass production of standardized goods. The importance of quality, speed of delivery, and adaptability to demand shifts and new technological opportunities call for long-term relationships between managers and workers, and between large firms and their subcontractors, which cannot be totally formalized with explicit contracts (Hage and Jing 1996). Minimal implicit agreements must be reached. This can only be done by building upon trust relationships, which are not derived solely from a particular core economic activity. Rich localized interactions between economic actors must occur. This conception emphasizes the importance of regional economies, and primary attention is devoted to the institutional arrangements at the local level within which firms are embedded (Benko and Lipietz 1989, 2000).

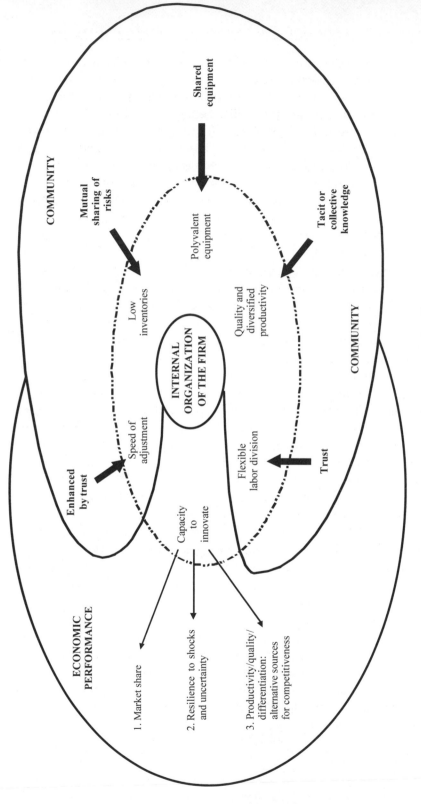

Fig. 2. The embeddedness of institutional regimes

Institutions As Social Constructs: State and Law Matter

Capitalism is an extremely dynamic form of economy that is dependent on the resilience of coordination mechanisms other than markets. Polanyi (1957; Polanyi-Levitt 1990; Streeck and Schmitter 1985) argues that if the market begins to dominate fundamental social relations involving land, labor, and money, there is a danger that the cohesiveness of society will erode (see also Gambetta 1988). This is because at some threshold, the domination of the market rationale challenges the viability of other institutional arrangements; pursuit of private interests by the individual can result in the deterioration of the values of the community, the family, and other forms of authority. Thus, unrestricted market activity will erode all kinds of traditional institutional arrangements.

Many of the traditional institutional arrangements are necessary for providing the trust forming the basis of transactions among economic actors. Institutional arrangements presenting an alternative to the market are required in order to control the market's corrosive nature. However, if traditional institutional arrangements impose social obligations too forcefully upon individual actors, the potential dynamism of the markets will be stifled. Conversely, without these external constraints in sufficient force, the market will bring about its own destruction. Hence, it is necessary that the market and these counterforces be held in a delicate equilibrium (Hollingsworth 1994; Hirsch 1977; Schumpeter 1976; Kumar 1983).

Some regulatory devices may challenge the conventional ways for organizing business activity and society, thereby enhancing innovations in order finally to deliver a viable economic regime closely shaped by each national regulatory style (Streeck 1997). Ex post, social values and dynamic economic efficiency can be reconciled. However, it is an extremely difficult task for social planners and societal elites to prepare blueprints for the institutional arrangements that will implement this type of delicate balance and to make a correct assessment of the impact of any radical departure from past institutional arrangements. Where such an equilibrium does exist, therefore, it is invariably the product of the path-dependent logic of the institutional history of a particular society.

The performance of a social system of production derives from the interaction of two contradictory forces. This perspective has definite consequences for the viability of institutional regimes (fig. 3). The logic of the company induces an expansion from its inner organization toward the surrounding environment, and these are the dynamics contemplated by the conception of the self-building of institutions portrayed in figure 1. Here, however, social groups struggle for the political recognition of their interests and values that might be damaged in the process of expansion. They may therefore turn to the state in order to exert a countervailing pressure directed toward maintaining the compatibility of the company with the social nexus upon which the related society is built. A conception of justice (implemented by the judiciary system and law, and embedded even into such things as a tax code and a welfare system), the structure of a society's industrial relations system, the organization of training for labor and management, the monitoring of the capital markets, and the viability of a national system of innovation are the key forces that constrain pure profit-maximizing. Initially, these regulatory mechanisms may hinder short-run efficiency, but over a long run, they facilitate innovative adaptations by firms, wage earners, and banks. Ultimately, such regulatory mechanisms may deliver a genuine pattern of development.

Major political events and structural crises lead to the emergence of new laws, rules, and norms, which places constraints on the behavior and performance of firms. Thus, inherent in this interpretation of institutional regimes is a strong sense of historicity. This is an eclectic vision constructed from two extreme representations of state intervention. Governments have power to intervene in economic activity, but at the same time they cannot unilaterally impose a particular economic pattern of behavior on private actors. Instead, state intervention may facilitate the emergence of social compromises and provide collective prerogatives for associations and other intermediate bodies in charge of monitoring the behavior and strategies of groups of actors (Schneiberg and Hollingsworth 1990; Campbell and Lindberg 1990).

The timing of public intervention is important: when the economy collapses or is facing unprecedented challenges (such as war or societal reconstruction), the radical uncertainty that paralyzes private agents can only be overcome by a clear statement about new institutional arrangements, legislation, or rules of the game that are both desirable and viable. The compatibility of a complete nexus of institutional arrangements defines the efficacy of public intervention. In other words, the choice of new strategies is limited by the logic of institutional

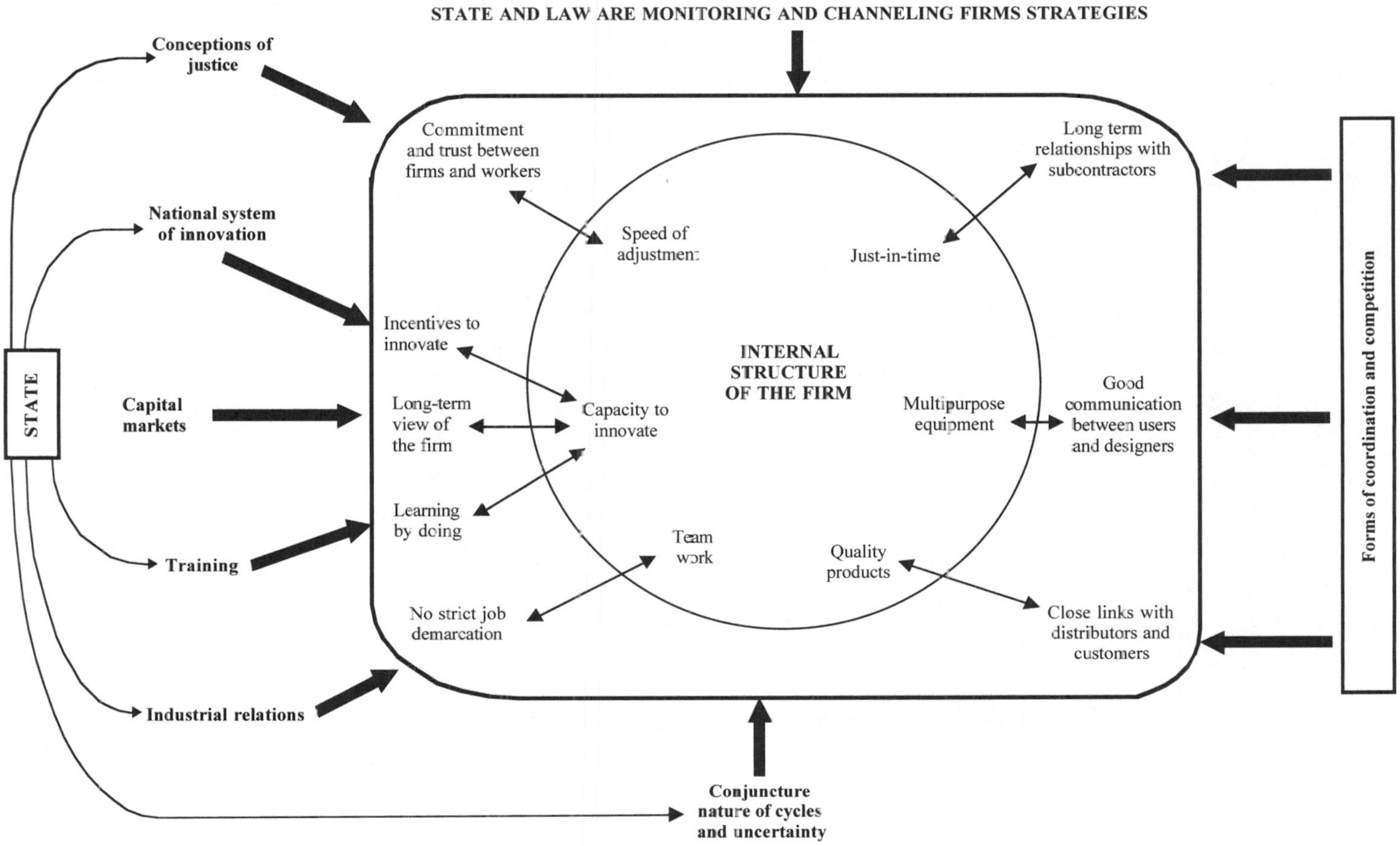

STATE AND LAW ARE MONITORING AND CHANNELING FIRMS STRATEGIES

Forms of coordination and competition

Long term relationships with subcontractors

Good communication between users and designers

Close links with distributors and customers

Just-in-time

Multipurpose equipment

Quality products

INTERNAL STRUCTURE OF THE FIRM

Speed of adjustment

Capacity to innovate

Team work

Commitment and trust between firms and workers

Incentives to innovate

Long-term view of the firm

Learning by doing

No strict job demarcation

Conjuncture nature of cycles and uncertainty

Conceptions of justice

National system of innovation

Capital markets

Training

Industrial relations

STATE

Power and polity are shaping institutional systems and partially the internal structure of the firm.

Fig. 3.   Power and polity are shaping institutional systems and partially the internal structure of the firm.

change within a particular society. Major new rules and institutional arrangements will in turn feed back and alter other institutional arrangements. Thus, the social and economic policies of Western countries have varied from country to country since World War II, since each has been constrained by its own traditional rules and norms, social cleavages, and social structures.

The Sources of Institutional Change: Three Visions and a Synthesis

A syncretic approach to the building of institutions combines three major interpretations, none of which, in isolation, can explain the shift from one institutional regime to another. From a theoretical point of view, each interpretation has its strengths and weaknesses (see fig. 4). The thinking of the new economic institutionalists (Williamson 1985) is based upon the central hypothesis that rational agents act in their own self-interest to build efficient institutions to govern their strategic interactions. Consequently, mixing full rationality (i.e., the ability to compute the outcome of even highly complex strategic interactions) with market competition should give rise to the optimal institutions required to coordinate a complex capitalist economy. This arrangement is such that the position of an actor cannot be improved without impairing the situation of another. Institutions involve the complementary behavior of individuals, and while it is intuitively very appealing to believe that the principles of the invisible hand of the market can be transposed to all kinds of institutions and organizational forms, they are far more difficult to monitor than pure market relations between individual actors. Costs invested in existing institutions provide them with a high degree of legitimacy. As a result, societies are hardly ever at liberty to renegotiate and rebuild institutions anew. Even when there have been violent revolutions, many norms, rules, and institutional arrangements persist and although actors may have a good sense of a superior institutional arrangement its implementation may be blocked by the habit and inertia of social interactions (Boyer and Orlean 1992; David 1986). Some form of collective action is usually needed in order to overcome the hysteresis of inefficient institutions. In short, the world simply cannot continuously be reconstructed anew as the new economic institutionalists would have us believe.

The second approach argues that the social embeddedness of rela-

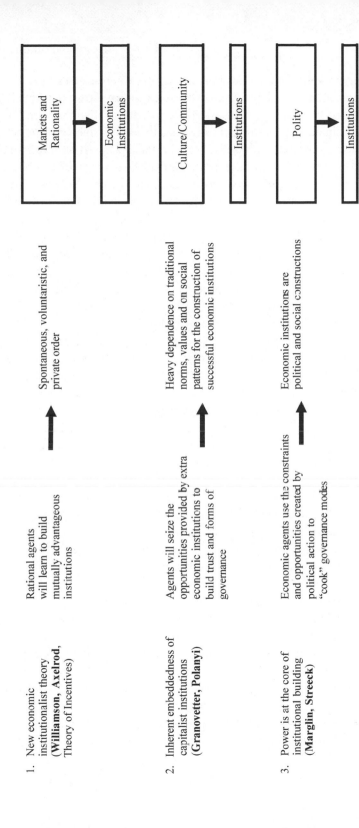

Fig. 4.   Three visions of institutional change

1. New economic institutionalist theory (**Williamson, Axelrod,** Theory of Incentives)

Rational agents will learn to build mutually advantageous institutions

Spontaneous, voluntaristic, and private order

Markets and Rationality → Economic Institutions

2. Inherent embeddedness of capitalist institutions (**Granovetter, Polanyi**)

Agents will seize the opportunities provided by extra economic institutions to build trust and forms of governance

Heavy dependence on traditional norms, values and on social patterns for the construction of successful economic institutions

Culture/Community → Institutions

3. Power is at the core of institutional building (**Marglin, Streeck**)

Economic agents use the constraints and opportunities created by political action to "cook" governance modes

Economic institutions are political and social constructions

Polity → Institutions

tionships in capitalist societies permits actors to circumvent the limits of pure rationality and the interactions of anonymous markets. For example, product and credit markets can exist because they are based on trust in the future fulfillment of transactions. When economic activity is tightly connected with dense social relations based on family, religion, school ties, and so on, the inherent tradition and trust can be used to build useful and efficient economic institutions. Whereas many observers have assumed that efficient institutions can exist only when traditional loyalties are abolished, a great deal of recent social science scholarship (Whitley 1992a, 1992b; Amsden 1989; Hamilton and Biggart 1988; Hamilton and Kao 1991; Hamilton, Zeile, and Kim 1990; Granovetter 1993) has demonstrated that many organizations—both public and private—operate effectively as a direct result of incorporating familial, feudal, and other traditional characteristics into their structure (Landes 1951; Zelizer 1988, 1989; Etzioni 1988).

Although this interpretation provides a partial explanation as to why some countries and regions cope better with the current phase of international competition, we are still confronted with the mystery of how trust is manufactured in a modern economy (Fukuyama 1996): why do individuals prefer to cooperate within a family or a group with strong school ties, for example, instead of being opportunistic? As Ronald Dore (1973) has suggested, today tradition is the unconscious outcome of yesterday's interactions and collective actions. Moreover, we are also faced with the question of why market relations have not more seriously eroded the loyalty of Japanese workers or the trust one observes in Italian industrial districts (Pyke, Becattini, and Sengenberger 1991; Pyke and Sengenberger 1992). Of course, no culture remains invariant and static, rather cultures are continuously reactivated and reinvented, and the Japanese and Italian cases are no exception.

The missing element in models one and two of figure 4 is an emphasis on power. In model three, power is at the core of institution building. Individuals interact as economic agents via market competition, but simultaneously they fight for political power, in order, for example, to gain control over the rules of the game and the building of asymmetries within the economic sphere (Marglin 1991). Modern economic theory (Stiglitz 1987) establishes the idea that some conflicting configurations call for collective interventions in economic activity to ensure better outcomes for all the participants. Moreover, considerable historical research exhibits an impressive series of economic interven-

tions by the state to overcome dead ends or to defend traditional societal values in an effort to promote effective economic institutions
(Streeck 1992; North 1981; Campbell and Lindberg 1990; Gerschenkron
1962). Given the coercive and persuasive power of modern states, this
process provides a substantial explanation for the development of new
institutional forms (North 1981, 1990). If the process of trial and error
with state power is sufficiently careful, a coherent "régulation" mode
may emerge and deliver a superior configuration of institutions for
almost all actors.

The polity is the sphere that allows for the recomposition of institutional forms, and this is why states and associations are so prevalent in
modern economic activity (Schneiberg and Hollingsworth 1990; Campbell and Lindberg 1990; Campbell, Hollingsworth, and Lindberg 1991;
Granovetter 1993). The concept of constitutional order (Sabel 1997)
provides another series of arguments for how political action enhances
institutional transformation. First of all, any institutional form has to be
organized with a clear distinction between two levels: the definition of
the rules of the game on one side, the interaction of individuals and
groups within a particular institutional setting on the other. This is an
interesting perspective with respect to the new economics of institutions (transaction costs economics, the theory of implicit contracts,
principal/agent theory, theory of incentives, and noncooperative game
theory). Economic agents do not simultaneously play within and outside the game according to a singular strategy. Only in cases of total
institutional breakdown do the tensions among actors become so
intense that they must fundamentally restructure most of the institutions of a society.

According to this interpretation, any institutional form exhibits a
hierarchy involving a constitutional order and the way constituent
members play the game. For example, within the state, a constitutional
court usually assesses the compatibility of rulings among lower-level
arbitration courts. Within large firms, a board is in charge of deciding
between the conflicting strategies proposed by competing plants or
functional divisions. Markets are governed or monitored by regulatory
agencies who are responsible for maintaining fair competition and/or
impeding the emergence of monopolies. Within associations, the same
hierarchical phenomenon prevails. For example, the statutes of a political party, a union, or a business association dictate the mutual responsibility and rights of constituents. Thus, all major coordinating mecha-

nisms imply a constitutional order, a political process of institutionalization that is something other than the pure routine of everyday interactions. In other words, the polity is a necessary component for the institutionalization of economic and social order.

There is a second reason for the importance of a constitutional order. For example, if the very functioning of a given institutional form generates some innovation that drastically alters the monitoring properties of the previous order or, depending on when the original constitutional order was constructed, if external shocks destabilize local systems, the players may have to confront a choice between continued cooperation, exit, or voice. If they continue to interact within the old constitutional order a rational decision might be to quit the game. By contrast, if they agree to deliberate about the ongoing problems, they might converge toward a redesign of the governance structure, possibly advantageous for every member. The constitutional, political, and economic histories of modern societies provide numerous examples of positive adaptations to new circumstances or issues (Hirschmann 1977; North 1990).

The possibility of voice, in contrast with exit, presents the possibility of social transformation. The ability to depart from a particular economic arena and to devise alternative rules of the game that better suit the new environment is clearly an important channel for economic reform, especially during crisis periods. Furthermore, a historical perspective suggests that this is the usual process for facilitating an increased division of labor and greater specialization of organizations and individuals, thereby promoting a long-run trend toward product and process innovations. A constitutional order may well be the best instrument for converting one set of institutional arrangements into another, but it is a choice usually neglected by standard neoclassical theory.

Markets may efficiently solve allocation problems when technological and economic changes are rapid, and institutional arrangements also have the ability to adapt when the issue concerns coordination and strategic interactions. It is erroneous to assume that simply because markets are flexible, all other institutions are inherently rigid. Everything depends on the nature of the problems to be solved (allocation/coordination) and the speed of change (moderate/fast).

The neoclassical vision now prevalent (at least among economists) is far from exclusive. Indeed, social research displays a complete spectrum of theories that can be ranked according to the answer given to two questions: (1) Are institutions selected according to economic efficiency or collective action? (2) Do institutions emerge out of a series of coordinated activities, or are they the outcome of a society-wide process? It might be useful to analyze how the present framework fits within those two axes (fig. 5) and how it relates to "Régulation Theory" (Aglietta 1982; Byer 1987, 1990; Boyer and Saillard 2001).

The first concerns the principle of *development and selection of institutions*. For many of the new neoclassical theories, the criterion of efficiency is essential to determine the viability and success of an institution, thus applying a rule which is equivalent to that used for competition in products, processes, and forms of organization. By contrast, it is necessary to insist on the role of *collective action,* and ultimately of *political authority,* in determining the emergence of institutional forms. For régulation theory, along with other institutionalist approaches, these most often result from conflicts and have displayed their viability only after the event. Does a mode of economic functioning exist which sustains the social compromise that has been instituted? This is the question that economists ought to be discussing, rather than indulging in their favorite question—what are the optimal institutions and why do governments not adopt them? Here we agree with the analyses of American institutional economics, as well as with certain approaches of the law, conceived as "an interlude between forces."

As a consequence, the major institutions of capitalism have not arisen from the aggregation of purely local and sectoral compromises, but from the *process of socialization* operating at the level of society as a whole and relating to the monetary regime, the market, and the wage-labor nexus, themselves objects of strong interventions by the state. While neoclassical theories seek a purely microeconomic origin for the regular macroeconomic features of capitalism, régulation theory applies itself to finding the macrosocial and political foundations of the strategies and behaviors of economic actors. For example, the forms of organization of firms depend very largely on the institutional context that defines not only the laws of ownership, but also the forms of competition, access to credit, or even the nature of industrial relations (see Boyer and Freyssenet 1999). This being the case, régulation theory agrees with some of the analyses of the political sciences (particularly Zysman et al. 1997; Hall 1997), of economic history (Greif 1996), or even of law (Bourdieu 1986; Trubek et al. 1994; Dezalay 1989; Dezalay and Garth 1995, 1996). In terms of method, it lays the foundations for a

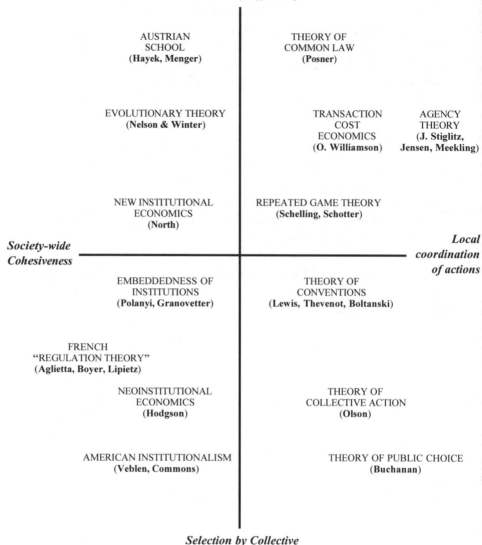

Selection by Efficiency

AUSTRIAN
SCHOOL
(Hayek, Menger)

THEORY OF
COMMON LAW
(Posner)

EVOLUTIONARY THEORY
(Nelson & Winter)

TRANSACTION
COST
ECONOMICS
(O. Williamson)

AGENCY
THEORY
**(J. Stiglitz,
Jensen, Meekling)**

NEW INSTITUTIONAL
ECONOMICS
(North)

REPEATED GAME THEORY
(Schelling, Schotter)

*Society-wide
Cohesiveness*

*Local
coordination
of actions*

EMBEDDEDNESS OF
INSTITUTIONS
(Polanyi, Granovetter)

THEORY OF
CONVENTIONS
(Lewis, Thevenot, Boltanski)

FRENCH
"REGULATION THEORY"
(Aglietta, Boyer, Lipietz)

NEOINSTITUTIONAL
ECONOMICS
(Hodgson)

THEORY OF
COLLECTIVE ACTION
(Olson)

AMERICAN INSTITUTIONALISM
(Veblen, Commons)

THEORY OF PUBLIC CHOICE
(Buchanan)

*Selection by Collective
Action*

Fig. 5.   Mapping the field of research on economic institutions. (Freely inspired and adapted from Marie Claire Villeval [1995: 485].)

'holistic individualism,' that is to say, for an approach in which the actors behave at their best within institutional structures born of past collective action, inherited by them and on which they cannot act at an individual level.

The third characteristic is that contradictions, conflicts, or disequilibria are always present, and finally reveal themselves through crises, during the course of which the acceptance and the viability of previous institutional compromises will be called into question. The hypothesis of rational expectations as applied to economic history conveys a form of idealized world, but, in reality, economic agents are not able to anticipate and frustrate crises that, in the long term, result from the interaction of their contradictory strategies. Even under the growth regime based upon mass production and consumption, i.e., Fordism, the contradictions of accumulation of capital finally revealed themselves, so we would be wise to anticipate that they will do the same within the economic regimes that we can predict for the early twenty-first century, such as a finance led regime (Boyer 2000) or a "new growth" pattern based upon Information and Communication Technology (Boyer 2001).

What Rules for International and National Regimes?

A Double Shift in Regulation Modes

The diffusion of a market ideology across the globe, the intensification of foreign competition, the increasing sophistication of financial markets, and the nation-states' loss of autonomy constitute a threat for many national institutional arrangements. In other words, some trends toward the internationalization of countries' individual economies suggest the emergence of transnational rules of the game (GATT, NAFTA, Maastricht Treaty), thus removing the space for nation-states to maneuver. On the other hand, the evolution of new social systems of production has prompted the call for more localized institutional arrangements—at least for some manufacturing sectors (Sabel 1988; Zeitlin 1994). Thus, the subject of subnational regional economies is very much part of our consciousness. These two opposite movements suggest a double shift from the nation-state to supernational institutional arrangements on the one hand and to reemerging subnational regional economies on the other. This double shift suggests a much more complex outlook than the simplistic vision of omniscient market mechanisms. Several examples illustrate the complexity of global trends during the 1980s and 1990s (see table 1).

The management of money continues to be an important function of the nation-state, but the degree to which the state can carry out this activity has been restricted, primarily due to the surge of financial innovations and short-run movements across national borders. For example, the stabilization of exchange rates within the European Monetary System has reduced the ability of member states to use interest rates and

TABLE 1. The Correspondence and Level of Coordination between Alternative Institutional Arrangements

Level of Coordination	Markets	Networks	Associations	State
1. Local district	*	** Third Italy Silicon Valley	** Guilds, craft unions, business associations	R&D** Education and training***
2. Regions	*	** South Germany	* Business associations	R&D** Education and training***
3. Nations	** (During Fordist era)	* Promotional networks in U.S. (1950–70)	** Labor Union, business association	Defense** Taxes*
4. Continental zones	** Financial services	*** Joint ventures, licensing agreements, sales and distributional ties	Formally existing but not very effective	Interest and exchange rates**
5. World	** Financial services	*** Joint ventures, licensing agreements, sales and distributional ties	Very weak when existing	Trade regulations** Interest and exchange rates**

* Coordination weak to moderately effective
**Coordination moderately effective
***Coordination very effective

exchange rates to solve internal problems. When European currency is instituted between 1999 and 2002, each national economy experiences a loss of national autonomy with regard to monetary seigniorage. Similarly, the idea of a single European market assumes that the rules of competition will be monitored at a continental level, which in turn assumes a shift in the form of competition toward supranationality. Moreover, when alliances and partnerships take place between multinationals operating in different countries, cooperation and competition among firms is transferred to the global level. Indeed, as a result of the General Agreement on Tariffs and Trade (GATT), trade regulations increasingly prevail at the international level and can interfere significantly with laws and industrial policies designed by particular states to enhance their society's competitiveness.

At the same time, some public interventions are easier to implement at a regional rather than at a national level. Research and development policies, training and education programs, public infrastructures, international marketing strategies, subsidies, and tax reductions increasingly appear to be more efficient when designed by a collaboration of local business associations, local or regional banks, unions, civil servants, and local governments. Indeed, one can observe that the more competitive manufacturing sectors in Germany, Italy, Denmark, and Japan have usually benefited from strong and reasonably coherent regional institutional configurations (Hollingsworth, Schmitter, and Streeck 1994; Pyke, Becattini, and Sengenberger 1991; Sabel 1988; Streeck 1991). When trust, solidarity, and exact delivery are required, local economies have many advantages over larger frameworks. Thus, even the most centralized countries such as France have been trying to organize the revival of small and medium-sized firms as well as regional and local districts in order to enhance competitiveness (Vickery 1986; Hage 1996).

Consequently, the nation-state is subject to a dual weakening, by supranationalization on one hand and regionalization on the other. Certainly, there remains a sense of national solidarity among citizens, and tax and welfare systems will long remain within the orbit of the state. Nevertheless, the intellectual and practical challenges associated with the double shift in regulatory modes is a significant factor in the political life of advanced industrial societies. Whereas a century has progressively shaped sophisticated political institutions at the nation-state level, the drastic transformations observed during the last two decades have created a double gap between the new economic requirements and the existing political order.

At the supranational level, it has been difficult to develop a set of institutional arrangements equivalent to the nation-state. To take a single example, the European Community institutions have not compensated for the erosion of each constituent nation-state, which has resulted from the internationalization of trade, production, and finance. One observes only partial or unstable international arrangements at both the sectoral level (microelectronics, car industry) and at the continental level (NAFTA, Maastricht Treaty) (Boyer and Drache 1996).

Subnationally, it has been very difficult for highly centralized states to organize the decentralization of political and economic decisions at an appropriate level, whether regional or local (industrial districts, large cities, and so on). In the early 1990s, the nations that exhibited the more efficient social system of production tended to benefit from densely organized regional economies: Germany, Japan, and Italy. If this diagnosis is correct, the double shift that undermines the adequacy of the previous nation-state configurations simultaneously alters the competitiveness of industrialized and industrializing countries. Similarly, the scope of various coordination mechanisms is altered by this two-directional movement away from the centrality of the nation-state. Some analysts think that the world system will be composed of global cities strongly interacting with one another, but increasingly disconnected from the hinterland and rest of the nation-state (Sassen 1991). This would require a dramatic shift from the post–World War II national embeddedness and state control of international relations.

Thus far, the history of European integration demonstrates that constructing the components of a supranational state is not an easy task and will require several decades before even the minimalist state-led regulations or principles have been implemented at the level of the European Union. In the meantime, the power of subnational regional states is still problematic in comparison with the power and omnipresence of the globalizing tendencies within financial markets—especially in the United States and the United Kingdom where industrial districts are weakly developed (Zeitlin 1994).

Markets, networks, associations, and states have unequal abilities to cope efficiently with transnationalization and regionalization. From a historical perspective, markets appear to be the most pervasive coordinating mechanism, having the capacity to be extended from the local marketplace to fully integrated financial markets operating continuously, twenty-four hours a day throughout the world. Consequently, economic policies designed by the state are very much influenced by financial traders, who continuously reassess the viability of public and external deficits, unemployment rates, the size of political majorities, and so on.

By contrast, networks can be extended at the international level, provided that the number of the constituents is restricted and there is a clear common interest. Strategic alliances between two or more multi-national firms have become increasingly common, some short-term in nature, while others appear to be long-lasting. Of course, strategic alliances at the global level are not a new phenomenon. Historically, however, they were aimed primarily at reducing the capital investment required by individual firms and at lowering the risks related to the entry into new markets. In the contemporary world, strategic alliances at the global level are also increasingly associated with the rising speed of technological change: partners increasingly participate in strategic alliances in order to diversify the risks involved in developing new technologies and to take advantage of other actors' developmental skills. However, there are many varieties of strategic alliance. Some involve technical exchange and cross-licensing, sales and distribution ties, while others involve joint development of products (Pucik 1988; Ohmae 1985; Contractor and Lorange 1988; Perlmutter and Heenan 1986).

Some types of networks are more easily developed at the regional or local level. The network of firms is so dense in some areas that they take on the character of industrial districts. Nevertheless, for these to exist there must be a configuration of regulatory institutions providing common services and the mechanisms for resolving internal conflicts. In short, firms must be embedded in a dense institutional environment that has the capability for providing collective goods for training, research and development, and the resolution of conflicts between labor and capital (Zeitlin 1994; Pyke and Sengenberger 1992).

Finally, it is relatively difficult to build business associations at a transnational level. Most business associations remain national, and their Europeanization is indeed limited, unless they already existed at a sectoral level in order to monitor competition. The organizational dilemma on the international plane is even more severe for labor unions, which are usually divided along political or religious lines as well as national frontiers. Thus, as the double shift in regulation occurs, trade unions and business associations may well weaken at the level of the nation-state and remain extremely weak at the global and transnational level, while their strength at the subnational regional level is more variable both within and across countries. All this suggests that regulatory modes at the level of the nation-state—whether the polity, unions, or associations—could experience a further decline in their efficacy in the future.

How to Govern a Complex Institutional and Spatial
Nested Structure

These observations raise the issue of the recombination of economic institutions at various spatial levels (e.g., subnational region, nation-state, global). The basic institutional arrangements of the 1990s differ vastly from those of the 1960s when they were embedded predominantly, if not completely, at the level of the nation-state (see fig. 6). During the 1960s, an international regulatory regime provided predictability and permitted ambitious national strategies, at least in OECD member countries. High growth dividends brought about an increase in welfare and tended to consolidate national compromises between labor and capital. It is true that regional economies experienced uneven growth, but undesirable consequences of such imbalances were minimized by redistributive mechanisms. With the passage of time, however, the embeddedness of economic institutions at the level of the nation-state has been progressively eroded. As the search for increasing returns to scale has made the domestic market too small, firms increasingly must compete in the international economy if they are to survive. In turn, the international economy has become an arena of fierce competition. Financial innovations have permeated and vigorously asserted themselves at the international level. The economic interactions among nations have increased, with rising interdependence among nations. National economies are now nested in a set of interdependent flows involving trade, finance, and technology, and this has created new problems for nation-states; the American economy, for example, is no longer shielded from other major economic competitors.

It is useful to contrast the post–World War II period of embeddedness of national institutions with the present nestedness of major institutions—a complex intertwining of institutions at all levels of the world, from the global arena to the regional level, including nation-states and such continental entities as NAFTA and the European Union. The concept of nestedness implies several distinct but currently interacting features.

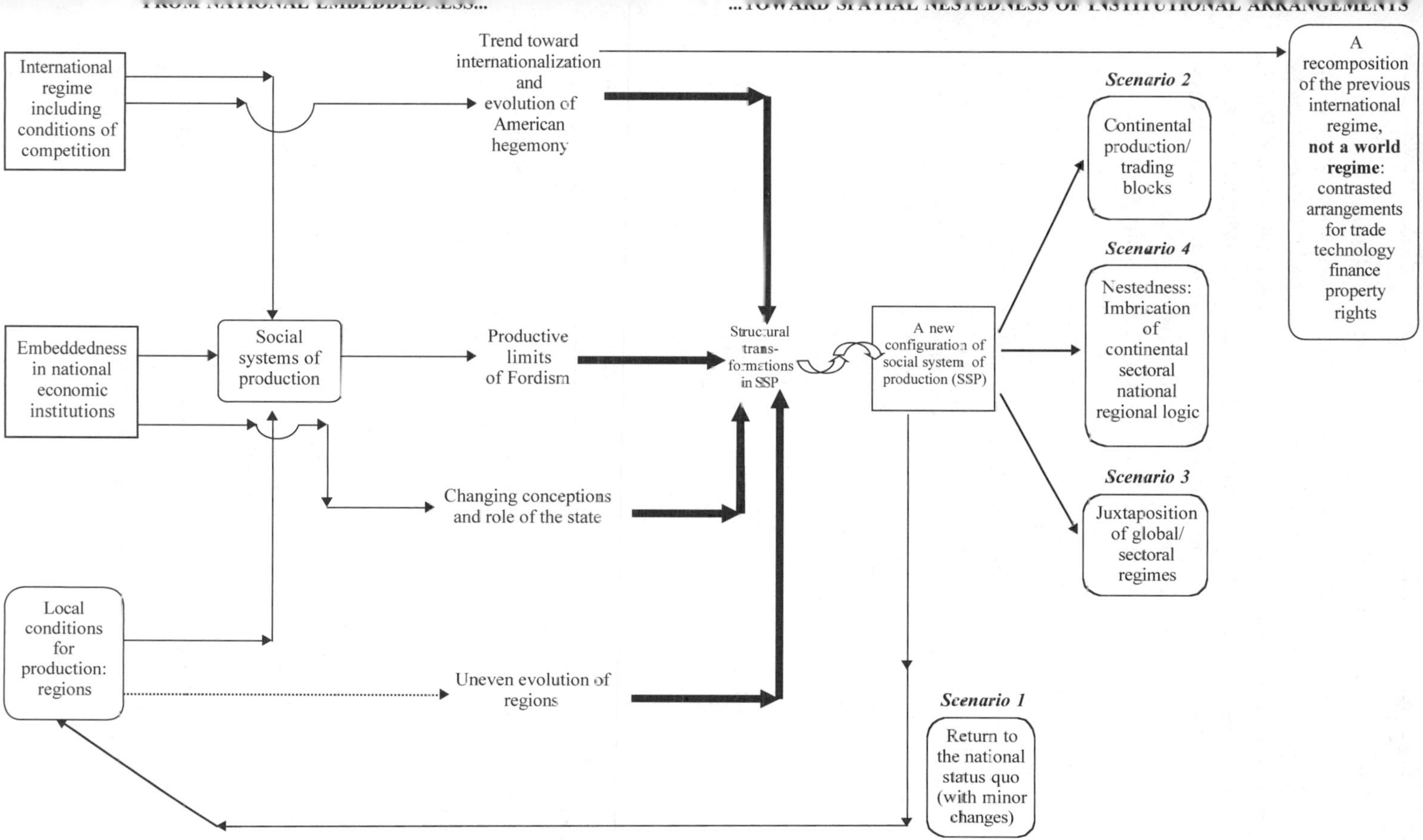

Fig. 6. The change in basic institutional arrangements

First, the institutional arrangements from the Fordist era, which tended to operate mainly at the national level with few constraints from the supernational or subnational levels, are now dependent on a variety of international trends as well as on the ability of subregional entities. This is the first and basic meaning for nestedness. Simultaneously, market-type activities tend to escape domestic boundaries and increasingly exercise more and more influence on regions and nations all over the world.

Second, nestedness implies that multifaceted causality runs in virtually all directions among the various levels of society: nations, sectors, free-trade zones, international regimes, supernational regions, large cities, and even small but well-specialized localities interact according to unprecedented configurations. This is a novelty with respect to most, if not all, past economic regimes. It is neither a bottom-up approach, from purely local competition toward an anonymous world market, as pure economic theory might imply, nor is it a top-down mechanism. Figure 7 illustrates the various levels of society interacting as an entire system.

The third feature of nestedness is that no single authority, whether supernational, continental, national, or local, has the power to monitor and to regulate such a complex system. The institutional arrangements for implementing the various functions of society do not occur at the same level. For example, finance and money tend to be highly internationalized, whereas welfare remains strictly limited to the national boundaries. Hence, possible conflicts between contradictory forces operate at different levels: business may prefer market freedom and may operate at the subnational, nation-state, and global level, while the overall population may look to the nation-state to protect them at the subnational level from the adverse effects of market logic. If, however, a national government wishes to curb the negative influences of highly speculative financial markets operating at the world level, its strategy might result in consequences worse than if they took no action, consequences such as substantial currency depreciation, higher interest rates, and/or foreign capital flight. This system has very different results from those that would have followed from similar regulations in the 1960s. The international forces currently emerging are generally unable to redefine extant national institutions completely. International trade agreements, for example, are concerned with the nature of products and public subsidies, but pay relatively little heed to the type of organizations, policies, and resources necessary to deliver social welfare services within a particular country. Competition wars between countries thus tend to be concerned with arguments of social dumping and have very serious consequences.

Nestedness makes economic policy and institutional change more difficult than ever, since no central supernational authority is able to monitor effectively a series of innovations. Some developments appear initially to be highly innovative but then turn counterproductive when inserted into the whole system. For example, financial deregulation in the late 1970s was initially assumed to promote more efficiency in capital allocation across countries and sectors. Twenty years later, however, the "short-termism" of financial markets increasingly permeated most areas of economic, social, and political life, thus introducing major new sources of instability in economic expectations. Consequently, the global effectiveness of financial deregulation may be mitigated. Some experts argue that the effects of financial deregulation have been negative, and they propose to tax short-run capital movements as a solution to the problem. However, no country has an interest in doing so alone, and so no country takes action to confront the problem. This Prisoner's Dilemma–type configuration is an indirect consequence of the nestedness of national and international institutions.

This argument about the diffusion of power leads to the speculation that the evolution of capitalist institutions will produce a series of governance modes at various levels of society, as shown in scenario four in figure 6. Competition might be coordinated partially at a continental level by free-trade agreements under the supervision of general rules of the game established worldwide. This, however, would not exclude some specific sectoral arrangements between two countries concerning the auto and textile industries, movies, and agriculture. While individual societies at the level of the nation-state may regulate the way health care and welfare benefits are distributed according to long-run national legacies, the most localized interactions are plugged into the world international system, as demonstrated by the problems of pollution, depletion of the ozone layer, biological diversity, and many other issues dealt with by the Rio world summit in the early 1990s. Acute conflicts of interest among industrialized and industrializing as well as rich and poor countries have made compromise especially difficult to achieve and still more to implement.

Given the structural character of such a shift from national embeddedness of economic institutions to their nestedness within a multilevel system, the national sources of competition have become much more complex. The quality of national systems of innovation, the nature of industrial relations systems, the level of skills, and the ability of economic actors to respond quickly to economic fluctuations and uncertainties mean that the kinds of interactions among firms, between employees and employers, and between private business and public authorities crucially affect the performance of national economies. Increasingly, the complexity and dynamism of these economies must be expressed at the subnational regional or local level. Nevertheless, the nature of the linkages between national and regional institutions plays an important role in shaping the ability of societies to evolve.

Contemporary research provides examples of how economic dynamism is influenced by the linkages between local and national institutions. For example, the high quality of differentiated production in Germany largely results from the combination of a decentralized system organized at the level of the Länder that is intricately linked with a national system of codetermination (Herrigel 1990). Like Germany, Japan used to be a good example of complementarity between dense localized networks (Nagoya City as a company town) and strong national institutions (such as major banks, spring offensives, and development agencies). In Britain, these tight linkages between regional and national institutions are not so well established; as a result, industrial districts are weakly developed, and the performance of the national economy is weak. This suggests how weakly developed regional structures may erode the vitality of previously successful institutional arrangements at the level of the nation-state (Zeitlin 1994). In the contemporary world, therefore, regional, national, and international institutions must be nested together.

In more analytical terms, the institutional arrangements that at one time were congruent at the national level are now more dispersed at multiple spatial levels (see fig. 7). Impressive economic performance now requires economic actors to be simultaneously coordinated in all spatial areas: actors must be nested in institutional arrangements that are linked at all levels. At the international level, for example, a trade regime is regulated by international agreements and tends to be more multilateral than bilateral in nature: rules are increasingly more of a constraint than a choice made by an individual nation-state. Increasingly, manufacturing and service firms are competing internationally. Moreover, monetary systems are becoming more transnational in nature. For example, currency adjustments are no longer a safety valve

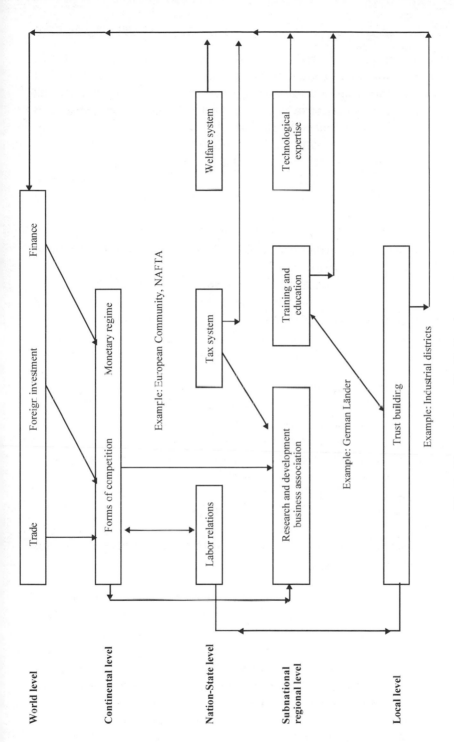

Fig. 7. The nestedness of institutional arrangements

to be manipulated in response to extra competition or inferior performance at the level of the nation-state. Indeed, nation-states have lost
much of their capacity to control interest and exchange rates (Hall
1997). Declining autonomy over these issues diminishes the capacity of
states to regulate social and other policy areas.

Conversely, the constitutional order that allocates power and
resources differently between central and local authorities increasingly
plays a role in shaping the ability of firms in a particular country to
compete in the international arena. Thus, the parts of each system have
become far more interdependent than during the 1960s, and the
increasingly complex distribution of power and resources across geo-
graphical levels is further evidence of economic institutions becoming
nested at multiple levels.

Nevertheless, coordination of economic actors at the level of the
nation-state has not completely disappeared and it is unlikely that it will
vanish, as this remains the level in which social solidarity, labor laws, a
national tax system, and many welfare services are still embedded.
However, the future of many national institutional arrangements continues to be extremely uncertain. So many contradictory forces are
operating that it is difficult to imagine that the institutional environment into which firms were embedded in the 1960s will survive another
generation. Irreversible forces have developed social systems of production that are transnational; they have shifted the division of labor
among regions and have transformed the relations between the state
and the economy.

Scenarios to Enlighten a Very Uncertain Epoch

As a result of these changes, one can imagine four different scenarios
(see right side of fig. 6).

Scenario One.   If the contradictions inherent in the internationalization of the economy, such as persisting mass unemployment in Europe,
rising inequality, major regional imbalances, xenophobic movements,
and speculation crises in Latin America and Asia, become too acute,
some governments may attempt to return to a so-called golden age by
becoming increasingly nationalistic and by erecting barriers to finance,
trade, and migration of persons. Given the interdependencies and
extreme division of labor that now operate at the international level,
such nationalistic policies for any particular country would lead to a

substantial reduction in productivity and standards of living. Should this occur, any state implementing such policies would be acting contrary to its society's general economic welfare. Indeed, if policies of internationalization could not be sustained, a state would suffer a major loss of legitimacy.

Scenario Two. Considering the emergence of the European Union, the North American Free Trade Area, and the further development of an Asian trading block, one can easily imagine that increased international economic uncertainty will foster the development of monetary and economic zones designed to minimize the discrepancies in interest and exchange rates between the zones of this triad. This scenario has been operating for more than a decade in varying degrees, and further developments along these lines are expected. Nevertheless, conflicting national interests within particular trading blocks might collide and provoke states to flirt with the first scenario, that is, the effort to seek more autonomy at the level of individual nation-states. One could clearly observe this type of tension operating between Britain and the European Community during the period between 1990 and 1993.

Scenario Three. This assumes that the juxtaposition of numerous different sectoral and/or global regulatory regimes will be sufficient to forge a compatible arrangement between conflicting interests, unequal competitiveness, and divergent trajectories among nations. For example, a GATT agreement on agricultural trade; bilateral self-restraint accords in the car, electronic, textile, and other industries; international regulation of banking and finance; a minimal social charter under the aegis of ILO; the development and implementation of an ecological tax for industrialized and industrializing countries; a codification of patents and intellectual rights; and a powerful group of seven to ten nation-states attempting to regulate interest and exchange rates could all eventually become a relatively coherent coordinated system, without any explicit design to do so. Institutions would be self-building at the international level, in accordance with an Austrian vision à la Hayek. However, the likelihood of such a pluralistic system of coordination without a powerful state or a single hegemony to orchestrate such behavior and to act as an enforcer appears to be problematic.

Scenario Four. This scenario is modeled on nestedness. Nestedness means that subnational regimes, sectoral, national, and international logics are intertwined—with none being dominant—in a two-sided type of causality. A complex system of regional, national, continental, and world institutional arrangements has left a legacy of national intervention, complemented by sectoral agreements, and has been emerging for at least a decade. For example, decisions in Brussels about economic regulations for the European Union have an increasing impact on the competitiveness of single nation-states, subnational regional dynamics, and the capacity of nation-states to shape their own economic and fiscal policies. At the same time the cohesiveness of national and subnational regional interests of member states plays a role in shaping the regulations designed in Brussels. Another example of nestedness refers to the links between product, credit, and labor markets at multiple spatial levels. In the 1960s, wage formation was embedded in a variety of national compromises between capital and labor, and monetary and exchange rate policies were designed to reflect the specificity of national political and economic institutions. In the 1990s, however, the intense international competition of product markets and the strong flows of money across countries have undermined the strength of national systems of industrial relations and labor contracts. In some advanced industrial societies, low wages are threatening to become a basic ingredient in shaping national competitiveness and the capacity of a society to attract foreign capital. All of this is intertwined at the subnational regional, national, continental, and global levels and feeds back and influences the degree of stability within the economy of any nation-state.

Thus in the 1960s, the way that institutions were embedded at the level of the nation-state influenced not only behavior and economic performance at the level of subnational regions but also the coordination of the international economy. In the 1990s and 2000s, however, the world trade regime and continental trade zones influence national policies and the structure and behavior of subnational regional groups. The flexibility and nature of national labor markets are subject to a double squeeze—from the outside by the international financial regime and from the inside by the ability of subnational regional groups to manufacture cooperation and trust among themselves.

Conclusion

How all of this fourth scenario will play out is uncertain, even though this scenario presently is extremely dynamic. Where is the theory that allows us to understand and guide such a process? Will public opinion accept such a complex set of institutional arrangements, especially in weaker countries that are more adversely affected by the ongoing transnationalization? What is the capacity of public authorities to build barriers to the process of transnationalization in order to preserve distinctive national institutions, macroeconomic performance, and high employment? Will the "satanic mills" created by the market Karl Polanyi discussed during the 1940s undermine the potential for social solidarity? Will nation-states have the capacity to respond to economic, social, and political innovations with sufficient speed to prevent economic crises—including the possible repetition of a great depression?

Long-term historical trends suggest that taming the market has always been more rewarding over the longer term than myopically following it. Moreover, modern economic theory is slowly converging toward such a vision: only short-run and marginal choices can be left to the market, whereas imaginative collective forms of coordination are addressing many of the more important social and political issues of our time. The World Bank has recently recognized that a relevant and efficient state is a necessary ingredient for institution building and development (World Bank 1997). The most competitive firms, regions, or nations are not mimicking the market; on the contrary, they are struggling to manufacture consensus, trust, collective forms of governance, and long-term vision. This essay suggests unconventional conclusions about economic policies for the future.

Following Polanyi, we must move away from the rhetoric of what free marketers promise and attempt to convince our societies to build more livable communities and to construct new forms of a mixed economy. But as our institutions are increasingly nested in a world of subnational regions, nation-states, and continental and global regimes, do we have the capacity to govern ourselves democratically? Clearly one of the major challenges of our time is to create a new theory of democracy for governing institutions nested in a world of unprecedented complexity, one in which subnational regions, nation-states, and continental and global regimes are all intricately linked.

NOTE

This essay is an adaptation and updating of the concluding chapter, "From national embeddedness to spatial and institutional nestedness," in J. Rogers

Hollingsworth and Robert Boyer, *Contemporary capitalism: The embeddedness of institutions* (Cambridge University Press, 1997), 433–77. By permission of Cambridge University Press.

REFERENCES

Aglietta, Michel. 1982. *Regulation and crisis of capitalism.* New York: Monthly Review Press.

Amable, Bruno, Rémi Barré, and Robert Boyer. 1997. *Les systèmes d'innovation à l'ere de la globalisation.* Paris: Economica.

Amsden, Alice. 1989. *Asia's next giant: South Korea and late industrialization.* New York: Oxford University Press.

Benko, Georges, and Alain Lipietz, eds. 1989. *Les régions qui gagnent! Districts et réseaux: les nouveaux paradigmes de la géo-politique.* Paris: PUF, Economie en Liberté.

Benko, Georges, and Alain Lipietz. 2000. *La richesse des régions: La nouvelle géographie socio-économique.* Paris: Presses Universitaires de France.

Bourdieu, Pierre. 1986. La force du droit. Eléments pour une sociologie du champ juridique. *Actes de la Recherche en Sciences Sociales* 64:3–19.

Boyer, Robert. 1987. Régulation. In John Eatwell, Murray Milgate, and Peter Newman, eds., *The new Palgrave: A dictionary of economics.* London: Macmillan.

———. 1989. Wage labor nexus, technology and long run dynamics: An interpretation and preliminary tests for U.S. In M. Di Matteo, R. M. Goodwin, and A. Vercelli, eds., *Lecture notes in economics and mathematical systems: Technological and social factors in long term fluctuations,* 321. New York: Springer-Verlag.

———. 1990. *The Régulation School: A critical introduction.* New York: Columbia University Press.

———. 1995. Capital-labour relations in OECD countries: From the Fordist Golden Age to contrasted national trajectories. In Juliet Schor and Jong-I You, eds., *Capital, the state and labour: A global perspective.* Aldershot: Edward Elgar.

———. 1997. Les mots et les réalités? In *Mondialisation au-dela des mythes,* 1–56. Paris: La Découverte les Dossiers de l'Etats du Monde.

———. 2000. Is a finance-led growth regime in viable alternative to Fordism? A preliminary analysis. *Economy and Society* 29, no. 1 (February): 111–45.

———. 2001. La diversité des institutions d'une croissance. In Center Saint Gobain for Economic Research, *Institutions et croissance.* Paris: Alain Michel.

Boyer, Robert, and Michel Freyssenet. 1999. *Le monde qui va changer la machine.* Mimeography. Paris: Gerpisa.

Boyer, Robert, and André Orlean. 1991. Les transformations des conventions salarales entre theorie et histoire: d'Henry Ford au fordisme. *Revue Economique* 42:233–72.

———. 1992. How do conventions evolve? *Journal of Evolutionary Economics* 2:165–77.

Boyer, Robert, and Daniel Drache. 1996. *States against markets: The limits of globalization.* London: Routledge.

Boyer, Robert, and Jacques Mistral. 1982. *Accumulation, inflation, crises.* Paris: Presses Universitaires de France.

Boyer, Robert, and Yves Saillard, eds. 2001. *"Régulation theory": The state of the art.* London: Routledge. Translation and updating of *Théorie de la régulation: L' état des savoirs.* Paris: La Découverte, collection recherche, 1995.

Calleo, David. 1982. *The imperious economy.* Cambridge: Harvard University Press.

———. 1992. *The bankrupting of America: How the federal budget is impoverishing the nation.* New York: William Morrow.

Campbell, John, J. Rogers Hollingsworth, and Leon Lindberg, eds. 1991. *The governance of the American economy.* Cambridge: Cambridge University Press.

Campbell, John, and Leon Lindberg. 1990. Property rights and the organization of economic activity by the state. *American Sociological Review* 55:634.

Chandler, Alfred D. 1969. *Strategy and structure: Chapters in the history of the American industrial enterprise.* Cambridge: MIT Press.

———. 1977. *The visible hand: The managerial revolution in American business.* Cambridge: Harvard University Press.

———. 1990. *Scale and scope: The dynamics of industrial capitalism.* Cambridge: Harvard University Press.

Contractor, F., and P. Lorange, eds. 1988. *Cooperative strategies in international business.* Lexington, Mass.: Lexington Books.

David, Paul. 1986. Under the necessity of QWERTY: The necessity of history. In W. N. Parker, ed., *Economic history and the modern economist.* London: Blackwell.

Dezalay, Yves. 1989. Le droit des faillites: du notable à l'expert. la restructuration du champ des professionnels de la restructuration des entreprises. *Actes de la Recherche en Sciences Sociales* 76–77:2–29.

Dezalay, Yves, and Bryant Garth. 1995. Merchants of law as moral entrepreneurs: Constructing international justice from the competition for transnational business disputes. *Law and Society Review* 29:27–64.

———. 1996. Building the law and putting the state into play: International strategies among Mexico's divided elite. ABF Working Paper 9509.

Dore, Ronald. 1973. *British factory, Japanese factory: The origins of diversity in industrial relations.* Berkeley: University of California Press.

————. 1983. Goodwill and the spirit of market capitalism. *British Journal of Sociology* 34:459–82.

Dumez, H., and A. Jeunemaitre. 1991. *La concurrence en Europe.* Paris: Seuil.

Eggertsson, Thrainn. 1990. *Economic behavior and institutions.* Cambridge: Cambridge University Press.

Etzioni, Amitai. 1988. *The moral dimension: Towards a new economics.* New York: Free Press.

Friedman, David. 1988. *The misunderstood miracle: Industrial development and political change in Japan.* Ithaca: Cornell University Press.

Fukuyama, Francis. 1996. *Trust: The social virtues and the creation of prosperity.* New York: Simon and Schuster.

Furubotn, Eirik, and Rudolf Richter, eds. 1991. *The new institutional economics.* Tübingen: J. C. B. Mohr.

Gambetta, Diego, ed. 1988. *Trust: Making and breaking cooperative relations.* Oxford: Basil Blackwell.

Gerschenkron, Alexander. 1962. *Economic backwardness in historical perspective.* Cambridge: Harvard University Press.

Gilpin, Robert. 1987. *The political economy of international relations.* Princeton: Princeton University Press.

Granovetter, Mark. 1984. Small is beautiful: Labor markets and establishment size. *American Sociological Review* 49:323–34.

————. 1985. Economic action and social structures: The problem of embeddedness. *American Journal of Sociology* 91:481–510.

————. 1992. Economic institutions as social constructions: A framework of analysis. *Acta Sociologica* 35:3–12.

————. 1993. Coase revisited: Business groups in the modern economy. Paper presented for ASSI Conference on hierarchies, markets, power in the economy: Theories and lessons from history. December 15–17. Milan, Italy.

Greif, Avner. 1996. Micro theory and recent developments in the study of economic institutions through economic history. In D. M. Kreps and K. F. Wallis, eds., *Advances in economic theory.* Cambridge: Cambridge University Press.

Hage, Jerald. 1996. The social system of production in France. In J. Rogers Hollingsworth, Richard Whitley, and Jerald Hage, eds., *Firms, markets, and production systems in comparative perspective.*

Hage, Jerald, and Zhongren Jing. 1996. Adaptive costs: A new paradigm for the choice of organizational form. In J. Rogers Hollingsworth, ed., *Social actors and the embeddedness of institutions.* New York: M. E. Sharpe.

Hall, Peter. 1997. The political challenges facing regional trade regimes. *La Lettre de la Régulation 22: Point théorique.* (September): 1–3.

Hamilton, Gary, and Nicole Biggart. 1988. Markets, culture, and authority: A comparative analysis of management and organization in the Far East. *American Journal of Sociology* Supplement 94:S52–S94.

Hamilton, Gary, and Cheng-Shu Kao. 1991. The institutional foundations of Chinese business: The family firm in Taiwan. In Craig Calhoun, ed., *Comparative social research*, vol. 12, *Business Institutions*. London: JAI.

Hamilton, Gary, William Zeile, and Wan-Jin Kim. 1990. The network structures of East Asian economies. In S. R. Clegg and S. G. Redding, *Capitalism in contrasting cultures*. Berlin: de Gruyter.

Hayek, Friedrich A. 1976–1982. *Law, legislation and liberty*. Chicago: University of Chicago Press.

Herrigel, Gary. 1990. Industrial organization and the politics of industry: Centralized and decentralized production in Germany. Ph.D. dissertation, MIT.

Hirsch, Fred. 1977. *Social limits to growth*. London: Routledge and Kegan Paul.

Hirschmann, Albert O. 1977. *The passions and the interests: Political arguments for capitalism before its triumph*. Princeton: Princeton University Press.

Hollingsworth, J. Rogers. 1994. Rethinking the theory of the liberal state: Towards a conception of collective responsibility, permanent mobilization, and citizenship. Paper presented before American Sociological Association, August 7. Los Angeles.

Hollingsworth, J. Rogers, and Robert Boyer, eds. 1997. *Contemporary capitalism: The embeddedness of institutions*. Cambridge: Cambridge University Press.

Hollingsworth, J. Rogers, and Leon Lindberg. 1985. The role of markets, clans, hierarchies, and associative behavior. In Wolfgang Streeck and Philippe Schmitter, eds., *Private interest government: Beyond market and state*. London: Sage.

Hollingsworth, J. Rogers, Philippe C. Schmitter, and Wolfgang Streeck, eds. 1994. *Governing capitalist economies*. New York: Oxford University Press.

Hollingsworth, J. Rogers, and Wolfgang Streeck. 1994. Countries and sectors: Performance, convergence, and competitiveness. In J. Rogers Hollingsworth, Philippe C. Schmitter, and Wolfgang Streeck, eds., *Governing capitalist economies*. New York: Oxford University Press.

Keohane, Robert O., and Helen V. Milner, eds. 1996. *Internationalization and domestic politics*. Cambridge: Cambridge University Press.

Kindleberger, Charles P. 1988. *The international economic order: Essays on financial crisis and international public goods*. Cambridge, Mass.: MIT Press.

Kumar, Krishan. 1983. Pre-capitalist and non-capitalist factors in the development of capitalism: Fred Hirsch and Joseph Schumpeter. In Adrian Ellis and Krishan Kumar, eds., *Dilemmas of liberal democracy*. London: Tavistock.

Landes, David. 1951. French business and the businessman: A social and cultural analysis. In Hugh Aitken, ed., *Explorations in enterprise*. Cambridge: Harvard University Press.

Lazonick, William. 1991. *Business organization and the myth of the market economy*. Cambridge: Cambridge University Press.

Lucas, Robert. 1988. On the mechanisms of economic development. *Journal of Monetary Economics* 72:3–42.

Marglin, Stephen A. 1991. Understanding capitalism: Control versus efficiency. In Bo Gustafsson, ed., *Power and economic institutions*. Aldershot: Edward Elgar.

Milward, Alan S. 1979. *War, economy and society: 1939–1945*. Berkeley: University of California.

North, Douglass C. 1981. *Structure and change in economic history*. New York: Norton.

————. 1990. *Institutions, institutional change and economic performance*. Cambridge: Cambridge University Press.

O'Connor, James. 1973. *The fiscal crisis of the state*. New York: St. Martin's Press.

Ohmae, Kenichi. 1985. *Triad power. The coming shape of global competition*. New York: Free Press.

Perlmutter, H. V., and D. A. Heenan. 1986. Cooperate to compete globally. *Harvard Business Review* 64:136–52.

Polanyi, Karl. 1957 [1944]. *The great transformation: The political and economic origins of our time*. Boston: Beacon.

Polanyi-Levitt, Kari, ed. 1990. *The life and work of Karl Polanyi: A celebration*. Montreal: Black Rose Books.

Pucik, Vladimir. 1988. Strategic alliances, organizational learning, and competitive advantage. *Human Resource Management* 27:77–93.

Pyke, F., G. Becattini, and W. Sengenberger. 1991. *Industrial districts and inter-firm co-operation in Italy*. Geneva: International Institute for Labour Studies.

Pyke, F., and W. Sengenberger, eds. 1992. *Industrial districts and local regeneration*. Geneva: International Institute for Labour Studies.

Raff, D. M. G. 1988. Wage determination theory and the five-dollar day at Ford. *Journal of Economic History* 48:387–99.

Rueff, Jacques, and X-Crise. 1932. Pourquoi, malgré tout, je reste libéral. In *De la récurrence des crises économiques*. Paris: Economica.

Sabel, Charles F. 1988. The re-emergence of regional economies. In Paul Hirst and Jonathan Zeitlin, eds., *Reversing industrial decline*. Oxford: Berg.

————. 1992. Studied trust: Building new forms of cooperation in a volatile economy. In Frank Pyke and Werner Sengenberger, eds., *Industrial districts and local economic regeneration*. Geneva: International Institute for Labor Studies.

————. 1997. Constitutional orders: Trust building and response to change. In J. Rogers Hollingsworth and Robert Boyer, eds., *Contemporary capitalism: The embeddedness of institutions*. Cambridge: Cambridge University Press.

Sabel, Charles F., and Jonathan Zeitlin. 1985. Historical alternatives to mass production: Politics, markets, and technology in nineteenth century industrialization. *Past and Present* 108:133–76.

Sargent, T. J. 1979. *Macroeconomic theory*. New York: Academic.

Sassen, Saskia. 1991. *The global city: New York, London, Tokyo.* Princeton: Princeton University Press.

Schneiberg, Marc, and J. Rogers Hollingsworth. 1990. Can transaction cost economics explain trade associations? In Masahiko Aoki, Bo Gustafsson, and Oliver E. Williamson, eds., *The firm as a nexus of treaties.* London: Sage.

Schumpeter, Joseph A. 1976. *Capitalism, socialism, and democracy.* 5th ed. London: Allen and Unwin.

Simon, Herbert. 1983 [1982]. *Models of bounded rationality: Behavioral economics and business organization.* 2d ed. Cambridge: MIT Press.

Stiglitz, Joseph. 1987. Dependence of quality on price. *Journal of Economic Literature* 25:1–48.

Streeck, Wolfgang. 1991. On the institutional conditions of diversified quality production. In Egon Matzner and Wolfgang Streeck, eds., *Beyond Keynesianism: The socio-economics of production and full employment.* Aldershot: Edward Elgar.

———. 1992. *Social institutions and economic performance.* Newbury Park, Calif.: Sage.

Streeck, Wolfgang, and Philippe C. Schmitter. 1985. Community, market, state—and associations? The prospective contribution of interest governance to social order. In Wolfgang Streeck and Philippe C. Schmitter, eds., *Private interest government: Beyond market and state.* Beverly Hills: Sage.

Tirole, Jean. 1988. *The theory of industrial organization.* Cambridge: MIT Press.

Trubek, David M., Yves Dezalay, Ruth Buchanan, and John R. Davis. 1994. Global restructuring and the law: Studies of the internationalization of legal fields and the creation of transnational arenas. *Case Western Reserve Law Review* 44:407.

Vatter, Harold. 1985. *The US economy in World War II.* New York: Columbia University Press.

Vickery, Lister. 1986. France. In Paul Burns and Tim Dewhurst, eds., *Small business in Europe.* London: Macmillan.

Wade, Robert. 1990. *Governing the market.* Princeton: Princeton University Press.

Weir, Margaret, and Theda Skocpol. 1985. State structures and the possibilities for 'Keynesian' responses to the Great Depression in Sweden, Britain, and the United States. In Peter B. Evans, Dietrich Rueschemeyer, and Theda Skocpol, eds., *Bringing the state back in.* Cambridge: Cambridge University Press.

White, Harrison. 1991. *Identity and control: A structural theory of social action.* Princeton: Princeton University Press.

Whitley, Richard. 1992a. *Business systems in East Asia: Firms, markets, and societies.* London: Sage.

———, ed. 1992b. *European business systems: Firms and markets in their national contexts.* London: Sage.

Whitley, Richard, and J. Rogers Hollingsworth. 1996. The industrial structuring of market economies. In J. Rogers Hollingsworth, Richard Whitley, and Jerald Hage, eds., *Firms, markets, and production systems in comparative perspective.*

Williamson, Oliver. 1985. *The economic institutions of capitalism.* New York: Free Press.

World Bank. 1997. *State in a changing world.* 1997 Development Report, Washington, D.C.

Zeitlin, Jonathan. 1990. *Industrial districts and local economic regeneration: Models, institutions and policies.* Geneva: International Institute for Labour Studies.

————. 1994. Why are there no industrial districts in the United Kingdom? In Arnaldo Bagnasco and Charles Sabel, eds., *Ce que petit peut faire: Les petites et moyennes entreprises en Europe.* Poitiers: Observatoire du Changement Social en Europe Occidentale.

Zelizer, Viviana. 1988. Beyond the polemics on the market: Establishing a theoretical and empirical agenda. *Sociological Forum* 5:614–34.

————. 1989. The social meaning of money: 'Special monies.' *American Journal of Sociology* 95:342–77.

Zysman, John, E. Doherty, and A. Schwartz. 1997. Tales from the "global" economy: cross-national production networks and the reorganization of the European economy. *Structural Change and Economic Dynamics* 8, no. 1: 45–83.

Between Liberalism and Neoliberalism: Law's Dilemma in Latin America

Jeremy Adelman and Miguel Angel Centeno

The essay by Jeremy Adelman, a historian, and Miguel Centeno, a sociologist, both at Princeton, takes a general look at a problem close to Boyer's institutional approach. Boyer, an economist, focuses on the need for harmony between the workings of the market and indigenous means of regulation, warning that poorly suited institutional innovations—including what we might believe to be legal universals—can lead to economic disaster. This essay takes up the issue of the unhappy coexistence of liberal markets and the legal order both throughout Latin American history and at the present time.

The essay confronts the question of why, given so much effort, the attempt to build a "democracy" and "rule of law" in Latin America has been unsuccessful. The efforts were first modeled on Europe after colonialism. Increasingly they have followed the international prestige and power of the United States, bolstered perhaps by various movements of law and development. The sociological and historical analysis in this essay points to the problems in moving new orthodoxies from the north to Latin American countries in the south.

There is a long history of law in Latin America, they note, but it has never achieved legitimacy domestically. It is imported, mostly tied to elites, and offers very little to ordinary citizens. The authors are sympathetic to an increased importance for law but they do not see immediate change on the horizon. In particular, they acknowledge the pressures that come from internationalization and models of a new state orthodoxy in the World Bank and among other transnational actors. They do not believe, however, that the currently legitimate exported institutions will be successful. In their words, "Lacking a set of institutions to convey the idea and its practice that 'ruled and rulers obey the same rules,' internationalization threatens to aggravate the uneven national development of the rule of law. Internationalization of law assumes that the rule of the state and its principles have been absorbed by civil society." The new prescriptions may lead to reform, but they may not.

The twin pillars of liberalism appear triumphant in Latin America: markets allocate resources, and elections define governments. And yet, Latin American societies remain crisis-prone. From Argentina to Mexico, not only is the legitimacy of the governments under assault, but the very girding of public authority is crumbling. Across the region, the shift to civilian rule has failed to solve many of the underlying troubles that undermined their progenitors. Deregulation, privatization, and internationalization of domestic markets have not licked rent-seeking habits, much less put regional economies on track to sustained upward growth.

The current malaise has historic roots in the record of liberalism in Latin America. The combination of market economics and republican rule, far from delivering on their upbeat prophecies, has usually resulted in polarized extremes: social upheaval against market rules or praetorian brutality. We argue that the troubled fate of liberalism can be ascribed to the way in which the two pillars of modern political and economic life have combined. In Latin America, the pattern of market allocation of resources and legal equality of political subjects proved to be, not a harmonious, self-reinforcing combination (in the idealized versions of what transpired in North America), but an explosive one. From independence onward, Latin America followed its own idiosyncratic course, not because the new republics did not sufficiently embrace liberal tenets, but because they did not consolidate the legal foundations for the coexistence of market competition and political legitimacy.

Much of Latin America's turmoil can be traced to the failure of the rule of law in Latin America. Rather than functioning as an institutional bedrock for markets and democracy, Latin American legality is a quicksand of rent seeking and contestation. Liberal theory concentrates attention on property rights—defining entitlements to use or dispose of resources—and citizenship—some degree of political representation. It presupposes the existence of a legal framework capable of enforcing rights and obligations flowing from private and public entitlements. This is what faltered in Latin America.

Why? In short, the independence struggles shredded the legal fabric of the ancien régime without bequeathing the means to create alternative legal systems. Liberals applied free-market dogmas without inscribing an underlying juridical order capable of legitimating public authority. Latin American states acquired the means for violence but did not forge regimes that could impose rule without force.

The result was a prolonged period of contestation, to which elites responded by revamping constitutional rules in favor of exclusive regimes capable of commanding only threadbare popular support. Citizenship was sacrificed to property. Yet, without legitimacy, this order—private property without public representation—was essentially unstable, always vulnerable to internal challenges to the rampant inequality and perceived injustices of the status quo.

By the twentieth century, Latin America—with important exceptions that more often proved the general rule—was rocking between regimes trying to unfetter market relations at the expense of public legitimacy, at one extreme, and reformist efforts that intruded on market autonomy, at the other. In effect, the legacy of the transition to modern republicanism set the region up for an openly contested relationship between political representation and private property.

Current neoliberal pieties replicate the earlier liberal fallacy of trying to combine markets and representation without the rule of law (O'Donnell 1994a). Reformers rushed to release markets without attention to the institutional life that would enable them to function. They were blind to a dilemma that dogged their precursors: bereft of public rules, wealth-seeking behavior often mutated into private rent-seeking; in turn, market activity aggravated social inequalities. All too often public authority was seen as and served as a mask for private enrichment.

As the recent triumphs of Hugo Chávez in Venezuela and Alberto Fujimori in Peru—and the horrified international reaction—suggest, the dilemma of inequality and citizenship persists. Even in the "mainstreamed" politics of Mexico and Argentina, the rule of law is not universally spread across the provinces and classes. Latin America's poor still reject the process and politics of technocratic decision-making. Those at the top perceive any participatory voice as a potential menace to their interests. The upshot of the dilemma is polarization and the frequent resort to plebescitary democracy.

The internationalization of the rule of law is not a solution to this dilemma. Our argument is that the precondition for any salutary effect of the internationalization of the rule of law is its nationalization. Lacking a set of institutions to convey the idea and its practice that "ruled and rulers obey the same rules," internationalization threatens to aggravate the uneven national development of the rule of law. Internationalization of law assumes that the rule of the state and its principles have been absorbed by civil society. In Latin America, where state authority was barely consolidated, legal transnationalism can only perpetuate the problems it claims to solve.

This essay challenges three common claims about the failure of liberalism and the rule of law in Latin America. The first, a "culturalist" critique, maintains that Latin America was a continent with no liberal heritage at all, a vessel for persistent authoritarian predispositions. A second "statist" argument claims that omnipotent public power suffocated private initiative, market-driven growth, and electoral democracy. Both of these arguments conveniently forget long periods of free-market policies and public commitment to liberal discourse in Latin American history. A third view uses the determinism of purely external factors—imperialism, international inequalities, or inescapable constraints of globalization—to account for Latin American troubles. However, while facts of everyday life, these are more results than causes of the pattern of liberal development. All of these types of arguments tend to argue that immutable structural factors weaken the rule of law; Latin America is genetically condemned to legal backwardness. We prefer a more historically and politically embedded account.

Republican Origins of Legal Dilemmas

Modern Latin America has the birthright of the Enlightenment—the clutch of ideas resting on notions of the legal equality of political subjects and the autonomy of the private sphere. From their inception, republican movements in Latin America shared the belief that the rule of law could protect this reordering of social relations. By the rule of law we mean that all subjects, including rulers, were beholden to the same general principles that formed baseline public rules; rulers and the ruled obey the same laws.

But on its own, the Enlightenment was not a foundational framework for a new order, nor a sufficient compass for a stable political community. This did not prevent late-eighteenth- and early-nineteenth-century proponents of change from treating it as a panacea. Indeed, the rather exceptional case of the triumph of republicanism in the Thirteen Colonies allowed them to idealize Enlightenment promises (Guerra 1993: 23–33; Langely 1996).

Such lofty aspirations were almost doomed to failure. They certainly promised disappointment. As Napoleon's occupation of the Iberian Peninsula in 1808 cascaded into a full collapse of the Bourbon transatlantic order, Creoles had to take charge of regimes for which they were not quite prepared. The champions of independence presented themselves as the makers of new political communities that would live up to the same principles as those of other revolutionary societies, principally France and the United States. Accordingly, the language of revolution broadcast a radically new order; free of kings, liberated from private guilds, and free from oppressive corporate privileges and obligations (like church or military *fueros*, or Indian tribute payments). In short, the notion of legal equality for all political subjects in an emerging public world was a cornerstone of early republican purposes.

Across the continent, the dual principles of reform spread. Legislators unencumbered property rights; anyone could trade, restrictions on contractual rights vanished, status-bound obligations to elites began to succumb. In the same spirit, suffrage spread—it was indeed the *citoyen* model and not Locke's that Creoles preferred (so property restrictions did not exist, with some prominent exceptions)—implying a daring degree of universal male representation, and aligning individualism with political citizenship. Across the continent, constitution-talk of the 1820s proclaimed the mutually reinforcing and harmonious logic of combining free markets with free political individualism, both now covered by principles of modern legality.[1]

It was, as proponents of reform soon discovered, much easier to proclaim ideals in the face of what they did not like than to translate imagined orders into constitutional realities. As has often been noted, the first stage of Latin American Liberalism was unable to resolve the difficult contradictions between its two central tenets: an emphasis on individual liberty and the creation of states strong enough to "humble any corporate groups that threatened individual liberty" (Bushnell and Macaulay 1994: 34; Peruzzotti 1996). Unlike their European equivalents that were contemporaneously constructing liberal regimes upon state machines that had been in the process of consolidation for a century or more, the Latin America republics needed to assure individual liberty while also constructing an administrative and political apparatus capable of enforcing the rule of law. The result was an often illiberal chaos. While the early liberals dreamed of a constitutional government, no legitimate force appeared that could enforce the law (Botana 1994: 478). Thus, for example, while all postindependence governments recognized the principle of private property, it was at least several decades before any of them (with the possible exception of Chile) was able to enforce such rights (Bushnell and Macaulay 1994: 49–50).

Furthermore, Creole republicans were far from like-minded about what the republic ought to resemble. Some trumpeted centralist, unitary frameworks, even constitutional monarchies to preserve some semblance of the old order so that the new order would not implode on itself. Others advocated a complete rupture with the past, arguing that only by cleansing the community of old vices would new virtues thrive. Constitutional congresses came and went. Revolution soon degenerated into civil war.

It is easy to take this account of infra–Creole elite discord at face value. But it does not exhaust the story. Republicanism discharged massive mobilization among subaltern sectors. Liberalism, in effect, was more than just a banner by which Creoles could trumpet an alternative to Bourbon absolutism and aristocratic privilege; it also stirred the political imagination, particularly among rural folk. The most dramatic (and, as far as elites across the region were concerned, horrific) episode was in Santo Domingo, where the principle of legal equality catalyzed a bitter war against the French and even the mulatto planter class.[2] If Haiti exemplified French revolutionary principles at the service of bringing down formal French rule, an entire arc of peasant society in mainland Latin America mobilized to the tune of popular sovereignty, freedom from onerous duties, and local self-rule. From the guerrillas of Father Morelos in Mexico to the *montonero* armies of José Artigas in the Rio de la Plata, rural folk found in elements of liberalism the possibility for realizing projects that did not easily square with the designs of more urban, elite publicists (cf. Thurner 1995; Guardino 1996). Thus, constitutional discord was more than a clash of ideas among revolutionary leaders to guide liberal communities into statehood; it was also the context for class, ethnic, and racial struggles over the meaning of community.

Disappointed republican leaders lost hope. Their despair led them to recast earlier faith in political subjects' ability for self-government. Consider Simón Bolívar's words: "The majority of the people have been led astray by religious fanaticism and reduced by the allurements of a devouring monarchy. To the torch of liberty, which we have offered to America as the guide and object of our efforts, our enemies have applied the incendiary brand of discord, of devastation, and the strong entice-ment of usurped honors and fortunes for men who have been debased by the yoke of servitude and reduced to brutishness by the doctrine of superstition" ("Manifesto to the People of Venezuela," Sept. 7, 1814: 82).

Despair eventually led many Creoles to blame their own liberated subjects for their inability to realize the double promise of freedom from absolutist monarchy. Bolívar himself bemoaned Latin Americans' "permanent infancy," and, by 1820, he advocated a temporary and benevolent dictatorship (not, it should be added, to be confused with the praetorian sort of the post–World War II years) to tutor the region out of its own backwardness. "The American states need the care of paternal governments to heal the sores and wounds of despotism and war" ("Reply of a South American to a Gentleman of this Island," Sept. 6, 1815: 115). By the 1850s, second-generation Creole statists, from Andrés Bello in Chile to Juan Bautista Alberdi in Argentina, advocated centralized, executive dominated polities to stabilize fractious republics and bring some order to fissiparous political communities. Alberdi, reflecting on the failures of the 1820s, once noted that "in the first cries of triumph, [liberals] forgot a word that is less sonorous than *liberty*, but which represents a counterweight that keeps liberty afoot: *order*" (1886: 237).[3]

It was Bello's adopted home, Chile, that offered something of a political template for the new order. Bello, active in legal and constitu-tional circles in Santiago from the 1830s, advocated a restorationist-type system, with a powerful presidency and laced through with a set of legal codes to defend private rights. Suffrage rights, however, took a beating: the 1833 Constitution scaled back the franchise by posing property and literacy requirements on the vote (some of these restrictions survived until 1970). The system, named after its chief political architect, Diego Portales, ushered in a comparatively long period of stability for the sin-uous republic. Indeed, from being a backwater, Chile emerged as one of the region's most powerful countries, devastating the older and once-richer heartlands of Bolivia and Peru in a series of wars of territorial expansion, culminating in the War of the Pacific (1879–83).

Brazil offered a similar example. Political authorities in Rio de Janeiro managed to steer the transition to independent statehood with a minimum of friction. This at least avoided the economic costs and social mobilization of waging a war of independence. While a representative monarchy, the Brazilian Empire was surprisingly open politically. The electoral laws of 1824 and 1846 provided for widespread suffrage rights and minimized property qualifications. As Richard Graham has noted, it is possible that the Brazilian Empire was technically speaking more "democratic" than the United States—until 1881, that is. With emancipation of Brazil's slaves on the horizon, constitutionalists recoiled at the prospect of enfranchising new ex-slave citizens and possibly imperiling Brazil's political "stability" and property rights. In a stunning coup de main, the Assembly radically gutted the electoral laws. By the time Brazil became a republic (1889), it boasted an extremely exclusionary regime (Graham 1990).

Across Latin America, principles and practices of political equality gave way to political inequality. Beginning with the second half of the nineteenth century, the pattern followed by Latin American liberalism changed dramatically. If the first half had been characterized by the chaos resulting from the contradictory goals of protecting individual liberty and the establishment of governmental authority, the second half saw the increasing abandonment of the first for the sake of the second. In the words of Venezuelan dictator Guzmán Blanco, the new ideology privileged above anything else "order, and moral and material progress." This shift was accompanied by a practically wholesale acceptance of liberal economic theory exemplified by the doctrines of free trade and comparative advantage. The Latin American variation on trasformismo unified elites into new historic blocs, solving the riddle of instability, while disassociating themselves from the integrative purpose of early liberals. This created the political basis for impressive market-led growth. From roughly 1880 to 1910, the region registered stunning economic performance but systematically turned its back on the challenge of legitimating local regimes. With nuances, the Chilean and Brazilian examples replicated in Mexico (which began restricting earlier suffrage rights in the 1830s—revoking some of these curbs under the Reforma), Colombia (which followed the Brazilian about-face in the 1880s Regeneración) and elsewhere. What is more, de facto exclusions reinforced these de jure exclusions through a series of widespread electoral practices, such as the prevalence of public voting, open fraud, even more open patronage and clientelism, and naked violence. All of this was supposed to ensure political stability without fully disbanding the original guiding principles of popular sovereignty (Sabato n.d.).

Our excursus into nineteenth-century Latin American history is meant to reveal three idiosyncratic aspects of Latin America's nineteenth-century liberal legacy. First, the breakup of Iberian (and especially the Spanish) empires shattered the ancien régime political economies and natural law systems without leading to an automatic liberal successor based on republican law. The revolutions shattered the juridical obstacles to capitalist development and remapped the personnel of the ruling class. But they did not imply consensus around alternative constitutional principles. Second, once independent, early liberals issued a flurry of reforms designed to uphold contractual freedoms and universal (male) rights to political representation. But the turmoil of economic dislocation, social militarization, and political fragmentation soon plunged the early republics into civil strife. Third, with the exemplars of Chile and Brazil, Latin American republics inverted the flow of political movement across the Atlantic of stabilizing market mechanisms and opening political channels.

This last point merits some elaboration through comparison. In North America and much of modernizing Europe, the franchise percolated downward as the century unfolded. With plenty of bumps and discontinuities (and, in the case of the United States, a full-scale civil war) along the way, these societies used extended suffrage to legitimate political economies (Macpherson 1977: 23–76; Marshall 1964: 65–122). Latin America, with very few exceptions, reversed this order: in order to stabilize market relations and bring order to representative systems, the political bases of regimes became less universal by the century's end. From Porfirio Díaz's Mexico to Julio A. Roca's Argentina, regimes were liberal economically (breaking up old, corporate property ownership, ushering their societies into the Atlantic circulation of goods and capital, and attentive to the needs of public institutions to promote private venture), but more conservative politically. In effect, regimes became more publicly exclusive as the private returns from world market integration began to climb. This, then, enabled local elites to claim larger shares of wealth and income without having to face a state actively supporting public goods, never mind trying to effect some relative material equality.

This had profound implications for the rule of law. If the early principles of republicanism promised to unite subjects under the shared banner of contractual and representative freedoms and equalities, the fallout of the revolutions uncoupled this dual mission. By the end of the century, law was manifestly designed to uphold private rights and freedoms, but deprived of the role of guaranteeing these features in the public realm. As order prevailed over liberty and as authority eclipsed freedom, legitimacy of the public domain waned in favor of its stability.

From Contestation to Social Citizenship

If law seemed less a field for protecting liberal public principles, it did not demobilize sectors that were excluded from republican representation. Indeed, it came as a shock for belle epoque elites that, in the throes of first-centenary festivities (ca. 1910), popular sectors raised the banner of legal freedoms to challenge conservative rule. In Argentina, sharecroppers denounced elite landowner power; in Brazil, syndicalists torched coffee cargoes to protest against infringements on bargaining rights; and in Mexico, most dramatically, a cross-class alliance brought down the kleptocratic Díaz regime in the name of restoring some semblance of constitutional propriety.

As the twentieth century unfolded, the legitimacy of the public order became a source of criticism among the excluded, and a subject of some anxiety among "elite" reformers. Governments began to tinker with very modest welfare concessions, many began to disband or condemn the exclusionary practices. Especially in the cases of Chile, Argentina, and Uruguay, some appeared to rejoin the Atlantic drift to secular universalization of the public domain. Some, like Brazil and Central America, made no progress.

For the most part, these reforms, when they occurred, represented cases of too little too late. The more tight-fisted regimes stomped openly on demands for suffrage, open collective bargaining, and urban reform. In Brazil, the planter political classes broke up unions, arrested neighborhood organizers, and silenced middle-class demands for incorporation into a cleaner political system. In El Salvador, Guatemala, and Nicaragua, patterns of exclusion were even more ruthless. But in most countries, tinkering was the prevailing rule. By 1930, however, no Latin American country could be said to have recalibrated the balance of universalizing private representation and protecting personal property. Market-driven capitalism flourished without addressing the legitimacy of the legal rules governing extraprivate relations. Indeed, the very economic success of outward-oriented development relieved pressure on the ruling classes to alter the rules of authority: rapid growth and high-pitched investment gave elites enough means to dispense patronage and favors to political clienteles.

The source of the imbalance's vibrancy was also its unforeseen debility. By the late 1920s, especially as export prices began to flatten, then drop, many had begun to wonder whether Latin America's idiosyncratic liberal regimes might survive. Their prescience anticipated the meltdown of 1929 and 1930. Export prices crashed, and international creditors called in loans. No Latin American society emerged from the Depression unscathed by the breakdown of gold standard internationalism (Cardoso and Faletto 1971; Thorp 1984).

In spite of the current distaste for economistic explanations, it would be hard to downplay the significance of the 1930s. The effects of economic turmoil were as multiple as they were profound. On the surface, the first victims were the civilian regimes, often already suffering from acute sclerosis. The Argentine army sent the senile President Yrigoyen into exile, a convergence of regional movements toppled the *paulista* planters from power in Rio de Janeiro, a radicalizing Liberal Party swept to office in Colombia, and even Plutarco Calles's emerging plutocracy (no pun intended) fell, giving way to the reformist Lázaro Cárdenas. The early 1930s destabilized the old republican equipoise. In few cases, however, did the full constitutional apparatuses of power collapse.

Below the surface, social and economic dislocations were even more seismic. The collapse of export sectors intensified the grievances lurking in the previous era's bounty. Syndicalists dusted off old claims about union recognition, and peasant seizures of estates began to climb. In perhaps the most extreme manifestation of export-led growth, in sugar-driven Cuba, cane-workers occupied mills and fields and began erecting sugar "soviets" and running their enterprises collectively (Carr 1996: 129–58). In some cases, such as López Pumarejo's "Revolution on the March" in Colombia and Lázaro Cárdenas' revival of *agrarismo*, regimes openly condoned (while trying to channel) assaults on the commanding heights of the hobbled export economies.

In the end, the combination of mobilized existing popular sectors and the emergence of new social actors, like the industrial proletariat (now grown thanks to import substitution), finally challenged the architectural makeup of nineteenth-century liberal constitutionalism.

By the 1940s, the earlier party machines and state apparatuses were clearly unable to absorb the blows from social claims from below. Sergeant Fulgencio Batista, having played the role of mediator in Cuba's febrile days of revolt in 1933 and 1934, finally helped break decades of fraudulent exclusion: in 1940 he invited workers, peasants, and Afro-Cuban delegates to assemble to rewrite the constitutional framework for the republic. Getulio Vargas began scuppering his own soft-authoritarian Estado Novo to don the mantle of friend of the Brazilian worker, only to have Brazil's potentates dislodge him from power. But perhaps the most celebrated case of this constitutional transformation propelled from below was the case of Argentina, where Colonel Juan Perón harnessed the power of the ever more aggrieved and dynamic trade unions. Elected to power in February 1946 by a slender margin, Perón set about dismantling the legal pillars of the old order and building a regime that would come to embody the quintessence of populism (e.g., Rock 1994).

The populist arrangement—with important nuances and variations that cannot be explored here—reversed the nineteenth-century pattern. If the previous century made the political arena more exclusive while defending private property rights, populism confronted the yawning legitimacy crises of the old model with an explicit effort to induct popular sectors back into the public arena.

Popular incorporation was partly achieved electorally. Perón, Vargas, Cárdenas, Batista, Arbenz, and others used the franchise and party politics to admit, or readmit, popular sectors into the public domain. They restored the republican notion that representation was a cornerstone of the rule of law, by resurrecting the idea that rulers and ruled should obey the same rules (of course, whether these principles were honored is quite another matter).

Populism also heralded another channel for popular induction: using public legal authority to create new private social rights. Trade unions, landless peasants, and mothers had all been clamoring, not just for formal political rights, but also for substantive social rights. Peronist trade unions radically shifted shop-floor property rights—inscribed in the matrix of collective bargaining laws—in favor of the rank and file. Guatemalan peasants pressed middle-of-the-road governments to broaden the peasantry's landholding stake, to the point of forcing the Arbenz administration to encroach on United Fruit Company territory (Handy 1994). Indeed, agrarian reform became, by the 1950s and 1960s, *the* wedge of social claims-making across the region. It was also the cause that most tested the internal stability of populist coalitions. Either way, it signified a high-water mark of a particular idiom of rights and entitlements in Latin America, one in which populist champions accepted the principle that a developing liberal regime had to address social and economic equalities in order to realize political liberalism. Substantive reform would induct popular sectors into the public domain while breaking down the calcified "feudal" obstacles to capitalism and modernity.

What made populism so remarkable was its explicit combination of political and social citizenship as the means to rebuild republican political communities. From the point of view of liberalism, however, populist regimes still failed to resolve the legal quandary of early independence. The Cárdenas *sexenio,* for example, represents one of the high points of Latin American populism. If this sought to reinclude the masses that had been abandoned in the nineteenth century, it did so not through the creation of a regime of citizens, but through a corporatist mechanism represented by the government party. The populist turn of the Mexican state was in part a response to the same economic crises facing other Latin American countries as a result of the Depression *and* the increase in labor and peasant militancy of the early 1930s. Whatever Cárdenas's ideological preferences, he, like his continental counterparts, had to come up with a political formula that would signal the inclusion of the masses who quite rightly had begun to question the benefits brought about by the Revolution of 1910.

The Cardenista response to demands from below included a massive expansion of agrarian reform, prolabor legislation, and the nationalization of vital sectors. While these did mark a break with the previous policies of exclusion, Cárdenas sought to respond to the needs of the mass of the population not through a defense of the rights of individuals, but through the representation of their social interests within the National Revolutionary Party (PNR)/Party of the Mexican Revolution (PRM) (precursors to the Partido Revolucionario Institucional (PRI)). Moreover, many of the most dramatic advances came thanks to the influence of the president himself using special decrees (Riding 1990: 21). While the Cardenista legacy included a remarkable political stability, this was not necessarily based on a strong regime of laws. Power was institutionalized through the PRI and the state bureaucracy, and the masses were at least formally included in the development of state policy, but this was done with little respect for formal law beyond the political expediency required for the protection of the institutional revolution. The articulation of this popular inclusion was therefore sensitive to the composition of the political leadership. Under Cárdenas, inclusion meant agrarian reform, but under Alemán, it meant the consolidation of a new dominant class linked to the regime.

Authoritarian Law

In retrospect, it is easy to pick apart the vulnerabilities of the populist démarche. Despite its inward reorientation, it did not insulate Latin American societies from international pressures. The real troubles, however, were domestic. Populism was no more successful at recalibrating the relationship between public representation and legitimacy with private property rights, which would place the republics on more stable constitutional foundations. In an effort to shore up the legitimacy of liberal capitalism in populist forms, governments intruded on the sphere of private property rights. If the belle epoque liberal mold suffered from underlying legitimacy problems, the latter-day populist reincarnation soon suffered from serious macroeconomic malaise. These troubles were, at heart, rooted in the failure of the revamped legal fabric to reconcile collective conflict.

It did not take long for contemporaries to see the warning signs. Inflation soared, balance of payments deficits plunged, and business sectors began to complain more loudly of persecution. When reforming regimes had to impose austerity, mobilized sectors balked. Populist experiments ended in tragedy. The assassination of Jorge Eliecer Gaitán, the ensuing bogotazo, and the restoration of revanchist Conservative rule in Colombia anticipated the reactionary tide in the rest of the region (Sánchez 1991: chap. 1). In a temporal span from the Guatemala coup in 1954 to the overthrow of Allende in 1973, populist projects to integrate workers and peasants into a republican model, by broadening representation with substantive rights, in some cases literally went down in flames. Collective violence became a political means to depoliticize society. Indeed, the scale of the public carnage and violation of personal liberties can only be understood as an effort to dismantle, forcibly, social alliances and political arrangements in formation since the 1930s. Authoritarian regimes aimed to dismantle the heritage of social citizenship.

On the eve of the modern authoritarian turn, Latin American societies hovered over a deep chasm between two irreconcilable positions.
Each one presented an alternative balance of the liberal mix between
public representation and the autonomy of private property. Each com-
manded polarized social allegiances and invoked opposing discourses of
rights. There were, to be sure, efforts to build bridges, as Kathryn
Sikkink has shown in the case of Brazilian and Argentine developmentalism (1991). This was a short-lived option. Some outliers used international rents (like oil in Venezuela after the fall of Pérez Jiménez) to
lubricate vast civilian patronage regimes. Others thwarted the populist
turn altogether and perpetuated the old civilian exclusionary model,
like Colombia, but condemned the regime to persistent legitimation
problems. Mexico, building on its revolutionary heritage, reinforced the
scaffolding of the PRI, bracing the state to the party while using oil rents
and political deals to palliate constituencies. Yet not even this archetype
of hegemonic rule could fully reconcile the divergent claims of political
participation and rights of property. The demons of liberalism finally
clashed openly in 1968.

The chasm between the populist-integrative alliance and the
authoritarian-exclusive camp widened in 1959 with the triumph of Fidel
Castro's rebels. Cuba, in fact, displayed the most concerted shift from
old republicanism, to populist incorporation, only to return to its earlier exclusive habits after 1952. Venal civilian, and later (under Batista)
soft-authoritarian rule (at least by comparison to what would begin to
seize Latin American societies after the Cuban Revolution) eventually
devoured itself in illegitimacy. The populist vision embodied in the 1898
and 1933 revolutions and the 1940 Constitution became the opposition's
rallying cry and eventually served as the *fidelista* banner. When Castro
entered Havana, he promised a return to the spirit of constitutional
integration—and as his regime sedimented into power, it institutionalized inclusionary policies of populism by claiming that the Party was the
total expression of the entire social spectrum. So universal was its
domain that principles of competitive elections were redundant. In the
meantime, bourgeois legal protection of personal property rights
became the emblem of what the Revolution sought to eviscerate: the
rights of particulars against the entitlements of the whole. Castro,
accordingly, used Party law to serve an entirely public purpose.

The victory of Cuban rebels hardened the resolve of other Latin
American elites to prevent populism from following the same course. As

guerrilla *focos* proliferated, rulers could use their presence as proof of an irreconcilable threat to bourgeois legal principles. Ironically, this threat to bourgeois legality prompted rulers to take a decisive turn to authoritarianism, treating the end of elections and the unimpeachable powers of the military as the necessary cost of defending private property rights. In dramatic fashion, propertied sectors swung Latin America to one side of the chasm. Doing so required unraveling the concessions made from the 1930s onward, crushing the mobilized constituencies of populism, and expunging even the nineteenth-century pretense of unequal public representation. Authoritarian rulers rejected the foundational logic of the rule of law; authoritarian law made explicit the disjuncture between the rules of the rulers and draconian rules for the ruled.

Law's Current Impasse

Authoritarian violence aimed to exorcise the demons of populism—even if these demons were themselves the progeny of liberalism. Efforts were made to reconcile the illegitimacy of constitutionalism by combining political and social claims-making in the collective language of incorporation. This was done by dispensing with concerns to legitimate public rules altogether. It is important, therefore, to distinguish the exclusionary patterns of the nineteenth century from contemporary models; the former seldom rejected the aspirational aspects of nineteenth-century liberalism, while the latter presented themselves (especially in the Southern Cone) as restorers of natural orders without the pretense of using the rule of law as a means to legitimate collective rules.

There were, however, affinities. Both models of exclusivism trumpeted the need for market integration. Dictators began tearing down the populist scaffolding of social citizenship: welfare rights, collective bargaining provisions, investment in public goods and a complex heritage of protection, fiscal inducement and financial backing for state and parastate firms. In the lexicon of 1970s economic orthodoxy, economic policy aimed to remove the sources of "financial repression" and to harmonize local and international prices.

But the similarities between the belle epoque model of market integration and political exclusion can be (and have been) exaggerated. Two important differences stand out. The first was the latter-day power and presence of international financial institutions that happily bankrolled the authoritarian models (they were, after all, pretty good business for a while—certainly considering the alarmingly low returns to capital after 1973). The second were the cold war and national security convictions that any surviving populist voices were nothing more than ventriloquists for communism (which, as Anastasio Somoza discovered to his dismay, only forced Nicaraguan elite reformers into the ranks of his opposition). Both differences provided contextual variables that eventually doomed the postwar dictators.

One remarkable aspect of the authoritarian recipe was just how much of a failure it was. There were, to be sure, some very long nightmares, Guatemala perhaps being the most gruesome. But, on the whole, efforts to tilt the balance of public and private rights in favor of the latter eventually collapsed under the weight of their own self-contradictions. In spite of the rhetoric of selfless, martial dedication to the health of the body social, rulers and their acolytes could not help but use their differential access to public power to line their private pockets. The very absence of checks and balances and of accountability—the thinnest veneer of homage to principles that the same rules applied to ruled and ruler—created an irresistible temptation to corruption. In the name of freeing market forces by unfree political means, dictators animated less profit seeking than collusive rent seeking. The sheer scale of corruption still awaits its historian. But its most evident outward form, capital flight, became rampant by 1978 and 1979 (Dornbusch 1990; Cumby and Levich 1987: 27–67). This behavior helps explain why, once in power, rulers recoiled from disabling the statist agencies which they rhetorically condemned as the Trojan horses of populism. They were simply too lucrative.[4]

There were also undertows of anxiety about the nonconstitutionality of military rule. The dictators (not unlike the vanguard Creoles of the Age of Revolution) found it easier to crush what they did not like than to nurture a new legal order. It did not take long for infraregime divisions over how to restore natural hierarchies on sounder footings to surface. Some coups were greeted with countercoups; others had to cope with constant internal squabbling (which, more often than not, was dealt with by giving disgruntled plotters access to the public trough). Under Ernesto Geisel, the Brazilian regime, not without some hesitation, tried to synchronize an eventual return to legality under the code word abertura or decompression. The Argentine generals feuded openly. Only Pinochet managed to keep a firm lid on internal discord while also constructing a pseudoconstitutionalist order.

If internal contradictions sapped authoritarians of their restora-

tionist ambitions, external shifts catalyzed their collapse. With variations, the eruption of the debt crisis in the summer of 1982 sundered the
feeble financial structures of authoritarianism. Then, with the ascent of
Gorbachev, détente across the cold war divide deprived rulers of their
claim to be the last defense against international communism. Like
dominoes, the dictators fell.

What did they leave behind? What did civilian regimes face? We
suggest three legacies. First, many new civilian governments sought to
insulate policymakers from popular claims-making, fearing that a
return to populist forms would destabilize their hobbled regimes. The
new democrats of the 1980s confided in the powers of technocratic solutions. They sought to remove crucial areas of decision making from
public, never mind deliberative, arenas altogether. So, rather than ani-
mating notions of a rule of law capable of using representation as a
means to reconcile collective conflict, new governments segmented the
powers of elected authorities from the authority of tutored experts. This
is not the same as authoritarian decision making, though there are some
continuities. Rather, new democrats invested in extrapolitical authority
the powers to make choices that representative authorities were deemed
incapable of making (O'Donnell 1994a, 1995).

Second, fundamental spheres where notions of legal equality were
supposed to be sanctified remained debilitated. This is especially true of
Latin American court systems. The glaring cases of military amnesties
and exemptions from due process only betrayed the reluctance of many
new civilian governments to rein in repressive forces. Moreover, the
mundane, day-to-day inefficacy and inequality of judicial dispensation
of rights is a reminder to Latin Americans of just how little judiciaries
can be relied upon to do the trench-work for defending even the most
formal and basic of rights (O'Donnell 1994b).

Third, Latin American economies inherited crippling debts and
massive pressure to restructure. These promise to leave entire swaths of
the populace outside active market participation, whether labor markets
or consumer markets. This not only saps elected regimes of their ability
to meet social claims-making and sows seeds for the very kind of fruit
that flourished under populism, but it also publicly removes pressures
on dominant classes to share the wealth (Altimir 1994: 7–32). In effect,
growing inequalities sharpen the dichotomy of market-allocated rewards
and a traditional discourse of social citizenship and substantive justice. It
remains to be seen just what political forms this disjunction takes.

These three issues reveal the troubled dimensions of neoliberalism. Neoliberals opted to withdraw the state from market regulation without reforming institutional makeups. Pulling the state out of market and even public activity, without assuring an underlying legitimate system to bind rulers and the ruled to the same rules, has perverse consequences in Latin America. It is one thing to dismantle state intervention in Western Europe or North America, where the history of liberalism has bequeathed a more deeply sedimented rule of law. Deregulation and privatization do not necessarily imperil baselines of civic equalities inscribed in legal rules and procedures. Rolling back substantive equality provisions at least does not scathe formal juridical equalities. In short, it may be argued that Thatcherite reforms did allow market forces to "work" in England (few across the political spectrum would contest this). But it is quite another matter to dismantle state powers in Latin America, where attacking substantive legal provisions cripples formal and procedural equalities. At the very least, populism sought to address formal equalities and notions of citizenship by tying them to substantive provisions. Taking down the substantive scaffolding only reveals the cracks and holes in the walls of the formal rule of law.

This has economic and social implications. Without baseline formal legal rules it is unclear whether market forces have been "unleashed" at all. It may be argued that the neoliberal language of market efficiency and private initiative is little more than the rhetorical arsenal for tightly bound grupos to obfuscate collusive arrangements. Deregulation and privatization have energized rentier behavior as much as competitive behavior. Paradoxically, "liberalization" on its own does not stabilize and protect private property rights, even though it transfers ownership from the public domain and vests more collective decision making in private hands. This is why the issue of corruption and public scandal across the region is so important: disclosure of dirty dealing exposes the neoliberal hypocrisy of putatively freeing agents from state constraint without forcing them to abide by common rules for all legal subjects. Perhaps of greatest relevance for the concerns of this essay, despite the considerable advances in promoting a more democratic politics, is that the rule of law and the accountability of the government remain tenuous. The personal corruption that appears in hindsight to have dominated the Salinas *sexenio* is a prominent example. The eight years of Menemismo in Argentina have seen increasing skepticism about whether members of the government are subject to the same laws

as the rest of the citizenship. Fujimori's *autogolpe,* his increasing auto-
cratic tendencies, and the ever-more-public role of the military and of
the mysterious Vladimiro Montesinos cast considerable doubt on
whether a state of law exists in that country. The impeachment of Col-
lor would indicate that Brazil could serve as an exception, but the widely
accepted corruption of the police forces, the considerable power of
regional political mafias, and the increasing threat to public security
make it difficult to see that country as one governed by laws.

In the end, the troubles with law in Latin America beg large contextual and historically derived questions. Embedded deeply in the
region's liberal heritage, the dilemma of legality in Latin America suggests a need for legal reform that cries out for more than technocratic
solutions. For many neoliberal apostles, rejuggling legal rules and better
enforcement will solve the riddle of insecure property and disgruntled
citizens. To be sure, incremental reform is important; many Latin
Americans would welcome even modest meliorative gestures. But the
persistence of rentier behavior is symptomatic of a deeper problem: bet-
ter-endowed classes use even the "reformed" rules to reinforce unequal
applications. With globalization upon us, the talk about state shrinkage
and unfettering market competition threatens to emaciate what
remains of legality in Latin America.

Ultimately, this points to the underlying issue of legitimacy. Latin
America's citizenry is not just dismayed at its governments, but at the
structure of state power altogether. Illegitimate rule only enhances the
incentives for individuals and groups to seek rents. In short, without an
effective and legitimately recognized rule of law, the result is not the
symbiotic activity in markets and public domains to which the liberal
aspired, but private preying on the weak, the powerless, and the disen-
franchised. In this context many Latin Americans face a growing popular sense that law serves private interests and is not a public benefit. The
rule of law, to the extent that it exists in Latin America, still faces its
foundational challenge: its inability to bear equally upon the rulers and
the ruled.

In this context, the internationalization of the rule of law threatens
to create entrepôt legal systems. Much like nineteenth-century liberalism, this enables a small elite to participate in a global legal order without dirtying its own hands in its own filthy courts (by which we mean
not just corruption, but the literal physical decay of courthouses). By
providing an institutional exit for the resolution of intraelite conflicts,

the internationalization of law strips the incentive to reform from the very people empowered to carry it out.

As Latin America's modern history suggests, the separation of the letter of the law from its enforcement was a dilemma that liberals, populists, and neoliberals alike sought to resolve. In the end, a system of law is only as strong as its legitimate enforcement. We do not see how an international order can enforce judgments with any authority when it is bereft of legitimate partners on the ground—whether national or subnational. If liberal architects of Latin American states were unable to create a rule of law for all citizens, postnational lawyers face the same dilemma as their national predecessors.

NOTES

1. Simón Bolívar announced to the Caracas Assembly in January 1814: "Compatriots, I have not come to oppress you with my victorious arms. I have come to bring you the rule of law" (Bierck 1951: 63).

2. Francisco de Miranda once confessed "that much though I desire the independence and liberty of the New World, I fear anarchy and revolution even more. God forbid that other countries suffer the same fate as Saint Domingue . . . better they should remain another century under the barbarian and senseless oppression of Spain" (Pagden 1990: 12).

3. For an elaboration on this constitutional theme, see Marcello Carmagnani 1993.

4. The wealthy also suffered from the underdevelopment of legal practice. Certainly their children could suffer the consequences of internal security apparatuses run wild. Less dramatically, the absence of legal protection may have retarded the organizational development of the Latin American private sector as it sought to create walls with which to protect firms from those whom it could never hope to take to court.

REFERENCES

Alberdi, Juan Bautista. 1886. La republica Argentina. In *Obras completas.* Buenos Aires: Imprenta de la Tribuna.

Altimir, Oscar. 1994. Distribución del ingreso e incidencia de la pobreza a lo largo del ajuste. *Revista de la CEPAL* 52:7–32.

Bierck, Harold, ed. 1951. *Selected writings of Bolívar.* New York: Colonial Press.

Botana, Natalio. 1994. Las transformaciones del credo constitucional. In Antonio Annino, Luis Castro Leiva, and François-Xavier Guerra, eds., *De los imperios a la naciones: Iberoamerica*. Zaragoza, Spain: iberCaja.

Bushnell, David, and Neil Macaulay. 1994. *The emergence of Latin America in the nineteenth century*. 2d ed. New York: Oxford University Press.

Cardoso, F. H., and E. Faletto. 1971. *Dependencia y desarrollo en América Latina*. Mexico City: Siglo XXI.

Carmagnani, Marcello. 1993. *Federalismos latinoamericanos: México/Brasil/ Argentina*. Mexico: Fondo de Cultura Economica.

Carr, Barry. 1996. Mill occupations and Soviets: The mobilisation of sugar workers in Cuba, 1917–1933. *Journal of Latin American Studies* 28:129–58.

Cumby, Robert, and Richard Levich. 1987. Definitions and magnitudes: On the definition and magnitude of recent capital flight. In Donald Lesard and John Williamson, eds., *Capital flight and third world debt*. Washington: Institute for International Economics.

Dornbusch, Rudiger. 1990. Capital flight: Theory, measurement and policy issues. IADB Occasional Papers No. 2.

Graham, Richard. 1990. *Patronage and politics in nineteenth-century Brazil*. Stanford: Stanford University Press.

Guardino, Peter F. 1996. *Peasants, politics, and the formation of Mexico's national state: Guerrero, 1800–1857*. Stanford: Stanford University Press.

Guerra, François-Xavier. 1993. *Modernidad e independencias: ensayos sobre las revoluciones hispánicas*. Mexico City: FCE.

Handy, Jim. 1994. *Revolution in the countryside: Rural conflict and agrarian reform in Guatemala, 1944–1954*. Chapel Hill: University of North Carolina Press.

Langely, Lester D. 1996. *The Americas in the age of revolution, 1750–1850*. New Haven: Yale University Press.

Macpherson, C. B. 1977. *The life and times of liberal democracy*. New York: Oxford University Press.

Marshall, T. H. 1964. *Class, citizenship, and social development*. Chicago: University of Chicago Press.

O'Donnell, Guillermo. 1994a. Delegative democracy. *Journal of Democracy* 5, no. 1.

———. 1994b. The state, democratization, and some conceptual problems (A Latin American view with glances at some post-communist countries). In William A. Smith et al., eds., *Latin American political economy in the age of neoliberal reform*. New Brunswick, N.J.: Transaction Books.

———. 1995. Illusions about consolidation. *Journal of Democracy* 7, no. 2.

Pagden, Anthony. 1990. *Spanish imperialism and the political imagination: Studies in European and Spanish-American social and political theory, 1513–1830*. New Haven: Yale University Press.

Peruzzotti, Enrique. 1996. *Civil society and constitutionalism in Latin America: The Argentine experience*. Ph.D. thesis, New School for Social Research.

Riding, Alan. 1990. Mexico, c. 1930–1946. In Leslie Bethell, ed., *Cambridge history of Latin America,* vol. 7. Cambridge: Cambridge University Press.

Rock, David, ed. 1994. *Latin America in the 1940s: War and postwar transitions.* Berkeley: University of California Press.

Sabato, Hilda. N.d. Relations between civil society and the political system in Latin America. Mimeo.

Sánchez, Gonzalo. 1991. *Guerra y política en la sociedad colombiana.* Bogotá: El Ancora Ed.

Sikkink, Kathryn. 1991. *Ideas and institutions: Developmentalism in Brazil and Argentina.* Ithaca: Cornell University Press.

Thorp, Rosemary, ed. 1984. *Latin America in the 1930s.* London: Macmillan.

Thurner, Mark. 1995. 'Republicanos' and 'la Comunidad de Peruanos': Unimagined political communities in postcolonial Andean Peru. *Journal of Latin American Studies* 27:291–318.

LEGAL EDUCATION AND THE REPRODUCTION OF THE ELITE IN JAPAN

Setsuo Miyazawa with Hiroshi Otsuka

Two Japanese sociolegal scholars, Setsuo Miyazawa and Hiroshi Otsuka, take the story of an increasing international focus on law in the state and the economy (seen in the previous essays) into one major domestic set-ting—legal education in Japan. They provide microlevel data related to a basic historical irony. After importation from Germany, the Japanese fac-ulties of law have continuously played a key role in the state and in the con-solidation of elite power around the state. But the law has played very little role in the state or the economy. The essay shows evidence of change, partly under the influence of international pressures. The number of graduates allowed to pass the bar examination, for example, has grown considerably. But the role of the law graduates and the leading faculties—especially the University of Tokyo—has not changed substantially. The embedded posi-tion of the faculties of law in the field of political power in Japan makes it quite resistant to major change.

C. Wright Mills wrote: "The power elite is composed of men whose positions enable them to transcend the ordinary environments of ordi-nary men and women; they are in positions to make decisions having major consequences," that "the drama of the elite is . . . centered in the command posts of the major institutional hierarchies," and that "there are now those command posts of modern society which offer us the sociological key to an understanding of the role of the higher circles in America." Since "within American society, major national power now resides in the economic, the political, and the military domains," it follows that "the chief executives . . . the political directorate . . . and the elite of soldier-statesmen . . . tend to come together, to form the power elite of America" (1956: 3–5, 6, 9).

Who, then, are the power elite in Japan? A standard answer to this question is that they are top members of the ruling party in the Diet, in the public bureaucracy, and in the business community (Sugimoto 1997: 193–219). However, such views have recently come under increasing criticism.

The Liberal Democratic Party continuously controlled the Diet of Japan for forty-eight years between 1955 and 1993 and returned to power in 1996 as the dominant party in the coalition government. *Zoku*, or its members representing special interests, "align with bureaucrats and interest groups in a kind of Japanese version of the iron triangle," but they "also play an autonomous role vis-à-vis the two other corners of the triangle" (Curtis 1988: 115). While "previously, former bureaucrats had played leading roles both in key private-sector organizations and in the ruling party," "after the 1970s, subtle barriers arose among different elite groups that were nearly obliged by experience and responsibility to represent separate spheres of Japanese society" (Allinson 1993: 29). The jurisdictional sectionalism of the ministries and agencies of the central government often prevents policy coordination (Sugimoto 1997: 195–96; Johnson 1995: 120–21), and indeed the whole relationship among the three groups is characterized by rivalry as well as cooperation. A fragmentation of the elite structure (Sugimoto 1997: 216–18) makes it increasingly difficult to argue that top members of the ruling party, the public bureaucracy, and the business community "command."

Nevertheless, no one denies that these top members still hold high positions in their respective sectors of Japanese society. Nothing important can be decided without their participation, even though they do not always get what they want. In this sense, they can still be called the elite of Japan, if not the power elite.

This essay analyzes the relationship between legal education and the reproduction of this elite in Japan. In the first section, we summarize the historical development of legal education in Japan in the context of the conscious modernization of Japan by the government. In each of the following three sections, we analyze more recent situations regarding politics, bureaucracy, and business, respectively. We show that the basic characteristics of the relationship between legal education and the reproduction of the elite established in the pre–World

War II era have largely survived in the postwar era. We then examine how both the law professors who teach that elite and the elite members of the judicial system are reproduced. In the conclusion, we discuss what reforms are required to change problematic aspects of the existing pattern.

1.   Legal Education and the Production of the Power Elite before World War II

The history of legal education and its political context in Japan before World War II is summarized in table 1 (Amano 1989; 1992; Aso 1991; Maeda 1970; Yoroi 1970). Legal education was highly fragmented until the Imperial University was established in 1886. Since there was not a sufficiently large pool of people educated in Western arts and sciences to meet the requirements of the rapid modernization of the country, various governmental ministries established schools to educate their own personnel. Students received scholarships and were required to work in their respective ministries for a certain number of years. The Justice Ministry, which not only had prosecutors on its staff, but also had the judiciary under its control, established its own law school in 1871. The Ministry of Education established the University of Tokyo in 1877 and opened its own faculty of law, mainly to educate teachers for various national schools. Graduates of this law faculty also became prosecutors and judges. Neither the graduates of the Justice Ministry Law School nor those of the University of Tokyo Law Faculty were required to take a qualifying examination to become attorneys, but that career was less attractive to them than a career in one of the ministries.

Private law schools started to appear in 1880. Their main purpose was to prepare students for qualifying examinations to become attorneys. They also produced members of the movement for increasing freedom and democracy in Japan (*jiyu minken undo*). However, since private law schools had to rely almost solely on tuition fees paid by students, faculty members were paid very little, if anything, and these schools had to admit a large number of students, often beyond their capacity. Not surprisingly, the quality of their legal education was far below that of the University of Tokyo, which was supported entirely by the government.

The gap between University of Tokyo Law Faculty and private law

TABLE 1. History of Legal Education and the Legal Profession in Japan until the Postwar Reform

1868	Meiji Restoration
	Kaisei School established
1871	Justice Ministry established Law School
1872	Representation by attorneys in civil litigation permitted; no qualification necessary
	Term *daigennin* introduced: 'person to speak on behalf of another'
1873	Formal regulations established for representation by *daigennin*
	Documents prepared by *daishonin:* 'person to write on behalf of another'
1875	*Bengokan* (defense officials) created for state-appointed criminal defenders
1876	Qualifying examination for *daigennin* introduced
1877	University of Tokyo established: faculties of Law, Letters, Science, and Medicine
	Attorney to the Ministry of Justice created to represent private parties and government
1879	Graduates of University of Tokyo Law Faculty obtained right to practice as *daigennin* without taking qualifying examination
	University of Tokyo gave first bachelor's degrees to graduates
1880	Establishment of Senshu School (Anglo-American Law; now Senshu University)
	Tokyo Law School (French Law; now Hosei University)
	Meiji Law School (French Law; now Meiji University)
	Control of examination for attorneys strengthened
	Bar associations established in jurisdictions of district courts
	Criminal code promulgated, right to counsel incorporated
1882	University of Tokyo Law Faculty permitted students to write graduation thesis in Japanese or Chinese language instead of English
	Tokyo Professional School (Anglo-American law; now Waseda University) established
1883	University of Tokyo abolished teaching in English; teaching in Japanese using German academic system
1885	University of Tokyo Law Faculty absorbed Faculty of Letters Dept of Politics and Justice Ministry Law School, became Faculty of Law and Politics
	English Law School (Anglo-American law; now Chuo University) established
1886	Decree on Imperial University issued
	University of Tokyo became Imperial University with Colleges of Law, Letters, Science, Medicine, Engineering
	Private law schools placed under supervision of President of Imperial University
	Kansai Law School (now Kansai University) established
1887	Rules of Civil Service Examination and Apprenticeship set
	Imperial University College of Law graduates exempted from examination
1888	Education Ministry extended privileges from Imperial University College of Law to graduates who had finished middle school before entering seven recognized private law schools

(continues)

TABLE 1. *Continued*

1889	Meiji Constitution promulgated
1890	Imperial University College of Law made Japanese law central purpose of education; foreign law became a supplementary subject
	Keio University and Nippon Law School (now Nippon University) established
	Examination for recruiting judges and prosecutors separated from that for high-ranked administrative officials
1891	Rules of Examination to Recruit Judges and Prosecutors set, graduates of recognized private schools allowed to take exam
	1,521 judges, 481 prosecutors, 1,345 attorneys
1893	Decree on Recruiting Civil Servants set. Imperial University College of Law graduates required to take only second part of examination for high-ranking civil servants; private university graduates required to start from first part.[a] Graduates of national or municipal middle schools were not required to take the examination for middle/low-ranking civil servants; graduates of private law schools were not granted that privilege
	Attorneys Law enacted; term *bengoshi* introduced for attorneys, a committee for annual qualifying exam formed with judges, prosecutors, and officials of the Justice Ministry, excluding attorneys
	Holders of a doctorate in law and graduates of Imperial University College of Law admitted without examination
1894–95	Sino-Japanese War
1895	Faculties of Law, Medicine, Engineering established in the Third High School in Kyoto
1897	Kyoto Imperial University established, including College of Science and Engineering and the Faculty of Letters in 1906
1899	Faculties of Law and Medicine of the Third High School became Colleges of Kyoto Imperial University
1900	1,244 judges, 473 prosecutors, 1,590 attorneys
1906	Faculty of Letters became College of Letters of Kyoto Imperial University
1907	Tohoku Imperial University established. Sapporo Agricultural School, the second school in Japan to grant Bachelor's degrees (est. 1872 by Hokkaido Development Agency) became its College of Agriculture
1910	Annexation of Korea
	1,125 judges, 390 prosecutors, 2,008 attorneys
1914–18	World War I
1918	The Decree on University issued, allowing establishment of private universities and single-faculty colleges.
	College of Agriculture of Tohoku Imperial University became Hokkaido Imperial University
1919	The Decree on Imperial University was amended. Colleges became faculties
1920	Establishment of several private universities authorized, including Keio, Waseda, Meiji, Hosei, Chuo, Nippon and Doshisha, enabling them to be recognized legally by government

TABLE 1. *Continued*

	Tokyo University of Commerce (now Hitotsubashi University) established (originally School of Commercial Law est. 1875, becoming Tokyo High School of Commerce in 1887)
	1,134 judges, 570 prosecutors, 3,082 attorneys
1922	Faculty of Law and Letters in Tohoku Imperial University established
1924	Faculty of Law and Letters in Kyushu Imperial University established
	Seoul Imperial University established
1925	Security Maintenance Law promulgated
1926	Students prohibited from studying social sciences
1927	Financial panic caused by austere fiscal policy
1928	Special High Police (*Tokubetu Koto Keisatsu*) established to investigate political crimes
	Taipei Imperial University and Osaka University of Commerce (now Osaka City University) established
1929	Great Depression started
1930	1,249 judges, 649 prosecutors, 6,599 attorneys
1931	Manchuria Incident occurred
	Osaka Imperial University established
1933	Professor Yukitoki Takigawa of Kyoto Imperial University Law Faculty expelled from faculty
	New Attorneys Law enacted. Attorney's role extended to services outside the court. Women admitted and apprenticeship similar to that for judges and prosecutors introduced. Prohibition of unauthorized practice not introduced because attorneys opposed giving more power to Justice Minister
1935	Professor Tatsukichi Minobe of Tokyo Imperial University Law Faculty expelled
1937	Federation of Economic Organization (Keieisha Dantai Rengokai or Keidanren) established
1939	Law for Total National Mobilization promulgated
	Nagoya Imperial University established
1940	1,541 judges, 734 prosecutors, 5,498 attorneys
1941–45	Pacific War
1949	Present Attorney's Law enacted as member bill in the Diet. National organization of attorneys, Japan Federation of Bar Associations (JFBA) established. JFBA and local bar associations obtained independence from Justice Ministry in admission of members, rule making, disciplinary actions. Qualifying examinations and apprenticeships for judges and prosecutors, and for attorneys, were combined. Justice Ministry responsible for annual law examination (*shiho shiken*), Supreme Court took over responsibility for newly created Judicial Research and Training Institute (*Shiho Kenshujo*)[b]
1950	1,533 judges (and 728 summary court judges), 930 prosecutors (and 743 assistant prosecutors), 5,863 attorneys

(continues)

TABLE 1. *Continued*

1985	2,001 judges (and 739 summary court judges), 1,173 prosecutors (and 919 assistant prosecutors), and 13,159 attorneys

Source: Nippon Hoshakaigakkai 1970: 191–93; Amano 1989; Amano 1992; Rabinowitz 1956; Haley 1991:102; Maeda 1970:114–17.

ᵃThe result of this was that in 1896, for example, 42 of 66 applicants from the Imperial University College of Law passed, while only 8 or 144 private law school applicants passed.

ᵇThose who pass the law examination spend two years at the Training Institute with their salaries paid for by the government. After finishing those two years, they are recruited by the Supreme Court as assistant judges, by the Justice Ministry as prosecutors, or they become attorneys.

schools was also reflected in the different academic backgrounds of their students. Until the 1910s, students had to finish four years of compulsory education in normal elementary school, two to four years in higher elementary school, five years in middle school, and three years in high school before they were admitted to the university. It was not uncommon to spend a year or two between middle school and high school preparing for entrance examinations. Therefore, it took ten to fifteen years of education in order to enter the University of Tokyo. The number of students who could afford to go through this process was extremely small. In contrast, private law schools, needing a large number of students, did not even require graduation from middle school. They admitted many students solely on the basis of their examination results.

In 1885 the University of Tokyo Law Faculty first absorbed the Justice Ministry Law School, and, when the University of Tokyo became the Imperial University in 1886, the Faculty of Law became the College of Law. These moves put an end to the hitherto amorphous situation and made the Imperial University the sole institution for training fast-track career bureaucrats, who were called *koto bunkan* or high civil servants.

The Decree on Imperial University (Teikoku Daigaku Rei) defined the purpose of the university as the teaching of arts and skills that satisfy the needs of the state. One such need was the training of trustworthy students to fill positions in governmental agencies, particularly the Finance Ministry and the Ministry of Home Affairs. The Ministry of Home Affairs was an extraordinary ministry since it encompassed an enormous range of policy areas presently covered by several ministries, controlled local governments by sending its officials as governors of prefectures, and most importantly, oversaw police forces. Another need was to develop legal studies that would both serve the interests of the state and shield its students from the influence of the liberal legal studies taught at private law schools.

Thus, the government established the Rules of Civil Service Examination and Apprenticeship (Bunkan Shiken Shiho oyobi Minarai Kisoku) in 1887, a requisite for all potential civil servants except graduates of the Imperial University Colleges of Law and Letters. The purpose was to recruit a small number of both highly talented and politically acceptable persons and place them in fast-track careers totally separate from middle- and low-ranking civil servants. Their highly privileged status was created to maintain loyalty to the government. In this sense, they clearly fit the definition of the power elite as defined by Mills. They were recruited, nurtured, and assigned responsibilities and powers specifically for the purpose of commanding the country.

At the same time, the government gave the power to supervise private law schools to the president of the Imperial University, in return allowing graduates of the seven recognized private law schools the privilege of taking the civil service examination if they had completed middle school. The reason for this was that the government lacked the resources needed to increase legal education under its direct control, and they therefore tried to co-opt private law schools as supplementary resources. The quality of private school legal education was definitely improved. However, since private school students included those who had not finished middle school, the number of students who enjoyed this privilege was limited. Moreover, the political tone of private schools' teaching also changed since they had to conform to that of the Imperial University. Nevertheless, other private law schools followed suit in order to obtain the same privilege. In 1893, however, the government's immediate needs had been met, and it therefore abandoned the private law schools by taking away the privilege to take the examination.

Of the 1,369 graduates from the Imperial University College of Law between 1886 and 1897, 375 became high-ranking administrative officers, and 300 became judicial officers. Only a small minority became attorneys.[1] In contrast, the occupations of a large number of graduates from private law schools are unknown, probably because they simply returned to their hometowns and villages. Only a small minority joined the government as high-ranking bureaucrats (79 out of 4,194), while the largest reported number (418) undertook "other" positions, namely, middle- and low-ranking governmental jobs. A similar number (357) became attorneys.[2]

Imperial University graduates who received a bachelor's degree did not need to take the employment examination for judicial positions, since relatively few wanted to become judges or a prosecutors. This was largely because the institutional reputation of the judiciary was lower, they had decidedly less power, and their initial salary was at least 50 percent lower than that of high-ranking administrative officers. Therefore, among approximately 1,700 judges and prosecutors in 1904, only 21 percent had a bachelor's degree. A vast majority of judicial officers were graduates of private law schools who had to take the employment examination. The popularity of a career as an attorney for university graduates was far lower; for instance, among approximately 2,000 attorneys in 1912, only 175 held a bachelor's degree.

The subordination of private school graduates, constantly discriminated against by the government, appears to have contributed, at least partly, to the development of the traditional professional ideology of those who define themselves as *zaiya hoso,* or lawyers in opposition to the government. This group is distinguished from judges and prosecutors who have been called *zaicho hoso,* or lawyers in the government. When attorneys obtained autonomy from the government during the reform after World War II, they enshrined this professional ideology in Article 1 of the Practicing Attorneys Act of 1949. It defined the mission of the attorney as "the protection of fundamental human rights and the realization of social justice," which was contrary to the reality that most of them were handling nothing but ordinary civil cases for paying clients.

Ultimately, the privileges given to Imperial University graduates sowed the seeds of *gakureki shugi,* or education-based elitism in Japan. However, this elitism applied only to bureaucratic careers until the end of World War II. In spite of the fact that the content of legal education would seem to be more clearly related to legal professions than to public administration (table 2), the professional education of legal practitioners, particularly attorneys, never became a major consideration for the government.

Because of its supervisory status, Tokyo Imperial University College of Law set the model curriculum for legal education. Table 2 indicates the amazing resilience of this initial model. In spite of its main purpose of training administrators, the curriculum was basically

TABLE 2. Subjects Taught in 1893 and 1974–75

Department of Law, College of Law, Imperial University, September 1893 (with no. of exams)		Faculty of Law, University of Tokyo, 1974–75
Constitutional Law	1	Constitutional Law I, II
		Comparative Constitutional Law
Civil Law	3	Civil Code I, II, III, IV
Commercial Law	1	Commercial Code I, II, III
Civil Procedure	1	Civil Procedure I, II, III
		Judicial Administration
Criminal Law	1	Criminal Law I, II
Criminal Procedure	1	Criminal Procedure
		Criminology
		Legal Medicine
Public International Law	1	International Organizations
Private International Law	1	Private International Law
Administrative Law	2	Administrative Law I, II, III
		Labor Law
		Intangible Property Rights
		Tax Law
Roman Law	1	Roman Law
Legal History	1	History of Legal Science
		Occidental Legal History
		Japanese Legal History
		Oriental Legal History
Jurisprudence	1	Philosophy of Law
		Sociology of Law
		Anglo-American Law I, II
		French Law I, II
		German Law I, II
		Soviet Law
		Chinese Law
		Theory of Comparative Law
Foreign Languages (English, German, French)	3	
		Political Process
		European Political History
		Political Science
		Japanese Political and Diplomatic History
		International Politics
		American Political and Diplomatic History
		Public Administration
		Comparative Government
		History of Political Theory
		History of Japanese Political Theory

(continues)

TABLE 2. *Continued*

Department of Law, College of Law, Imperial University, September 1893 (with no. of exams)	Faculty of Law, University of Tokyo, 1974–75
	History of International Politics
	Asian Political and Diplomatic History
	Marxist Principles of Economics
	Modern Economic Theory
	Public Finance
	Economic Policy
	Social Policy
	Accounting

Source: Yoroi 1970: 157; Abe 1976: 579–80.

designed to provide doctrinal training in *roppo:* the six basic codes of constitutional law, civil law, commercial law, civil procedure, criminal law, and criminal procedure. Eighty years later, the same basic structure is maintained.[3]

Between 1894 and 1895, Japan won the Sino-Japanese War, and the government felt the need to train students who would work in expanding the economy and managing the colonies. This purpose was clearly identified by the president of the university when the Kyoto Imperial University and its College of Law were established in 1897. It resulted in legal education at national universities being further removed from the training of legal professionals and had an influence that would last more than forty years. In addition, there was a growing trend for law graduates to enter private companies. By 1925 about 68 percent of law graduates adopted careers in business, further compounding the separation of legal education from the training of legal professionals.[4] The shift in emphasis is illustrated by the fact that of the law graduates in 1939, Tokyo Imperial University produced a far larger number of bureaucrats, judicial officers, and military officers, while only Kyoto produced attorneys and government employees who worked in foreign countries, mainly Manchuria.[5]

Since the law faculties of Imperial Universities trained future high-ranking bureaucrats, considered the most prestigious people in Japan, business corporations also gave their highest positions to law graduates from Imperial Universities. Salary differences at a major company among graduates from different types of schools reveal this discrimination (table 3). Even when compared to Imperial University graduates in other fields, law graduates were particularly coveted. Therefore, the status of Imperial University Law Faculties, particularly that of Tokyo Imperial University, was firmly established within both the government and big business. In other words, Tokyo Imperial University Law Faculty became the institution to train the power elite in both the public and private sectors in prewar Japan.

The main task of the following three sections will be to examine to what extent this role of elite reproduction through legal education has been maintained. However, since the number of law students radically increased after World War II (see Taniguchi 1994: 312), it has become far less meaningful to talk about all law graduates in Japan. The focus will therefore still be the University of Tokyo Law Faculty and, to a lesser extent, Kyoto University Law Faculty.

2. The Elite in Japanese Politics

When Mills said that "the center of initiative and decision has shifted from the Congress to the executive," he was arguing that fifty-odd men of the executive branch of the government were "now in charge of the executive decisions made in the name of the United States of America."

TABLE 3.   Monthly Salaries at Mitui Mining Company in the 1920s

School	Technical Staff	Clerical and Management Staff
Imperial University (including Tokyo College of Commerce, now Hitotsubashi University)	70 yen	75 yen
Waseda	65 yen	65 yen
Keio		65 yen
Other private university	60 yen	60 yen
Kobe High School of Commerce (now Kobe University)		60 yen
Engineering High School	55 yen	
Other high schools of commerce		55 yen
Vocational School		55 yen

Source: Maeda 1970: 118.

They include "the President, the Vice President, and the members of the cabinet; the head men of the major departments and bureaus, agencies and commissions, and the members of the Executive Office of the President, including the White House staff" (Mills 1956: 229, 231). Their Japanese counterparts to be discussed here will be the prime minister and cabinet members. Top bureaucratic members within the ministries will be discussed separately below.

We must note that there is an increasingly strong argument that the formal powers of the prime minister and cabinet members are severely constrained (Richardson 1997: 97–108). Under the parliamentary cabinet system, the prime minister and the cabinet have power to propose legislative bills formulated by ministries and other agencies. However, the prime minister has enemies within his own party. Richardson argues that "under LDP [Liberal Democratic Party] rule, the prime minister was the temporary head of an intraparty, interfactional coalition. . . . Factional competition was consequently pervasive. . . . Exposure to faction and policy group challenges made him abnormally vulnerable. The result was limited, sometimes weak leadership" (1997: 98). Moreover, the prime minister and his cabinet ministers have to rely on bureaucrats whom they are supposed to lead. Richardson says that "because the cabinet and prime minister have only a limited staff, much of the policy research needed by the central organs of government is performed within the bureaucracy. . . . In theory, Japanese cabinet ministers have the authority to decide on internal personnel assignments. . . . But the matter of control over appointments is hard to trace" (1997: 102).

Nevertheless, we may still argue that at least institutionally, the prime minister and cabinet ministers occupy key positions. No important decisions can become final until they decide, approve, or at least consent. The way ministers use that position may be contingent upon various conditions. For instance, Richardson acknowledges that different prime ministers left different marks on the Japanese political landscape according to their respective priorities and leadership, although none have been able to realize even half of their priorities (1997: 105–7). In short, they may still be called the elite of Japanese politics, although they do not necessarily command. Therefore, we will examine how legal education, particularly that at the University of Tokyo, is related to production of prime ministers and cabinet ministers.

Of the twenty-one prime ministers between 1946 and 1996, fourteen were law graduates, and of those nine graduated from the Tokyo

Law Faculty, four from private law faculties, and only one from the Kyoto Law Faculty. The dominant position of the Tokyo Law Faculty among the prime ministers is due to the fact that high-ranking bureaucrats have been the main and most stable source of new Diet members for the LDP, which controlled the government from 1955 to 1993. The six Tokyo Law Faculty graduates who became prime ministers during that period were former high-ranking bureaucrats, and the sole Kyoto Law Faculty graduate was also a former high-ranking bureaucrat. However, after the LDP's loss in 1993, this dominant position of the Tokyo Law Faculty appeared to fade quickly. While two of the eight prime ministers since 1993 have been law graduates, neither came from the Tokyo Law Faculty, nor did they formerly hold bureaucratic positions. It would appear that the recruiting of the political elite in Japan has become more diverse.

Turning to lesser members of the political elite, namely, cabinet ministers, table 4 examines changing patterns of their educational background over a forty-year period. In the Kishi cabinet in 1957, fourteen out of the twenty ministers were law graduates, of which twelve graduated from the Tokyo Law Faculty. The Fukuda cabinet in 1976 had nearly the same proportion of law graduates, but the proportion of Tokyo Law Faculty graduates declined slightly. The Hashimoto cabinet shows further that not only the number of Tokyo Law Faculty graduates, but also the number of law graduates in general has further reduced. Only nine out of the twenty-two ministers are law graduates, and there are only four Tokyo Law Faculty graduates. While graduates of the Tokyo Law Faculty are still the largest group, their lead is now slight.

These trends, of course, do not negate the fact that law graduates, particularly those of Tokyo Law Faculty, have long dominated conservative politics in postwar Japan. For instance, table 5 shows that in the first half of the postwar period, when former bureaucrats were a main source of Diet members, University of Tokyo graduates, particularly those of the Law Faculty, really dominated. Nevertheless, the situation seems to have changed.

On the other hand, it is interesting to note that tables 5 and 6 show that the proportion of law graduates did not decline much in the forty years since 1955. While the number of Tokyo Law Faculty graduates declined drastically, graduates of law faculties other than Tokyo and Kyoto radically increased in number. This change may reflect the fact that more people have received legal education in postwar Japan than

TABLE 4. Cabinet Ministers of Selected Years

University/Faculty	Number
1st Cabinet under Prime Minister Nobusuke Kishi (as of 7/57)[a]	
Tokyo/Law	12 (including Prime Minister)
National/Other	2 (no Tokyo; 1 Kyoto)
Private/Law	2 (no Waseda; no Keio)
Waseda/Other	3
No University	1
Total	20
Cabinet under Prime Minister Takeo Fukuda (as of 11/76)[b]	
Tokyo/Law	9 (including Prime Minister)
Kyoto/Law	1
National/Other	3 (no Tokyo; 1 Kyoto)
Private/Law	3 (no Waseda; no Keio)
Private/Other	4 (no Waseda; no Keio)
No University	2
Total	22
2nd Cabinet under Prime Minister Ryutaro Hashimoto (9/97)[c]	
Tokyo/Law	4
Kyoto/Law	1
National/Other	4 (1 Tokyo; 1 Kyoto)
Waseda/Law	1
Keio/Law	1 (Prime Minister)
Other Private/Law	1
Private/Other	9 (1 Waseda; 3 Keio)
No University	1
Total	22

Source: For cabinets of 1957 and 1977, *Gaimusho Gaiko Shiryokan Nippon Gaikoshi Jiten Hensan Iinkai* 1992; for cabinet of 1997, *Sankei Shimbun* 9/12/97, morning.

[a]The cabinet was formed in February 1957 and reshuffled in July 1957.

[b]The cabinet was formed in December 1976 and reshuffled in November 1977.

[c]The cabinet was formed in November 1996 and reshuffled in September 1997.

in prewar Japan (Taniguchi 1994: 312). This might imply a new, less elitist function of legal education in postwar Japan, which we will discuss below.

Another interesting finding in table 6 is the small and declining number of attorneys among Diet members. Of course, given that we have only approximately 16,000 attorneys for the 93 million people between twenty-five and seventy-five years of age (*Asahi Shimbun* 1996: 48, 228), 4.3 percent of Diet members is an overrepresentation. Nevertheless, their number is too small to be consequential. Moreover, table 7 indicates that a vast majority of those attorneys belong to the Communist Party. This reflects the fact that the candidate must have an independent source of income if he is going to run for election in a district where his chance of winning is slight. Another interesting finding from this table is that the Communist Party is nearly as elitist as the LDP in terms of the proportion of University of Tokyo graduates, although their professional backgrounds may be markedly different. Many Communist University of Tokyo graduates are attorneys, while those in the LDP are former bureaucrats.

To recapitulate, while the dominant position of University of Tokyo Law Faculty is steadily declining, the dominant position of law graduates has not declined significantly. However, this steady presence of law graduates has had little effect on the number of attorneys. Therefore, it is uncertain whether the content of legal education itself has made any significant contribution to prepare students for political careers. What is clear is that the significance of legal education as a background for Diet members cannot be a professional one. We will discuss this point further below.

TABLE 5.   Former Career Bureaucrats among Cabinet Ministers, 1946–78

University/Faculty	House of Representatives	House of Councilors	Total
Tokyo/Law	58	34	92
Tokyo/Other	12	3	15
Kyoto	6	2	8
Other National and Municipal	4	4	8
Private	3	2	5
Other	3	1	4
Total	86	46	132

Source: Kitagawa and Kainuma 1985: 124.

TABLE 6.   Members of the Diet

University/Faculty	Number (percentage)
House of Representatives 2/55	
Total	467
Tokyo/Law	98 (21.0)
Tokyo/Other	16 (3.4)
Kyoto/Law	19 (4.1)
Other/Law	70 (15.0)
Attorney	63 (13.5)
House of Representatives Election 10/96	
Total	500
Tokyo/Law	68 (13.6)
Tokyo/Other	16 (3.4)
Kyoto/Law	9 (1.8)
Other/Law	107 (21.4)
Attorney	23 (4.6)
House of Councilors 4/53 and 7/56 Elections combined	
Total	255
Tokyo/Law	60 (23.5)
Tokyo/Other	25 (9.8)
Kyoto/Law	1 (0.4)
Other/Law	15 (5.9)
Attorney	12 (4.7)
House of Councilors 7/92 and 7/95 Elections combined	
Total	253
Tokyo/Law	26 (10.3)
Tokyo/Other	18 (7.1)
Kyoto/Law	5 (2.0)
Other/Law	44 (17.4)
Attorney	11 (4.3) (including one barrister)

Source: various newspapers reporting election results.

3.   The Elite in Japanese Bureaucracy

Mills wrote that "the United States has never and does not now have a genuine civil service . . . effectively above political party pressure" and that "there is no civil-service career that is secure enough, there is no administrative corps that is permanent enough, to survive a change-over of political administration in the United States" (1956: 239, 241). Hence, professional bureaucrats are not at the center of decision making.

In the Japanese bureaucracy the opposite appears to be true. Johnson argues that "the postwar bureaucracy . . . has had fewer rivals for power [comparable to the military and the monopoly capitalists] than did the pre-war bureaucracy" and that "the bureaucracy does not rule in a vacuum in Japan, but it does hold an ascendant position and is likely to continue to do so" (1995: 126, 140). Moreover, careers of bureaucrats do not stop when they leave the government. Their "life begins at fifty" when they retire (Johnson 1995: 142). They can move to leading business corporations, industrial associations, semigovernmental organizations, or to politics (Johnson 1995: 141–56; Sugimoto 1997: 196–98). Therefore, some bureaucrats can reach top positions in at least two sectors: either in bureaucracy and in business, or in bureaucracy

TABLE 7. Backgrounds of Members of the House of Representatives of the Diet

Party (Year of Founding)	Liberal Democratic (1955)	Japan Socialist (1955)	Japan Communist (1946)
All members until 1982	N = 732	N = 362	N = 90
University graduate	74%	44%	54%
University of Tokyo graduate	29%	10%	20%
Local politician	26%	26%	14%
High-ranked bureaucrat	21%	2%	0%
Business executive	15%	3%	1%
Politician's staff	11%	1%	0%
Attorney	4%	3%	21%
Party functionary	1%	14%	34%
Union official	0%	37%	10%
Elected in 1983	N = 258	N = 111	N = 26
University graduate	83%	44%	69%
University of Tokyo graduate	29%	4%	31%
Local politician	26%	33%	23%
High-ranked bureaucrat	20%	0%	0%
Business executive	16%	1%	0%
Politician's staff	19%	2%	0%
Attorneys	3%	3%	31%
Party functionary	1%	7%	23%
Union officials	0%	44%	7%

Source: Okimoto 1988: 189.

and in politics. If this is the case, it is highly ranked bureaucrats who provide the connection between the three sectors of the elite in Japan.

Such a view of Japanese bureaucracy has been the subject of much recent criticism. For instance, Reed argues that "it is autonomy, not power, that the bureaucrats are protecting" (1993: 120). Allinson argues that "after the early 1970s, the majority of Keidanren's [Federation of Economic Organizations] leaders consisted of business managers who had served their entire careers in the private sector" and that "lifelong politicians came to dominate the highest ranks of the party [LDP]" (1993: 29). Furthermore, it has been suggested that "firms hire bureaucrats to increase their influence in the bureaucracy" (McKean 1993: 82), rather than the bureaucracy influencing firms.

On the other hand, however, "the two great powers of the bureaucracy are the initiating of legislation and the compilation of the budget" (Johnson 1995: 122). Legislation and the budget cannot be introduced into the Diet without the involvement of bureaucrats, and we may still argue that they belong to the elite in Japan, even if they do not wield the same power as their predecessors in prewar Japan.

It was said in the 1980s that law students at the University of Tokyo ranked their possible career paths as follows (Kitagawa and Kainuma 1985: 125):

> *Special 1:* Those who pass both the Law Examination and the examination for fast-track career bureaucrats within four years and join the Finance Ministry (including the Bank of Japan), the Ministry of Home Affairs (in charge of local governments), the Ministry of International Trade and Industry (MITI), or the National Police Agency.
>
> *Special 2:* Those asked by their professors to remain in the Faculty as research associates (*joshu*).
>
> *Special 3:* Those who pass the Law Examination within four years.
>
> *Special 4:* Those who rank within the top twenty on the examination for fast-track bureaucrats.
>
> *Second rate:* Others who somehow manage to join the government.
>
> *Bottom:* Those who intend to go into the private sector from the beginning.

Assuming this to be true, the legacy of the historical origin of the University of Tokyo Law Faculty is still very strong. An anecdote reported recently said that when University of Tokyo law students ask classmates about their career plans they ask, "The Law Exam (*Shiho*)? National Civil Servant Class One (*Koku Ichi*)? Then, the private sector (*minkan*)?" (AERA 1997: 14), implying the perceived status of these careers, in descending order of their respectability. It is particularly interesting to note that the students have already aligned themselves with the government and mention business careers as something outside of their realm. Another interesting aspect of this anecdote is that the prestige of the legal profession among University of Tokyo law students appears to be markedly improved from that before the war, a point we will discuss in more detail below.

It is clear that the domination by Tokyo Imperial University law graduates was firmly established before the war. Higher civil service positions virtually existed for them, with 5,653 law graduates becoming highly ranked civil servants between 1894 and 1947. The second largest source of top administrative staff was Kyoto Imperial University with only 795 graduates passing the Higher Civil Servants Examination for Administrators over the same period (Kitagawa and Kainuma 1985: 101). The Tokyo Imperial University law graduates were particularly well represented in the two key ministries, namely, the Ministry of Finance (85.6 percent) and the Ministry of Home Affairs (75.79 percent). The question is how the situation has changed since the war.

Table 8 shows that as far as bureaucrats in top positions of ministries are concerned, the situation has barely changed in fifty years after the war. The proportions of law graduates and of Tokyo law graduates has not changed, with all the top bureaucrats at the Finance Ministry and the Home Affairs Ministry in 1995 being Tokyo law graduates.

The upper half of table 9 indicates the situation in the mid-1970s. The proportion of Tokyo graduates was largest among top bureaucrats, followed by middle-management bureaucrats, and lowest among new recruits. It is safe to assume that an overwhelming majority of them were law graduates. Moreover, even among the new recruits, more than half of them were Tokyo graduates, and their proportions were larger in more powerful and hence more popular ministries and agencies, such as finance, home affairs, international trade and industry, and the police. Kyoto graduates, if they were in evidence at all, represented only a small percentage. None of them was among top bureaucrats at the Finance Ministry. In this sense, too, the legacy of the different historical backgrounds of the establishment of Tokyo and other national universities remained very strong.

It is often said that, once they are hired, members of the same entry class are promoted at the same speed until one of them becomes a vice minister, then all other members retire. However, the data indicate that differences already appear at the middle-management level; Tokyo law graduates are promoted faster than others.

Given that Tokyo is the largest national university and attracts the smartest high school students, it is surprising that among those who passed the civil service examination for fast-track positions, only 25 percent in 1994 were Tokyo graduates. More surprising is that the proportion of Tokyo graduates among those who were actually hired was 51.9 percent in the same year.[6] Simply passing the civil service examination, therefore, does not guarantee appointment. Actual hiring is determined by the personnel department of each ministry or agency that applicants must visit if they wish to join. The data imply that personnel departments still favor Tokyo graduates when they finally decide to hire. After all, these officials are likely to be Tokyo graduates too, and applicants from Tokyo can expect a friendly reception, while those from other schools cannot. Those from other schools may even hesitate to visit ministries and agencies where there are no former graduates from their

TABLE 8.   High-Ranked Bureaucrats in the Postwar Period

University/Faculty	Number (percentage)
1954	
Tokyo/Law	63 (71.6) (7 out of 8 at Finance)
Tokyo/Other	10 (11.4)
Kyoto/Law	2 (2.3)
Other/Law	3 (3.4)
Other/Other	10 (11.4)
Total	88
1995	
Tokyo/Law	75 (69.4) (9 out of 9 at Finance; 5 out of 5 at Home Affairs)
Tokyo/Other	11 (10.2)
Kyoto/Law	6 (5.5)
Other/Law	6 (5.5)
Other/Other	10 (9.3)
Total	108

Source: Kokusei Kyokai 1954, 1995.
Note: Those at the rank of bureau chief (*kyokucho*) or higher in ministries (*sho, fu*) are counted. Those in agencies (*cho*) are not counted for the sake of simplicity.

school in the personnel department and limit their job search to less prestigious ministries and agencies from the beginning.

It is likely that such personnel practices favor Tokyo law graduates throughout their career. In fact, Tokyo graduates can work in an environment that is almost an alumni organization of their university and can feel more confidence about their future prospects, while those from other universities are constantly reminded that they are minorities and do not have the same supporting networks among elite bureaucrats.

The Finance Ministry proudly announced that the proportion of Tokyo law graduates to be employed by them in 1996 was smaller than before, and that even two women were included—nevertheless, of the seventeen new recruits, a total of eleven were from the University of Tokyo, with six of those being from the law faculty. Tokyo graduates still account for nearly two-thirds of the total number, which is not markedly different from the situation in 1976.[7] It should be clear from

TABLE 9.   National Civil Service Examination, Recruitment by Ministries, and Universities of High-Ranked Bureaucrats (1976)

New recruits and graduates of the University of Tokyo among them			
Total	573	Tokyo 265 (46.2%)	
Finance	32	Tokyo 20 (62.5%)	
Home Affairs	12	Tokyo 12 (100%)	
MITI	37	Tokyo 29 (78.3%)	
National Police Agency	24	Tokyo 16 (66.7%)	
Universities of those at the rank of section chief (*kacho*) or higher of major ministries			
Total	1,600	Tokyo 1,001 (62.6%)	Kyoto 137 (8.6%)
Finance	105	Tokyo 93 (88.6%)	Kyoto 6 (5.7%)
Home Affairs	41	Tokyo 31 (75.6%)	Kyoto 5 (12.2%)
MITI	113	Tokyo 93 (82.3%)	Kyoto 7 (6.2%)
National Police	49	Tokyo 22 (44.9%)	Kyoto 2 (4.1%)
Tokyo and Kyoto graduates at the rank of bureau chief (*kyokucho*) or higher of major ministries			
Total	155	Tokyo 126 (81.3%)	Kyoto 16 (10.3%)
Finance	11	Tokyo 11 (100%)	
Home Affairs	5	Tokyo 4 (80%)	
MITI	10	Tokyo 8 (80%)	Kyoto 2 (20%)
National Police	8	Tokyo 7 (87.5%)	

Source: Konaka 1978: 112–14.
Note: Only fast-track career bureaucrats are counted.

these data that the production of the bureaucratic elite is still over-whelmingly carried out by the University of Tokyo. Then, what about the domination by law graduates?

Table 10 indicates the proportions of the three main fields of spe-cialization among the new recruits in 1981 measured according to the types of examinations they took. The largest group is always those who took the examination for *horitsu-shoku,* or law-related staff. The most extreme example is the Ministry of Home Affairs, where fourteen out of the fifteen new recruits were in that category. The group of *keizai-shoku,* economy-related staff, came close at the Ministry of International Trade and Industry, but remained a distant second at most other ministries. Oddly enough, the group of *gyosei-shoku,* administration-related staff, is smallest in spite of its apparent expertise in administration.

These data imply that they are not exactly hired for their expertise in law, economics or administration. A good example is the Finance Ministry. Eighteen of its twenty-seven new recruits were hired as law-related staff. However, this does not mean that they were hired as pro-fessional lawyers. It is more accurate to say that they were hired as human resources smart and trustworthy enough to receive on-the-job training designed to mold and grow them as generalists who can efficiently handle any assignments.[8]

TABLE 10.   Fields of Civil Service Examination of Recruits of Major Ministries in 1981

Ministry	Administration	Law	Economics
Finance	1	18	8
Education	2	11	1
Health	3	8	1
Agriculture	0	12	4
MITI	1	15	13
Transportation	0	14	3
Post	0	7	4
Labor	2	6	2
Construction	0	11	4
Home Affairs	0	14	1
National Police Agency	3	16	1

Source: Kitagawa and Kainuma 1985: 147.
Note: Only clerical staff (*jimukan*) among fast-track career bureaucrats are counted. Tech-nical staff (*gikan*) are not counted.

After they have familiarized themselves with the culture in the Ministry, elite bureaucrats are sent to prefectural governments for two to three years. They return to the Ministry headquarters as sub-department heads. In the seventh or eighth year, they are sent to prefectural governments as heads of key departments such as general affairs, tax, and planning for two years. They return to the ministry headquarters as assistant department heads.

Every ministry or agency, including the National Police Agency where the speed of promotion of elite recruits is faster than other ministries and agencies, has its own pattern of training, rotation, and promotion. Since nearly every promotion is coupled with relocation or a change of departments, what is expected of them is not specialization or technical expertise but the ability to adapt their skills to suit the environment. This point can be better understood by examination of the different status of clerical (*jimukan*) and technical staff (*gikan*). Those technical staff include holders of master's and doctoral degrees or even medical doctors, such as those in the Health Ministry. However, technical staff rarely reach top positions. For example, at the Ministry of Agriculture in 1981, the vice minister and seven out of the nine bureau chiefs were clerical staff. Twenty out of twenty-nine heads of the most important departments within each bureau were also clerical staff. It is safe to assume that a vast majority of those clerical staff were initially recruited as law-related staff (see table 9).

The struggle between clerical staff and technical staff was exposed in the aftermath of the HIV infection of hemophiliacs in Japan by contaminated blood products (Mainichi Shinbunsha 1997: 57–77, 92–97). In this scandal involving the Health Ministry, medical profession, and pharmaceutical industry, there were one ministry official, one medical doctor, and three past and present presidents of the largest blood products manufacturer arrested and indicted for criminal negligence causing death. When the story broke, the health minister formed a task force to search for documents relating to the case, the existence of which ministry officials had denied. The task force, headed by the vice minister, who was a clerical staff member, found crucial documents including those of a former head and a medical doctor of the Department of Biology and Antibiotics in the Bureau of Pharmacological Affairs. The indicted ministry official was his predecessor who was also a medical doctor. While the responsibility of the bureau certainly requires medical and pharmacological expertise, the bureau chief was always a clerical staff person, and the head of the planning department, considered the most important department in the bureau, was also a position reserved for clerical staff. In this case, the former bureau chief who was responsible for the final decisions of the bureau escaped investigation. Therefore, we can observe that clerical staff of the Health Ministry seized this scandal as an opportunity to further their already dominant position in the ministry (Feldman 1997: 6).

In any event, it is quite evident that law graduates are hired by the bureaucracy neither as professional lawyers nor for their legal expertise. Ever since the College of Law of Tokyo Imperial University was designated as the central institution to train future elite bureaucrats, law faculties have been the most competitive departments in nearly all universities. Law graduates are hired essentially because they are considered to be more intelligent than students from other departments. Legal education, particularly that at the University of Tokyo, is playing a decisive role in the reproduction of the elite in Japanese bureaucracy. This does not mean, however, that legal education per se is directly related to the reproduction of the elite. Legal education of elite bureaucrats has not contributed, for instance, to the advancement of the rule of law in Japan.

It is widely known that extralegal measures called administrative guidance (*gyosei shido*) are the main instruments by which bureaucrats carry out their policies (Upham 1987: 166–204).[9] Of course, an enormous number of statutes are enacted every year, and a vast majority of them concern activities of the bureaucracy. Nevertheless, they are essentially designed as instruments of the bureaucracy and rarely provide the public with the legal rights to challenge bureaucratic decisions. In other words, the rule by law, not the rule of law, still prevails in Japan.

As far as the bureaucratic elite are concerned, we have found that the situation has not changed between the prewar and postwar periods: the bureaucratic elite are largely reproduced by legal education at the University of Tokyo.

In 1981, of the 595 law graduates from the University of Tokyo, 122 took up positions in national government, and a further 47 were employed by public corporations and local governments.[10] Table 11 shows the same information for 1997, in comparison with Kyoto and Kobe Universities. One can clearly see that excluding the Judicial Research and Training Institute, the largest individual employers of Tokyo law graduates were government ministries and agencies or other organizations closely related to the government, such as Nippon Tele-

TABLE 11. Largest Employers of Graduates of the Law Faculties of the University of Tokyo, Kyoto University, and Kobe University in 1997

Tokyo
    48 Professors, 23 Associate Professors, 5 Lecturers

Number of Graduates	ca. 700
Judicial Research and Training Institute	56
Nippon Telephone and Telegraph	18
Ministry of International Trade and Industry	13
Ministry of Finance	12
Ministry of Home Affairs	12
National Police Agency	11
Bank of Japan	10
Ministry of Transportation	10
Industrial Bank of Japan	9
Tokyo Marine and Fire Insurance	9

Kyoto
    36 Professors, 14 Associate Professors, 1 Lecturer

Number of Graduates	ca. 400
Judicial Research and Training Institute	no data
Sumitomo Bank	11
Kansai Electric	8
Nippon Life Insurance	8
Mitsubishi Bank	6
Sanwa Bank	6
Prime Minister's Office[a]	5
Kyoto City	5
Daiichi Kangyo Bank	5
Industrial Bank of Japan	5
Sumitomo Trading	5

Kobe
    31 Professors, 15 Associate Professors, 1 Lecturer

Number of Graduates	ca. 220
Judicial Research and Training Institute	no data
Nippon Life Insurance	6
Kobe City	6
Nippon Telephone and Telegraph	4
Sekisui Chemical	3
Daiei	3

Source: Shukan Asahi 1997: 306, 463, 506.

[a]Although it is indicated that five graduates from Kyoto Law Faculty were hired by the Office of the Prime Minister in 1997, the office is actually divided into several agencies including the National Policy Agency, and combining all those agencies does not really make sense.

phone and Telegraph, the Bank of Japan, and the Industrial Bank of Japan. It is surprising that while Kyoto was the second Imperial University and is definitely the second most competitive national university in Japan, the distance between the two law faculties with regard to the reproduction of elite bureaucrats is staggering.

When the entrance examinations for national and municipal law faculties were ranked according to their level of difficulty (Shukan Asahi 1996), the hardest was deemed to be Tokyo Law Faculty, which had 73 points. Kyoto scored 70 points, Osaka was ranked third with 69. Kobe, Tokyo Metropolitan, Nagoya, and Hitotsubashi were jointly ranked fourth with 65 points. Kyushu was awarded 64 points, and 50 points were awarded to the lowest ranking institution. Moreover, table 11 implies that the differences in the institutional status of Tokyo, Kyoto, and Kobe Law Faculties have been deliberately maintained by the Ministry of Education. Tokyo has the largest number of students and faculty members, Kyoto is allowed to have only two-thirds of what Tokyo has, and Kobe and other national law faculties are allowed even less. Since national universities are part of the Ministry of Education, any expansion or reform must be authorized by the ministry: no national university is allowed to surpass Tokyo. As long as the present system of recruiting elite bureaucrats remains, the position of the University of Tokyo Law Faculty will remain unassailable.

4.   The Elite in Business

The most conspicuous players in prewar Japanese business were *zaibatsu*, namely, conglomerates controlled by family-owned holding companies.[11] The postwar economic reform dissolved these, and individual capitalists were no longer regarded as the elite in Japanese business. Institutional share holding replaced share holding by families. Gerlach calls the social organization of Japanese business in the postwar period "alliance capitalism" (1992). While 95 percent of stock in the United States is controlled by market investors, including both individuals and institutions, 70 to 75 percent of the stock in Japan is controlled by stable investors, namely, affiliated companies (Gerlach 1992: 55). Affiliated companies mutually hold each other's stocks. The proportion of stock owned by the top ten reciprocal shareholders is nearly 20 percent among the top sixty companies in Japan, compared to less than 1 percent in U.S. companies in general (77–78). In this alliance economy, the most powerful business elites are the top executives who control institutional investment in affiliated companies and who form and maintain alliances, although most of them are not major individual shareholders (78–79). It is this group, therefore, that may be considered the Japanese counterparts of what Mills called the "chief executives" (1956: 118–46).

We collected information on the presidents of the largest corporations in 1975 and 1995. The purpose was to examine which schools dominate the top positions of major companies and whether any changes have happened recently. Taking the top companies of 1975 as those having capital of thirty billion yen or more, and those of 1995 as having capital of 100 billion or more, Tokyo law graduates were the largest group in both years, representing 22.9 percent of presidents in 1975 and 22.2 percent in 1995. Further, Tokyo graduates from other faculties make up an additional 30 percent of presidents in 1975 and 27.2 percent in 1995. Kyoto graduates represent only 2.9 and 6.2 percent in 1975 and 1995 respectively (Daiyamondosha 1975; 1995). If you combine Tokyo law graduates with other Tokyo graduates, they control half of the largest companies in Japan. While going to private companies has been the least popular career choice for Tokyo law graduates from the faculty's very beginning, they have still ended up controlling one-fifth of the largest companies in Japan.

Of course, the proportion of Tokyo law graduates in top positions in corporations is far smaller than that in the government bureaucracy. In that sense, as happens in politics, personnel practice in corporations may be more democratic. Nevertheless, it is clear that the Tokyo Law Faculty has not relinquished its leading position in the business world. We must note here that some of those Tokyo graduates may not have started their corporate careers immediately after graduation. Some of them may have joined the government bureaucracy and moved to companies in a "descent from heaven" (*amakudari*) (Johnson 1995: 141–56). It has been argued that the proportion of *amakudari* business leaders has decreased since the 1970s, and the majority of more recent business leaders have spent their entire careers in the private sector (Allinson 1993: 28–30). Nevertheless, *amakudari* does exist, particularly in the more heavily regulated industries. For example, as most vividly revealed in the scandal of HIV infection of hemophiliacs, the three past and present presidents of Green Cross, the main manufacturer of blood products in Japan, were all former bureaucrats, including a former bureau head of the Health Ministry (Mainichi Shinbunsha 1997: 83–91). Those *amakudari* bureaucrats function as personal links that connect the elite in public and private sectors.

Business leaders can also form ties with leading conservative politicians. For instance, each time the prime minister changes, several groups of business leaders are formed around the new prime minister. They meet regularly, exchange views, and discuss policy issues. Table 12 shows the membership of one such group formed around Zenko Suzuki, who was prime minister between 1980 and 1982. Neither a former bureaucrat, nor a Tokyo graduate, nor even a university graduate, Zenko Suzuki was not considered a particularly powerful prime minister. Nevertheless, this group included top leaders of all four business organizations in Japan, namely, the Japan Chambers of Commerce and Industry (Nippon Shoko Kaigisho), the Japan Federation of Employers' Associations (Nippon Keieisha Dantai Rengokai), the Federation of Economic Organizations (Keizai Dantai Rengokai), and the Japan Association of Corporate Executives (Keizai Doyukai). One-third of the group were Tokyo law graduates and two-thirds were Tokyo University graduates. We should note that the proportion of Tokyo graduates is larger in this circle, which is closer to the power center in Japan, than among presidents of the largest corporations in general.

Just as the civil service does not hire Tokyo law graduates for their legal expertise, so business corporations hire them for their intelligence and their potential to be inculcated by the corporate culture. There is no evidence that their presence in the leadership of Japanese business has promoted a corporate culture that respects law.

5.   The Elite in the Judiciary

Possibly because he wrote before the advent of the liberal activist Warren Court, Mills did not pay any attention to the judiciary in his analysis of the American power elite (1956). We may also ignore the Japanese judiciary in our discussion of the elite in Japan. The Japanese judiciary is hardly activist in the sense that it actively examines the legality and constitutionality of the actions of the other two branches of the government.[12] Nevertheless, such a passive judiciary has played a significant role in proclaiming the legality and constitutionality of various arrangements produced by the elite in the legislative and executive branches of the government and business. In other words, the judiciary's role as a rear guard for the conservative status quo is not insignificant, and it deserves our attention in that sense.

The institutional status of the Japanese judiciary was markedly improved during the postwar reform, when they were separated from the Justice Ministry, given the power of judicial review, and judges became the best-paid government employees (Watanabe et al. 1997: 95). These alterations may have caused some changes in the educational background of top members. For example, the top judges (Supreme Court justices, bureau chiefs or higher judges in the Supreme Court General Secretariat, chief judges of high courts, and chief judges of Tokyo and Osaka district courts) in 1954 graduated from universities before World War II. Tokyo law graduates formed the overwhelming majority, 74.2 percent of all high-ranking judges, including the chief justice. The top judges in 1995 were likely to have graduated around 1960. Tokyo law graduates still made up 51.6 percent of the total, but the proportion was much smaller than in 1954.

The most striking change is the rise of Kyoto law graduates from 6.5 percent in 1954 to 35.6 percent in 1995. The chief justice between 1985 and 1990 was a Kyoto law graduate, and the present chief justice who was appointed in October, 1997 is also a Kyoto law graduate. In the same

TABLE 12. Members of a Business Leaders' Group for Prime Minister Zenko Suzuki in 1981

Tokyo/Law	10	including presidents of the Japan Chambers of Commerce and Industry and the Japan Federation of Employer's Associations
Tokyo/Other	11	including president of the Federation of Economic Organizations and representative secretary of the Japan Association of Corporate Executives
Kyoto/Other	1	
Other National/Law	1	
Other National/Other	7	
Private/Law	1	
Private/Other	0	
No University	2	
Total	33	

Source: Kitagawa and Kainuma 1985: 141.

month, another Kyoto law graduate was appointed as a supreme court justice, and still another Kyoto law graduate has been appointed the chief judge of a high court. It appears that under the continuing domination of the administrative bureaucracy by Tokyo law graduates, Kyoto law graduates have made inroads into the judiciary, almost as if to compensate for their inferior status in the more powerful branches of the government.

If this is true, it is probable that the key person to open many top positions in the judiciary to Kyoto law graduates was Koichi Yaguchi, a Kyoto law graduate who successively served as the head of the personnel bureau (1970–76), vice secretary general (1976–77), and secretary general (1980–82) of the General Secretariat of the Supreme Court, as well as supreme court justice (1984–85), and, ultimately, chief justice (1985–90) (Nippon Minshu Horitsuka Kyokai Shiho Seido Iinkai 1990: 16–17). Since elite judges who repeatedly serve in the General Secretariat virtually appoint and promote each other (Miyazawa 1994: 267–68), Yaguchi's long reign may have assisted in the promotion of many Kyoto law graduates in the judiciary.

Alternatively, the surge of Kyoto law graduates may simply reflect relative proportions of Tokyo and Kyoto graduates among those who passed the law examinations around 1960. Table 13 provides data pertinent to such a possibility. In 1961, the ratio of Kyoto graduates to Tokyo graduates was only three to four, almost identical to the ratio among top judges in 1995.

Another interesting finding is that graduates from other law faculties virtually disappeared from top positions in 1995. The virtual exclusion of students from schools other than Tokyo and Kyoto from top positions may have resulted from either the selective hiring process or the selective promotion process, or both. In any event, the reproduction of elite judges has become the oligarchy of Tokyo and Kyoto Law Faculties, in contrast to the monopoly of top positions in the administrative bureaucracy by the Tokyo Law Faculty. However, given the most recent results of the law examination (in 1996) in which Tokyo law graduates were one-quarter of all those who passed, more than double the number of Kyoto law graduates, it might be possible that Tokyo will regain an overwhelmingly dominant status thirty years from now.

Incidentally, approximately 34,000 people took the law examination in 2001. The pass rate is approximately 3 percent. This enormous popularity of the law examination totally contradicts the accepted wis-

TABLE 13.   Top Universities in the National Law Examination in Selected Years

1961		1975		1996[a]	
Chuo (private)	106	Tokyo (national)	108	Tokyo (national)	191
Tokyo (national)	41	Chuo (private)	77	Waseda (private)	115
Kyoto (national)	32	Waseda (private)	52	Kyoto (national)	90
Waseda (private)	19	Kyoto (national)	42	Keio (private)	74
Meiji (private)	18	Meiji (private)	19	Chuo (private)	52
Kyushu (national)	17	Osaka (national)	16	Hitotshubashi (national)	35
Tokoku (national)	12	Hitotsubashi (national)	16	Osaka (national)	23
Nippon (private)	11	Keio (private)	13	Sophia (private)	19
All other universities	77	Tokoku (national)	13	Meiji (private)	17
		Kyushu (national)	11	Kyushu (national)	17
		Osaka City (municipal)	11	Nagoya (national)	15
		Nagoya (national)	10	Kansai (private)	10
		Kansai (private)	10	All other universities	110
		All other universities	74		
Total	333		472		768

Source for 1961 and 1975: Abe 1976: 572, 578; *source for 1996:* Hogaku Semina 1996: 119.
[a]The data for this year indicate those who passed the essay examination. A final oral examination was to be administered after it, but only a few usually fail at that stage.

dom of Japanese legal culture. The popularity of the examination reflects the difficulty in becoming an independent person in Japan where employers are likely to demand total devotion to the interests of the organization (Haley 1991: 111–14). One of the best ways to escape from such organizations is to become an attorney.

6.   The Elite in Legal Academia

Tokyo law graduates make up an overwhelming majority of elite bureaucrats. Their share is smaller among elite politicians, elite business people, and elite judges, but they still form the largest group in all of them. What, then, is the educational background of those who taught

Tokyo law graduates? Table 14 provides the pertinent statistics. Until the 1970s, Tokyo Law Faculty professors were exclusively Tokyo law graduates.[13] The Tokyo Law Faculty started to hire graduates of other schools in 1985. But the proportion of those non-Tokyo graduates still remains minuscule, at around only 5 percent.

University legal education in Japan is at the undergraduate level.[14] A vast majority of junior faculty members were initially recruited as *joshu* (research associates) immediately after finishing their undergraduate legal education. They were promoted to *jokyoju,* or associate pro-

TABLE 14.   Last Schools of Law Professors in Selected Years

Faculty	No. of Faculty Members	Tokyo Graduates (%)	Kyoto Graduates (%)
1996			
Nine National[a]	236	48.3	25.4
Tokyo	46	100.0	
Kyoto	43	4.7	93.0
Six Private[b]	212	6.6	10.2
1976			
Nine National	262	50.0	22.5
Tokyo	54	100.0	
Kyoto	37		100.0
Six Private	290	10.0	7.6
1986			
Nine National	337	45.4	22.3
Tokyo	56	94.6	
Kyoto	41	2.4	97.6
Six Private	288	9.0	8.0
1996			
Nine National	360	43.6	19.4
Tokyo	71	94.4	1.4
Kyoto	47	6.4	89.4
Six Private	305	11.1	7.2

Source: Kojunsha Henshubu 1966, 1976, 1986, 1996.

Note: Full-time faculty members at the rank of lecturer or higher are counted. Faculty members in subjects other than law, politics, and international relations are excluded. The school listed as the last school of each faculty member is counted.

[a]The "nine national" law faculties are those at the seven former imperial universities (Hokkaido, Tohoku, Tokyo, Nagoya, Kyoto, Osaka, and Kyushu) and Hitotsubashi and Kobe Universities.

[b]The "six private" law faculties are those at Waseda, Keio, Chuo, Sophia, Doshisha, and Ritsumeikan Universities.

fessor, at either Tokyo or other universities after three years. Those who entered the graduate program working toward master's and doctoral degrees were considered second-rate; therefore, a vast majority of Tokyo Law Faculty professors do not have advanced degrees. Nevertheless, they examine graduate students and award graduate degrees. The first graduate student who was hired as an associate professor directly from the graduate program was Kahei Rokumoto in 1970, which was considered revolutionary. The similarity of this *joshu* system to the fast-track career system in the bureaucracy is striking. In fact, the *joshu* system has been justified by the need to compete against the bureaucracy and retain bright young students in academia.

The situation at Kyoto Law Faculty is not much different. Their inbreeding rate has always been slightly lower than that of Tokyo; nevertheless, graduates of non-Kyoto universities constitute only about 10 percent of its academic staff. Moreover, Kyoto also uses the *joshu* system. The similarity between Tokyo and Kyoto in this respect is also striking.

Tokyo graduates and, to a lesser extent, those from Kyoto also control sizable proportions of faculty members at other major national law faculties. Including their own school, Tokyo graduates occupy more than 40 percent of faculty positions, while Kyoto occupies nearly 20 percent. These proportions have declined slightly in the last twenty years. Nevertheless, they jointly control 63 percent of faculty positions in major public law faculties in 1996. The remaining 37 percent are divided among other national and private schools.

The share of Tokyo and Kyoto graduates is far smaller at major private law faculties. The reason is obvious. Major private law faculties also tend to inbreed. This is particularly true at the two most prestigious private law faculties, namely, Waseda and Keio. However, the proportion of their graduates in elite positions in Japan is still negligible. In that sense, these private law faculties cannot be considered major players in the reproduction of the elite in Japan.

Conclusion

The following conclusions emerge from the analysis above:

(1) The educational institution that is most strongly related to the reproduction of the elite in Japanese society is still the Univer-

sity of Tokyo, most notably in the reproduction of the bureaucratic elite.

(2) Within the University of Tokyo, the Faculty of Law occupies an
overwhelmingly dominant status.

(3) It does not appear, however, that graduates of Tokyo and other
law faculties are recruited by government ministries and agencies for their legal expertise. They are more likely to be
recruited as raw materials to be molded to the needs of their
ministry.

(4) The domination by the University of Tokyo and its Law Faculty is strongest among the highest level of the elite in Japan.

(5) The mobility of the bureaucratic elite to the political elite or to
the business elite has been declining in recent times, but is still
recognizable. Hence, the old boy networks of the University of
Tokyo and of former bureaucrats are still important ties con-
necting the elite in bureaucracy, politics, and business.

(6) The elite law professors teaching in the Tokyo Law Faculty
have themselves been recruited in a manner similar to the
recruitment of their students by government bureaucracies.
They are recruited directly from the undergraduate program
with a guaranteed position in legal academia.

We may draw at least two implications from these conclusions. One is
directly related to the function of university legal education in Japan,
and the other is related to a much broader question of the stratification
of Japanese society. Let us first discuss the former. If our conclusion is
correct that students of those elite law professors are not exactly
recruited for their legal expertise by the government and business, an
interesting question arises with regard to the relevance of the content of
legal education provided by those elite law professors. It is as if students
are ready to forget whatever they learned in the university immediately
after joining the government and business, and begin eagerly to incul-
cate themselves with the specific cultures of their respective employers.

It is, of course, arguable that university legal education more
closely contributes a theoretical understanding of law to those who
eventually pass the national law examination to become attorneys,
judges, and prosecutors. However, even that contribution is debatable.
Masao Sorimachi, president of LEC, Inc., the largest chain of cram
schools for students preparing for the national law examination, the

national civil service examination, and various other qualifying examinations, boasts that "even Tokyo law students do not go to the university these days. Why? That is because study at our school takes precedence over study at the university" (Kubori 1997: 257). He goes on to say that "students from faculties other than law pass the examination rather faster than law students, because the former do not have preconceptions," and that "many students pass in their junior year recently . . . [because] they start studying [at my school] when they are still in high school" (260). He is, of course, exaggerating. Nevertheless, his exaggeration is only slight: one of us recently met a group of such students who passed the law examination in their junior year. While they were intelligent and confident, they could not say which professors they liked most and did not even know where the law library was in their university. They had spent the entire time in their cram schools.

Sorimachi's chain is not the only one, for there are several competing national chains. In this situation, the name of the law faculty from which the student graduated does not mean much. It should be considered mainly as a proof of the fact that he was smart enough to pass the entrance examination to the faculty. For him, the real legal education is provided by his cram schools. Legal education at cram schools is followed by training at the Judicial Research and Training Institute. Those who pass the law examination spend one and a half years (until 1998 it was two years) there as judicial trainees with salaries paid by the government. The Institute is managed by the Supreme Court, and education there is dominated by career judges who were carefully selected by the General Secretariat to teach mainstream doctrines and forms of practice. Since judges, who are called assistant judges in their first ten years, as well as prosecutors, are directly recruited from the Institute, judge-instructors in the Institute also serve as the recruitment panel for the judiciary. Therefore, in spite of the fact that the university's legal curriculum is overwhelmingly geared toward the national law examination, its relevance in reality is highly doubtful.

Moreover, professional training in the practice of law is only provided in the Judicial Research and Training Institute. It is done in the twelve months in the eighteen-month training at the Institute. Trainees spend their time at a local court, a local prosecutor's office, and a local bar association. The university legal education offers nothing in areas such as professional responsibility, professional ethics, the practice of law, legal research and reasoning, or clinical legal education.

Of course, unless most students are likely to become professional lawyers, presenting such courses in universities would not make sense, and students would not take them seriously even if offered. In that sense, the present situation may be rational. Nevertheless, it also means that there is no place in Japan that constantly examines issues, theories, and skills concerning lawyering itself. It would appear that the university legal education is simultaneously redundant and wanting, even in the training of legal professionals. Furthermore, since theoretical legal education is provided at the undergraduate level to those who have not studied any other subjects at the university level, it is virtually impossible to have a wide variety of people in the legal profession who have academic backgrounds outside law. In a legal market that is becoming increasingly international and in which a greater degree of sophisticated and innovative legal service is required, the Japanese legal profession and their clients will suffer seriously.

What should be the future of legal education in Japan? Japan now has approximately 90,000 law students in each entry class. One logical possibility may be to professionalize their undergraduate education like undergraduate legal education in European countries. However, since that possibility requires that a majority of those 90,000 students pass the law examination, it is totally unfeasible.

An alternative possibility may be to expand it into liberal arts education. Since political science is always part of the law faculty curriculum, this route of reform is more feasible. What is needed is to remove highly technical courses of doctrinal analysis and replace them with less technical courses that simply outline the major characteristics of the legal system and various fields of law and examine their social, political, and economic implications. The aim would be to educate students to be wiser citizens and consumers of legal services. Compared to the American liberal arts education, which teaches virtually nothing about law, such a law-related liberal arts curriculum has merit. Moreover, since neither the government bureaucracy nor businesses are recruiting law graduates as legal professionals, such a change would not cause them a serious problem.

If we can change the undergraduate legal education into a more clearly defined liberal arts education, legal education aimed at educating students for law-related occupations could be provided at a graduate level. Technical doctrinal courses should be elevated to the graduate level, and they should be combined with courses on legal practice, professional ethics, clinical education, and so on. Internship and other field training should also be incorporated into university legal education.

Table 15 indicates that Japan has a large number of law-related occupations other than judges, prosecutors, and practicing attorneys. Since judicial scriveners, administrative scriveners, patent agents, and tax agents all include retired government employees who have never taken qualifying examinations, we believe that these positions would be better conceived as extensions of government agencies that supplement manpower and reduce the work load of these agencies. If automatic admission of retired government employees were to be abolished, the boundary between these occupations and that of attorney might be blurred or lowered like the reform that has been going on in the United Kingdom. University legal education at the graduate level could become the basis for those legal professionals, too.

Nevertheless, the number of such graduate programs would have to be far smaller than that of undergraduate law faculties that exist now. Otherwise, the situation will continue where only a small proportion of students have a realistic expectation of becoming legal professionals, so that taking legal education at the graduate level will lose meaning for a majority of students.

Are there any institutions presently that might become bases of such graduate-level, professional-oriented legal education?

TABLE 15.   Persons Doing Legal Work in Japan in 1982

Judges	2,700
Prosecutors	1,173
Practicing attorneys	12,233
Company employees doing legal work	1,320
Judicial scriveners	14,572
Administrative scriveners	30,121
Patent agents	2,600
Tax agents	40,860
Total	105,579
Population of Japan (12/81)	118,107,000
Population per person doing legal work	1,119
France (1965)	4,026
West Germany (1971)	1,561
United Kingdom (1971)	1,023
United States (1978)	505

Source: Kato 1996: 290.

Several leading law faculties recently established graduate programs, geared toward experienced practitioners and government employees, that grant master's degrees in one or two years. Since these graduate programs have no clear purpose, they are presently nothing more than a mixture of various courses of continuing education (Taniguchi 1994: 306–7). Providing professional training in universities at the graduate level will give a clearer function to these programs. The present law examination for those who finished at least two years of university education consists of three parts: multiple choice, essay, and oral. Therefore, the multiple-choice portion, for instance, should be waived for graduates of these programs.

Naturally, the universities that are allowed to have such graduate programs will obtain a tremendous advantage over other schools. Hence, most schools are likely to oppose the establishment of such graduate programs if those programs were only allowed in a limited number of universities.

An alternative strategy would be to establish completely new practice-oriented graduate legal studies programs. For instance, the Japan Federation of Bar Associations could start a Japanese version of accreditation like that of the American Bar Association and encourage newer universities to establish programs designed to meet its conditions. Such programs would also have the merit of destroying the present hierarchy among the existing law faculties. However, even presuming the universities wanted to collaborate with the Japan Federation of Bar Associations, there is another source of resistance: the Supreme Court might want to maintain its control over professional training.

For instance, when it was decided to increase the number of people who may pass the law examination from 750 to 1,000 in 1998, the Supreme Court proposed to reduce the duration of traineeship from two years to one. Then, the Japan Federation of Bar Associations tried to seize this opportunity and proposed that it would provide training for the lost period by itself. Both the Supreme Court and the Justice Ministry rejected the bar's proposal. Nevertheless, if the duration of professional education at the Judicial Research and training Institute is further reduced while the number who pass the law examination is further increased, a real opportunity for the Bar to take over professional training would appear.

In any event, the legal profession is the only well-established profession in Japan that has failed to use universities for the professional training of its future members. Medical doctors, dentists, and veterinarians all use universities, and there is no reason for the legal profession not to join them. The Judicial Research and Training Institute could then survive as a place for on-the-job training of judges, and basic professional training of legal practitioners would be set free from central control to become more flexible and diversified.

Let us now turn to the second implication of our conclusions, namely the stratification of Japanese society. Entrants to the University of Tokyo are now dominated by graduates of private or national high schools that combine the three-year junior high school curriculum with that of the three-year high school in a unified curriculum, so that students are able to finish their high school curriculum in their fifth year and to devote their sixth year entirely to entrance examinations for universities. In 1989, for instance, among the top twenty high schools of the entrants of the University of Tokyo, only two were regular three-year public high schools (Amano 1990: 9), fifteen were private six-year high schools, and three were six-year national high schools. Therefore, those students whose parents are wealthy enough to send them to such schools are the ones able to aspire to enter the University of Tokyo. The proportion of six-year high schools has been constantly increasing.

It is well known that the average socioeconomic status of parents of students at the University of Tokyo is higher than that of parents of other university students (Amano 1990: 19–20). Moreover, even among those parents, the socioeconomic status of those whose children attended six-year high schools is higher than that of parents of other students. Therefore, if the present elite-reproduction system continues, the number of students from higher socioeconomic statuses will increase further, and it is arguable that the policies and behaviors they carry out as government bureaucrats, politicians, and corporate executives may simply reflect the ideology and interests of their own socioeconomic status.

Furthermore, since entrance examinations to those six-year high schools take place at the end of elementary school, the competition to get into the University of Tokyo will take place when children are still at the elementary level. Therefore, in a survey of students in the University of Tokyo in 1988, 78 percent of those who came from six-year high schools had gone to cram schools during their elementary school years (Amano 1990: 20), while only 48 percent of the entire student body had gone to cram schools when they were in elementary schools. These data imply that a higher socioeconomic status provides students with a greater possibility of joining the elite in Japan. If such a cycle continues, the existing social stratification will not only be reproduced, it will also be strengthened.

The question then is whether we should introduce some form of reverse affirmative action that either prohibits government agencies from hiring more than a specified number of graduates from one school or else prohibits universities from admitting more than a certain number of students from a single high school. Such proposals have been regularly made and persistently rejected. Moreover, given the relatively small income inequalities in Japan compared with other developed countries and the general lack of sensitivity to class structure or stratification, the public may not care much about the reproduction of the elite being confined within the elite themselves. Furthermore, so long as the decision-making process in the government is transparent, and government and business are held accountable for their behavior, the self-reproduction of the elite by the elite probably will not cause serious problems to the public.

Therefore, a more meaningful reform from the public's perspective is probably to increase transparency and accountability of government agencies. Although it has various limitations that require improvement, the enactment of the Administrative Procedure Act in 1993 was a positive step in that direction, and the expected enactment of the Freedom of Information Act would be another step forward. Reformers of Japanese society must continue their fight to strengthen the rule of law.

Postscript (as of January 2002)

The Freedom of Information Act was enacted on May 14, 1999. Furthermore, the government established the Justice System Reform Council (JSRC) under the Cabinet for a two-year term from July 27, 1999. Article 2 of the Law Concerning Establishment of the Justice Reform Council stipulates that "the agenda of the Council may include the realization of a more accessible and user-friendly judicial system, public participation in the judicial system, redefinition of the legal profession and reinforcement of its function" (see "The Points at Issue in the Judicial Reform" at <http://www.kantei.go.jp/foreign/judiciary/ 0620reform .html>). The Council presented its final opinions (*Ikensho*) to Prime

Minister Jun'ichiro Koizumi on June 12, 2001 (see <http://www.kantei
.go.jp/foreign/judiciary/2001/0612report.html>). The Council emphasized that the production of a larger number of better-educated legal
professionals is the basis of the entire reform.

Specifically, the Council proposed the following in the area of legal
education and the production of legal professionals:

(1) establishing graduate professional law schools (*hoka daiga-
    kuin*) in 2004, with both standard programs requiring three years
    and shortened programs requiring only two years for those who
    have already acquired a high level of legal knowledge;
(2) introducing a new national law examination, and increasing
    the number of those passing to 3,000 people per year by 2010,
    in contrast to only 994 in 2001; and
(3) increasing the total population of active legal professionals
    (judges, prosecutors, and attorneys) to approximately 50,000
    by 2018.

The JSRC urged the concerned agencies to set standards for recognizing law schools and allowing graduates to sit in the National Law
Examination as soon as possible. However, there are various problems
in details. First, undergraduate law faculties will remain in some revised
forms. Therefore, universities with an undergraduate law faculty will be
tempted to create a graduate law school mainly with a two-year program and fill it with its own undergraduate law students, unless some
clear guidelines are set to prevent it.

The JSRC proposed to introduce an LSAT-style aptitude test for
admission, but it also mentioned the possibility of introducing a preliminary examination on legal knowledge for students who apply to
two-year programs. If such an examination is introduced in the form of
a single national examination, undergraduate law students will simply
go to cram schools to prepare for it without learning much in universities, as they do presently for the national law examination.

Although graduation from a law school will be the main
qualification to be able to sit in the national law examination, the JSRC
also mentioned the need to create a "bypass," where those who cannot
afford to go to a law school and those who have already acquired practical legal experience will be allowed to take the exam without satisfying
the law school requirement. Is it possible to introduce such a bypass

without creating general disincentive to go to graduate law school? How should we screen people who will be allowed to sit in the National Law Examination without going to a law school? If the JRC introduced a preliminary examination of legal knowledge, people would again simply go to cram schools.

Finally, although the JRC proposed to create new law schools as "professional schools," it also proposed that practical apprenticeship (*jitsumu shushu*) be maintained. If the Legal Research and Training Institute were maintained, would it not become a bottleneck that artificially limits the number of people who pass the national law examination? Therefore, details still remain undecided. Much will depend on the legislative process that commenced in December 2001.

NOTES

This essay was originally written in 1997 when Setsuo Miyazawa was a professor at Kobe University and a visiting professor at Harvard University. At Kobe University Faculty of Law, Ken'ichi Yoneda, a lecturer, Keiichi Ageishi, a doctoral student, and Masashi Kanno, a master's student, helped the authors in data collection. In Cambridge, Hans Van Der Sande, a J.D. student at Harvard Law School, edited most of the text and table 1, and Roy Freed, Esq., edited the conclusion. The authors are most grateful to them. An earlier version was published in *Asian-Pacific Law and Policy Journal* 1, no. 2 (2000). This is a slightly shortened and revised version.

1. For statistics of occupations of all graduates from Tokyo Imperial University College of Law between 1886 and 1897, see Aso 1991: 85.

2. For statistics of occupations of all graduates from private law schools surveyed in 1897, see Amano 1992.

3. It is interesting to note that the assumption seems to be that those who did well in a curriculum suited to the training of legal professions would also do well as administrators. The Civil Servant Examination of 1929 required that administrative officers take constitutional law, administrative law, civil law, and economics, while judicial officers were required to take constitutional law, civil law, commercial law, criminal law, and civil or criminal procedure.

4. For statistics, see Maeda 1970: 135.

5. Tokyo produced 151 administrative officers, as opposed to Kyoto's 12; 24 judicial officers against Kyoto's 5; 93 military officers against Kyoto's 11 (Yoroi 1970: 147).

6. *Asahi Shimbun,* August 10, 1994, evening; October 5, 1994, morning.

7. For statistics see *Asahi Shimbun,* International Satellite ed., October 3, 1997.

8. Such on-the-job training at the Finance Ministry is as follows:

Year 1–2: Time spent in the corridors of the Diet finding out what questions the Diet members are going to ask so the finance minister and top bureaucrats can prepare answers. They are expected to learn during these first years how to handle information, what politicians are, and how the Diet works.

Year 3–4: Sent to foreign or domestic universities to learn economic theories and obtain other specialized knowledge.

Year 5–6: Work as chief sub-department heads (*kakaricho*).

Year 7: Work as heads of local tax offices while they are still only twenty-eight or twenty-nine years old. They supervise older subordinates and deal with local leaders, often entertained as the guest of honor by the latter. They are expected to learn leadership.

Year 8: Return to the ministry headquarters as assistant department head (*kacho hosa*). They are expected to show their ability in defending the turf of the ministry by arguing against bureaucrats of the same rank from other ministries, in drafting bills and designing policies, in negotiating, and in obtaining a broader perspective.

A similar pattern exists in the Ministry of Home Affairs (Kitagawa and Kainuma 1985: 149–51).

9. Haley, in contrast, argues that Japanese governmental agencies have been forced to use administrative guidance because they were not given legally enforceable instruments (1991: 139–68).

10. For further statistical data relating to the career directions of Tokyo University law graduates, see Kitagawa and Kainuma 1985: 126.

11. Edward Lincoln (1992) discusses the Japanese economy from the 1920s to the 1980s.

12. See generally Okudaira 1993; but, for a view that the Japanese judiciary has been activist in its own sense, see Foote 1995, 1996.

13. The recruitment and promotion of faculty members at Tokyo Law Faculty was analyzed by Feldman (1993).

14. Yasuhei Taniguchi (1994) provides an interesting discussion of legal education.

REFERENCES

Abe, Haruo. 1976. Education of the legal profession in Japan. In Hideo Tanaka, ed., *The Japanese legal system.* Tokyo: University of Tokyo Press.

AERA. 1997. Contemporary personality of Tokyo Law Faculty students (in Japanese). June 2, 1997.

Allinson, Gary D. 1993. Citizenship, fragmentation, and the negotiated polity. In Gary D. Allinson and Yasunori Sone, eds., *Political dynamics in contemporary Japan.* Ithaca: Cornell University Press.

Amano, Ikuo. 1989. *Kindai nippon koto kyoiku kenkyu* (A study on the higher education of modern Japan). Tokyo: Tamagawa University Press.

———. 1992. *Gakureki no shakaishi* (Social history of education-based elitism). Tokyo: Shinchosha.

Asahi Shimbun. 1997. *Japan almanac 1997.* Tokyo: Asahi Shimbunsha.

Aso, Makoto. 1991. *Nippon no gakureki erito* (The education-based elite in Japan). Tokyo: Tamagawa University Press.

Curtis, Gerald L. 1988. *The Japanese way of politics.* New York: Columbia University Press.

Daiyamondosha, ed. 1975. *Daiyamondo kaisha shokuinroku 1976* (1976 Directory of company executives). Tokyo: Daiyamondosha.

———. 1995. *Daiyamondo kaisha shokuinroku 1996* (1996 Directory of company executives). Tokyo: Daiyamondosha.

Feldman, Eric A. 1993. Mirroring minds: Recruitment and promotion in Japan's law faculties. *American Journal of Comparative Law* 41:465–79.

———. 1997. Deconstructing the Japanese HIV scandal. Japan Policy Research Institute Working Paper 30.

Foote, Daniel H. 1995. Resolution of traffic accident disputes and judicial activism in Japan. *Law in Japan* 25:19–39.

———. 1996. Judicial creation of norms of Japanese labor law: Activism in the service of—stability? *UCLA Law Review* 43:635–709.

Gaimusho Gaiko Shiryokan Nippon Gaikoshi Jiten Hensan Iinkai, ed. 1992. *Shinpan Nippon gaikoshi jiten* (Dictionary of Japanese diplomacy: New edition). Tokyo: Yamakawa Shuppan.

Gerlach, Michael L. 1992. *Alliance capitalism.* Berkeley: University of California Press.

Haley, John Owen. 1991. *Authority without power.* New York: Oxford University Press.

Hogaku Semina. 1996. *Hogaku semina* (Law seminar). No. 504.

Johnson, Chalmers. 1995. *Japan: Who governs.* New York: W. W. Norton.

Kato, Masanobu. 1996. The role of law and lawyers in Japan and the United States. In Kenneth L. Port, ed., *Comparative Law.* Durham: Carolina Academic Press.

Kitagawa, Ryukichi, and Jun Kainuma. 1985. Nippon no erito (The elite of Japan). Tokyo: Otsuki Shoten.

Kojunsha Henshubu, ed. 1966. *Zenkoku daigaku shokuinroku 1966* (National directory of university faculty members). Tokyo: Kojunsha.

———. 1976. *Zenkoku daigaku shokuinroku 1976* (National directory of university faculty members). Tokyo: Kojunsha.

―――. 1986. *Zenkoku daigaku shokuinroku 1986* (National directory of university faculty members). Tokyo: Kojunsha.

―――. 1996. *Zenkoku daigaku shokuinroku 1996* (National directory of university faculty members). Tokyo: Kojunsha.

Kokusei Kyokai, ed. 1954. *Kokusei soran 1954* (1954 National directory). Tokyo: Kokusai Rengo Tsushinsha.

―――. 1995. *Kokusei soran 1995* (1995 National directory). Tokyo: Kokusai Rengo Tsushinsha.

Konaka, Yotaro, ed. 1978. *Todai hogakubu* (Tokyo University Faculty of Law). Tokyo: Gendai Hyoronsha.

Kubori, Hideaki. 1997. *Hoka shakai e Nihon ga kawaru* (Japan is becoming a legalized society). Tokyo: Toyo Keizai Shinbunsha.

Lincoln, Edward J. 1992. The Showa economic experience. In Carol Gluck and Stephen R. Graubard, eds., *Showa: The Japan of Hirohito*. New York: W. W. Norton.

Maeda, Tatsuo. 1970. Japanese capitalism and universities and law faculties (in Japanese). *Ho-shakaigaku* 22.

Mainichi Shinbunsha Shakaibu Yakugai Eizu Shuzaihan. 1997. *Koseisho no hanzai: Yakugai.* (Crime of the health ministry: Injury by medication). Tokyo: Nippon Hyoronsha.

McKean, Margaret A. 1993. State strength and the public interest. In Gary D. Allinson and Yasunori Sone, eds., *Political dynamics in contemporary Japan.* Ithaca: Cornell University Press.

Mills, C. Wright. 1956. *The power elite.* London: Oxford University Press.

Miyazawa, Setsuo. 1994. Administrative control of Japanese judges. In Philip S. C. Lewis, ed., *Law and technology in the Pacific community.* Boulder: Westview.

Nippon Hoshakaigakkai, ed. 1970. *Ho-Shakaigaku* 22.

Nippon Minshu Horitsuka Kyokai Shiho Seido Iinkai, ed. 1990. *Zen saibankan keireki soran* (Directory of careers of all judges). Tokyo: Kojinsha.

Okimoto, Daniel I. 1988. Ex-bureaucrats in the Liberal-Democratic Party. In Daniel I. Okimoto and Thomas R. Rohlen, eds., *Inside the Japanese system.* Stanford: Stanford University Press.

Okudaira, Yasuhiro. 1993. Forty years of the constitution and its various influence. In Percy R. Luney and Kazuyuki Takahashi, eds., *Japanese Constitutional Law.* Tokyo: University of Tokyo Press.

Rabinowitz, Richard W. 1956. The historical development of the Japanese bar. *Harvard Law Review* 70:61–81.

Reed, Steven R. 1993. *Making common sense of Japan.* Pittsburgh: University of Pittsburgh Press.

Richardson, Bradley. 1997. *Japanese democracy.* New Haven: Yale University Press.

Shukan Asahi. 1996. *Daigaku ranking '96* (University ranking '96). Tokyo: Asahi Shimbunsha.

————. 1997. *Daigaku ranking '97* (University ranking '97). Tokyo: Asahi Shimbunsha.

Sugimoto, Yoshio. 1997. *An introduction to Japanese society.* Cambridge: Cambridge University Press.

Taniguchi, Yasuhei. 1994. Legal education in Japan. In Philip S. C. Lewis, ed., *Law and technology in the Pacific community.* Boulder: Westview.

Upham, Frank K. 1987. *Law and social change in postwar Japan.* Cambridge: Harvard University Press.

Watanabe, Yasuo, et al. 1997. *Textbook gendai Shiho* (Textbook of the contemporary judicial system) 3d ed. Tokyo: Nippon Hyoronsha.

Yoroi, Takayoshi. 1970. The faculty of law at Imperial universities and 'national-social demand' (in Japanese). *Ho-shakaigaku* 22.

Cultural Elements in the Practice of Law in Mexico: Informal Networks in a Formal System

Larissa Adler Lomnitz and Rodrigo Salazar

Larissa Adler Lomnitz and Rodrigo Salazar, anthropologists at the National University of Mexico, continue the theme developed in the previous essay. They concentrate on the local pressures, while taking into account international ones, transforming the position and practice of law in Mexico. Here, as in Japan, the faculties of law—especially the one at the National University of Mexico in Mexico City—have been prominent sources of leadership in politics and the state, and the practice—in the general sense applied to all legal roles—of law itself depended much more on personal relations than technical law.

The authors also show how careers in legal practice have depended greatly on where individuals started in terms of resources and personal relations. Even success in court might depend more on personal relationships than the quality of legal arguments. The Mexican legal system has historically been far from the models promoted in the United States and elsewhere as necessary to the legitimacy of the state.

In recent decades, the authors suggest, domestic and international factors have begun to transform the position of law in Mexico, and the transformation is seen in the careers of Mexican law graduates. The authors point especially to "the rise of a new legal technocratic elite—closely related to the rise of an elite of economists—that is displacing the traditional political elite trained at UNAM." The change has tended to exacerbate certain inequalities in Mexico, since access to foreign degrees is even more stratified than domestic education. Pressures for change, furthermore, have not changed the role of the courts in any major respects. They have created a relatively small technocratic group.

There is continuity in the continuing importance of social networks, but increasingly the networks "are not the traditional ones made up of UNAM classmates and professors, but rather networks established among their classmates abroad. The nickname 'the Chicago boys' exemplifies this phenomenon of clique formation among Latin Americans trained in certain universities in the United States."

The question, reminiscent of the challenge Boyer and Adelman and Centeno presented in their essays, is whether the mix of imported expertises and Mexican practices will promote stability and economic growth or will exacerbate divisions in Mexican society.

This essay contends that the normal practice of the law in Mexico (in private practice as well as the public sphere) has traditionally conformed to what Dezalay and Garth (1997) describe as "relational" as opposed to rule of law, in that professional success depends to a large degree upon the lawyer's ability to construct and use personal social networks. These networks are needed for an exchange of favors based on reciprocity and patronage, as well as to understand when and how to offer payment to obtain services required to complete a case successfully. Hence, for professional success a lawyer has to be immersed and skilled not only in the (often subtle) practices of sociability and rules of etiquette determined by the national culture, but also in specific vocabularies, interpretation of signals, and informal professional practices, in order to become an artful network builder and a successful manipulator of those networks.

The essay will describe the dominant structure of social networks in Mexico (horizontal and vertical) and relate it to the types of services informally exchanged in actual practice in order to acquire formal results. It will also offer ethnographic examples of the culturally expected forms (the etiquette) of soliciting services and of the situations for which they are needed and used. Needless to say, this sort of knowledge is not formally taught at the universities, although most professional networks are built there. Where and how, then, is this know-how acquired? In what stage of a lawyer's training is it brought in? How do the lawyers themselves define the parameters that distinguish moral or legal practices from those that are not? How do these same lawyers resolve the contradictions between the definitions of morality and legality and the actual requirements for successful practice? How have the changes brought about by globalization affected the balance between the rule of law and the need for relational capital in professional practice?

Through interviews and readings we have collected empirical material that describes the informal practices typically carried out in order to overcome the stumbling blocks inherent in Mexico's formal legal system. One implication of this study is the importance of traditional informal practices, which depend upon cultural characteristics, in the practice of law.

Rule of Law versus Relational Capitalism

According to Dezalay and Garth (1997), the practice of law requires a combination of, on the one hand, knowledge and legal rationality (the rule of law) and, on the other, relational resources, such as *guanxi* (relations), which have been studied mainly in Asian societies. Furthermore, the authors claim that the importance of personal relations has not been adequately recognized or understood: "The starting point for developing new theoretical tools must be the recognition that legal practice is itself a combination of technical knowledge and relational resources" (139). We might add that the entire practice of law is susceptible to the influence of personal relations. Furthermore, business, the state apparatus, and academia are all interrelated within the practice of law. As an example, Dezalay and Garth present the case of Japan, where public and private networks have a common base in the faculty of law of the University of Tokyo, and (as also occurs in Mexico) individual lawyers may become informal brokers or interlocutors between these different sectors of society. To understand these informal aspects of the practice of law, empirical studies are necessary. In this essay we will describe the case of Mexico, placing particular emphasis on the cultural elements involved in the construction of the social networks that individual lawyers and firms need in order to succeed in their practice of law.

Social Networks as the Basis of Relational Capital

Social networks are the basis of relational capital, and it is from an individual's complete network that specialized clusters of relationships, such as those related to the practice of law, are formed. Social networks have been defined as social fields constituted by relationships between people (Barnes 1954: 39–58; Meyer 1962: 576–92; Mitchell 1969). After defining networks, sociologists began formalizing a social network paradigm in which social relations are structured into a systematic pattern of social organization, composed of sets of social networks or fields of exchange, which appear as abstract constructions defined by a researcher according to specific underlying criteria. Hence, social network studies allow the identification of informal social structures that are not formally defined by society; relational data are conceptualized as the concretion of the social network (Leinhardt 1977: xiii). One can create a diagram of relationships between individuals or groups among which an exchange of goods, services, and/or information takes place. Examples related to the subject of this essay are exchanges of bureaucratic favors and of information.

Following Karl Polanyi (1957: 234–69), Lomnitz (1982: 64–66) has proposed a conceptual model of the structure of interpersonal and group relationships in Mexico. The model entails the following variables: (1) direction of the flow of exchange (horizontal and vertical), (2) kinds of resources exchanged (capital, power, work, loyalty, services, information, and so on), and (3) mode of articulation within the structure (formal or informal). Every ego may be placed at the center of a social network that extends in all directions within the social structure. Horizontal bonds are between relatives, friends, and peers or associates at the same hierarchical level. The existence of horizontal bonds conditions, and is conditioned by, the flow of reciprocal exchange in both directions; in toward ego and outward from ego. This flow consists of goods, services, and information.

The structure also has a vertical dimension, which we call hierarchy. A vertical bond between ego and a subordinate or a superior differs fundamentally from the horizontal relation between peers; it is a patron-client relationship. These vertical relationships are the main channels that distribute the resources of the system throughout the structure; capital and power flow downward, and work and loyalty are suctioned upward. The asymmetry of what is exchanged conditions the asymmetry of the relationship; individuals receive loyalty and service from their subordinates and render loyalty and service to their superiors. As a corollary of these services and loyalties, individuals receive material rewards and power from their superiors and yield material rewards and power to their subordinates. The quantum of material rewards and power retained by ego defines individual status as a broker in the structure.

In Mexico there exists a formal vertical segmentation of society (private, public, and labor; formal and informal) defined by the kinds of resources they generate. In the public sector, the resource that is generated is political power. In the private sector, it is capital. Thus, one sector controls and the other produces, while a third sector, labor, supplies labor and political loyalty to the other two and therefore is a client to both.

Articulation between the three sectors is provided at a formal level by the state through legal or even compulsory organizations of capital and labor, formal instances of mediation and conflict solving, political mediation, and so on. Such a system of formal articulations, however, may lead to a society of castes permanently battling against each other. Therefore, individual networks of reciprocal exchange that informally cut across hierarchical boundaries between the sectors provide flexibility and fluidity. These networks circulate resources from one pyramid to another; bureaucratic information is passed on to the private sector, and economic information to the public sector. Political support, vital services of a bureaucratic or economic nature, jobs, and other opportunities all circulate among members of different networks. Indeed, it is advantageous to have relatives or friends in all three sectors. Labor union leaders may hold business investments and, at the same time, be running for Congress and perhaps have a son or daughter in the civil service or in business. Industrialists may have sons who become technocrats in the public sector. Politicians have been known to become investors or officeholders in private corporations, while private businessmen may be appointed to executive positions in state corporations and agencies. Liberal professionals may temporarily occupy high-level technocratic positions in the state apparatus. The examples are endless and merely serve to underscore the fact that horizontal networks of college mates, relatives, and friends provide a tangled web of bonds within and between sectors. Thus, while social energy is largely channeled along vertical lines within each sector, lubrication and fluidity in the manipulation of resources is largely provided by these horizontal reciprocal exchanges.

Dezalay and Garth offer an example of this relation between sectors: "The arbitration world, like the large law firms, stands at a crossroads where the representatives of three great powers—the university, business and the state—intersect and serve to construct authority and legal legitimacy. Each serves as a marketplace of exchange. Academic lawyers can acquire familiarity and contacts in the worlds of business and politics—and vice versa. These institutions, furthermore, are also at the crossroads of the national and international, which allows them to facilitate the conversion of their members' local competence—legal and relational—into a capital of cosmopolitan expertise and prominence" (1997: 140–41).

From the point of view of ego, a reciprocity network is not merely a useful mechanism for obtaining certain resources, it is a resource in itself. The network may be mobilized on behalf of ego's job and may enhance his or her performance, thus making ego more valuable to his or her superior and increasing his or her prospects for promotion. The entire system benefits from the existence of such informal contacts, since they serve to check and diminish sources of conflict at all levels, while a diffuse tacit solidarity is generated that helps secure the stability of the system. This is the social background in which the profession we are dealing with in this essay develops, and with which it interacts.

To sum up, the social structure of Mexico may be described as a system of domination—or an authority structure—based on pyramidal corporate entities called *sectors*. The share of each individual in the resources of the system is determined by his or her position in the hierarchy and by his or her mode of articulation. The dominant groups are organized into two sectors, the public sector and the private sector, which vie—sometimes competing, sometimes cooperating—for control of the system. Both are organized into hierarchies. Beyond their rivalry, however, both sectors (as well as the leaders of the labor sector) are primarily interested in the continuance of the system as such. Complex horizontal hierarchies cut across sectors and promote the interests of the system as a whole.

The Profession of Law

A total of 142,774 lawyers graduated between 1945 and 1997, most of whom obtained their degrees in public universities throughout the country. The National University of Mexico (UNAM) stands in first place, producing nearly one-third (28.9 percent) of the total population of lawyers—more than four times the number produced by the university in second place. On the other hand, the five main private universities of Mexico City (Escuela Libre de Derecho, Universidad del Valle de México, Universidad Iberoamericana, Universidad Panamericana and ITAM) have graduated a mere 5 percent of the total (SECIC 1997b).[1] In the centralized society of Mexico, the UNAM is clearly the most important university, not only in terms of the number of students who graduate from it, but also because of the notorious influence these graduates have had on the country's leadership. In order to understand the development of the legal profession, therefore, it is necessary to describe the history of the UNAM.

The National University of Mexico

Now a mass university, the National University began, at the turn of the century, as an elite institution oriented toward the training of liberal professionals.[2] Traditionally, the main areas of recruitment were medicine, law, and engineering. As the middle class rose to prominence with the advent of industrialization and city growth, however, this elitist university ceased to satisfy all the aspirations of the leading strata of society. After 1940, the avalanche of students aiming toward the National University simply could not be contained. The need arose for a greater diversity of professional careers, in accordance with the requirements of modern society. Research institutes were organized, and research became a central activity in the university, second only to teaching. As faculties grew, so did their teaching staff. Academic teaching jobs, which once belonged exclusively to senior professionals who taught a few specific courses, mostly for prestige, have increasingly become a full-time career in their own right. Thus, two distinct new professional careers were defined: professors, who teach full time at the schools and faculties, and researchers, who research full time in the institutes.

At the same time, as the middle class rose in political importance, the university became a training ground for the new state elites, as well as an "ideological battlefield and center of revolutionary critique" (C. López 1974: 3). The functions of the National University were not limited to the strictly academic roles of its organic law such as teaching, research, and cultural extension, but included other important implicit functions. It provided informal political training to future political and technocratic leaders (the "new class"), channeled social criticism, provided new options for social mobility, and helped build the ideological,

moral, and political functions of the Mexican national postrevolutionary ethos.

Such diverse functions imply the possibility of conflict between
groups that uphold contradictory ideals concerning the very nature of
the university (as related to its *explicit* vs. *implicit* functions). In opposition to those who strive for an academic and professional university
stand those who vie for a politically concerned university. This results in
the existence of different life careers or functional specialization in relation to the national system.

What do we mean by a *life career*? Each student in the university
undergoes a training process that is not limited to formal academic curricular content, but actually includes a number of activities and experiences that prepare him or her for a certain role within the national system. Thus, we can distinguish between two types of life careers: (1)
formal academic careers according to the explicit functions of the university, such as careers oriented to the civil service, business, and the liberal professions; and (2) careers that relate to the university's implicit
functions, such as the practice of politics, the training of political leaders, and the general reproduction of the society's political culture.

Groups geared toward different life careers tend to defend their
interests, which may compete or conflict with those of other life careers.
The activities of political pressure groups may interfere with the quality
of academic training through strikes and other disruptions. Conversely,
the passive resistance of academically oriented students tends to inhibit
political participation and limit the objectives of politically oriented
student groups. Each life career is represented by a social group with
characteristic features, which include an internal structure, a set of initiation rites, a set of norms and values, and, finally, characteristic mechanisms that govern the process of their members' integration into a
specific role in national life. All life careers may coexist within each faculty, thus making it possible for individuals to acquire broader networks, which may be put to use later on in their professional lives.

Lomnitz (1977: passim) has identified three main life careers: academic, professional, and political. All three are present within the faculty
of law at the university.

1. *The academic career.* Academics are members of the university
community who develop a preference for research and teaching as a
way of life. They are concerned with the explicit functions of the university and may eventually seek academic positions in this or another

university. Their recruitment is based upon an unofficial semitutorial system, which begins for some of the better students when they attract a professor's attention. Typically, the professor will personally direct their theses, help them to obtain scholarships, and use them as assistants. The result is often an enduring relationship of scientific and personal loyalty between the tutor and his or her assistant. The student's next step is to become hired as a member of the research staff of an institute.

2. *The professional career.* This is a life career clearly oriented toward a role outside the university. In the UNAM—as in other universities—many professors are practicing professionals who only teach a few hours per week (on the side, as it were) and who may, therefore, lack the necessary dedication to update their courses. On the other hand, however, they represent a link between the student body and the professional market. The university's separation of teaching and research has tended to produce a static curriculum that considerably lags behind the newer scientific and technical results in a given field. This is particularly true today in the faculty of law. To counter this problem, there is a new tendency to supplement the teaching staff with full-time academics, although many part-time professors are distinguished professionals whose practical experience is also invaluable to the student. They quickly single out the more competent students in each class and provide personal opportunities for job training in public or private corporations, private firms or offices, or public administration. Such tutorial supervision represents a major complement to curricular teaching, as well as a selective recruiting mechanism for the liberal professions. While it is true that the interests of these professionally oriented students lie mainly outside the university, such alumni typically stay connected to their schools by means of occasional teaching, as well as through their professional associations, many of which do carry considerable political weight. Thus, the political influence of professional groups is felt in university politics—particularly in the law school—as well as in national politics as a whole.

3. *The political career.* Members of the academic community who have shown an active interest in political affairs from their student days take up this life career. Their interest is initially expressed through participation in student movements and other power conflicts—whether for or against the current political regime. They tend to support a current of thought that holds that a major, if not essential, function of the National University is to take a stand in matters of public affairs. Some

of these political leaders are drawn from student activists of the high schools affiliated with the UNAM, while others become attracted to political participation after entering the university. Eventually, the so-called student bases—made up of sporadic or potential activists and politically oriented students—become differentiated from the mass of the politically passive student body. These relatively small bases represent the proper field of action for the "politicians." The life career of a politician is as demanding and time-consuming as that of an academic. In fact, at the higher echelons the two careers are mutually exclusive, since a student will rarely have enough time to be an academic and a political activist at the same time. The typical structure of a political group has a leader, followed or surrounded by members of his immediate staff and supported by activists who gather and work with some regularity, but not full-time. Promotion within such groups depends upon loyalty, dedication, and leadership. The main qualifications for political leaders are, basically, access to relevant information and an ability to attract and recruit other students. Furthermore, they must be able to maintain efficient personal contacts with members of the university administration. These contacts enable them to play a brokering role in conflicts that arise between students and administration on matters such as registration, examination fees, changes in curricula, and other complaints regarding a number of academic issues and problems. A capable political leader knows how to control student strife. This ability represents his or her basic power resource and major drawing card. The essential quality of a true political leader, however, is the ability to perceive and channel the true fears and desires of the bases. It is the political leader's task to interpret and translate into words and actions the basic aspirations and objective problems of the student body.

The preceding description of the complex model found within the university fits the general structural description previously proposed for the national political culture, defined in terms of horizontal and vertical social networks. In the faculty of law all three life careers intermingle in a diverse student body that will eventually differentiate into various occupations: liberal professionals, civil servants, politicians or members of the political elite, government technocrats, employees in large private firms (including international trade firms), and researchers working for the Instituto de Investigaciones Jurídicas, as well as lawyers involved in socially oriented practices such as human rights, NGOs, union work, and so on. During their formal training period, at school, these students have the opportunity to interact and socialize with each other within the whole range of horizontal relations. Whether as friends, political comrades, classmates, or mere acquaintances, the opportunity exists to incorporate others into their general social networks. The same is true with regard to the vertical networks that professors build with selected students, which often result in a relationship of clientele—particularly important in the recruitment of students in the job market.

This network-building process eventually allows the individual the possibility of contacting other individuals identified with entirely different life careers when the need arises in his or her professional life. Within the state apparatus, for example, political leaders constitute their work teams with technical practitioners—individuals who followed a professional life career. In order to include these professionals in an action group, a political leader needs not only to be acquainted with who they are, but also to be able to trust them to a certain degree. Conversely, technocratic leaders may well require political knowledge from lawyers well versed in conflict resolution, political analysis, and so forth. Finally, professional lawyers, working as liberal professionals, will perform and succeed better in their cases if they have made the judge's acquaintance beforehand, have had access to important information from friends or relatives working in related areas, and so on.

In conclusion, the university provides training for different life careers. During their formal training period, individuals have a chance to build their social networks by interacting with other students interested in pursuing different life careers, as well as with professors who can provide vertical connections and introduce them to the labor market. A basic professional social network is thus developed and then completed with external personal relations such as family, friends, and neighbors. These relations—this social capital—is the basis for the construction of specific social networks to be used in the individual's professional practice, according to his or her particular post. The UNAM's tendency to recruit a large percentage of socioculturally deprived students affects the constitution of the graduates' social networks, their recruitment into the labor market, and their possibilities of participating in the new technopolitical elite, which is increasingly produced by the private universities. On the other hand, the National University still maintains a monopoly on research and the training of high-level interpreters of the law. It continues to offer an academic career and researchers linked to the Institute of Juridical Studies.

The Social Origins of Students at UNAM and Its Faculty of Law

The National University, aware of its own importance in contributing to social mobility, recruits a large proportion of lower- and middle-class students coming from economic and culturally deprived families. As table 1 shows, the percentage of students entering the university from families belonging to a very low economic category (income less than three times the minimum wage) has increased from 21 percent in 1965 to 68.6 percent in 1985. This group belongs to a category that may be termed as lower and lower-middle class. The next category of students (family income between 3 and 4.6 times the minimum wage) has also increased in number between 1965 and 1985, from 18.7 to 25.7 percent. This group may be classified as middle-class. Finally, the number of students from the upper middle class has sharply decreased. While 37.8 percent of the total incoming student population in 1965 came from families that earned between 4.6 and 9.1 times the minimum wage, in 1985 a mere 5.7 percent came from families that earned over five times the minimum wage. The number of upper-class students has similarly decreased, representing a mere 3.2 percent of the total by 1975. This means that people belonging to the upper middle and upper classes began choosing to go to other universities, particularly after 1975.

Using a different form of classification,[3] by the Dirección General de Estadística y Sistemas de Informática e Información, UNAM (DGESII), information for 1995 is shown in table 2. Again we find a minority of students whose family income is greater than eight times the minimum wage, while the category with the largest percentage is that of students whose families earn between two and four times the minimum wage. The bulk of the student body is middle-class, and we now find a new increase in the number of upper middle class students with family incomes greater than ten times the minimum wage. On the other hand, only 13 percent of these first-year students come from families earning less than twice the minimum wage, which may mean that fewer students from poor families studied in universities in the 1990s. In 1997 the minimum wage was equivalent to 3.3 dollars a day, and therefore families in this lowest category have an income of less than 100 dollars per month.

The major jumps that may be distinguished (see table 3) are related to the years in which the peso underwent devaluation. For example, in 1980 (during the oil bonanza), the minimum wage was 7.11 dollars a day.

In 1982, however, a very drastic devaluation took place, which explains the dramatic drop in the minimum wage for 1985.

The UNAM's tendency to attract mainly lower- and middle-class students can also be seen by examining the occupational pattern of the parents of students entering the university. From 1958 through 1985 an average of approximately 18 percent of the students belonged to typical working-class categories (blue-collar workers, artisans, and farmers), while an average of 30 percent belonged to what we might consider middle to lower middle class. An average of 16 percent may be classified as upper-middle class (professionals and technicians, executives, and public employees). By 1995 the situation had changed; 38.6 percent of the students' fathers carried out working-class activities, whereas 53.6 percent had middle-class occupations, and a mere 4.8 percent belonged to what might be classified as upper middle and upper classes (Covo 1990: table 15; DGESII a).

TABLE 1. Family Income of Students entering the UNAM (1965–85)

1965		1970		1975		1980		1985	
Income	%	Income	%	Income	%	Income	%	Income	%
0.95–3	21	0.65–3.1	52.3	0.5–3.1	69.9	0.6–1.5	55.8	1–2.5	68.6
3–4.6	18.7	3.1–5.1	25.3	3.1–5.2	20.7	1.8–3	32.5	2.5–5	25.7
4.6–9.1	37.8	5.1–10.2	17.5	5.2–7.8	6.1	>3	11.9	>5	5.7
>9.1	22.7	>10.2	5.4	>7.8	3.2				

Source: Basedon Covo 1990: table XIII.
Note: Family income expressed in relation to the minimum wage at the time.

TABLE 2. Family Income of Students entering the UNAM in 1995 (in percentages)

Multiple of Minimum Wage	
less than 2	13.2
2–4	35.5
4–6	23.0
6–8	13.4
8–10	7.5
more than 10	7.3

Source: DGESII a

TABLE 3. Daily Minimum Wages (equivalence in U.S. dollars)

Year	Minimum Wage (dollars)
1965	1.72
1970	2.56
1975	5.08
1980	7.11
1985	2.63
1990	3.21
1995	2.47

It is easy to understand the great demand that exists to enroll in the National University of Mexico. It costs nothing and promises social mobility (real or virtual) within the middle classes (García Salord 1997). The demand to enter the UNAM in general, and the faculty of law in particular, as well as the university's inability to respond to this demand, can be observed in table 4.

The Training of Law

Although the aim of this essay is not to analyze the theoretical basis of the practice of law in Mexico, it is necessary to point out the differences between lawyers' formal training and their acquisition of informal skills. The basis of formal civil law in Mexico is the Napoleonic Code, which is a modernized version of Roman law. The practice of law in Mexico is based on the constitution and the laws that derive from it. Each particular case requires the execution of specific articles that apply to it. This contrasts with Anglo-Saxon law, where the judges are constantly interpreting and making the law (common law). One informant explained to us that "the U.S. juridical culture is more pragmatic. Mexican juridical culture is very formalistic. What are important in Mexico are formalities, which hide reality; the law's mission is not to regulate reality, but to categorize it. In the U.S., the tendency is to solve problems, which results in a pragmatic culture situated in a system in which lawyers have relative autonomy within the administrative apparatus."

TABLE 4.   Demand and Admission to the UNAM and Its Faculty of Law, 1990–96

	Students Requesting Admission		Students Admitted		Percentage Admitted	
	UNAM	Law	UNAM	Law	UNAM	Law
1990–91	43,373	6,540	30,091	4,243	69.3	64.8
1991–92	41,373	6,547	28,500	3,809	69.0	58.1
1992–93	93,217	14,575	29,510	3,664	31.7	25.1
1993–94	100,022	15,655	32,950	3,615	32.9	23.0
1994–95	115,587	18,445	30,941	3,396	26.7	18.4
1995–96	152,833	19,485	40,082	3,409	26.2	17.5

Source: Based on on Nieto 1997.

Common law is developed constantly, based on practical grounds. The U.S. Constitution consists of a very short written list of civil rights and principles, interpreted through jurisprudence based on precedent. In Mexico, the basis is a written constitution that must be applied in every case. Only in cases where no applicable written law exists is an open interpretation of the law acceptable. These cases do not constitute binding precedent unless there have been five consecutive cases solved in the same way. Thus, the practices of law in Mexico and the United States follow different principles, which correspond to different juridical and political cultures. In Mexico, which has an authoritarian and vertically oriented political culture, the written law dictates what citizens should and should not do. In the United States, which is more democratic and horizontally oriented, commoners make the law by their practice.

All law students must follow the same basic program (table 5) and receive the title of *licenciado en derecho*. Specialization, in general, is acquired through practice. Certain optional courses are offered, "but mainly in the job you end up in, you learn how to be a specialized lawyer. In some cases, lawyers pursue a master's degree or even go abroad to take specialized courses. Specialization comes once you've finished your career. You can specialize in any area of the law you like, although the assertion that you choose that area is somewhat of a lie. In reality, life takes you to it; that is, at some point you find a job solving labor problems, and then you find yourself being a labor lawyer; or the first job that you find is in a notary, and you'll probably end up as one."

Although the basic training at school is the same, lawyers fulfill a large number of roles, and, as the findings of the Chicago study by Heinz and Laumann (1994: 28–36) illustrate, they specialize in many fields of law. Originally a jurist could fulfill different roles, such as that of legislator (who makes the laws), judge (who applies the law to particular cases), and lawyer (who advises and defends clients before the courts and authorities). Other legal professions existed as well, such as state lawyers, notary publics, researchers, and university teachers. The growth of the Mexican state during the twentieth century, however, and the leadership role it has assumed, have led the government to regulate many aspects of social life with excessive detail. The expansive phenomenon of international law (after World War II) has also contributed to these internal dynamics. These factors produced a great range of juridical specialties, and it became essential to add theoretical and practical

TABLE 5. The Basic Curriculum of Studies in the Faculty of Law

1st Semester
•Introduction to the Study of Law
•Sociology
•Introduction to Civil Law
•Introduction to Penal Law
•Roman Law I
•Contemporary Juridical Systems
•Economic Theory
•Techniques in Juridical Research

2nd Semester
•Legal Theory
•Political Theory
•Property
•Theory of Crime
•Roman Law II
•History of Mexican Law
•History of Economic Thought
•Techniques for Expression

3d Semester
•Constitutional Law I
•State Theory
•Obligations
•Particular Offenses
•Contemporary Political Systems
•Juridical Methodology
•Juridical Ethics
•Juridical Lexicology

4th Semester
•Constitutional Law II
•Trial Theory
•Obligations and Contracts
•Particular Offenses II and Special Offenses
•Administrative Law I
•Individual Labor Law
•Introduction to Economics Law
•Mathematics Applied to Law

5th Semester
•Individual and Social Guarantees
•Civil Trial Law I
•Contracts
•Public International Law I
•Administrative Law II
•Collective Labor Law
•Trade Law

6th Semester
•Habeas Corpus I
•Civil Trial Law II
•Family Law
•Public International Law II
•Administrative Law III
•Social Security Law
•Charters of Credit

7th Semester
•Habeas Corpus II
•Penal Trial Law
•Inheritance Law
•Fiscal I
•Administrative Law IV
•Labor Trial Law
•Credit Operations

8th Semester
•Law and Philosophy
•Private International Law I
•Fiscal II
•Ecology Law
•Agrarian Law
•Trade Contracts

9th Semester
•Private International Law II
•Judicial Processes and Procedures
•Juridical Regulations for External
  Commerce
•Agrarian Trial Law
•Bank and Stock Law

10th Semester
•Economic Integration Law
•Business Law
•Thesis Elaboration Workshop

specialization to the basic and general training (De la Madrid 1993: ix–x). Among the best-known specialties are family, fiscal, labor, penal, international, business, civil rights, and civil law.

Once the students finish their course program, and before they write their mandatory dissertation, a short period of fieldwork experience called *pasantía* is required. As *pasantes,* students get recruited by private firms, as well as by the government or the academic world. Those in practice learn all the practical steps needed to handle a case. One informant states:

> Most of the students begin to work even before finishing their educational careers, because in their *pasantías* they help the lawyer in litigation by doing the dirty work, such as going to the courts, checking the agreements, making photocopies, etc. During this experience they become familiarized with their profession. . . We may have a wonderful knowledge of the judicial procedure and an excellent academic level, but what we see in the books does not correspond necessarily to what goes on in reality. It's not the same thing to go to court to ask for a dossier as to know whom and how you should ask for it. . . . those things you can only acquire through practice.

Besides the term of *pasantía,* students must perform a six-month period of unpaid work, which is called social service. Normally, it is done in a governmental institution where the student has an opportunity to see how the bureaucracy works. The purpose is to force students who have attended a free university to repay society with some of what they have learned. Sometime during this period, students begin collecting data to write their *licenciatura* dissertation. This dissertation is a research exercise that must be directed by an authorized professor and eventually receive the approval of five other faculty members; it also must be presented in an open oral examination. After that, the student gets a degree in law, although he or she is still required to obtain a *cédula profesional* from the federal Ministry of Education. UNAM certifies the new lawyers' acquisition of knowledge and skills. There is no professional association to certify it, and neither does the *cédula profesional* given by the state fulfill the role of final examiner. Once the graduate obtains the title of *licenciado en derecho* from the university, he or she is a lawyer, and once the *cédula profesional* is obtained the individual is a certified practicing lawyer.

Certain types of activities require formal specialization through *diplomados* at a master's or sometimes Ph.D. level, which may be acquired from Mexican universities or abroad. The importance of acquiring such a specialization abroad will be addressed later in this essay, when we examine the "modern" technocratic tendency.

The Labor Market

The importance of social relations among young new lawyers can best be appreciated by looking at the way in which they are recruited into the labor market, a process that is dependent upon each individual's class origin (from which his or her basic social network derives). As we pointed out in the previous section, lawyers can fulfill a wide range of activities in the public, private, and academic sectors of society, corresponding to the different life careers found in the university (see table 6).

The Public Sector

(a) A large share of graduating lawyers end up working for the state apparatus. This percentage dropped somewhat after 1991, due to the introduction of new (neoliberal) state policies. We find a considerable number of lawyers occupying the lower and middle echelons of the civil service or state bureaucracy,[4] as the state is the largest provider of mid-

TABLE 6. Social Sector in Which Graduates Find Work: All of UNAM vs. Faculty of Law, 1988–95 (in percentages)

	Public Sector		Private Sector	
	UNAM	Faculty of Law	UNAM	Faculty of Law
1988	54.1	60	45.9	40
1989	52.4	62	47.6	38
1990	48.8	63	50.5	37
1991	42.8	54	57.2	46
1992	42.1	56	57.9	44
1993	43.8	60.7	56.2	39.3
1994	43.7	48.1	56.3	51.9
1995	44.4	48.2	55.6	51.8

dle-class jobs, not only in the judicial system (in the tribunals, for example), but also in different levels and specialties within the offices of the state apparatus (e.g., international law for the Ministry of Foreign Affairs, labor specialists for the Ministry of Labor, taxation laws, electoral laws). These civil servants do not occupy decision-making positions, but deal with the technical issues needed to support the whole legal system and apply it to the different roles of the state. In other words, they do not belong to the political or technical elite.

(b) The process of modernization of society has produced a need for specialized professionals, including lawyers. Some occupy leadership positions (the technocracy), while others make up the professional teams working under them. They require specialized technical training, for example, in economics or public administration. Technocratic lawyers are those who occupy the middle to higher levels of the state apparatus, combining specific legal know-how with political decision-making power. This technocratic elite includes the Supreme Court judges, magistrates, and other highly specialized legal advisers of the state apparatus (the legal designers of NAFTA, to cite but one example). It is at this level that, according to Dezalay and Garth (1996: 77), the public and private sectors interact.

(c) Traditionally, ambitious young men who wished to enter high-level politics would study law at the National University. All of the country's presidents (except the current one), as well as their higher echelon ministers, studied at the UNAM. Furthermore, professors and classmates normally recruited the future leaders into political action groups (and social networks), precisely during their student years. In his book *Labyrinths of Power*, Peter Smith provides the following hypothetical advice (based upon his study of political careers in Mexico) to a young man who wishes to enter the national elite: Go to UNAM. "The National University is an excellent place for making contacts, alliances and friendships. . . . Professors and students were able to observe each others' talents, they often met informally, they introduced each other to friends and acquaintances, they provided one another with *palancas* for subsequent use. . . . Nearly one half of the total 1946–71 elite studied at UNAM, and the figure might have been as high as 70 percent of the upper level office holders. . . . Once at UNAM . . . choose a discipline with care. Law has traditionally offered the optimal prospect for a political career, and economics has steadily gained importance over time" (1979: 245–50).

Analyzing the secretaries of state in the different administrations from Porfirio Díaz to Zedillo, Camp (1995; 1996: 131, 137) shows not only the traditional importance of having a law degree, but also a steady rise in the status of economists from Díaz Ordaz's regime to the present. In fact, in the last two administrations the number of economists equals (with Salinas) and then surpasses that of lawyers. At the same time, the predominance of UNAM graduates over those of private universities has faded. From the term of President Echeverría (1970–76) to that of Zedillo, the number of members in the original cabinet of each given term who graduated from private universities has shown a dramatic increase of 100 percent per year.

The Private Sector

In the last decade, some private universities have concentrated their efforts upon improving their training in law and economics, aiming to place their graduates in elite positions, both in private enterprises and high-level technocracy. One informant who graduated from the Universidad de la Salle declared: "I come from a middle class family that could afford to send us all to private schools and universities. . . . I did not choose to go to UNAM because, in those days, there were many strikes and whole semesters were lost. So from the very beginning I decided to choose a private university. . . . Although we had the freedom to choose which type of career to follow, it is true that most of my classmates ended up working for private firms and corporations, rather than the public sector. Many of their parents owned businesses, and they were planning to work for them. I can say that in UNAM students were more interested in social problems than we were. In my university [in contrast with UNAM] we received an education in economics and in English; most of the students came from private schools, and had a more diversified education, including having traveled with their families. I can say that in my university we focused toward preparing ourselves for a good working position in society."

The liberal practice of the profession represents an important area of work for lawyers. These lawyers specialize in litigation, defending private interests, whether against other private parties or against the state. Private lawyers also carry out civil matters such as divorce and inheritance. According to one informant, "Some students begin to work for family firms, and, when they finish their studies, they might open up their own firm. Or they can join their own family firm, if they belong to such a family."

Another informant continued, "There used to be a time in which every family or every business had a private lawyer, just as they had a private doctor. However, as the complexity of the knowledge of the law grew, individual lawyers had to join or create firms in which a wider field of specialties would be represented. The small individual firms are disappearing."

In the business world the tendency is either to work with large law firms or to create a juridical department, with lawyers working exclusively for the firm. "The lawyer's role in the corporation is, on the one hand, to help the corporation comply with legal regulations in the most profitable manner, and, on the other, to prevent the firm's potential conflicts from reaching the point of litigation—which is considered pernicious to the firm's image and prestige" (Pérez Perdomo 1996: 132–34).

Historically, there have existed important family firms working in the field of international business. Before the revolution, Cansino and Riva was the most important international firm in Mexico. They represented Petróleos El Águila, one of the largest oil companies in the world. Three other family firms followed in importance, but they dissolved after the deaths of their respective family heads. Other firms were created in the 1930s such as Goodrich Dalton, Mijarrés y Sepúlveda, and Mackenzie, Baker and Botts. Most of them were subsidiaries of American firms, although some of them were independent. One example of the latter was Noriega y Escobedo, a Mexican firm that opened an office in New York and associated with a Canadian firm. Today, the firm deals almost entirely in international business. Its clients are basically foreign companies. Including partners and employees, fifty lawyers have belonged to the firm, and through the years it has given rise to ten other firms. This type of corporation is mostly contacted by American law firms representing foreign companies who seek lawyers in Mexico in order to establish themselves legally in the country and also seek their counsel to prevent possible conflicts that may arise. On the other hand, according to a member of Noriega y Escobedo, Mexican entrepreneurs usually consult a law firm only when they find themselves already in a jam.

Academia

Lawyers who dedicate themselves to academic work constitute a select elite. Juridical research constitutes the basis of all lawyers' professional development (at least at a formal level) and of the legal framework of the nation (Soberanes 1993: 171). Furthermore, there are few institutions where this type of research is done, the most important of which is the Instituto de Investigaciones Jurídicas of UNAM, which continues to hold a virtual monopoly on the legal research produced in the country.

Usually, a small group of students interested in following an academic career participates enthusiastically in the theoretical courses taught by the professional academicians. If a student's talent is acknowledged by a professor, the student may continue to write his or her professional thesis under the professor's direction and may end up as the professor's assistant. The students can then enter graduate studies, in order to be hired finally as permanent members of the institution. Often, academic lawyers are eventually invited (by their tutors, or even by their former students) to take on governmental positions in state agencies, for example, or in the Supreme Court. The academic career carries moral status and prestige, but can be long and difficult because of the scarce number of positions.

Building Social Networks

The construction of professional social networks begins at the faculty of law, as students of every grade follow the same curricula for several years. This gives them the opportunity to meet a variety of students and professors and in time to choose a close circle of friends. The construction of a friendship group (or eventually a clique) follows the cultural rules of friendship in Mexico, as well as the particular psychological tendencies of the people involved. One might say that the faculty provides a hidden curriculum, complementing the formal one, which teaches how to make friends and how to ask services from them.

Smith (1979: 253) advises young politicians to make all the friends they can, "especially among your superiors . . . This is crucial because jobs are distributed on a personal basis. Contacts from the UNAM, if you have them, can provide useful entry and introductions." Grindel (1977: 43) showed that, in the case of CONASUPO, no high-level official obtained his a her post without some sort of introduction or *palanca,* and 80 percent of the middle-level administrators obtained their position through a direct or indirect personal bond.

According to one informant, it is through practice that a young lawyer learns to create social networks. "A lawyer needs to be a social person, with good manners and an interest in people, beginning with his own clients, because in the first interview it is very important that they trust the lawyer. . . . Having relations is basic everywhere. In the USA lawyers also need to have clients, and a good portfolio gives them prestige, and this is mainly achieved through social relations. There, however, it is handled more discreetly, because society, ideologically, doesn't value personal relations as much as the lawyer's own ability."

Another informant said: "Making friends depends on your personal abilities to communicate with others. If you are a wild person, and you yell at anyone who stands in your way, you won't make friends. So, your ability to make friends is important. Also, your knowledge and education. Good manners are very important too, since you can be very nice and very refined, but if you become a real beast when you sit down to eat, no one will invite you to a business lunch, since you will discredit the whole group" (notice that business lunches are often mentioned among informants as the place to discuss at length the most important aspects of a given case with lawyers, judges, and others).

Informants, however, declared a total absence of any practical intentions when making friends or socializing with classmates and colleagues, as well as a lack of consciousness regarding the importance of personal relations when choosing friends, even though they may later become the basis for an exchange of favors and information related to their professional practice. "I don't think any one designs or plans or programs the need to make friends. . . . I don't know of anyone who thinks, 'Let's see: I must make so many friends, I need to know that many judges in six months.' I don't think anyone is going to stop to make those calculations regarding their future need. It's rather the opposite: you simply make friends because you like to socialize. Maybe [those calculations are done by] those lawyers who want to get into politics, who usually try to please everybody, to organize people, etc."

Other sources of relational capital are the professors with whom the students take courses and those they work with when writing their professional dissertation. As we mentioned previously in relation to life careers within the university, students are introduced into the labor market by their professors. This is particularly true for the academic career, but professors are also known to recruit assistants for their private firms, or even for civil service and technocratic teams.

Family relations are an important source of social capital. In a previous study, Lomnitz and Pérez-Lisaur (1971) showed that the basic unit of solidarity is the three-generational family group, which results in a very large kinship network for most individuals. Among this pool of people, a practicing lawyer may have access to a variety of people related to their specialized needs. We often find that lawyers belong to families of lawyers. Family firms, in fact, are normally an extension of one private lawyer whose children or nephews have joined the firm over the years. The studies of Smith and Camp on political and technical elites also show the importance that family connections play in Mexican politics (Camp 1976: 75–78; Smith 1979: 254).

Finally, another source of networks (even if not originally related to professional practice) is friends, including family friends, neighbors, high school classmates, voluntary club associations, and so forth. In time, these too become instrumental for the practitioner.

Recruitment into the Labor Market

Recruitment into the labor market is directly related to the social origin of the students, as well as to the life careers they choose during their time as students. Although the National University is open to all social classes, students begin to differentiate from the very beginning, forming groups based upon factors such as social class, color of skin, and the high school where they studied (one student of the faculty of law talked about a separation between the "beautiful people" and the "uglies"). This is the initial instance where the professional future of the students will be determined. In these early stages, professors also begin to detect which particular students they will eventually recruit when the need arises.

One professor identified three distinct levels of students, relating their social origin to their professional opportunities: "At UNAM, we are talking about students who generally come from the lower-middle classes, who expect to experience a strong upward mobility in comparison to their own parents, but will themselves only be able to reach certain limited positions . . . since they lack the social relations needed to have access to Big Business or to the middle and higher levels of the public administration." He adds, "Many students choose law as a career guided by the hope that a university degree will rescue him and his family from poverty, or even place him in the Presidential Chair. The student finishes his studies and finds out that he does not know anyone that can give him a case or a job. . . . What can he expect from a fruit seller, a taxi driver or a porter? That is his milieu. . . . So, if you have no relations, you won't get a job . . . and he ends up with a small-time job in the public sector. . . . They would have to meet people of a different social level to aspire to a higher level job or income. . . .

"Then come a second level of students whose social relations are better, and their work opportunities greater. These are middle class young men that have better contacts (relations), and therefore can work in family firms, or open small firms who can work for companies or banks, handling consulting or litigation, in a middle level status. The third level consists of upper-middle class students (mostly studying at private universities, and one very small group at UNAM). Through their friends or relatives in high places, they enter directly into large firms or corporations, those that carry out litigation or consulting of importance, receive the cases that earn the most money, etc. Large enterprises hire those firms for consulting and the administration of important business. . . as do international consulting firms who deal with totally different businesses, dealing with large amounts of money."

Another informant describes the importance of social networks in the first steps of professional life: "I believe that human relations are always important in every sense. They are necessary because the young lawyer who is starting professional practice and has no social relations that can provide him or her with a case will have no work and will end up in small-time jobs, perhaps as the last secretary of a tribunal, or checking papers in a public office, and that's where he or she will remain. . . . In order to establish yourself, you need a case, and if you don't have it, you'll have to get a job in a firm or in the government, and for that you'll also need to know people. . . . Once you get your first case (which some relation gave you) and you solve it, you can start getting more cases. And then, if you have enough relations because you are socially well connected (your parents or friends) then you have easy access to easy cases, but you'll also have to prove you're capable."

For students without appropriate social relations, it is easier to enter the lower echelons of the public administration. Indeed, this represents social mobility for them: "In the university they will have classmates whose parents may be public employees or union leaders, or a professor with whom they get along well, who at the same time may be a public employee. So at the university it may be easier to get these types of jobs. The largest employer in this country is the government, and if you are a public employee, you have a steady income, social and medical security and a pension. So for people who don't have anything, it's ideal." The normal way for students to enter the state apparatus is through their social service, but there are also students with relations in higher-level public administration who will be recruited directly into higher-level positions.

Thus, students originating from lower classes find their opportunities constrained by "inadequate" social networks, often despite their personal capabilities. In the words of another informant: "A lower middle class student can become a good lawyer (if he studies hard), but because of his lack of contacts he must limit himself to unimportant cases and to a certain level of bureaucratic activities. A private university student may be a mediocre lawyer but, because of his family and friends, may have access to better levels of employment and professional practice."

In the private labor market, social relations also play a crucial role. Students may, for example, begin by collecting bills for friends of the family, or as clerks in notaries and firms. One informant noted with regard to practice in a tribunal that "litigation is not included in the formal curriculum of the university. Students usually start working (sometimes years before graduating) in a firm as assistants to an individual lawyer, who starts instructing you. He shows you how to be in contact with the tribunals, how to ask for documents, how to write your first draft." Their access to the firm is either through their professors or their family social networks.

In the case of one private university student, her first job was in a private firm where one of her professors sent her to one of his friends. "I had an interview with one of the partners of the firm, and he sent me to solve small problems on my own (obtain an agreement in court), for which I had no official authorization. I was lucky it was a man who was in charge, and when he saw how upset I was about not being able to get a copy of the agreement, he allowed me to get a copy." The same informant also did litigation cases on her own. "My first boss gave me a case to litigate for him by myself, a case of land expropriation. . . . I learned a lot and won the case on my own. That person was unselfish in giving me his knowledge in advice, and gave me confidence."

The main partner of a large international corporation describes their recruitment policies in the following manner: "We used to recruit students from UNAM. Now the best ones come from ITAM [a private university]. We take ten students from the second year on until they are *pasantes*. After three years, when they receive their degree, we will decide if we want them. Normally only one remains. The main problem we have in recruiting young lawyers is their training and education. We need intelligent, multilingual and transcultural lawyers. A purely Mexican lawyer that doesn't understand what foreigners want is useless. And UNAM usually does not give that sort of education. We end up selecting young people that, because of their family background and experience, have a knowledge of languages, and understand not only what it is to be Mexican, but also the foreign point of view."

Although a large percentage of private lawyers study at UNAM, the private universities (which are particularly interested in improving their law schools) have been recruiting students from high-class families, who end up working for private enterprises and not for the government. Table 7, although it does not distinguish between the private and public sectors, gives us an idea of the occupational distribution of UNAM graduates. We can state that farm workers, inspectors and supervisors, artisans and blue-collar workers, assistants and the like, transportation drivers, domestic workers, watchmen, and guards—which together make up 7.2 percent of the total—clearly represent the working class. We might also venture that teachers, public officers, and office workers—around 41 percent—work in the public sector as bureaucrats. The largest single work category, *profesional*—equivalent to liberal professionals—can apply to either sector, and the same is true for the "technical" category.

The Importance of Social Relations in Normal Practice

Social relations are particularly important in the practice of law since it is a field that deals precisely with people and their relations. "Relations are vital because they allow us to get ahead in many things. It's not the same thing to go to an unknown person and ask him for something (even if it's legal), than to go with a personal reference, as they are fundamental in Mexico. Perhaps it shouldn't be so, but personal reference is the key that opens every door. This actually has negative consequences, since it results in the fact that many people who are not capable get decision-making jobs."

After relatives, friends from school are particularly important. Eventually, during their careers, classmates who follow different paths or enter different levels of the administration may find themselves in need of each other's help in a particular case. A private litigant, for example, might find out that the public attorney (usually a low-level lawyer stemming from low-class origins) who has information on a case he or she is working on is also an old classmate from their faculty years. That person is then activated as an important social resource. "With social relations, doors are opened. But relations [alone] will not sustain you entirely in your work, since it is your capacity to positively solve the cases [that] will keep you going."

Social networks are necessary in all aspects of the practice of law. First of all, most cases involve more than one specialty, and therefore a

TABLE 7.   Occupational Distribution of UNAM Law Graduates (1990)

Line of work	Number	(%)
Professional	61,048	51.3
Technical	1,880	1.6
Teaching	7,993	6.7
Arts	954	0.8
Public officers or directors	14,550	12.2
Farming	943	0.8
Inspection and supervising	633	0.5
Artisans and blue-collar work	1,052	0.9
Machine operators	224	0.2
Assistants and similar	174	0.1
Transportation drivers	711	0.6
Office work	20,335	17.1
Commerce and sales	5,457	4.6
Traveling worker	434	0.4
Domestic employment	13	0.01
Supervision	623	0.5
Watchman and protection services	970	0.8
Not specified	970	0.8
Total	118,964	100

Source: Nieto 1997.
Note: Of the above, 1.1 percent are employed in the Primary Sector, while 89.5 percent are employed in the Third Sector; 15 percent earn more than 10 times the minimum wage.

particular lawyer has to consult other specialists. "A divorce case, for example," says an informant, "can have fiscal implications, or the couple might decide to donate property to their children, and that donation might be free of tax, or the divorce might be complicated by the fact that the husband beat his wife and sent her to the hospital, and that has penal implications. You have to know people involved in those types of cases in order to solve them. . . . Then one needs to have good relations with the authorities, because that can help facilitate the work. He will permit the case to be resolved sooner, or give you a chance to talk to him. . . . It is not a good idea to have a bad relationship with a judge."

"If one knows a judge and has been his friend since childhood, " said another informant, "it is easier, within the framework of friendship, to invite him to lunch and explain your case in full. This is not considered corruption, but friendship."

It is common knowledge that low-level lawyers who deal with small matters depend more on their social networks than on technical knowledge to solve problems. The use of networks, however, is extremely important among elite lawyers as well. According to a corporate lawyer, for example, foreign firms subcontract with Mexican firms because they do not have social or political contacts and do not know how to do business in Mexico. In Mexico, social know-how is just as important as social know-who. "Business here is done differently. You need to know whom to deal with; the moral solidity of a potential partner. If you are going to do business with the government, you need to know how the government acts. . . . In Mexico, political corruption exists, but in the form of social contacts. If you have a friend who is a friend of a government officer who makes decisions regarding contracts, you might get the contract. . . . You can't do that with foreign clients, because if they catch you, they'll make a big scandal."

Informal Transactions

In Mexico, it is considered normal practice to give small *renumeraciones* or *mordidas* to poorly paid public clerks (administrative personnel, secretaries, etc.) in order to speed up the paperwork. These tips or gratuities are not classified as corruption, but it is important to know how to offer them, and how much to offer. "Since there is a long queue to get copies, for instance, it helps to give a tip to the clerk so as to have him rush it for you." One of the most common practices before recent restraints were imposed on the tribunals was the misplacing of the file by the clerks, so that one's client had more time to complete a procedure.

Large payments to political actors used to be, according to public opinion, a common practice. Now things have changed, said one corporation lawyer: "You used to have to know how to give a million dollars to a politician. . . . Now you have to know how to deliver your 'sales pitch' or convince him of your project with reasons, such as the political and economic advantages of introducing a big productive enterprise into the country. One role of the firm is to help the project succeed in the most transparent manner possible."

There also exists a more flagrant practice of corruption—informal payment for a legal service—that also requires certain formalities to be followed and a certain know-how, including which judges are approachable. Every judge has a reputation, and it is known which ones are willing to accept payment for his or her favors.

The question of professional ethics becomes, therefore, a complex one. A good lawyer is the one who wins the case for his or her client. This has two moral implications for the litigant: First, he or she should not question whether the client is right or wrong. The lawyer is morally blind in the sense that he or she could be helping "evil" to win. Second, given the priority mentioned, the lawyer may consider it justifiable to turn to unethical practices, such as bribery and favoritism, to mention the most common. Important high-level firms might prevent individual lawyers from using graft practices directly by hiring low-level practitioners ad hoc (called *coyotes*). However, as far as social relations are concerned, the question is, should we consider the use of social relations a corrupt practice even if, by not using them, the client may lose his or her case vis-à-vis a less "touchy" practitioner?

When asked whether the word *honesty* applies to lawyers, one informant—an academic lawyer—answered, "By definition I don't believe so. What is the lawyer's role? To defend his or her client. On the other hand, the law is a corpus to be interpreted. It is not a dogmatic corpus. And each side interprets it to his or her convenience, for the correct benefit of one's client. A good lawyer is one who knows how to present a good juridical argument, so as to convince a judge that the interpretation he or she is proposing is *the* correct interpretation. Hence, to talk about honesty is very relative, as it depends whose side I am on. From an operational point of view, there is always the problem of contradictory argumentation. That is the essence of this business. So, how do you establish your professional prestige? If you are a good arguer, you do serious work, you are convincing and you get efficient results. . . . Many lawyers do not know how to defend a case, and try to fix everything under the table. That means that there is a difference between good lawyers and corrupt lawyers—those are the ones that win their cases by a lot of money. In other words, a good lawyer is one that can win cases by good argumentation."

This quotation shows the ambiguity that exists in the practice of law, in Mexico and elsewhere. To be a good lawyer implies defending the interest of the client, even if from a truly legal point of view that client is wrong, or guilty. Lawyers are clearly able to distinguish when they are defending a case through corrupt practices (graft) and when their success is based on knowledge and ability for argumentation. What is less evident is the peer judgment that is placed upon the use of social capital (connections). We did not find a clear attitude toward the issue. This fact makes us think that there is a relatively tolerant view toward the practice, which, after all, is based on a different moral system: loyalty toward relatives and friends.

The Opening-up of International Practice of Law in Mexico: Changes and New Generations

Mexico closed its doors to international law after the Revolution of 1910. During the revolutionary process, two currents of thought evolved. One was a theoretical nationalistic ideology that advocated isolating the country in order to concentrate on national values. By closing the Mexican territorial juridical system, cases could only be resolved through the application of Mexican law. As an example, the nationalization of the oil industry was carried out thanks to a law specially created for that purpose. The second current was a pragmatic attitude on behalf of the leaders of the country, who realized that Mexico had to answer to the claims presented by foreign companies against damages caused by the revolutionary process, particularly when countries such as the United States, Holland, and England began to get involved. As a result, international mixed commissions were created.

These two currents, theoretical and pragmatic, kept the Mexican juridical system isolated until 1975. During that time, the postrevolutionary governments did not want to join the international game and become the object of criticism. As a result, Mexico was the last Latin American country to accept the practice of private international law, other than a few international firms established in Mexico to advise foreign enterprises on how to invest in Mexico (always according to Mexican law).

In 1975, Mexico participated for the first time in a conference on private international law, which included international contracts, family concerns (including adoptions and weddings), and even international criminal law. Consequently, and for the first time, Mexico ratified eight international conventions in private matters. In 1985 Mexico joined GATT, and in 1986 the *apertura económica* (the economic opening-up of the country) began. As an example of the result and speed of this *apertura* process, we may note that before 1978 Mexico had ratified only two conventions on private international law, and since 1978 fifty have been ratified. This explosion implies the integration of Mexico into the international context in the practice of law. Along with this, many large Mexican firms have begun to practice law internationally, not only in matters of foreign investment, but also in the legal aspects of exportation (which has grown enormously), mainly in the area of contracts. According to one international lawyer, "the Mexican trade operators are exporting more and more every day, and they need to know how to do it, what kind of contracts they have to make. The contracts must include arbitration clauses not directed to Mexican tribunals, but to be submitted unto international commercial forums."

The training of lawyers at the National University of Mexico followed the original postrevolutionary nationalistic ideology. The regime's intent was to modernize the country by supporting a national industrialization project (import substitution) centered in the cities. This project promoted social mobility and the creation of new middle classes, through a large educational effort and the creation of middle-class jobs by both industry and the state apparatus. The state was perceived not only as the agent for organizing society, but also as a market for middle-class jobs related to social policies, such as education and health. This helped enlarge the job market, particularly for university students and graduates.

The introduction of neoliberal policies in the 1980s, the country's admittance into the international market, and the shrinking of the state apparatus have had a clear effect on the educated middle classes and on the previously protected family enterprises. A new group of technocrats (known as the *técnicos*) has appeared and taken command of elite positions within the state apparatus. At the same time, the state apparatus has closed its doors to the traditional middle-level professionals. This has created a division between these traditional practitioners (trained in national universities, as described above) and the new "globalized-transnationalized" group, which stands for firms that have teamed up with financial institutions of foreign investors (López Ayllón 1997). Furthermore, governmental institutions felt a need for technically trained young lawyers. These young lawyers are confronting the traditional ones, who previously had a monopoly on the private professional field of activities and now feel threatened by this new breed of technical lawyers. The traditional lawyers also feel threatened by the NAFTA agreement and by the possibility that American firms, together with the new breed of Mexican lawyers, may compete for foreign clients and win.

One of the first manifestations of the current process of globalization is the opening-up of the international market. This circumstance has boosted the importance of possessing new technical knowledge in several professions. Currently, a greater technological knowledge is needed to complement or support the political management of countries generally. In the case of Mexico, new demands are being placed upon careers such as economics and law, due to factors such as the NAFTA agreement and the recent opening-up of the legal profession. Thus, the different professions have been affected internally, with new values and knowledge being introduced even while traditional mentalities continue to dominate the majority of the guild. "When the political elites were all lawyers, they understood each other, because they were educated with the same concepts regarding the use, as well as the symbolic and political values, of the law. When the economists arrived, wanting to change the economic model, the first thing they found was that the lawyers kept telling them 'this cannot be done because of the constitution'. The economists said 'of course it can be done'; they don't perceive the law as an essential value, but as an instrumental value. Some lawyers of the new type begin to view the law without taboos and with no secret values, but in a different way. And this is a new elite that comes with the changing generation, since about ten years ago."

One informant who embraces the new mentality stated, "When one lives in a closed economic system, as we did before, there is little need for communication with the outside world, particularly juridical communication. We had a legal system that was completely shut off, impermeable, and self-sufficient. The moment the *apertura* happened, some sectors of the legal profession introduced new elements and expectations, new practices related to the new social uses of the law. A change took place. At least in the sectors that have more contact with the outside world, there has been a progressive modification of professional practices: the practice of law is becoming more technical and less relational. Before, the practice of law was fundamentally based on social relations. The technical element was important, but much more important were [personal] relations: which friends do I have in the government? Who will be the judge? Today, at least in certain sectors, the practice of law is beginning to function in a different manner, because the activity has to be regulated by technical norms. In certain sectors, such as investments, contracts, the financial sector, trade, customs—in other words, all sectors related to the *apertura*—the function of the law had to change, in its professional practice, towards more technical lawyers who base their practice less on relationships and more on knowledge."

As a result, there is a new generation of lawyers, between the ages of twenty-eight and forty, who already feel the need to be trained in ways that differ radically from those of past generations. This has introduced a struggle within the juridical field, in which traditional lawyers (mostly trained at UNAM) feel displaced by young technicians with new ideas and concepts. Typically, these young lawyers did not study at UNAM, but in one of three small private universities (Escuela Libre de Derecho, ITAM, Universidad Iberoamericana).

Thus, the UNAM Law School, which continues to have the largest enrollment in the country, is losing ground in the training of the new elites, particularly the technocratic state elite. As a result, there is a displacement of potentially high-level students from the UNAM toward two or three small private universities. Therefore, while most political career–oriented networks are still being developed at UNAM, the technocratic elite networks are currently being created, for the most part, in a few private universities. Private university graduates, who were once recruited almost exclusively into the private market, are now being recruited in vast numbers by the public sector. Graduates of the Escuela Libre de Derecho, for example, took control of the Banco de México and from there moved on to the juridical departments of the secretary of treasury and other key offices within the state apparatus. These new lawyers are characterized not only by their formal training but also by their social origins and their personal social networks. In fact, the small minority of UNAM graduates that do belong to this new elite do so because they share the same social origins and social networks with the elite private school graduates.

Students of the technocratic type—who have gone to private universities, come from the upper middle classes, and have traveled abroad for specialization—attain high-level positions without having to climb up the bureaucratic ladder. They do, however, also enter the state apparatus through other types of networks, mainly created during their postgraduate training in American universities (Lomnitz and Morán 1976). A young economist who has no political networks, for example, but owes his advanced position to his technical knowledge, will in turn bring in lawyers or economists from other networks. What he looks for are people who are technically able, quick learners, can speak English, and are unburdened by political commitments. As a result, a new technical elite network of young people, independent of the traditional political apparatus, is created.

These technical groups tend to become politicized, since because of their function and position in the government they must rally the support of other political groups. Due to their own personal and social characteristics, however, their members usually do not aspire to remain in the public sector for the rest of their lives. By having studied mostly in the United States, they have acquired knowledge that allows them to enter both the public and the private spheres. In other words, a young lawyer who has received postgraduate training abroad may be recruited, through various different networks, directly to a high-level technocratic position, fulfill a number of years of technical service in the government, and eventually establish him- or herself in private practice.

As one informant concludes, "the Mexican lawyer has become Americanized, meaning internationalized. . . . This implies learning English, learning legal terms in English, and possessing a more cosmopolitan education. As a result, the UNAM students are lagging behind, covering the national fields, particularly as civil servants of the state apparatus, and as individual or family-firm liberal professionals."

Conclusion

In this essay, we have sought to describe the traditional relational aspect of the practice of law in Mexico, as it is embedded in its cultural configurations. We tried to show how a practitioner's success depends not only on his or her formal knowledge of the law, but also to a large degree on what we call an informal ability to construct new social exchange networks. Exchanges of favors are based on reciprocity and patronage among relatives, acquaintances, and friends, as well as a cultural knowledge of how to hand out marketlike payments (corruption) to obtain services needed to successfully complete a case.

It is important to stress the fact that the use of *guanxi* (relations) is considered the informal aspect of the practice of law and generally accepted as necessary. It is much less criticized than corrupt market practices, the existence of which is shamefully recognized by everybody. This acceptance is partly due to the fact that lawyers' ethics are based on loyalty to the client, which may justify the use of social practices in order to solve a case favorably. Moreover, social exchange networks find acceptance because they function through a deeper morality, one that upholds primary loyalties to one's kin and friends vis-à-vis impersonal bureaucratic rules. Thus, it is the professional loyalty of the lawyer toward the client, along with the personal loyalties of others toward the lawyer, that allows the informal exchange of favors.

Traditionally, most lawyers in Mexico were trained at the National University of Mexico, UNAM. For most of this century they concentrated their practice on a series of functions within a closed system characterized by its nationalistic ideology. During their training period, UNAM students all followed (and continue to follow) the same curriculum in order to learn the formal principles of Mexican law. At the same time, outside the classrooms, they learn about informal personal practices such as the construction and use of social relations. Polanyi's three forms of exchange are the basis of these informal practices: reciprocity among equals, redistribution within vertical patron-client relations, and, finally, market exchange.

Graduating lawyers are recruited into the system according to their socioeconomic level and their social networks within the levels and sectors that compose the Mexican state (public, private, and labor sectors). The fact that they have all shared the same training allows each lawyer to have contacts with other lawyers working in different sectors and levels of society, whom they can contact when necessary. An exchange of favors of this kind rarely occurs between graduates of private universities and those of UNAM, unless they happen to be personally connected through kinship or some other way.

In the last decades many changes have begun to take place in the country, both internally and as a result of global tendencies. Mexico has opened up its frontiers, and a "new modernity" (López Ayllón 1997: 317) is emerging. Within the legal system, particularly important changes, which López Ayllón has called a "silent revolution," have taken place. This is reflected in the rise of a new legal technocratic elite—closely related to the rise of an elite of economists—that is displacing the traditional political elite trained at UNAM.

There is an increasing demand for a new type of a highly specialized legal technician. This new breed of lawyer needs to be more cosmopolitan and open to the outside world, must speak English and understand other legal systems, and requires specialized technical expertise, particularly in areas of international trade such as investments, contracts, financing, trade practices, and customs. This new elite is currently being trained in two or three private universities in which upper-middle-class students enroll. Thanks to their own background, these students possess a cosmopolitan education, come from private bilingual high schools, have traveled abroad since they were teenagers, and so on. The private universities have introduced a number of courses in economy and business administration into their curricula, with the idea of preparing their graduates specifically for private practice. Ironically, though, many of these very graduates, after spending time in highly specialized training at exclusive universities abroad, form the technocratic elite that currently rules the state. Thus, as Dezalay and Garth have pointed out, the opening-up of the market has produced a certain convergence of two traditionally separate elites: private and public. After some time, however, these high-level technocrats tend to abandon public administration and return to private practice.

Although members of this new elite require specialized technical knowledge for their law practice (especially those involved in international law), the use of social networks continues to be necessary in order to obtain positions and perform successfully within them. Obviously, these networks are not the traditional ones made up of UNAM classmates and professors, but rather networks established among their classmates abroad. The nickname "the Chicago boys" exemplifies this phenomenon of clique formation among Latin Americans trained in certain universities in the United States. Because they are an elite, their use of networks corresponds to a higher-level exchange of information and services.

How far-reaching are these changes of practice with respect to all members of the profession? We believe that the process of globalization, which in the case of Mexico has brought about internal neoliberal economic policies (including the privatization and shrinking of the state apparatus), has had a negative effect on the economic situation of the new and growing middle classes (García Salord 1997; Lomnitz and Melnick 1991). As a result, profound political changes are currently taking place in Mexico—changes that, while positive from a democratic point of view (e.g., the 1994 and 1997 elections), imply a questioning of those same neoliberal economic policies that produced the present crisis for the majority of the population. The middle-class sectors, who in the present case are represented by most UNAM trained lawyers, are precisely the ones defending their traditional class interests against the "modern" group of technically trained elite lawyers, who in most cases come from well-to-do families and private universities.

In conclusion, we agree with Dezalay and Garth that this new situation is erasing the borders between the public and private elites, as private technicians are recruited into elite state positions, but eventually can return to private practice. At the same time, these changes have produced a new division between the traditional nationalist middle-class practitioners and the new technocratic elite. The new elite bases its practice on strict knowledge of the law and imported technical knowledge of economics and business administration. The traditional lawyers, on the other hand, base their practice not only on their knowledge of Mexican law, but also on informal means, complementing their skills with the traditional administration of social relations. In both cases, a combination of technical formal knowledge and skills regarding the upkeep and use of social relations is needed, but in different proportions. Moreover, the formal knowledge of each group is of a different nature: one based on the internal constitution of Mexico, the other on international practices. Finally, their social networks are based on different social class relations.

NOTES

1. As we will describe later on, these private universities produce most of the new technocratic elite.

2. The following considerations on UNAM and life careers are taken from Lomnitz 1977.

3. The department of statistics at UNAM performs a yearly survey of the first-semester students. The criteria used to aggregate data vary each year. This explains the discontinuity in the tables that we present here.

4. According to a knowledgeable informant, a large proportion of lawyers do not enter the labor market as lawyers, but in other activities such as taxi drivers, insurance salesmen, and so on. The census of 1990 shows that nearly 20 percent work as technicians, teachers, manual workers, salesmen, etc. (in other words, the informal sector; see Nieto 1997).

REFERENCES

Barnes, J. A. 1954. Class committee in a Norwegian island parish. *Human Relations* 7:39–58.

Camp, Roderic. 1976. El sistema Mexicano y las decisiones sobre el personal político. *Foro Internacional* 27:137–51.

———. 1995. El cabinete de Zedillo: ¿Continuidad, cambios o revolución? *Este País* 51:46–54.

———. 1996. *El reclutamiento político en México*. Mexico City: Siglo XXI.

Covo, Malena. 1990. *Apuntes para el analisis de la trayectoria de una generación universitaria*. Mexico City: ENEP, Acatlain.

De la Madrid, Miguel. 1993. Prólogo. *El papel del abogado*, ix–xii. Mexico City: Porrúa/UNAM.

Dezalay, Yves, and Bryant Garth. 1996. *Building the law and putting the state into play: International strategies among Mexico's divided elite*. ABF Working Paper no. 9509.

———. 1997. Law, lawyers and social capital: 'Rule of Law' versus relational capitalism. *Social and Legal Studies* 6:137–69.

DGESII a. *Perfil de aspirantes y asignados a bachillerato, téxnico en enfermería y licenciatura de la UNAM*. Mexico City: UNAM, several years.

García Salord, Susana. 1997. *Estudio socio-antropológico de la clase media en México: El capital social y el capital cultural como espacios de constitución simbólica de las clases sociales*. Doctoral dissertation (mimeo).

Grindel, Merilee. 1977. Patrons and clients in the bureaucracy: Career networks in Mexico. *Latin American Research Review* 12:37–66.

Heinz, John P., and Edward O. Laumann. 1994. *Chicago lawyers: The social structure of the bar*. Evanston, Ill.: Northwestern University Press/American Bar Foundation.

Leinhardt, Samuel. 1977. *Social networks: A developing paradigm*. New York: Academic Press.

Lomnitz, Larissa. 1977. Conflict and mediation in a Latin American university. *Journal of Interamerican Studies and World Affairs* 19:315–38.

————. 1982. Horizontal and vertical relations and the social structure of urban Mexico. *Latin American Research Review* 17:51–74.

Lomnitz, Larissa, and Ana Melnik. 1991. *The Chilean middle class: A struggle for survival in the face of neoliberalism.* Boulder: Lynne-Rienner.

Lomnitz, Larissa, and A. Morán. 1976. Estudio a Mexicanos graduados en el extranjero. *Revista del Conacyt* 2:45–50.

Lomnitz, Larissa, and Marisol Pérez-Lizaur. 1971. *A Mexican elite family 1820–1980.* Princeton: Princeton University Press.

López, Cámara. 1974. Hacia una concepción dialéctica de la autonomía universitaria. *Deslinde* 53.

López Ayllón, Sergio. 1997. *Las transformaciones del sistema jurídico y los significados sociales del derecho en México. La encrucijada entre modernidad y tradición.* Mexico City: UNAM/IIJ.

Meyer, P. 1962. Migrancy and the study of Africans in town. *American Anthropologist* 64:576–92.

Mitchell, J. C. 1969. *Social networks in urban situations.* Manchester: Manchester University Press.

Nieto, Gerardo. 1997. *Agenda estadística del orientador 1997.* Mexico City: UNAM/Dirección General de Orientación Vocacional.

Pérez Perdomo, Rogelio. 1996. De la justicia y otros demonios. In María E. Boza y Rogelio Pérez Perdomo, *Seguridad jurídica y competitividad.* Caracas: IESA.

Polanyi, Karl. 1957. The economy as an instituted process. In K. Polanyi, C. M. Arensberg, and H. N. Pearson, eds., *Trade and market in the early empires.* New York: Free Press.

Smith, Peter. 1979. *Labyrinths of power: Political recruitment in twentieth-century Mexico.* Princeton: Princeton University Press.

Soberanes, José Luis. 1993. El abogado como investigador. *El papel del abogado.* Mexico City: Porrúa.

The Discovery of Law:
Political Consequences in the
Argentine Case

Catalina Smulovitz

The prior two essays focused especially on strong domestic institutions quite resistant to change. Neither the practice of law in Mexico nor the faculties of law in Japan have moved very much in response to international pressures. This essay provides a similar story with respect to the judiciary in Argentina. This case study by Catalina Smulovitz, a political scientist at the University of Torcuato di Tella in Buenos Aires, highlights the impact of international factors on the historically very weak role of the courts in the Argentine state.

In particular, in the wake of the human rights movement in the 1970s, the democratization of the 1980s and 1990s, and international patterns of "judicialization of conflicts," Argentines began to expect much more from law and the courts. The trials of the military junta especially highlighted the new possibilities for redressing rights through the courts. As the essay shows, the pressures and hopes have not produced effective improvements in the judiciary. The role of the judiciary has become a matter of domestic political debate, but the practical results of the new focus have been an intense politicization and a "mediatization" of the courts. The courts have escalated political fighting—using the media to promote themselves and their positions as well—rather than providing a forum for resolving conflicts.

In the Argentine context, therefore, where political compromise has often been difficult to obtain, all the entities of the state have historically been objects of intense political fighting. The essay shows that the results of the domestication of the pressure to conform to a new legal orthodoxy have so far not provided the kind of political and economic stability and pre-

dictability that proponents of reform have imagined. The author suggests that the future is still uncertain.

In Argentina, less than fifteen years ago, rights were systematically violated by the state and judicial power was regarded as an unreliable institution for resolving state-society conflicts. At present two perplexing developments can be observed. On the one hand, political conflicts and social demands that used to be "solved" in the political arena are now transformed into judicial contests and into demands by the media. On the other, opinion polls register a continuous decrease in the prestige of judicial institutions (see table 1).

This new situation poses a series of questions: (1) Why has a society with a political system that had good historical reasons to disregard the judicial system and the law begun to employ them? (2) What are the political consequences of the discovery of judicial procedures? (3) How has this process changed the relationship between citizens and the law and between citizens and the political system? (4) Has the fact that citizens are now relating to the political scene through legal claims changed the process of representation? (5) What are the consequences of this displacement from the political scene to the courts and from the courts to the media? These are some of the questions to be addressed in this essay.

The Discovery of Law

Let us consider our first question: why has a society with a political system that had good historical reasons[1] to disregard the judicial system and the law begun to employ them? In the early 1980s, Argentine society and its political system seemed to discover the benefits of the law. This acknowledgment was costly. Only after the damage caused by state terrorism became evident was it possible to conclude that the rule of law was useful for settling conflicts and avoiding public and private violence. Conversely, the accusations of human rights violations demonstrated the way in which the rhetoric of law can be both a mobilizing and subversive force.

The liberalization process initiated after the Malvinas/Falklands

War was characterized by the prominence achieved by human rights issues.[2] In that context, the establishment of the rule of law became not only a demand for justice but also a political program. Trials and legal punishment for those responsible for state terrorism were the main issues of the democratic transition. To satisfy the demand for justice that had set the tone of the electoral campaign, the first democratic government designed a strategy oriented toward a limited self-judgment by the military for the human rights crimes committed during the military administration. The government's plan included the repeal of the so-called Law of Self-Amnesty and the enactment of a new law that was to specify both the scope of penal liability and the jurisdiction in which the trials were to be held. In the early stages of the Alfonsín administration, therefore, Congress repealed the military's self-amnesty law and sanctioned a reform of the Military Code. This law gave the Supreme Council of the Armed Forces initial jurisdiction to prosecute military personnel, established an automatic appeal mechanism in civilian courts, and precluded the indiscriminate use of the concept of due obedience in cases involving aberrant crimes.

In September 1984, after the Supreme Council of the Armed Forces decided to absolve the ex-military commanders of any criminal responsibility, the Buenos Aires Federal Court of Appeal took the case into its own hands. This act had several consequences: it reintroduced the judiciary to the center of the human rights conflict, and—given the prominence this issue had achieved during the transition—it gave judicial power a strategic place in the political scene. The judiciary had to satisfy society's demand for justice, and, at the same time, it had to show that the rule of law was an authoritative and legitimate mechanism for solving political conflicts.

The trial of the junta commanders was the first opportunity for the judicial system to show its capacity to mediate political conflict and its autonomy from political power. The spectacular character of the trial,

TABLE 1. Confidence in the Judiciary: Survey Results (in percentages)

	1984	1991	1995	1996
High and medium confidence	57	26	26	11
None and low confidence	42	75	74	89

Source: Gallup. La Nación, November 3, 1996.

in which weak citizens held powerful individuals accountable, helped to build the image of a judiciary that could discipline the powerful and defend the rights of the weak. The event acquired dramatic overtones due to the type of confrontation and to the fact that its development was observed not only by the victims and the victimizers but also by the national and international media. The public character of the hearings and the continuous journalistic reports of the trial had a double consequence: they assured the relatively autonomous operation of the court, and they gave public exposure to the benefits of legal procedures.

Independent from the opinions that the sentences generated,[3] the trial of the ex-commanders allowed legal logic to transform historical information into legal evidence, producing in the process legitimated information about the Argentine past. The legal discourse was able to order the past and to give credibility to the witnesses' stories becoming, in turn, an effective mechanism for a historical and political judgment of the dictatorial regime. Therefore, the decision of the Buenos Aires Federal Court made the courts the stage upon which the promise of the newborn democracy was to be fulfilled. The political impact and high visibility of this decision began to transform perceptions of the traditionally subordinate role of the judiciary. Judicial powers and abilities were reexamined. As a result of this "spectacular" and "unexpected" public event, the conservative judiciary appeared to become a place where the rights of citizens could be realized.

In the following months other highly publicized trials and judicial decisions claimed the attention of the citizenry: the extradition of López Rega,[4] the threat of resignation by judges of the Federal Court of Buenos Aires,[5] a Supreme Court decision compelling the government to pay overdue retirement pensions,[6] the massive initiation of human rights cases after the approval of the Punto Final Law[7] (Ley de Punto Final), the oral trials of members of the military who participated in the Aeroparque[8] uprising, the trial of an ex-police chief for violations of human rights, and the public trial of a famous world champion boxer. All these trials and public judicial interventions exposed the citizenry to the disciplinary and equalizing capacity of judicial procedures. The central effect of these events was the social revelation of an institutional mechanism for the resolution of disputes that hitherto "the silent propriety of the judges" had hidden.

However, this theatrical entry of judicial procedures into the public scene brought about several misunderstandings. It obscured the fact that by chance those trials had evolved by oral procedures, and with a speed that was unusual for the Argentine judiciary. Some people were tried under military procedures, and the boxer's case had taken place in a provincial state that admitted oral procedures for criminal cases. Thus, the first misunderstanding was the appearance of relatively efficient judicial procedures. This confusion derived not only from the spectacular character of the cases but also from the use of exceptional[9] oral procedures. This error prevented the acknowledgment of the judiciary's real difficulty in confronting the growth of a litigious system that maintained ancient procedural codes and did not renew its working procedures.

The spectacular entrance of the judiciary into the political scene had another consequence: suddenly the fulfillment of the promise of justice seemed to depend on the conversion of some judges into loquacious activists. Some judges abandoned the low profile they had previously cultivated and appeared to become advocates of civic causes. This activist style contributed to the credibility of the system's effectiveness (*Periodista* 1988). However, this initial enthusiasm deferred a diagnosis and debate about the real institutional capacities of the judiciary. In addition, when expectations were left dissatisfied, enthusiasm devolved into skepticism.

As another consequence of this initial enthusiasm for the abilities of the judiciary and its judges, a process of judicialization of conflicts[10] appeared. In the Argentine case, this process entailed the appearance of social and individual actors who opted to submit the definition of the legitimacy of their petitions to the courts. In the past some of these conflicts would have been solved without the intervention of an external third party. A corporatist logic—in which parties confront each other through the exercise of political resources—used to be the chosen route for conflict resolution. Disputes among army officers about the illegal sale of airplane parts, disputes among union members in regard to pension funds, and demands of army officers in relation to the tax exemptions of their salaries are just a few examples of this new process of the judicialization of conflicts. Increasing litigation is not the only indicator of this phenomenon. However, the fact that the number of initiated legal disputes has increased consistently across different jurisdictions and chambers in recent years must be considered a significant indicator of this trend (see tables 2, 3, and 4).

The process of judicialization of conflicts can also be observed in

TABLE 2. Total Number of Files Received by the National Judiciary, by the National Supreme Court, and by the Federal District and Interior Courts and Appeal Courts

	National Judiciary[a]		National Supreme Court		Federal District Courts and Appeals Courts		Interior Tribunals and Chambers	
	Number of Files	Annual Variation	Number of Files	Annual Variation	Number of Files	Annual Variation	Number of Files	Annual Variation
1991	621,613		5,332		473,710		142,371	
1992	681,534	9.64%	6,546	22.77%	446,101	−5.83%	158,887	11.60%
1993	779,194	14.33%	24,507	274.38%	589,968	32.25%	164,719	3.67%
1994	1,016,202	30.42%	36,657	49.58%	690,884	17.11%	288,661	75.24%
1995	1,070,399	5.33%	16,880	−53.95%	736,502	6.60%	305,334	5.78%

Source: Estadística de la Corte Suprema de la Nación.

[a]The total number of files received by the National Judiciary includes the sum of the total number of files received by: Corte Suprema de la Nación, Cámara de Casación Penal (si corresponde), Tribunales Orales de la Capital Federal (si corresponde) Juzgados de Ejecución Penal, Fueros de Capital Federal (Cámaras), Juzgados de Capital Federal, Tribunales Orales en lo Criminal Federal del Interior, Tribunales Orales del Interior de Ejecución, Cámaras de Jurisdicciones del Interior, and Juzgados de Jurisdicciones del Interior.

TABLE 3. Total Number of Files Received by the Interior Courts and Appeal Courts

	Paraná	Annual Variation	Rosario	Annual Variation	Posadas	Annual Variation	Resistencia	Annual Variation	Tucumán	Annual Variation
1991	3,642		13,965		4,703		9,002		12,504	
1992	5,521	51.59%	16,522	18.31%	5,096	8.36%	10,522	16.89%	13,795	10.32%
1993	5,400	-2.19%	19,520	18.15%	5,560	9.11%	13,426	27.60%	10,008	-27.45%
1994	12,041	122.98%	40,511	107.54%	10,060	80.94%	19,464	44.97%	16,212	61.99%
1995	12,746	5.85%	44,403	9.61%	8,668	-13.84%	17,847	-8.31%	18,095	11.61%

	Cordoba	Annual Variation	Mendoza	Annual Variation	Gral Roca	Annual Variation	Cornodoro Rivadavia	Annual Variation	Bahia Blanca	Annual Variation
1991	9,330		12,287		4,932		6,417		4,642	
1992	13,008	39.42%	13,878	12.95%	5,776	17.11%	8,358	30.25%	4,425	4.67%
1993	16,133	24.02%	13,494	-2.77%	7,392	27.98%	11,362	35.94%	7,375	66.67%
1994	29,017	79.86%	33,104	145.32%	13,811	86.84%	13,775	21.24%	11,783	59.77%
1995	38,090	31.27%	28,491	-13.93%	16,190	17.23%	12,703	-7.78%	12,237	3.85%

	San Martin	Annual Variation	La Plata	Annual Variation	Total Juzgados del Interior	Annual Variation
1991	18,803		28,065		123,292	
1992	24,080	28.06%	22,708	-19.09%	143,689	12.00%
1993	21,782	-9.54%	18,709	-17.91%	150,161	4.50%
1994	36,891	69.36%	40,492	116.43%	277,161	84.58%
1995	49,341	33.75%	46,523	14.89%	305,334	10.16%

Source: Estadística de la Corte

TABLE 4. Total Number of Files Received by the Federal District Courts and Appeal Courts

Year	Civilian Courts and Appeals Courts	Annual Variation	Administrative Courts and Appeal Courts (fuero contencioso administrativo)	Annual Variation	Commercial Courts and Appeal Courts	Annual Variation
1991	98,581		16,670		51,645	
1992	132,238	34.14%	26,694	61.75%	59,517	15.24%
1993	137,371	3.88%	34,890	29.39%	83,616	40.49%
1994	139,765	1.74%	79,009	126.45%	102,382	22.44%
1995	157,763	12.88%	112,034	41.80	136,257	33.09%

Source: Estadística de la Corte

other areas where citizens' claims and petitions take place. In this sense, it is worthwhile to consider the way in which citizens have related to two ombudsman agencies that were created recently,[11] as well as ways in which citizens qua consumers have exercised their rights. In 1994 the Defensoría del Pueblo de la Nación (a national ombudsman office) received 779 claims in only 75 days. In all of 1995 it received 7,511. This implies that between 1994 and 1995 the number of daily claims received by the Defensoría del Pueblo de la Nación doubled. The record of the municipal ombudsman, the Controladuría General Comunal, shows a similar trend[12] (see table 5). The behavior of citizens qua consumers also shows an increase in the number of claims. The statistics of several regulatory councils of recently privatized public enterprises, as well as the data registered by the most important consumer association in Argentina, confirm this tendency (see table 6). These data show not only an increase in citizens' activities but also that their behavior and claims are made and based on the rhetoric of legal rights. In other words, it seems that the judicialization process has extended to other areas where citizens' activities are taking place.

One other factor must be considered in order to understand the changes in society's perception of the Argentine judiciary. In most cases the process of judicialization has taken place along with an increase in the media coverage of conflicts. The media's discovery of the judiciary

TABLE 5. Claims Received by the National Ombudsman Agency (Defensoría General de la Nación) and by the Municipal Ombudsman Agency (Oficina del Ombudsman Municipal)

	Claims Initiated at the National Ombudsman Agency	Claims Initiated at the Municipal Ombudsman Agency	Annual Variation
1988		1,021	
1989		934	−8.5
1990		1,058	13.2
1991		1,511	42.8
1992[a]		848	−43.8
1993		1,478	74.2
1994	779	2,851	92.8
1995	7,511	2,713	−4.8

Source: Defensor del Pueblo de la Nación. Informe Anual 1994 and 1995. Controladuriá General Municipal.
[a]In 1992 the permanence of the head of the Municipal Agency was questioned.

TABLE 6. Claims and Inquiries Received by the Customer Offices of the National Transport Commission (Comisión Nacional del Transporte Automotor, CONTA), by the Gas Regulatory Commission (Ente Nacional Regulador del Gas, ENARGAS), by the Electricity Regulatory Commission (Ente Regulador de le Electricidad, ENRE), and by the Communication Regulatory Commission (Comisión Nacional de Telecommunicaciones, CNT)

Year	National Transportation Commission[a]	Annual Variation	Gas Regulatory Commission	Annual Variation	Electricity Regulatory Commission	Annual Variation	Communication Regulatory Commission[b]	Annual Variation
1993	3,207		6,029		5,554		29,129	
1994	8,855	176.1	28,070	365.5	16,371	294.7	31,060	6.6
1995	37,979	328.8	68,740	144.8	11,255	−68.7	16,052	48.3

Source: CONTA, ENARGAS, ENTRE, CNT.

[a]Including claims regarding public transportation at the federal district and at the Gran Buenos Aires and claims regarding long distance public transportation.

[b]Including claims received by ADELCO until May 31, 1995.

had a somewhat bastard origin. Although controlling public power is an unexpected outcome of increasing media attention and one that cannot be underestimated, it was not the will to oversee public acts but rather the theatrical lure of the judicial genre that explains the increasing interest the media has shown in the operation of the judicial system. As Oscar Landi and Inés Gonzalez have asserted, the structure of the judicial genre, where mysteries, crimes, and melodramas converge, lent itself to appropriation by the press and television (1995). In most cases there are heroes, villains, and ultimately a knight in shining armor. Even though media interest can be attributed to the seduction of mystery rather than to public or civic virtues, the result was the media's discovery of an arena in which a silent power was at work. When reporters began to watch what was going on in the courthouse, the hidden face of power was revealed. Thus, the media, and some journalists in particular, became public prosecutors and defenders of the public interest.

The media discovered the judiciary, and citizens subsequently discovered the power of the media to petition for their rights, to accelerate juridical decisions, and/or to condemn presumed or real violators of the law. Thus, when the media revealed itself as an effective mechanism for controlling and accelerating public decisions, citizens used this discovery to access an alternative route, diverting attention from the public authorities and informally passing judgment on suspected illegal activities (Peyrú and Ciamberlani 1992).

Finally, there was a series of institutional initiatives oriented toward the *aggiornamento* of the judicial institutions coupled with a number of decisions that restricted the autonomy of the judiciary. During the administration of the Union Cívica Radical, judicial policy concentrated on the update of the legal codes.[13] In addition, a series of important projects were sent to Congress, although they were not approved. Among them were the creation of a Family Court, the creation of a small claims court, and the modification of the criminal justice procedures. Some of these projects were later approved during the Menem administration in watered-down versions. One of Menem's ministers of justice sent projects oriented toward the introduction of plea bargaining in certain criminal procedures, the reform of the parole system,[14] the strengthening of the judiciary's budgetary autarchy,[15] and the introduction of public hearings in nomination procedures.[16]

This *aggiornamento* of judicial institutions took place simultaneously with a series of measures that restricted judicial autonomy and citizens' capacity to petition for granted rights. This second trend can be observed in a number of laws and "extraordinary decrees"[17] that reverse judicial decisions or limit the ability of the judiciary to recognize certain rights. It has also made itself apparent with political interventions in the appointment of the functionaries in charge of watchdog agencies. In addition, functionaries of the executive branch have explicitly advocated the need politically to control the decisions of the courts,[18] and a law increasing the number of Supreme Court judges was passed in order to control the Supreme Court.

Given the prominence of the judicial question, these attempts politically to subordinate the decisions of the courts have in turn resulted in even higher visibility and politicization of conflicts. The judicial bureaucracy has become the arena for disputes between the government and its opposition. The control of appointment, promotion, and removal of judges has become an important component of political strategies. At present, the judiciary is a political power not only because its decisions have political consequences, but also because the control of its internal organization has become the center of political struggle. These conflicts have made evident that something is at stake in the control of the judiciary that, in turn, has increased media and political attention.

This politicization has had conflicting effects. While in some cases it has promoted judicial compliance, in others it has resulted in certain judges and prosecutors exhibiting their independence. The judicialization process has thus become an instrument for individual citizens and social actors to bypass the state's ability to transform certain social conflicts into nonevents, which forces the state to intervene in disputes. Had these issues endured as political conflicts, they could have remained unresolved, as there are no institutions that compel the state to define its position. Therefore, from the perspective of civil society, the strategy of judicialization can be seen as a resource for breaking political impasses. When insurmountable difficulties prevent citizens from organizing effective collective action, the judicialization strategy allows them to protect their rights, even though this protection may not be guaranteed. However, the strategy has its drawbacks: at the same time as it allows citizens to avoid some of the difficulties collective actors confront when they have to articulate and coordinate social actions, it impels the transformation from potentially collective social actors to atomized citizens.

From the perspective of the government, this strategy can be used to delay the treatment of some controversial issues. Indeed, the judicialization of certain topics allows the government to create the image that issues brought to the courts are being considered by the public powers. However, once these disputes enter the judicial system, citizens are less able to control the development of their petitions. The government can then use the judicialization of conflicts to postpone the actual resolution of disputes. Therefore, while the judicialization of disputes appears to be an efficient path for citizens to "voice" (Hirschman 1970) their demands, for the government, it may become a means by which to control the increasingly vocal claims of the public, in addition to being a mechanism for postponing, and in some cases even eliminating, the need to take action on certain issues.

From the point of view of the political system, the attraction of the citizenry to this strategy seemed, at first, to offer one important advantage: governmental actions could appear disconnected from the actual resolution of specific conflicts. However, when the judicialization of conflicts was combined with high visibility in the media and with a large number of the cases and conflicts surrounding the government's political initiatives, the government attempted to ignore, suspend, or obstruct judicial resolutions or to restrict the citizens' ability to make claims. Signs of this governmental behavior were the creation of certain laws and "extraordinary decrees" (*decretos de necesidad y urgencia*) intended to reverse judicial decisions or to limit the capacity of the judicial power to implement the rights it had acquired. The government was also guilty of manipulating appointment procedures of administrative agencies in charge of controlling governmental activities. Specific examples include the "extraordinary" decree no. 2196/86 declaring the discontinuation of pension fund trials against the state, the Due Obedience Law,[19] the presidential pardons of 1989 and 1990, the Convertibility Law that established, insofar as it pertains to the public interest, that nobody can claim previously granted rights against the state, an increase in the number of members of the Supreme Court, the removal of the national attorney general and of members of the Accounting Office, the "promotion" of judges in charge of controversial causes and the appointment of judges to the recently created Criminal Cassation Chamber.[20]

The reversal of judicial decisions and the lack of resolution in conflict cases have not been without consequences. They have resulted in confrontations with other state powers and have made evident the attempts politically to subordinate judicial decisions. The events that followed the "Instruction to the Military Prosecutors"[21] after the sentencing of ex-military commanders and the extraordinary decree declaring the emergency of the pension system show the political cost these types of actions may have for the government. In other cases, costs to the government occurred as a consequence of the nonresolution and accumulation of well-known cases against political officials and successful entrepreneurs.[22] Therefore, the initial political benefits to be derived from the apparent willingness to discipline powerful entrepreneurs and corrupt officials were diluted when it became evident that these cases were not going to be solved due to judicial inefficiency and/or due to obstructive interventions of the executive branch.

Initially the judicialization of conflicts allowed the political power to disentangle itself from the results and to delegate responsibilities to the judiciary. However, when the nonresolution of cases, the passing of time, and the use of obstructive actions became evident, the judicialization ended, thus repoliticizing disputes and canceling the initially promising effects. The consequences of these last developments can be observed in the decreased prestige of the judiciary registered by the opinion polls.

A skeptical interpretation of these facts will take them as proof of the weakness of the transformations that have taken place, and as confirmation of the return to old traditions. However, one significant element distinguishes the current situation from past experiences: the initiatives oriented toward the obstruction of judicial procedures and the weakening of the rule of law have acquired an openly conflictual character. Examples of this new situation include the politicization of disputes surrounding rights issues, the public visibility of discussions about the institutional design of judicial power, and debates about the merits of its personnel and about its nominating procedures. Rather than a return to the past, all of these conflicts reveal that the fate of the practice of the law has become a matter of concern for the public in general and not only a topic for specialists. Therefore, and insofar as the judicial question has become part of the public agenda and an object of public scrutiny, it is to be expected that the traditional practices of political subordination will not be as easily tolerated as they have been in the past.

Next I would like to consider the consequences of the increased media attention to the judicial system. At first, it appeared to be an effective means of bypassing the difficulties that characterize access to regular juridical procedures. This seems to have been successful in a series of recent events in which citizens have made accusations through the media in order to obtain quick attention from public authorities. However, this method has raised certain problems that must be considered.

At the same time that the journalistic construction of a juridical case tells a story, it necessarily produces judgments. Therefore, independent from the intention of the reporters, many accusations published in the media automatically become public sentences. This problem arises from the fact that the main instrument of media justice is public scandal. However, the scandal needed to draw public attention to a case is simultaneously the mechanism of punishment. Consequently, when the media is effective in drawing attention to a case, it inverts the steps of the legal process; it condemns first through scandal and, at times, proves guilt afterward. At this point, however, those who were unjustly touched and sentenced by the scandal will not be able to avoid the punishment already inflicted, nor will they be able to avoid being followed by suspicion. In this situation, which in effect inverts the rules of evidence, "reasonable doubt" does not protect the accused; rather, it summarily sentences them.

It is also worth mentioning that since the scandal is also the punishment, the media's procedures cannot determine penalties proportional to the presumed violations. The scandal and the resulting ostracism are diffuse and incontrovertible outcomes. Consequently, if the formal outcomes do not conform to the sentences established by the media, this public sentence violates the right to a just defense. Therefore, the recognition of the media's new role as a mechanism for control and accountability must pay heed to the threat it presents to individual rights.

A recent study (Poder Cuidadano 1996) analyzes the relationship between the journalistic and legal treatment of a series of notable cases. It shows how the right to receive accurate information, the right of the imputed to the presumption of innocence, and the right of the judges to make decisions without external pressures are affected by media involvement. Research has established that, with few exceptions, the information provided by the media for juridical cases has differed from the information gathered and accepted by the courts. There are several explanations for these differences. To maintain public interest in the case, the media not only dramatizes the news but also tends to advance conjectures that have not been or cannot be proven by the courts. In addition, and insofar as journalistic coverage is especially heavy during the first stages of the process when procedural restrictions are greater, the media has a structural incentive to advance unverified data provided by interested parties. Therefore, the conflictive relationship between the media and the courts may not only affect individual rights but may also have serious systemic effects. As previously mentioned, in many cases the public arrives at prima facie sentences on the basis of unverified information. When the actual legal sentences contradict those achieved through journalistic conjectures, the chances are that the public ends up with a negative opinion of the way the judicial system operates. It is important, while recognizing the watchdog function of the media in an open society, to acknowledge the ambiguous effects of the transposition of judicial procedures into the realm of the media—not only on individual rights, but also on the prestige of legal institutions and public perception of their performance.

Finally it should be mentioned that some analysts attribute the surprising emergence of "media justice" to the slowness and inefficiency of regular legal procedures. However, even though some of the present shortcomings of the system may be improved, it is worth noting that formal procedures are by definition slower and less responsive to immediate demands. Consequently, even though the performance of the judiciary may improve, it can be expected that the attention of the media will persist.

At this point I would like to consider one last issue. We have already mentioned that the statistics for claims initiated by the Judiciary, in the Defensoría del Pueblo de la Nación (National Ombudsman Agency), in the Controladuria General Municipal (Municipal Ombudsman Agency), and in the different customer service agencies of recently privatized enterprises, show a significant increase in the number of claims made by individual citizens. In a context where the utility of making claims is uncertain and where the impartiality of the judiciary is in doubt, we must wonder about the reasons citizens may have to make use of this instrument. Why, in spite of the disdain of the judiciary, have judicial claims and individual complaints increased?

Let us consider some hypotheses. Perhaps citizens have opted to bring their demands to the courts because although they know that the impartiality of the outcome is not guaranteed, this strategy allows them to legitimate their claims and to obtain institutional acknowledgment for what they consider to be their rights. In that case, the increase in the number of claims must be understood as a search for legitimacy and public recognition of their problems and endangered rights rather than the achievement of actual results. Unlike consumers, citizens do not have "exit" (Hirshman 1970) as a possible strategy; consequently, "voice," transformed now into claims in the judiciary or in the media, becomes their only strategy. Rather than practical goals, then, it seems the judicialization strategy has expressive ones.

Alain Minc has suggested another possible explanation for the rise of the judicialization strategy. He asserts that in a world where the limits between good and evil have dissolved, the discourse of rights serves as a comfortable substitute for the moral one. In such a world, the judge intervenes in institutional and social conflicts to seek compromise, and in moral conflicts his or her judgment can become a way to face "the corruption of traditional values." Thus, when citizens appeal to the judiciary, they are simultaneously seeking legal and moral legitimation for their claim (Minc 1995: 154). If this is the case, then the judicialization strategy is attractive because at least it allows the petitioners to express their moral resistance.

In addition, the judicialization strategy can be seen as a convenient tool by which to receive attention; thus, it has practical effects. Judicialization becomes the necessary credential to promote media scandal. Some authors have concluded that the emergence of media justice is a consequence of the growing distrust of politicians and the lack of faith in the efficiency of representative institutions. However, although claims made through the media imply a certain distrust of the judicial institution's ability to perform its task, it is worth noting that to be effective, the claims of the media seem to require judicial validation. The media can accelerate the fate of or guarantee attention to a claim, but a claim only acquires public legitimacy if it can be converted into a judicial demand. Therefore, even though the judicialization and media processes can be differentiated analytically, they seem to operate jointly. While the legal discourse gives legitimacy to the claim, the media "happening" establishes the topic in the public agenda and accelerates the need to solve it. Thus, the two processes must be considered as codependent, rather than alternative strategies.

Final Comments

Today, in spite of reversals in juridical decisions and infamous cases of inequality before the law, it is possible to observe that governmental policies and opposition claims attempt to legitimate themselves by using legal discourse. On the other hand, displacement of the petition mechanisms—from politics to the courts, and from the courts to the media—can be verified. This displacement is affecting the way citizens exercise their rights and the ways they are politically represented. Before addressing the possible consequences of these changes on the ability of citizens to use the judicial system and its relationship to political representation, one comment is in order regarding the way the Argentine case fits within the global judicialization of politics.

The emergence of this process in the Argentine case has been explained as a result of the specific dynamic of its political process. It has to be emphasized, however, that most of the Argentine historically based elements are related to the different facilitating conditions Neal Tate has mentioned to explain the process of judicialization as a global phenomenon (1995). Indeed, the judicialization of politics in Argentina could not have taken place without the presence of a "politics of rights," nor without the belief among certain interest groups that court decisions could be beneficial to the achievement of their goals. The reconstruction of the Argentine case also shows the presence of some other facilitating factors: the existence of citizens and civic associations that resort to the courts in order to bypass "ineffective majoritarian institutions" and of political actors who use the courts as an alternative way of pursuing a politics of opposition. Therefore, even though the process of judicialization of politics is evolving with local color and is having specific and novel consequences in this particular scenario, its emergence is related to the global character of the phenomenon.

The politicization of the judiciary that can be observed in the Argentine case can also be explained through domestic and general reasons. On the one hand, the recent conversion of the judiciary into a strategic space for decision making in the local political game has transformed it into a valuable arena and has led, therefore, to open and visible partisan political struggles to control it. On the other hand, and in spite of the more scandalous features that have tarnished the politicization of the judiciary in Argentina, recent analyses of court actions have stressed the impact of external political variables on judicial decisions. Indeed, recent political science explanations of court actions have argued that judges' expectations about the preferences of political actors determine the orientation of their decisions. If that is the case, then the politicization can be explained as the result of the usual strategic decisions made by judges in any political context (see Helmke 1998 for an interesting application to the Argentine Supreme Court). Therefore, although specific local factors explain the particular dynamic of the Argentine case, its development is not foreign to the global process of the judicialization of politics.

Finally, two comments concern the future of judicialization and mediatization of politics in the Argentine case.

1.   In light of the increasing discredit of the judiciary, at least two possible scenarios can be visualized. On the one hand, if the perception that "all is rotten in the state of Denmark" consolidates itself, and if the accusations and successive scandals make the courts seem useless mechanisms for modifying the current situation, it is likely that citizens' interest in the fate of the judiciary will recede. If expectation cannot be fulfilled, it is likely that the judiciary will return to that subordinate and obscure role that had characterized its relationship with the citizenry in the past. Knights in shining armor will disappear, the name of the villains will remain unknown, and conflicts will cease to hold public interest once more. Even though there are good reasons to be skeptical, some of the elements that distinguish the present situation from past experiences allow us to imagine a moderately optimistic alternative.

First, we have seen that the implementation of initiatives that obstruct judicial procedures and weaken the law has begun to be publicly contested. The politicization of the debates regarding judicial issues, the public visibility of the discussions about the design and reform of judicial institutions, the agitation over the professional merits of its personnel, and the confrontations regarding nomination procedures indicate an increasing, rather than decreasing, interest in juridical issues on the part of the citizenry. Instead of returning to a past in which questions of rights were the business of specialists, these questions have become an object for societal attention. Citizens seem to have discovered that the way in which these institutional disputes are solved can affect their daily lives. Therefore, in spite of the negative perceptions about the performance of the judiciary, it can be expected that the courts will remain a viable space for engaging in political competition and obtaining political attention.

Another element justifies this moderate optimism. The guarantees and predictability provided by a strong legal system are vital for the implementation of effective economic reform. The rule of law is thus demanded, not only by individual citizens, but also by economic groups and firms who have benefited from recent market reforms. Since 1992, business associations, individual entrepreneurs, and even the U.S. ambassador have demanded legal security and transparency in legal procedures in order to encourage future investments. In 1992, for example, the central topic of the IDEA[23] Annual Seminar was a discussion of the impact of legal security on the evolution of business. A recent study written by a think tank supported by the main Argentine corporations (FIEL) was also dedicated to this matter (FIEL 1994). The choice of topic was symptomatic, and the political signal unequivocal. It was the first time the business sector specifically addressed the issue. In the new economic context, without a stable and transparent judiciary there are no chances for consolidating newly acquired economic benefits, nor are there incentives to plan for future investments. In other words, the judicial issue has become not only a normative need for the Argentine democracy, but also a functional requirement for the stability and success of its economic reforms, as well as a political demand of its "business establishment." These other events allow us to speculate that judicial issues will not disappear quickly from the political spotlight.

2.   In the next paragraphs, we will consider some of the consequences that these changes have had on the way citizens are being represented. Bernard Manin has indicated that at the end of the twentieth century the basic feature characterizing changes in political representation is its personalization (1992). This has resulted in party identity losing its significance as a central mechanism in the organization of political relationships. There are two fundamental reasons for this metamorphosis. On the one hand, improvements in communication techniques reduce the candidates' dependence on the mediating role of parties. On the other, as the increasingly complex and uncertain conditions promote the emergence of politicians unbound to party programs, they call for the appearance of politicians that must present themselves as reliable and flexible individuals rather than as representatives of rigid party platforms. Beyond the consequences that these transformations may have on the future of political parties, it is also worth emphasizing that the personalization of representation affects the capacity of citizens to impact the public agenda.
    A first interpretation of these phenomena might lead one to think that a closer relationship between citizens and their representatives can be expected. However, this image obviates the fact that this apparent

closeness results in a situation whereby citizens have fewer resources to ensure their preferences are considered and weighted by the political system. Because party identity has lost its significance, citizens are less able to have their demands weighted. In many cases, there is no way to measure how many citizens are aggregated behind a certain demand. Therefore, the erosion of the importance of party mechanisms is resulting in the erosion of the citizens' ability to have their preferences heard.

As a consequence of the weakening party mediations, some alternative mechanisms for the defense of citizen rights have emerged, based upon individual legal claims and media resources. With the displacement of political claims to the courts, citizens have an incentive to realize their preferences through individual strategies, rather than through associative tactics based on their shared solidarities.

This type of exercise of rights, which appears to celebrate the autonomy of the liberal citizen, has disconcerting effects, as well. It is known that contemporary democracies, where in principle all individual adults have the same rights and obligations, do not automatically generate the conditions required for the effective exercise of these rights and obligations. Necessary requirements for the exercise of citizenship—such as material security, education, and access to information—are not guaranteed by the existence of democratic institutions. Indeed, one of the characteristics of contemporary democracies is that extended positive rights coexist with a "low intensity citizenship" (Przeworski 1995; O'Donnell 1994). On the other hand, it should be remembered that the exercise of individual rights does not necessarily result in egalitarian outcomes. As Danilo Zolo has mentioned, the exercise of citizens' rights produces inequality and freedom in the same way in which the market produces inequality and wealth (1993).

Why is this the case? The exercise of citizens' rights requires not only individuals who know their rights (Felstiner et al. 1980) and how to exercise them, but also individuals able to dedicate a significant part of their lives to defending their rights or to controlling the actions of their representatives. However, not all citizens know how to do this. Furthermore, not all citizens, even if they do know, can dedicate their time to advocate for themselves. Dedication to public activity competes with time citizens need to devote to their private affairs (Hirschman 1982; Constant 1814). Indeed, extended dedication to public activities reduces the time that could be devoted to the production of income. Given inequality in income distribution, the cost of this reduction is also unequal. While for some citizens the cost of devoting their time to public activities may imply a substantial reduction of essential resources, for others the cost of doing so does not significantly affect their well-being. Consequently, even if citizens are willing to dedicate an important share of their time to public activities, we know that the costs will be extremely unequal. If only a few citizens have the time to exercise their rights on a permanent basis, it can be inferred that rights will be distributed unequally. Indeed, if these are the conditions under which rights are being exercised, it is likely that citizens' rights will be restricted to those individuals who can meet the costs in effort, time, and revenue that involvement in public activities demands. It is likely, therefore, that only a few will be able to exercise their rights and participate effectively in public affairs. Therefore, the atomization and individualization resulting from changes in the form of representation may produce highly unequal distributions of rights.

We know that judicial and media strategies may have both defensive and expressive outcomes. We know that sometimes these strategies can even be successful. However, they place claimants of rights in a weak position. The use of these strategies reveals difficulties citizens encounter when making claims in the political realm or their inability collectively to organize their demands. Paradoxically, this weakness is hidden behind an action (litigating or publicizing in the media) that, as it appears to be confronting power, creates a deceptive perception about the actual strength of citizens' practices.

A final comment regarding the effects of the media process. We know the media has an important role as a watchdog of public affairs. We also know of its abilities to create an agenda and a public stage. As mentioned previously, the journalistic style, by choosing the form of telling stories and by selecting which stories to tell, is creating the current political spectacle (Edelman 1988). With these considerations in mind I would like to draw attention to one specific aspect of the problem. The media has flooded the public space. We are constantly exposed to war reports, crimes, and other disasters. This continuous exposure not only "naturalizes" and "normalizes" anomalous events, but also creates a false sense of participation (Hart 1996). We can attend a presidential inauguration while simultaneously being with the troops invading an occupied territory. All these images can make us believe that we are participating in the public and social scene. However, participation in the virtual scene ends up removing citizens from the real situation.

Thus, the combination of these two phenomena (judicialization and media) configures a complex scenario with atomized and weakened citizens who believe that they are conscious and autonomous participants in the public realm. The result could not be more discouraging.

NOTES

1. For the historical reasons behind this perception of the judiciary in Argentina, see Catalina Smulovitz (1995).

2. An analysis of the human rights policy implemented by the Alfonsín and Menem governments can be found in Acuña and Smulovitz 1995. An abridged version in English is in Acuña and Smulovitz 1997.

3. As a consequence of this trial, General Jorge Rafael Videla and Admiral Emilio Massera were given life sentences, General Viola was given seventeen years in prison, Admiral Lambruschini was given eight years, and Brigadier Agosti was given three years and nine months. The members of the junta that governed between 1979 and 1982 were acquitted because the court found the evidence against them to be inconclusive. All of them were set free by a presidential pardon signed by President Menem in December 1990.

4. López Rega had been minister of social action during the Isabel Perón government and had been accused of creating a paramilitary organization and of embezzling public funds.

5. The judges threatened to resign when the government attempted to override the sentence of the trial through "Military Instructions." The "instructions" were intended to reduce radically the number of prosecutions by exempting from accountability cases where those accused of torture, kidnapping, or murder could prove that they had acted according to orders.

6. Reported in *La Nación*, October 3, 1986.

7. The Ley de Punto Final established a deadline for summoning the presumed violators of human rights. When the law was approved, seven federal courts suspended their January holidays to work on the pending cases. By February, when the lapse of time determined by the law ended, more than 300 high-ranking officers had been indicted.

8. In one of the military rebellions that took place during the Alfonsín government, a group of "Gendarmerie officers" took control of the Buenos Aires Airport known as Aeroparque.

9. The Argentine federal judiciary has been characterized by the use of written procedures. In 1991, oral procedures were introduced in the criminal federal justice. In the other chambers written procedures are still being used. Several state justice systems have adopted oral procedures: Córdoba, Mendoza,

Salta, La Pampa, Entre Ríos, Misiones, Chubut, Chaco, Neuquén, Río Negro, San Luis, La Rioja, Corrientes, Jujuy, Formosa, Santiago del Estero, and Tucumán. See Cámara de Diputados 1992.

10. The *International Political Science Review* dedicated an issue (1994, vol. 15, no. 2) to the phenomenon of the judicialization of politics. In this volume Torbjorn Vallinder defined the process as the expansion of the jurisdiction of the courts and of the judges at the expense of politicians and/or administrators, that is, the transfer of decision-making rights from the legislature, the cabinet, or the civil service to the courts (Vallinder 1994: 91).

11. The Defensoría del Pueblo de la Nación, a national ombudsman agency, was created in July 1993, and it acquired constitutional status in 1994. Its mission is to defend and protect human rights and other rights and guarantees protected by the Constitution. The municipal ombudsman office, Controladuría General Comunal, was established in 1985, but it only started to operate in 1988. Since 1983, ombudsman agencies have been established in Córdoba, La Rioja, Salta, San Juan, San Luis, Rio Negro, Buenos Aires, and Formosa.

12. Additional information regarding the performance of these two agencies and comparison with the performance of other national agencies can be found in Smulovitz 1997.

13. The following codes were updated during the Alfonsín administration: Código de Procedimiento Penal (Gaceta Legislativa 1, 1: 5, January 11, 1984); Código de Justicia Militar; Código Penal de Excarcelación (February 9, 1984); Código Penal (March 15, 1984); Régimen Penal y Contravencional (May 30, 1985); Código Aduanero (August 14, 1986); Código Civil; Código Electoral.

14. This project was sent to the Legislative Power on August 6, 1992.

15. The budgetary autarchy was finally approved on September 28, 1990.

16. Public hearings for nomination procedures were approved on August 27, 1993. However, it should be noted that the first time the procedure should have been used, the Senate authorities did not submit the information requested by journalists and citizens. Reported in *La Nación*, September 29, 1990.

17. Between July 1989 and December 1992, the Menem administration sanctioned 244 extraordinary decrees (*decretos de necesidad y urgencia*). This number can be compared with the 20 extraordinary decrees that were sanctioned between 1853 and 1983 and with the 10 decrees sanctioned during the Alfonsín administrations (Rubio Ferreira and Goretti 1993).

18. In 1989, the then technical and legal secretary and later justice minister Raul Granillo Ocampo mentioned the need to modify what he called an "Alfonsínista judiciary." It was not his intention to designate "men identified with a particular governmental policy but with its big goals" (Verbitsky 1993: 78). In September 1989, Eduardo Bauzá, general secretary of the presidency, reaffirmed this goal, and member of the House of Representatives Manzano

added that the homogenization of the Supreme Court was not motivated by the pending military trials but by the need to guarantee the orientation of judicial resolutions in cases related to the economic emergency laws and to the reform of the state administration (reported in *La Nación,* September 26, 1989, and *Pagina* 12, March 30, 1990).

19. The Due Obedience Law established that those individuals who at the time of the military government were chief, junior, or noncommissioned officers, soldiers of the armed forces, members of security forces or police, and penitentiary personnel were not punishable for crimes that violated human rights, provided that they had acted within the scope of due obedience to the authorities above them.

20. For coverage of the conflicts that took place during the nomination process for judges of this chamber, see newspapers from the last two weeks of October 1992.

21. See note 5.

22. Reported in *Noticias,* May 3, 1992.

23. IDEA (Instituto para el Desarrollo de Ejecutivos de la Argentina) is an organization integrated by the CEOs of the main corporations.

REFERENCES

Acuña, Carlos, and Catalina Smulovitz. 1995. Militares en la transición Argentina: Del gobierno a la subordinación constitucional. In Carlos Acuña et al., *Juicio, castigos y memorias. Derechos humanos y justicia en la política Argentina.* Buenos Aires: Nueva Visión.

———. 1997. Guarding the guardians in Argentina. Some lessons about the risks and benefits of empowering the courts. In James McAdams, ed., *Transitional democracies and the rule of law in new democracies.* Notre Dame: University of Notre Dame Press.

Cámara de Diputados de la Nación. 1992. *Trámite Parlamentario* 74, August 13, 1992.

Constant, Benjamin. [1814]. In Benjamin Constant, *De l'esprit de conquête et de l'usurpation: dans leurs rapports avec la civilisation européenne.* Paris: Imprimerie national.

Edelman, Murray. 1988. *Constructing the political spectacle.* Chicago: University of Chicago Press.

Felstiner, William, Richard Abel, and Austin Sarat. 1980. The emergence and transformation of disputes: Naming, blaming, claiming. *Law and Society Review* 15:631–54.

FIEL. 1994. *La reforma del poder judicial en la Argentina.* Buenos Aires.

Hart, Roderick P. 1996. Easy citizenship: Television's curious legacy. *Annals of the American Academy of Political and Social Science* 546.

Helmke, Gretchen. 1998. *Toward a formal theory of an informal institution: Insecure tenure and judicial independence in Argentina, 1976–1995*. Paper presented at the Thirtieth International Congress of the Latin American Studies Association.

Hirschman, Albert. 1970. *Exit, voice and loyalty*. Cambridge: Harvard University Press.

———. 1982. *Shifting involvements: Private interest and public action*. Princeton: Princeton University Press.

Landi, Oscar, and Inés Gonzalez. 1995. Los derechos en la cultura política. In Carlos Acuña et al., *Juicio, castigos y memorias. Derechos humanos y justicia en la política Argentina*. Buenos Aires: Nueva Visión.

Manin, Bernard. 1992. Metamorfosis de la representación. In Dos Santos Mario, ed., *Qué queda de la representación política?* CLACSO: Nueva Sociedad.

Minc, Alain. 1995. *La borrachera democràtica. El nuevo poder de la opinión pública*. Madrid: Ediciones Temas de Hoy.

O'Donnell, Guillermo. 1994. On the state, democratization and some conceptual problems. In William Smith, ed., *Latin American political economy in the age of neoliberal reform: Theoretical and comparative perspective for the 1990s*. New Brunswick: Transaction Books.

El Periodista. 1988. Los jueces suben a escena. *El Periodista 4*.

Peyrú, Graciela, and Lilia Ciamberlani. 1992. Cuando la prensa cumple el rol de la justicia. *Clarín*, February 14.

Poder Ciudadano. 1996. *Jueces y periodista. Como se informa y se juzga*. Fundación Poder Ciudadano.

Przeworski, Adam. 1995. *Sustainable democracy*. Cambridge: Cambridge University Press.

Rubio Ferreira, Delia, and Matteo Goretti. 1993. The emergency and the relationship between the executive and the congress during President Menem's administration in Argentina: Use and misuse of prerogative powers. Working Papers on Comparative Legislative Studies. Appleton, Wisc.: IPSA, Lawrence University.

Smulovitz, Catalina. 1995. Constitución y poder judicial en la nueva democracia Argentina. La experiencia de las instituciones. In Carlos Acuña, ed., *La nueva matriz política Argentina*. Buenos Aires: Nueva Visión.

———. 1997. Ciudadanos, derechos y política. In Felipe Gonzalez Morales, ed., *Las acciones de interés público. Argentina, Chile, Colombia y Perú*. Santiago de Chile: Cuadernos de Análisis Jurídico, Universidad Diego Portales.

Tate, C. Neal. 1995. Why the expansion of judicial power? In C. Neal Tate, ed., *The global expansion of judicial power*. New York: New York University Press.

Vallinder, Torbjorn. 1994. The judicialization of politics: A world-wide phenomenon. *International Political Science Review* 15:91.

Verbitsky, Horacio. 1993. *Hacer la corte.* Buenos Aires: Planeta.

Zolo, Danilo. 1993. Democratic citizenship in a post-communist era. In David Held, ed., *Prospects for democracy.* Stanford: Stanford University Press.

Hybrid(ity) Rules: Creating Local Law in a Globalized World

Heinz Klug

Heinz Klug, a law professor at the University of Wisconsin and former South African activist, takes the relationship between international and domestic factors to a different setting—the making of the South African Constitution of 1996. Drawing on his own experience in addition to research, he shows the way that South African actors drew on foreign sources of legitimacy to try to support their own points of view in the process. The authority of expertises imported and exported from abroad, in particular, led the African National Congress ultimately to accept a very different property clause in the Constitution than their party program had long advocated. Indeed, the entire process of producing the Constitution was very much framed by the authority and the hierarchy of authorities legitimating and delegitimating certain approaches and norms. What was accepted, therefore, was an internationally legitimate hybrid, but it did not put to rest the potentially explosive issue of how to address the vast racial inequalites in the ownership of property.

Similarly, in the South African context, the new constitution gave a large role to the Constitutional Court that in effect internationalized South African constitutional doctrine. As other authors in this book have suggested, this process potentially places the leading judges of the South African courts in an international context that facilitates exchange and dialogue—perhaps ultimately an international consensus on particular norms and approaches. Again, however, Klug's analysis makes it clear that participation in an international "community" of jurisprudence will not necessarily lead to solutions to the problems that still deeply divide South African society. The political struggles have been transformed by international events. As suggested by several other essays, the incorporation of the

prescriptions embodying the "best" international thinking in politics (or
economics) will not necessarily lead to the desired changes. The impact of
the changes will depend on how the international expertises interact with
the local structures of power.

The construction of new rules, in the late twentieth century, is both
unique and ubiquitous. Whether it is the making of a new constitution
for South Africa or the negotiation of new regulations for the electronic
transfer of capital in the global marketplace, the new rules reflect both
unique attempts to address particular social, economic, or political
problems and the historical and comparative experiences of our
increasingly globalized world. I will argue in this essay for a dialectical
understanding of the relationship between the global and local in which
local agency deploys global forms and is both reshaped in the process
and contributes to the continuing reformulation of global alternatives.

This dialectical interaction—between a global text constituted by
the histories, practices, and normative prescriptions of nation-states,
international bodies, and organizations (such as the United Nations,
World Bank, and, increasingly, transnational corporate and nongovernmental organizations) and the local struggles and processes
through which new rules are created and applied—may be identified
through the explication of five specific elements. These elements when
taken together comprise the metaphorical life cycle/evolution of the
"globalization of the rule of law." First, there is the deployment of existing global forms by local actors attempting to reformulate local rules.
Second, this deployment has the effect of shaping the local imagination,
whether posed as the only alternative or as a weight against local alternatives. Third, this deployment of global forms, whether as norms or as
stories of success or failure, has the ultimate effect of setting the limits of
available options—on pain of global marginalization, an isolation
imposed by capital markets, governments, or the international human
rights community. Fourth, while local options may be circumscribed by
"global insistence" and the limits of "bounded imaginations," this does
not prevent the emergence of a particularized and even "unique" local
rule, shaped by the specificities of cultures, histories, and the politics of
the moment. Finally, and completing the "life cycle," this adoption of

any local rule or process provides an experience that adds to the global text, both influencing the continuing reformulation of global forms and providing yet another example for the constant refrain "international experience shows . . ."

In short, these five elements or metamorphic stages may be characterized, in neither temporal nor hierarchical order, as, first, "local agency"; second, "bounded alternatives"; third, the pervasiveness of the global, or "global insistence"; fourth, the "hybridity of outcomes"; and fifth, local impact on the shape of the global, or "international experience shows . . ." A crude example of this process at the global level has been the use and reformulation of the story of Korea and the "Asian economic miracle" in which the experience of South Korean economic development was formulated and presented simultaneously as: culturally specific; a paradigm of modernization and free-market development from accumulation to takeoff; and, more recently, as the inefficient paradigm of state intervention, labor security, corruption, and personal patronage (*guanxi*).

Law and Development or Cut, Paste, and Tinker?

In the first half of the 1990s well over a billion dollars was spent on rule of law projects in every conceivable corner of the globe. A host of different institutions, from local and nationally based nongovernmental organizations through to the UN Human Rights Committee are engaged in this new rule of law movement.[1] While legal reform is not restricted to the dramatic developments in public law accompanying the enormous political reconstructions of the post–cold war era, the adoption of new, justiciable constitutions has been a major product of this movement.

The response of many scholars has been to herald a new age. David Beatty, a Canadian scholar of comparative constitutionalism, describes ours as "an age of constitutionalism" (1994: 1), while Bruce Ackerman (1997) has recently published an essay entitled "The Rise of World Constitutionalism." For these scholars, the significance of this new age is the adoption, by nations creating justiciable constitutions, of the universal principle—central to understandings of modern constitutionalism—of a "commitment to limitations on ordinary political power" (Greenberg et al. 1993: xxi).

That a "globalizing constitutionalism" should take this form, right now, is rather unremarkable in an age where the state is in retreat and where constitutionalism provides a means to attain the goals of both those struggling for human rights and those who argue that the market most efficiently mediates the demands of autonomous individual needs. While this confluence of antistate interests explains the popularity of this latest constitutionalist wave, it does not give us any reason to believe that this latest commitment to the rule of law should fare any better than the multitude of past law and development or judicial reform programs. Even if we accept the empirical evidence that more and more nations have adopted written constitutions with bills of rights and have empowered their courts to uphold these new charters as the supreme law of the land, it is not self-evident that the outcome or even the meaning of these new institutions is the same in all these societies. While we may recognize a globalizing constitutionalism, the challenge is to understand the specifics of its incorporation into particular national legal systems as well as to understand the potentially multiple roles that constitutionalism is playing in the reconstruction of different polities.

Law and development scholarship traditionally looked at this process in terms of a cultural diffusion model, at the motives behind and consequences of transporting legal systems to new contexts. In earlier debates over the transfer and imposition of law, scholars raised troubling concerns about the goals, consequences, and effects of these processes. On the one hand it was argued that local legal cultures "proved remarkably resilient in the face of American legal models" with the effect that "legal-transfer mechanisms" attributed to the law and development movement were seen as ineffective (Gardner 1980: 9). On the other hand, stinging critiques were mounted, condemning the movement as "an exercise in 'cultural imperialism,' one more manifestation of a desire to extend United States cultural and economic 'domination' through foreign aid and development assistance programs that reinforced American influence by strengthening the role of cooperating local elites, in this case local legal elites" (283). Questioning their own motives and roles in the law and development movement, some scholars withdrew from active participation and through their critiques played an active role in the movement's demise (see Trubek and Galanter 1974). Recent contributions to this debate, however, have looked beyond the particular experience of the law and development movement in the United States. Accepting that efforts to export law have at times been the product of "misguided 'missionary' notions of sharing with the Third World the legal modernity and 'know-how' thought to have been realized in the United States" (Gardner 1980: 7), these new participants have called for continuing engagement "in concrete work in developing countries," as a way to get beyond the persistent crisis in law and development theory (see Tamanaha 1995).

While these criticisms and reevaluations may reveal some of the underlying motivations and problems of the law and development movement, they fail to acknowledge that "legal transfer" or the exchange of legal forms has been a hallmark of the creation and practice of law since at least the twelfth century, with the "revival" of the study of Roman law at European universities, particularly Bologna (von Mehren and Gordley 1977: 7). Indeed, the incorporation of new legal doctrines, in particular within the Anglo-American system, is a basic form of the common law method (Schlesinger et al. 1988: 231). Within the civil law system the transfer or adoption of complete legal codes, beginning with the Napoleonic Code itself, has also been unremarkable (Lawson 1955: 48–51). The widespread adoption of justiciable constitutions and bills of rights in the 1990s merely reflects, from this perspective, a continuation of legal exchange or the adoption by particular states or local elites of legal forms most applicable to their present goals and circumstances.

While critics of the law and development movement recognized that local elites in the host countries were deeply implicated in the transfer of legal forms, there has been little attempt to explore the role of local actors in shaping the reception of particular legal doctrines, or how these doctrines were deployed locally to achieve particular aims or to gain advantage in particular local contests over power and resources.[2] Thus, instead of focusing on the imposition of law and the competing interests of those engaged in the export of the rule of law, I wish to explore the specific contours of legal incorporation and exchange from an opposite, internal perspective, in order to understand the extent to which participants in postcolonial settings draw on and reinterpret legal forms (rules, doctrines, standards, and codes) from a variety of jurisdictions to suit their own locally defined ends. This will involve both an exploration of how different interests (social, economic, and professional) are furthered and shaped by the deployment of different incorporated rules and practices, as well as how the sources and local articulation of these different rules and practices lend specific weight to their successful incorporation and hybridization.

While this focus may be compared to an earlier literature that focused on the reception of law and legal institutions (see Elias 1965; Seidman 1968; Thompson 1968), I believe that there is a clear distinction between the earlier phases of reception and the process of incorporation inherent in this latest "global" wave of political reconstruction. Both the colonial reception of imperial law and the postcolonial imposition of bills of rights in independence constitutions adopted at Westminster may be clearly contrasted with most of the recent democratic transitions. These transitions have been driven by social and political movements demanding the incorporation of human rights that have gained international recognition in the period since World War II.[3] The embrace of constitutionalism in the context of these democratic transitions is, in this view, a complex form of reception where local competitors draw on available international resources in order to pursue their own local and ultimately transnational agendas.

In developing this analysis I will argue that the adoption locally of a globally bounded notion of democratic constitutionalism both enables political reconstruction or transition to proceed and tests the institutional capacity of the incorporated framework to address the conflicts arising from often irreconcilable political demands. The realm of bounded possibilities created by the introduction of constitutionalism is constantly infused with the incompatible constitutional imaginations of local contestants. In order to demonstrate this process of incorporation and to explore how it circumscribes the bounds of legitimate alternatives, I will focus on the construction of the property clause and the place of property in South Africa's new Constitution.

At the Core Is Property

The conflicts, debates, and final compromise on the inclusion of a property rights clause in the South African Constitution provide a window through which this particular interaction between global and local imperatives may be viewed. While the internationally endorsed process for the transition away from apartheid included a commitment to the rule of law and the inclusion of a justiciable bill of rights, there was no clarity on the contents of this commitment. As a result, the different political parties and interest groups entered into a process by which they sought to shape the meaning of these commitments so as to achieve their particular goals. While this "debate" over the content of particular commitments or rights reflected the political goals and assumptions of the different parties, it was also substantially framed by the available intellectual resources. These included primarily the historical text of local experience as well as the text of international and foreign jurisdictions, which served simultaneously as exemplary resources in the pursuit of particular goals and as the bounded universe constraining the choices and options of the parties.

My own introduction to the debate over property coincided with de Klerk's February 1990 public announcement of the political opening that would set the stage for South Africa's democratic transition. At that moment I was at the headquarters of the African National Congress (ANC) in Lusaka, Zambia, helping to organize a workshop on the Land Question that had been initiated by fellow ANC activists Bongiwe Njobe and Helena Dolny. While the workshop focused on analyzing the state of rural South Africa, all the participants—ANC members who ranged from scholars and traditional leaders to peasant activists— seemed to assume that nationalization of existing landholdings, given the history of dispossession and the vast inequalities in landholdings between black and white (Claassens 1991; Robertson 1990), would be high on the agenda of an ANC government. This shared assumption was based in no small part on our commitment to the 1955 Freedom Charter—recognized by the ANC as expressing the will of the South African people—which declared in part that the "national wealth of our country . . . shall be restored to the people" and "all the land redivided amongst those who work it, to banish famine and land hunger" (ANC 1989a: 319).

Despite our assumptions and the liberation movement's general rhetoric on the Land Question, activists at the workshop had a realistic view of the low priority rural issues had on the mainly urban-based ANC's political agenda in the late 1980s. We were encouraged, however, by the "Economy and Land" sections of the ANC's Constitutional Guidelines, which had been issued in 1988 as part of the ANC's preparations for negotiations with the apartheid regime. Here, the ANC signaled its future intentions to both the international community and the apartheid regime, by announcing its intention to protect property constitutionally. While this promise went further than might have been expected, given the rhetoric of socialization, nationalization, and redistribution so dominant in the ANC at the time, the limited focus on property for "personal use and consumption" allowed these conflicting visions of redistribution and property rights to coexist. This coexistence was aided by the document's commitment to "devise and implement a land reform programme . . . in conformity with the principle of affirmative action, taking into account the status of victims of forced removals" (ANC 1989b: 323–24). With the exact modes of implementation still open to debate, the Lusaka workshop opted to institutionalize the issue within the ANC by calling for the formation of an ANC Land Commission to address the lack of specific policies within the organization.

It was as a member of the ANC Land Commission's secretariat (first alone and joined later by two others)[4] that I returned to South Africa in June 1990. In setting up the Land Commission we soon began to work with the already well-established community of lawyers, NGOs, and activists who had long struggled against forced removals in the courts and on the land.[5] This informal coalition provided the organizational basis, knowledge, and experience that sustained the struggle for the recognition of dispossessed land rights during the political transition and constitution-making process. While the ANC Land Commission had access to the ANC's internal policy-making processes and could evoke strong public reaction as a voice of the ANC,[6] it was the return to land campaigns of land claimants, and their lawyers' continued engagement with the de Klerk government, that frustrated the apartheid regime's attempts to preempt future claims. This the apartheid government attempted to do by repealing the Land Acts (Abolition Act 1991) in 1991 and establishing an Advisory Commission on Land Allocation (Section 89–96) with the purpose of settling all claims before the political transition to democratic rule could be completed.

It was from this perspective, then, that I was able to both participate in[7] and view the debate over property rights and how the rules of the game were framed for the new South Africa. At first, discussion centered on the ANC's draft bill of rights, which was published in 1990 and contained a single article addressing the "economy, land and property" (ANC Constitutional Committee 1990: Article 11). Within the ANC, the Land Commission began hearing from its constituency and opening debates on land reform, nationalization, and restitution. This process began with newly formed ANC branches and communities locked in land conflicts around the country, but increasingly focused on a series of internal discussions. Joined at times by activists and lawyers of the land movement, the Land Commission engaged with members of the Constitutional Committee[8] as well as with other activists and sectors in a series of conferences initiated by the Constitutional Committee—at which special sessions or subgroups focused on the issue of land and property. Outside the ANC, the Land Commission built links and worked closely with lawyers and activists of the return to land movement and became engaged in wider public debates over land claims and land redistribution. Central to these debates was the status that property rights would have in a future constitution.

Although the ANC's draft bill of rights only protected, in our view, limited rights to personal property, it became clear at the May 1991 conference convened by the ANC Constitutional Committee that the ANC was under a great deal of pressure to grant greater recognition to property rights. In fact, attempts at that conference to question whether there should be any constitutionally protected property rights at all elicited a highly charged response from one member of the Constitutional Committee who warned that the rejection of property rights would directly endanger the democratic transition. In response the participants at the conference called for a reworking of the draft in which land would be recognized as a specific form of property and treated separately from property in general. Concern was expressed about the recognition of property rights as such before the implementation of the necessary process of redistribution. Furthermore, participants made a commitment to include positive rights to land for the landless (Centre for Development Studies 1991: 129–32).

While this internal debate sought simultaneously to limit the reach of existing property rights and to secure a more equitable distribution of property in the future, the response of the regime and the existing economic interests was expressed most clearly by the South African Law Commission—a nominally independent statutory body. In its August 1991 "Interim Report on Group and Human Rights," the Law Commission launched a sustained attack against the ANC Draft, charging that the "ANC's bill . . . provides, in a manner which hardly disguises the aim, for nationalization of private property without objectively testable norms for compensation," and that what the ANC intended was "in fact nothing but nationalization under the cloak of expropriation . . . designed to secure state control over property" (359–65).

Instead, the Law Commission called for the protection of private property and for the payment of just compensation in the event of expropriation in the public interest. Likewise, the Democratic Party, traditionally the party of big capital and white liberals, proposed a comprehensive right to property that could only be derogated by lawful expropriation in the public interest, and only then when subject to the "proper payment of equitable compensation, which in the event of dispute, shall be determined by an ordinary court of law" (Democratic Party 1993: Article 9). Neither of these proposals provided for the restitution of property taken under apartheid and as such failed to comprehend the threat to property rights, and even the very notion of constitutional rights, that the legal entrenchment of the apartheid's spoils entails.

While attention was focused on the question of property rights, the ANC Land Commission continued to hold meetings around the country to discuss land issues,[9] both as a means to increase awareness within the ANC, as well as to begin the formulation of a land policy for adoption by the movement. The first target of this campaign was to commit the organization to a set of principles upon which a policy could be built. With this as its goal, the ANC Land Commission held a national conference in June 1991 at which we produced a set of guidelines for the development of land policy. These guidelines were then presented and adopted at the ANC's National Conference in July 1991. The most important features of the Land Manifesto were its simultaneous commitment to both land restitution and land redistribution, its recognition of a diversity of land tenure forms, and the advancement of a policy of affirmative action as the main device to achieve specific policy goals (ANC 1991). With these guidelines the ANC effectively endorsed a strategy against the simple constitutional recognition of private property as acknowledged by the apartheid state. First, by demanding both restitution and land reform, it questioned and threatened the legitimacy of existing property rights. Second, the acceptance of different forms of tenure decentered private land ownership and provided a basis for the recognition of communal and other forms of land tenure. Finally, the manifesto recognized that affirmative action–type policies would provide a structure in which the multitude of specific policy goals and claims of different constituencies within the ANC could be accommodated and targeted to address land issues and the interests of the rural poor.

At the October 1991 National Conference on Affirmative Action, convened by the ANC Constitutional Committee, I reported back to the plenary session that the subgroup on land had concluded that a wealth tax would be necessary to fund land redistribution. Given the demand that any expropriation be compensated, we concluded that the only way to achieve the redistribution of land necessary to overcome the legacy of the 1913 Land Acts was to create a specific compensation account. In order to achieve the equitable redistribution required, this dedicated account would need to be funded by those who benefited from the limited land market created by the Land Acts, which had reserved 87 percent of land for white ownership and control. This could be achieved, I argued, by the imposition of a wealth tax, similar to the equalization tax adopted in the Federal Republic of Germany in the aftermath of World War II. While the idea of special taxes to overcome the vast disparities created by apartheid has continued to raise interest, in 1991 the reaction was immediate—the major white-controlled newspapers went ballistic, and within hours I was once again receiving death threats from those who had attempted to silence opposition during the height of apartheid. Although senior ANC leaders supported our right to conduct a debate on the wealth tax it also became clear that any attempt to conduct an effective redistribution of land rights would meet extremely stiff opposition from the ancien régime as well as conflict with alternative demands for resources among the ANC's own constituencies.

Despite this fierce public exposure, when formal negotiations began at Codesa in December 1991, it seemed as if the land issue would once again be pushed into the background as the parties clashed over the very nature of the political transition. As far as property issues were concerned, they were subsumed in the larger debate over whether the purpose of Codesa was to produce a detailed interim constitution or broad constitutional principles that would guide, but not frustrate the work of a future democratically elected constitution-making body. Despite this marginalization of substantive issues in the negotiations, for land claimants and those active in support of their demands, the struggle over land and property rights continued simultaneously on two planes: first, in actual land occupations and attempts to return to land from which communities had been forcibly removed—whether by occupation or legal and administrative negotiations with ACLA[10] and the de Klerk government; second, at the level of ideas, with debates over different policy options continuing at a series of conferences and meetings, either organized by the ANC Constitutional Committee together with various university-based institutes or directly by the academy. One of the most important of these was organized by longtime land activist Aninka Claassens through the Centre for Applied Legal Studies (CALS) to discuss "the effect that a constitutionally entrenched right to property might have on future land reform legislation and programmes" (1992: v).

The opening of a discussion on particular options for the recognition of land rights and the consequences a property clause might have on land claims was, at this stage, a vital intervention, making it clear that the issue of land rights could not be divorced from the wider question of property. Furthermore, when this conference is placed in the context of the series of conferences, meetings, and workshops held in this period,[11] its significance, as one in a series of intellectual loci of the South African transition, may be recognized. At these events, new substantive ideas were introduced into the public debate while simultaneously being framed through their presentation in the context of different international histories and examples. Among the important substantive interventions made at the CALS conference was the public floating of the suggestion for a land claims court—in the form of a report to the conference from a group of lawyers and activists from the "land claims movement" who were working on this option at the behest of the ANC Land Commission (Swanson 1992).[12] Other important substantive interventions at this conference included Geoff Budlender's construction of a legal right to land for the landless (1992),[13] as well as the work of Catherine Cross, who demonstrated the continued vitality and existence of an alternative understanding of land rights in opposition to the prevailing legal notions of individual private property rights (1992). Presentation of the Canadian decision to preclude the explicit recognition of property rights from their 1982 Charter of Rights (Bauman 1992) and the history of constitutional conflict over land reform in India in the postindependence years (Murphy 1992) both introduced substantive examples of alternative approaches and provided grist for debate over the dangers of, and alternatives to, the constitutional enshrinement of property rights.

It was these interventions that forced the ANC to reevaluate its own proposed "Draft Bill of Rights." After several meetings with land activists and members of the Land Commission, Albie Sachs proposed new sections on land and the environment as well as a separate property clause for the revised text of the ANC draft bill of rights. These new sections essentially expanded the ANC's proposals, making it clear that

land rights would remain a central claim of the antiapartheid movement and that the protection of property would remain subject to these
claims. While property rights were given separate recognition for the
first time in the new text, the text also suggested that these references to
property, along with all other "principles governing economic life,"
might be better placed outside the bill of rights in a nonjusticiable section of the Constitution defined as "Directive Principles of State Policy"—which is the case with similar sections of the Irish and Indian
constitutions.

By the time this revised text was first published in May 1992, negotiations with the de Klerk government had formally broken down—col-
lapsing Codesa into a morass of mutual recriminations (Friedman
1993). At the same time, the government's land claims forum was being
rejected by communities (Statement 1991) who were threatening to
physically reoccupy their lands,[14] and the ANC Land Commission was
being thrust into an engagement with new actors—both national and
international—who had recognized the centrality of land to the struggle
over property rights. The first engagement, which culminated in a
meeting in December 1992, was with the Urban Foundation, a policy
institute funded by South African big business, which asked for a meeting with the ANC Land Commission to discuss land claims and the
question of creating a land claims court. At this meeting the ANC delegation, which included members of the Constitutional Committee as
well as the Land Commission and its allies in the land movement, was
presented with the argument that while some form of limited land
claims process might be necessary to legitimate future property relations, both the demand for land among the African majority and the
reality of resource needs and allocations for future development
required that this process be tightly circumscribed. While we recognized the problem of competition over resources under a future democratic government, we argued that any attempt to engage in an all but
symbolic process of restitution would fail to build the legitimacy they
seemed to recognize was needed to secure property relations in the new
South Africa.

The second of these new engagements began in mid-1992 when the
World Bank launched its own initiatives in South Africa. Our immediate response was to ask who had invited them to South Africa and to
reject the notion of engagement with this institution. Soon, however,
we realized that the World Bank was developing its own strategy toward

the "new" South Africa[15] and would continue to do so whether or not we engaged. Refusal by definition meant lack of knowledge and influence. The Bank, at the same time, had been rebuffed by other sectors of the antiapartheid movement—particularly the urban sector activists—and responded to our own hesitations by organizing an initial seminar outside South Africa, in Mbabane, Swaziland, in November 1992. To this event they invited representatives from different South African political groupings, both government and nongovernment bodies, to discuss a set of papers prepared by the World Bank and its consultants (World Bank 1992).

These two engagements presented radically alternative possibilities and opportunities. While the Urban Foundation (UF) was convinced that the demand for land reform among Africans was being grossly exaggerated, Hans Binswanger, the senior World Bank adviser who dominated the Swaziland seminar, presented a vision of world development dependent upon the carrying out of a successful land reform.[16] While the UF suggested a limited process of restitution in order to legitimate property rights, Binswanger argued that land claims and even land invasions would drive a process of land reform and suggested that by facilitating land reform the government would be providing an essential catalyst for sustained economic development. Although the ANC Land Commission remained extremely skeptical of the equities of the World Bank's proposals—for a market-driven reform focused on small-scale producers—we realized immediately that the World Bank's position could be deployed as a way to keep the issue of land reform on the political agenda. With this aim, we encouraged Hans Binswanger to persuade the de Klerk government that land reform was and should remain an essential part of South Africa's political transition. At the same time, we introduced Binswanger to members of the ANC's leadership, including the Constitutional Committee, facilitating ANC agreement to engage with the World Bank on these issues.

This engagement was pursued through the newly formed Land and Agricultural Policy Centre (LAPC) and was structured by the tension between the ANC's historic concerns about the role of the Bretton Woods institutions and by our concern to retain some influence over the Bank's activities in the political transition. As we began to negotiate our working relationship with the Bank's representative, Robert Christiansen, I attended a meeting of NGOs in Johannesburg at which Martin Khor of the Malaysian-based Third-World Network and representatives of a World Bank monitoring group from Washington, D.C., explained the structure and workings of the institution. Although we had already experienced the dramatic impact that interest by the Bank could have on an issue, the understanding we gained from these activists of the manner in which the Bank's missions operated convinced us of the need to engage the Bank closely and to retain some influence over the Bank's own information-gathering and analytical process.

While the World Bank both wanted and needed our endorsement of their plan to prepare a rural restructuring program (RRP) for South Africa, we demanded that the initial research work be conducted by and remain under the control of South Africans. This was made possible through the creation of terms of reference for the preparation of a series of background reports that would form the basis of the preparation of the RRP. The resulting aide-mémoire was concluded on June 15, 1993; in it Robert Christiansen committed the Bank to a process that would "be fully transparent, consultative and collaborative at all stages" (1993). To this end, I was asked to head the legal research team and to prepare the report on the constitutional requirements of a land restitution and reform process. Later, as a member of the World Bank's mission to South Africa in late 1993, I participated in the formulation of the Bank's proposal for a rural restructuring program for the country. While there were many parts of the report with which I was not in complete agreement, its importance from the perspective of the ANC Land Commission lay in its clear assertion that both land restitution and land reform were central to rural restructuring (World Bank 1994c). Furthermore, even though our argument that a constitutionalized property right would impede land redistribution was excised at the last moment, in favor of the Bank's ideal of a market-driven process, we were able to obtain a clear statement in the report to the effect that land restitution and even redistribution were so important that in the event of market failure, government intervention would be both justified and necessary.[17]

However, prior to the beginning of substantive constitutional negotiations in early 1993, the ANC and government still held dramatically alternative notions of how property should be constitutionally protected. On the one hand, the ANC was willing to protect the undisturbed enjoyment of personal possessions, so long as property entitlements were to be determined by legislation and provision was to be made for the restoration of land to people dispossessed under apartheid (ANC 1993: Article 13). The government's proposals, on the other hand, aimed at protecting all property rights and would only allow expropriation for public purposes and subject to cash compensation determined by a court of law according to the market value of the property (Republic of South Africa 1993). In response the ANC suggested that no property clause was necessary.[18]

As negotiations with the de Klerk regime gained momentum in 1993, conflict over the property clause began to focus on specific issues. Although the ANC had initially insisted that an interim constitution contain only those guarantees necessary to ensure an even political playing field, the momentum for entrenching rights could not be slowed, and before long we recognized that we were in the process of negotiating a complete Bill of Rights. It was in this context that the apartheid government insisted that property rights be included in the interim constitution and that the measure of compensation include specific reference to the market value of the property. In response the ANC insisted that the property clause not frustrate efforts to address land claims and that the state must have the power to regulate property without being obliged to pay compensation unless there was a clear expropriation of the property. Although the regime agreed that explicit provisions guaranteeing and providing for land restitution should be included, its negotiators insisted that such provisions should not be located within the property clause. Instead, it was proposed that if they were to be included, they should be incorporated into the corrective action provisions of the equality clause.

Mass action played an important part in the ANC alliance's campaign to shape the transition, and various forms of public display of claims, outrage, and strength were employed by groups on all sides to ensure that their concerns or demands be placed on the agenda at the multiparty talks. Marked by protests, demonstrations, campaigns, and even an invasion of the World Trade Centre in Kempton Park, the site of the multiparty negotiations, mass participation in the constitution-making process exhibited both a diversity of claims and a degree of popular frustration with an undemocratic negotiating process. Among these were representatives of communities who were forcibly removed under apartheid, who marched on the World Trade Centre protesting the proposed constitutional protection of property (which they saw as an entrenchment of the apartheid distribution of property), and who demanded constitutional recognition of their right to return to their land.[19]

Answering these demands and conflicts, the interim 1993 Constitution provided a separate institutional basis for land restitution, which was guaranteed in the corrective action provisions of the equality clause (Constitution 1993: Section 8(3)(b)), and compromised on the question of compensation by including a range of factors the courts would have to consider in determining just and equitable compensation (Section 28(3)). Significantly, as Matthew Chaskalson argues, the final outcome in terms of the specific wording adopted was as much a result of serendipity, legal ignorance, and the particular quirks and concerns of the individual negotiators as the logical product of an informed or even interest-based political debate and compromise (1995). This is demonstrated most aptly in the choice of the terminology of public purpose over public interest in the expropriation clause despite agreement among the parties to give the state as much leeway as possible in this regard.

Even then, however, the substance of the outcome reflects both the general contours of the political conflict over the property clause and the bounded alternatives available to the parties—from the recognition of existing property rights on the one hand to the recognition of land claims on the other. Significantly, the factors to be considered in the determination of just compensation reflect this outcome. On the one hand, they were directed at the problem of land claims and included "the use to which the property is being put, the history of its acquisition, the value of the investments in it by those affected and the interest of those affected" (Constitution 1993: Section 28(3)), while, on the other hand, the insistence of the ancien régime made possible the inclusion of other factors, in particular "market value." It was under this constitutional regime that Mandela's government and South Africa's first democratic parliament began to address land claims. Acting in terms of the specific clauses of the 1993 Constitution, which provided for the establishment of a land claims process, parliament passed the Restitution of Land Claims Act in 1995, setting up regional Land Claims Commissions and the new Land Claims Court (Klug 1996b).

Despite predictions that there would be very little change in the Constitution during the second phase of the constitution-making process, particularly on such sensitive issues as the property clause and the bill of rights, the property issue, in fact, once again became one of the unresolvable lightning rods in the Constitutional Assembly. Although the committee charged with reviewing the Bill of Rights was at first reluctant to change the formulation of the 1993 compromise, challenges centered on the question of land restitution and reform (see Constitutional Assembly 1995b; Constitutional Assembly, Theme Committee 1995b, 1995c) once again forced open the process. In this case the impetus came from the Workshop on Land Rights and the Constitution organized by the Constitutional Assembly's subcommittee, Theme Committee 6.3, whose task was to resolve issues related to specialized structures of government such as the Land Claims Commission and Court provided for in the 1993 Constitution. Focusing on the land issue, this meeting once again raised the problem of property rights in the Constitution. While some participants raised the question whether there should be any property protection within the final Constitution, the major change from the period in which the 1993 Constitution was negotiated was that the participants in this workshop, even those representing long-established interests like the National Party and the South African Agricultural Union, now agreed on the need "to rectify past wrongs" and for land reform. Disagreement here was over the means. The South African Agricultural Union, for example, continued to assert that "it should be done in a way without jeopardising the protection of private ownership," while the National Party now embraced the World Bank's proposals, arguing that land reform should "be accomplished within the parameters of the market and should be demand-driven."

The outcome of this workshop and the submissions made to Theme Committee 6.3 was a report to the Constitutional Assembly that both challenged the existing 1993 formulation of property rights and called for a specific land clause to provide a "constitutional framework and protection for all land reform measures" (Constitutional Assembly 1995b: 13). While Theme Committee 4, which was responsible for the Bill of Rights, had thus far uncontroversially adopted a property clause that merely incorporated the 1993 Constitution's restitution provisions into the property clause itself, the report on Land Rights threw the proverbial cat among the pigeons. Some objected to Theme Committee 6.3's discussion of property rights, while others sensed an opportunity to reopen the debate on property rights and to once again question their very inclusion in the Bill of Rights. As a result, the Draft Bill of Rights published by the Constitutional Assembly on October 9, 1995, included an option that there be "no property clause at all."

It was in this context that an alternative option, a property clause that included specific land rights as well as a subclause insulating land reform from constitutional attack, began to gain momentum. While a strategy to insulate land restitution and land reform from constitutional attack had been implicit from early on in the debate, it was my suggestion in a submission to Theme Committee 6.3 that the property clause include a specific subclause insulating state action aimed at redressing past discrimination in the ownership and distribution of land rights, which the negotiators were able to rely upon as a compromise between those demanding the removal of the property clause and those, like the Democratic Party, who remained opposed to even the social democratic formulation modeled on the German Constitution (Constitutional Assembly 1995c: 13–41). Still the debate raged, and the draft formulations of the property clause continued to evolve.[20] Political agreement on the property clause was only finally reached at midnight on April 18, 1996, when subsection 28(8), the "affirmative action" or insulation subclause of the property clause, was modified so as to make it subject to section 36(1), the general limitations clause of the Constitution (Nicol and Bell 1997).

The final property clause reflects the democratic origins of the Constitutional Assembly. It not only guarantees the restitution of land taken after 1913 (Constitution 1996: Section 25(7)) and a right to legally secure tenure for those whose tenure is insecure as a result of racially discriminatory laws or practices (Section 25(6)), but also includes an obligation on the state to enable citizens to gain access to land on an equitable basis (Section 25(5)). Furthermore, the state is granted a limited exemption from the protective provisions of the property clause so as to empower it to take "legislative and other measures to achieve land, water and related reform, in order to redress the results of past racial discrimination" (Section 25(8)).

Despite agreement in the Constitutional Assembly, the property clause was presented to the Constitutional Court as violating the Constitutional Principles and therefore grounds for denying certification of the Constitution.[21] Two major objections were raised: first, that unlike the interim Constitution the new clause did not expressly protect the right to acquire, hold, and dispose of property; second, that the provisions governing expropriation and the payment of compensation were inadequate (Ex parte chairperson of the Constitutional Assembly 1996: Paragraph 70). The Constitutional Court rejected both of these arguments. First, the Court noted that the test to be applied was whether the formulation of the right met the standard of a "universally accepted fundamental right" as required by Constitutional Principle II. Second the Court surveyed international and foreign sources and observed that "if one looks to international conventions and foreign constitutions, one is immediately struck by the wide variety of formulations adopted to protect the right to property, as well as by the fact that significant conventions and constitutions contain no protection of property at all" (Paragraph 71). In conclusion the Court argued that it could not "uphold the argument that, because the formulation adopted is expressed in a negative and not a positive form and because it does not contain an express recognition of the right to acquire and dispose of property, it fails to meet the prescription of CPII" (Paragraph 72). The second objection met the same fate, with the Court concluding that an "examination of international conventions and foreign constitutions suggests that a wide range of criteria for expropriation and the payment of compensation exists," and thus the "approach taken in NT 25 [new text section 25] cannot be said to flout any universally accepted approach to the question" (Paragraph 73)

Although it may be argued that the property clause in the final Constitution is unique to South Africa and is the product of South Africa's particular history of dispossession, it is also important to note how resolution of the property question was framed by international options. While the Constitutional Court could argue that the particular formulation of the clause was compatible with global standards—given the variety of formulations in existence—it is also true that those who advocated that there should be no property clause in the Constitution were compelled by the politics of recognition of property rights to accept its inclusion.

The politics of constitution making in this instance were thus bounded on both sides. Both the option of widespread nationalization initially advocated by the African National Congress, which may have been facilitated by the exclusion of a property clause, and the demands for a strict protection of property guaranteeing market-value compensation for any interference were silenced. Instead the parties were able to use the international and foreign lexicon of treaties, constitutions, and case law to formulate a specifically South African compromise. This resolution both enabled the political transition and left open, for future fact-specific confrontations, the exact interpretation to be given to the new Constitution's property clauses.

Globalized?

While South Africa's "final" 1996 Constitution has been profoundly shaped by the struggles—political, social, and intellectual—that continue to be waged over fundamental political and social arrangements, including the nature and extent of property rights, the adoption of a common constitutional framework has begun to trace the boundaries of these at times irreconcilable differences. Focusing on the making of the property clause, I have tried to demonstrate both the complexity of the interaction of "local agency" and "global insistence" through the emergence of "bounded imaginations" and the resultant "hybridized outcomes," as well as the particular role that constitutionalism played in South Africa's democratic transition by supporting and giving hope to those who held fundamentally conflicting goals.

This harnessing or civilizing of political conflict is, it seems, achieved in two primary ways. First is the inherently open form of the constitution, which, despite all attempts to the contrary, is interpreted by opposing factions as supporting, at least in part, their particular vision of what is either possible or mandated. Second, by incorporating external formulations of constitutional rights and structures, as well as explicitly providing for the use of international and foreign legal sources, the constitutional framework implicitly silences options that cannot be justified in terms of the constitution read in a global context.

While the new constitutional framework has enabled the political transition by allowing opposing forces to imagine the possibility of achieving, at least in part, their particular vision within the terms of the Constitution, it has also worked to shape these imaginings through the creation of external reference points that delegitimate incompatible alternatives or visions. There remain, however, fairly large and incompatible differences between the alternative yet viable interpretations advocated in the context of these different political and social struggles. The incorporation of "global rules and practices" of constitutionalism here provides the institutional space for repeated attempts to advance any particular vision that may conceivably be presented as a compatible interpretation of the Constitution. The courts and in particular the new Constitutional Court thus perform an essential political role by keeping alive alternative possibilities while employing globally legitimated "rules" and "practices" to establish the outer boundaries of competing constitutional imaginations.

Political conflicts over property rights were thus projected into the future where their resolution will continue to depend on local responses to, interpretations of, and remakings of global standards. The outcome is a forever changing but bounded interaction in which the legal standards will represent at once a hybridized incorporation of global standards and the local formulation and production of global options. Once framed locally in response to both local and global possibilities, the property clause in the 1996 Constitution is now an example to be globalized and hybridized by others.

Conclusion

While I have tried to trace the contribution that international forces, examples, and legal sources made to the property clause in South Africa's new Bill of Rights, as well as the impact of local histories, ideas, and struggles on its ultimate form, I will conclude by trying to specify the conditions that made such hybridity possible and the often unintended consequences of these developments. First, it is important to recognize why "the international" might have had such valence in South Africa's transition. While the specific examples drawn upon by the particular players had no individual significance—from the United States, German, and Canadian constitutional formulations, to the histories of the Indian Claims Commission in the United States, land reforms in Taiwan and South Korea, and the equalization tax in postwar Germany, to constitutional conflicts over land reform in postcolonial India and the affirmative land-rights provisions in the Papua New Guinean Constitution—their role as part of an international text had a major impact on the shaping of the alternatives open to the South African participants. The power of "international experience," I would suggest, came not only from a fundamental belief that international norms provide an external point of reference for conflicting parties, as well as the ANC's strategic commitment to international norms as a means of precluding some of the ancien régime's most cherished claims, but also from a history in which the antiapartheid movement had long looked to international norms to sustain its critique of apartheid. As Nelson Mandela argued in explaining the ANC's adoption of a "human rights programme" at the opening of the ANC's workshop on a future bill of rights in May 1991, "international human rights standards have provided the legal and moral inspiration for the struggle against the antithesis of civilised values: apartheid. By characterizing apartheid as a crime, by protecting our combatants, by describing certain aspects of apartheid as genocide, international rules have validated our struggle. As a result, the apartheid regime has treated such developments with disdain and contempt. We have been cut off from full membership of the international community through South Africa's refusal to adhere to the basic international texts governing human rights" (1991).

Second, the process of negotiation and even serendipity (whether political or intellectual), in which the different interest groups and players posited alternative and often conflicting examples and formulations, created an unconscious process of hybridization. As some possibilities—such as nationalization or the total protection of all existing property rights—were precluded, other imaginable alternatives were produced from the remnants of past hopes and viable possibilities. These alternatives then became the building blocks of each successive formulation and reimagining.

Third, the two-stage constitution-making process adopted in the South African transition enabled the recognition of legitimate claims to restitution, even if narrowly defined, in the first phase, to become the basis for the explicit limitation of property rights in the final constitution. Not only was it possible to bring the right of restitution into the property clause, where it logically belonged, but the shift in power enabled the Constitutional Assembly—despite desperate struggles to the contrary—to include positive rights to land and an explicit affirmative exception for future land and water reform to be included within the property clause of the final constitution.

Finally, despite the obvious gains made by those of us who participated in the struggle for the restitution of land taken by the apartheid regime through acts of forced removal, which will always represent the darkest face of the crime of apartheid, we must also face up to the unintended consequence of our victory—the protection of the wealth of apartheid's beneficiaries. While it may be argued—and indeed was argued, at the ANC conference on a future bill of rights in 1991—that a peaceful transition to democracy required important compromises including the recognition of existing property rights, it is also true that the focus on land left the country's real wealth—now in companies, mines, stocks and bonds, as well as urban housing—completely unchallenged.

NOTES

Parts of this essay have been taken and elaborated from Heinz Klug, *Constituting Democracy: Law, Globalization, and South African's Political Reconstruction* (New York: Cambridge University Press, 2000), by permission of Cambridge University Press.

1. Programs range from that of the Ford Foundation, which has historically supported social movements struggling for democratic rights; to the United States Agency for International Development's programs "designed to support the creation of legal and political environments that will promote processes of democratization and market-based reform" (Rule of Law Consortium 1994: 1) in the former Soviet Union; to the World Bank's 1994 Economic Law Reform Project, assisting China in the reform of its legal framework. The World Bank noted that the "key to any market system is the reliance on a fair and credible legal framework: legal norms and procedures are needed to substitute for government control of economic decisions and to demarcate government's regulatory role in many areas of economic activity" (World Bank 1994a: 1).

2. For example, the work of Yves Dezalay and Bryant Garth on the construction of the field of international commercial arbitration is an example of recent sociolegal scholarship that has begun to examine the construction and transformation of particular systems of justice (1995, 1996).

3. For example, Boaventura Santos discusses the globalization of law and the role of counterhegemonic social forces in the advancement of human rights (1995: 250–377).

4. Bongiwe Njobe, now a senior civil servant in the Department of Agriculture, and Derek Hanekom, minister of land affairs and agriculture in Mandela's cabinet.

5. Richard Abel (1995) gives an excellent account of this activity.

6. As we experienced in the public furors over a suggested wealth tax to pay for compensation to landowners whose land would be expropriated for redistribution, or when suggestions were made about claims on land within the national parks.

7. Dolny and Klug (1992) give an example of an early contribution to the land reform debate from the perspective of the ANC Land Commission.

8. The Constitutional Committee was chaired by Zola Skweyiya, head of the ANC's legal department, under whose authority the land commission initially fell. Skweyiya's interest in and commitment to these issues are reflected in his 1990 article "Towards a Solution to the Land Question in Post-Apartheid South Africa."

9. It should also be noted that, at the same time, activists working in or identified by the ANC Land Commission were being exposed to international

experiences of land reform, including a Ford Foundation–funded six-week minicourse organized by the Land Tenure Center at the University of Wisconsin–Madison.

10. Elsewhere I have criticized the government's Advisory Committee on Land Allocations (ACLA) (Klug 1996a: 166–71).

11. These included the following conferences: "Towards a Non-Racial, Non-Sexist Judiciary in South Africa," Constitutional Committee of the ANC and the Community Law Centre, University of the Western Cape, Cape Town, March 26–28, 1993; "Structures of Government for a United Democratic South Africa," the Community Law Centre, University of the Western Cape, ANC Constitutional Committee, Center for Development Studies, University of the Western Cape, Cape Town, March 26–28, 1992; "National Conference on Affirmative Action," University of the Western Cape, ANC Constitutional Committee and Community Law Centre, Port Elizabeth, October 10–12, 1991; "Conference on a Bill of Rights for a Democratic South Africa," Constitutional Committee of the ANC and the Centre for Socio-Legal Studies, University of Natal, Durban, Salt Rock, Natal, May 10–12, 1991; "Constitutional Court for a Future South Africa," ANC/CALS/Lawyers for Human Rights, Magaliesberg, February 1–3, 1991; and "Seminar on Electoral Systems," Centre for Development Studies (CDS)/ANC Constitutional Department, Stellenbosch, November 2–4, 1990.

12. While I participated erratically in the meetings of this group, I did submit a memorandum on the experience of the Indian Claims Commission in the United States as both an example of a land claims process and as a warning against limiting the claimants' remedies to monetary compensation instead of the return of land that was the basic demand of claimants. In the debates that followed we were able to use the experience of the ICC to argue that cash settlements could never satisfy demands for the return of land, pointing to the fact that after thirty years and millions of dollars Native American claims remained unsatisfied.

13. Budlender was director-general of the Department of Land Affairs, the highest-ranking civil servant in the department, from 1995 to 2000.

14. For example, a letter dated July 31, 1991, from J. De Villiers, minister of public works and land affairs, responding to a letter from lawyers representing a claimant community, stated in part, "I do appeal to you to advise your clients not to take the law into their own hands because that would unnecessarily complicate consideration of possible claims. It would only serve to increase the temperature of the debate rather than to arrive at a solution."

15. The World Bank published the series "Informal Discussion Papers on Aspects of the Economy of South Africa" between 1992 and 1994, including, for example, *World Bank Southern Africa Department, South African Agriculture: Structure, Performance and Options for the Future* (1994b).

16. This article was eventually published (Binswanger and Deininger 1993).

17. When the World Bank's Rural Restructuring Programme was presented in South Africa at the LAPC-organized Land Redistribution Options Conference in October 1993, it had to compete with a range of suggestions and received serious academic and political criticism. As a result, the program never gained a life of its own, but became yet another source of the smorgasbord of alternatives both enabling and constraining the options available to policymakers in the new South Africa. Its most enduring impacts may be its endorsement of land restitution and reform on the one hand, and the emphasis upon the market in achieving these reforms on the other.

18. As late as October 1995 the Draft Bill of Rights being considered by the Constitutional Assembly's Theme Committee 4 included as Option 2 "No property clause at all" (Constitutional Assembly, Theme Committee 1995a). The Constitutional Assembly, Constitutional Committee Sub-Committee Draft Bill of Rights includes a discussion of the nature of the right to property in international law (1995a: 126–40).

19. A group marching on the World Trade Centre in June 1993 delivered a land rights memorandum to the negotiators. It was followed by a march in central Pretoria in September 1993 in which about 600 people from 25 rural communities threatened to reoccupy land from which they had been removed by the apartheid government. Marchers demanded the unconditional restitution of land, the establishment of a land claims court, and guaranteed security of tenure for farmworkers and labor tenants. The Transvaal Rural Action Committee, which organized the march, also called for the rejection of the proposed property clause in the constitution (Adrian Hadland, "Demonstrators hand govt land ultimatum," *Business Day*, September 2, 1993).

20. New versions were published in the October 30, 1995, Refined Working Draft (2d ed.) of the Constitution (Constitutional Assembly 1995d). Another ANC proposal was published in the February 9–16, 1996, edition of *Constitutional Talk*—the official newsletter of the Constitutional Assembly. Still another was published in the April 22–May 18, 1996, edition of *Constitutional Talk*.

21. Under the original political compromise, the Constitutional Assembly was to be constrained by the Constitutional Principles negotiated between the parties and appended to the 1993 interim Constitution. The Constitutional Court was empowered to certify whether a draft constitution prepared by the Constitutional Assembly met the requirements of the Constitutional Principles. The Constitutional Court in 1996 first declined to certify the draft and then certified the new text adopted in response to the Court's first certification judgment.

REFERENCES

Abel, Richard. 1995. *Politics by other means: Law in the struggle against apartheid, 1980–1994.* New York: Routledge.

Ackerman, Bruce. 1997. The rise of world constitutionalism. *Virginia Law Review* 83:771–97.

ANC (African National Congress). 1989a [1955]. The Freedom Charter. Reprinted in *Hastings International and Comparative Law Review* 12:318–21.

———. 1989b [1988]. Constitutional guidelines for a democratic South Africa 1988. Reprinted in *Hastings International and Comparative Law Review* 12:322–24.

———. 1993. *Draft Bill of Rights: Preliminary Revised Version.* February.

ANC Constitutional Committee. 1990. *A Bill of Rights for a new South Africa: A working document of the ANC Constitutional Committee.* Bellville: University of the Western Cape Centre for Development Studies.

ANC Land Commission. 1991. *Land Manifesto for ANC National Conference.* July. Durban, South Africa.

Bauman, Richard W. 1992. Property rights in the Canadian constitutional context. *South African Journal on Human Rights* 8:344–61.

Beatty, David M. 1994. Human rights and the rules of law. In D. M. Beatty, ed., *Human rights and judicial review: A comparative perspective.* Dordrecht: M. Nijhoff.

Binswanger, Hans P., and Klaus Deininger. 1993. South Africa land policy: The legacy of history and current options. *World Development* 21.

Budlender, Geoff. 1992. The right to equitable access to land. *South African Journal on Human Rights* 8:295–304.

Centre for Development Studies. 1991. *A Bill of Rights for a democratic South Africa: Papers and report of a conference convened by the ANC Constitutional Committee.* May. Durban, South Africa. Bellville: University of the Western Cape Centre for Development Studies.

Chaskalson, Matthew. 1995. Stumbling towards section 28: Negotiations over property rights at the multiparty talks. *South African Journal on Human Rights* 11:222–40.

Christiansen, Robert. 1993. *Aide memoire: Preparation of a rural restructuring program.* June 15. Document in author's possession.

Claassens, Aninka. 1991. For whites only: Land ownership in South Africa. In Michael De Klerk, ed., *Harvest of discontent: The land question in South Africa.* Mowbray, Capetown: Institute for a Democratic Alternative for South Africa

———. 1992. Editorial. *South African Journal on Human Rights* 8:v.

Constitutional Assembly. 1995a. *Constitutional Committee Sub-Committee, Draft Bill of Rights,* vol. 1, *Explanatory memoranda.* October 9.

————. 1995b. *Constitutional Committee Sub-Committee, Documentation: Land rights.* October 9.

————. 1995c. *Constitutional Committee, Documentation,* vol. 2A, *Land rights.* September 15.

————. 1995d. Refined working draft. 2d ed. of the Constitution. October 30.

————. 1996a. *Constitutional talk.* February 9–16.

————. 1996b. *Constitutional talk.* April 22–May 18.

Constitutional Assembly, Theme Committee 4. 1995a. *Draft Bill of Rights.* October 9.

Constitutional Assembly, Theme Committee 6.3. 1995b. *Specialised structures of government: Land rights, documentation.* September 11.

————. 1995c. *Specialised structures of government: Documentation,* vol. 2A, *Land rights.* September 15.

Cross, Catherine. 1992. An alternative legality: The property rights question in relation to South African land reform. *South African Journal on Human Rights* 8:305–31.

Democratic Party. 1993. Freedom under the rule of law: Advancing liberty in the new South Africa. Draft Bill of Rights, May 1993.

Dezalay, Yves, and Bryant Garth. 1995. Merchants of law as moral entrepreneurs: Constructing international justice from the competition for transnational business disputes. *Law and Society Review* 29:27–64.

————. 1996. *Dealing in virtue: International commercial arbitration and the con struction of a transnational legal order.* Chicago: University of Chicago Press.

Dolny, Helena, and Heinz Klug. 1992. Land reform: Legal support and economic regulation. In Glenn Moss and Ingrid Obrey, eds., *South African Review 6: From 'Red Friday' to Codesa.* Johannesburg: Ravan Press.

Elias, T. O. 1965. The evolution of law and government in modern Africa. In Hilda Kuper and Leo Kuper, eds., *African law adaptation and development.* Berkeley: University of California Press.

Ex Parte Chairperson of the Constitutional Assembly. 1996. In *Re Certification of the Constitution of the Republic of South Africa, 1996* (4) SA 744.

Friedman, Steven. 1993. *The Long journey: South Africa's quest for a negotiated settlement.* Johannesburg: Centre for Policy Studies.

Gardner, James A. 1980. *Legal imperialism: American lawyers and foreign aid in Latin America.* Madison: University of Wisconsin Press.

Government of the Republic of South Africa. 1991. *Abolition of racially based land measures Act 108.*

————. 1993. *Constitution of the Republic of South Africa, Act 200.*

————. 1996. *Constitution of the Republic of South Africa, Act 108.*

Greenberg, Douglas, et al., eds. 1993. Introduction. *Constitutionalism and democracy: Transitions in the contemporary world.* New York: Oxford University Press.

Klug, Heinz. 1996a. Bedevilling agrarian reform: The impact of past, present and future legal frameworks. In Johan Van Zyl, Johann Kirsten, and Hans P. Binswanger, eds., *Agricultural land reform in South Africa: Policies, markets and mechanisms.* Capetown: Oxford University Press.

———. 1996b. Historical claims and the right to restitution. In Johan Van Zyl, Johann Kirsten, and Hans P. Binswanger, eds., *Agricultural land reform in South Africa: Policies, markets and mechanisms.* Capetown: Oxford University Press.

Lawson, Frederick H. 1955. *A common lawyer looks at the civil law.* Ann Arbor: University of Michigan Law School.

Mandela, Nelson. 1991. Address, on the occasion of the ANC's Bill of Rights Conference, May. In *Papers and report of a conference convened by the ANC Constitutional Committee.* Bellville: University of the Western Cape Centre for Development Studies.

Murphy, John. 1992. Insulating land reform from constitutional impugnment: An Indian case study. *South African Journal on Human Rights* 8:362–88.

Nicol, Mike, and Paul Bell, eds. 1997. *The making of the constitution: The story of South Africa's Constitutional Assembly, May 1994 to December 1996.* Claremont, South Africa: Churchill Murray.

Republic of South Africa. 1993. *Government's proposals on a Charter of Fundamental Rights.* February 2.

Robertson, Michael. 1990. Dividing the land: An introduction to apartheid land law. In Christina Murray and Catherine O'Regan, eds., *No place to rest: Forced removals and the law in South Africa.* Capetown: Oxford University Press.

Rule of Law Consortium. 1994. *ARD/Checchi joint venture, program circular.* November 18. Washington: United States Agency for International Development (USAID).

Santos, Boaventura de Sousa. 1995. *Towards a new common sense: Law, science, and politics in the paradigmatic transition.* New York: Routledge.

Schlesinger, Rudolf B., ed. 1988. *Comparative law: Cases, text, materials.* 5th ed. Mineola, N.Y.: Foundation Press.

Seidman, R. B. 1968. Law and economic development in independent, English-speaking, Sub-Saharan Africa. In Thomas W. Hutchison, ed., *Africa and law: Developing legal systems in African Commonwealth nations.* Madison: University of Wisconsin.

Skweyiya, Zola. 1990. Towards a solution to the land question in post-apartheid South Africa: Problems and models. *South African Journal on Human Rights* 6:195–214.

South African Law Commission. 1991. *Interim report on group and human rights.* August.

Statement. 1991. Statement from 19 Communities on the Government's Advisory Commission on Land Allocation, September 15.

Swanson, Edward. 1992. A land claims court for South Africa: Report on work in progress. *South African Journal on Human Rights* 8:332–43.

Tamanaha, Brian Z. 1995. The lessons of law-and-development studies. *American Journal of International Law* 89:470–86.

Thompson, Cliff F. 1968. The sources of law in the new nations of Africa: A case study from the Republic of the Sudan. In Thomas W. Hutchison, ed., *Africa and law: Developing legal systems in African Commonwealth nations.* Madison: University of Wisconsin.

Trubek, David M., and Marc Galanter. 1974. Scholars in self-estrangement: Some reflections on the crisis in law and development studies in the United States. *Wisconsin Law Review* 1974:1062–1102.

von Mehren, Arthur T., and James R. Gordley. 1977. *The civil law system: An introduction to the study of comparative law.* 2d ed. Boston: Little, Brown.

World Bank. 1992. *Experience with agricultural policy: Lessons for South Africa.* Washington, D.C.: World Bank.

———. 1994a. Press release October 18. Washington, D.C.: World Bank.

———. 1994b. *Southern Africa department, South African agriculture: Structure, performance and options for the future. Informal discussion paper on aspects of the economy of South Africa.* Washington, D.C.: World Bank.

———. 1994c. *Summary: Options for land reform and rural restructuring, in land redistribution options conference October 12–15, 1993: Proceedings.* Land and Agricultural Policy Centre.

Legitimating the New Legal Orthodoxy

Yves Dezalay and Bryant G. Garth

The preceding essays reveal a number of theoretical approaches to account for recent transformations in the rules governing the state and the economy. The competing theories tend to agree about the importance of the rule of law and the judiciary as well as legally oriented nongovernmental organizations. The essays on national stories in Argentina, Japan, Mexico, and South Africa also apply the same criteria for assessing local changes. The converging criteria, evident in all the essays, point to a new orthodoxy—a legal one. The potential new orthodoxy is in part sustained and legitimated through academic theories. Since one of the major purposes of this book is to try to develop theoretical approaches to understanding the various phenomena previously depicted, this concluding essay will focus more on how the production of theories relates to the processes that we have seen.

What appears as the best legal and social scientific expertise is the product of national and academic hierarchies that serve to make certain approaches legitimate and others illegitimate. Theoretical approaches tend to be blind to the processes that create and legitimate them and to similar processes that determine how and why some are exported and imported. Our own approach—described and to some extent exemplified in this essay—seeks to find tools to overcome these problems. We recognize, of course, that we cannot completely eliminate them. Our own emphasis on "Americanization" as a key aspect of the new legal orthodoxy, for example, may make the process appear to be inevitable. Our aim, however, is to see what makes it seem inevitable, which includes processes involving our own work. A close analysis of the processes of import and export can reveal how a new state orthodoxy privileges and highlights law—and even certain approaches to law—in state governance.

From our perspective, the content and the scope of rules produced to govern the state and the economy cannot be separated from the circumstances of their creation and production. That is not to say that the rules are somehow the inevitable products of a set of social forces, but the circumstances of production shape the range of possibilities that are likely to be contemplated and implemented—or ignored. These *national* markets for the production of rules, moreover, are central to the production of rules that govern in *transnational* contexts, including the rules exported by transnational institutions. Transnational battles about the appropriate rules of the game are therefore continuations of national battles about the governance of the state and economy. The setting of the transnational rules of the game, in particular, requires that we study the field of state power in the United States, the leading exporter of rules, as well as in competing countries and countries that are more likely to be considered net importers of legal rules.

Consistent with our emphasis on the circumstances of production, we have found that, following Bourdieu, the best way to understand the rules and institutions that are imported and exported is to examine their genesis—where they come from, what material was used to create them, and what conflicts were present at the time.[1] To understand these processes, drawing again on Bourdieu, we use the conceptual tool of the field—in particular, the field of state power, which can be defined as the semiautonomous space where the competition for state power and for shaping the rules governing that competition takes place. The field of state power is a site where different expertises and know-how compete for ascendancy. Accordingly, the best position in the competition is to succeed not only in promoting a particular expertise, but also in dictating the value of that particular currency in relation to the offerings of competitors. This contest thus involves the relative values of, among other things, particular languages, academic disciplines, professions, and national credentials.

Law in the United States historically has been able—indeed expected and desired—to gain the position of setting the key terms of legitimacy.[2] Given this position, it is not too much of an exaggeration to say that the processes of promoting the "rule of law" today can be understood to a great extent as an effort to promote a U.S. product as the lingua franca for business and politics. This is not the result of a national plot or conspiracy.[3] It follows from the structure of the field of state power in the United States. Again, that does not mean that all U.S.

actors try to export a U.S. style of the law, but those who have advanced or seek to advance in the field of state power in the United States quite often and naturally choose to invest in the law. It is then natural to use variations on the same approach—internalized as a habitus in Bourdieu's terms.

What is often described as "globalization" involves competition in laws, approaches to law, and approaches to the state and governance. Sometimes, of course, the competition in models or rules is quite self-conscious. In the conference at which these essays were first presented, several of the commentators showed how this competition affected their own careers and practices. James Carter, a lawyer with Sullivan and Cromwell in New York and a practitioner in international transactions, highlighted a competition between particular legal systems:

> There is, of course, competition among national legal systems that is relevant to our civil court system. The competition that my colleagues in the corporate side get involved in, and then when things go wrong I get involved, are the mega-deals of the world. Building the infra-structure in places from Argentina to Kazakhstan, privatizing government enterprises across the globe, accessing capital markets in connection to those activities, and in terms of selling securities internationally more generally. Among those issues, the first question is whether it is going to be governed by New York law or English law: There are only two choices. Even if all of this is taking place in Kazakhstan, because the actors are multinational banks, organizations, and so on, there will be aspects of this that will affect the United States. And the English will say, when making their arguments, that somehow if you have New York law you might get drawn into the U.S. court system, and that is something you do not want to do, and they will say, no, we do not.

According to Carter, therefore, there are two dominant sets of rules for private legal systems, and only they can gain the legitimacy of actors around the globe.

Similarly, Jacques Werner, a Swiss lawyer and international arbitrator, spoke of competition for the business of international commercial arbitration among new centers opening practically every week. The competition historically has involved particular laws and the rules used to handle the arbitrations. He also suggested, however, that the competition in some respects was diminishing. According to Werner,

The United Nations (UNCITRAL) United Nations Commission for International Trade Law whose seat is in Vienna, Austria, has constructed the Model Rules of International Arbitration and the Model Law on International Arbitration, in order to give countries of the world a model upon which to base legislation. More and more countries of the world have adopted legislation which if not a carbon copy of the UNCITRAL Rules, still very closely resembles the UNCITRAL Model Law, in the sense that they have grounded their rules in the same . . . basic principles which all Model International Arbitration Laws have.

Competition among different nationally produced models and approaches helped to produce a more uniform system with international legitimacy. But a story of competition does not fully explain the construction of an international field. There was also a strong story of cooperation within the field of international commercial arbitration (Dezalay and Garth 1996). The UNCITRAL Model Rules and the Model Law were thus the product of competition and cooperation among those who worked together at the international level to reinforce the power and credibility of international commercial arbitration within the national settings from which they came and to which they returned. A "consensus" developed, but of course it represented a consensus that favored the dominant approaches of the major centers of power in arbitration.

Outside of the business area, particular nationally produced positions can also be promoted quite explicitly. A U.S. position on the rule of law, for example, has been promoted almost self-righteously in much of the literature about the role of NGOs, about democratization, and especially about proper government-business relations. The current denunciations of an illegitimate "crony capitalism" in Asia are nearly always coupled with an argument for particular legal prescriptions. While Robert Rubin and Jeffrey Sachs were arguing vehemently in the media over what economic recipes were necessary to solve the Asian crisis, for example, they agreed in speeches to Yale Law School alumni in November 1998 that the long-term solution was to bring the rule of law to Asia.[4]

The individuals who analyze these debates and activities concerning the production of national and transnational rules and convert them into scholarly theories and descriptions are themselves actors in the production of governing rules. They are participants in the contests of expertise and value. Whether from dominant or dominated groups, these analysts are embedded in specific national settings and in specific professional disciplinary homes. After all, their careers are national. Further, as part of their national careers, analysts quite often seek to export the wars that they are fighting domestically. For example, in the 1950s, the "foreign policy establishment" in the United States, led by elite lawyers associated with the Council of Foreign Relations in New York City, developed a strategy for the cold war that involved finding and even creating allies among their counterparts abroad. Leaders abroad who were friendly to the United States could help the United States in the cold war against the Soviet Union and, not insignificantly, help to maintain the influence and power of those at home who formed the strategically important friendships abroad. Similarly, labor unions and environmental groups in the United States today take their fights for influence over domestic policy into transnational arenas such as NAFTA[5] and the Multilateral Investment Agreement.[6] Success in the transnational arena helps particular groups build domestic legitimacy and protect their national power and influence from erosion through transnational decision making and rule construction.

Those who participate in these debates as analysts and policymakers are not all in the same position. In particular, relatively dominated individuals—pure academics, for example—must compensate for their lack of power by overinvesting in scientific or moral authority. In making such investments, as already suggested, they necessarily embed themselves as actors and producers in the story that has also produced them. That is to say, what defines moral or scientific authority is provided by the national histories in which they are educated and formed. It is not surprising, therefore, that specifically national actors come to believe quite naturally that their universals—again the product of very particular local histories—should be regarded as universally valid. The result is a faith in such exports as, for example, democracy, the rule of law, or recipes for economic development, and this faith can make it very difficult to study the processes of rule making and exportation critically. There is a natural tendency especially for academic idealists to suspend some of their academic skepticism when they mobilize on behalf of specific objectives consistent with their accepted universals. In such cases, they tend to rely less on their scientific tools and more on the authority of the professional expertise or discipline they represent.

The contradiction is that everyone is fighting in the name of "universals" that are defined by national histories and disciplinary evolutions. A further complicating factor is that we are in a period when the hierarchies and maps of the disciplines are changing. As Wallerstein has noted (1991), the division of the roles of the disciplines is the product mainly of the nineteenth-century state. Political science thus focuses on national government, for example, while anthropology focuses on colonial relationships. Since international strategies today are contributing to reshape the state, perhaps, as many argue, even promote its disappearance, the division of labor between disciplines—and scientific discourse about the state and government—is also at stake. The sense of concern with these issues is apparent in the current general interest in the notion of "governance"—which allows all disciplines to meet and to fight (Dezalay and Garth 2002). The term *governance* refers to nothing more specific than the domain of institutions and rules, but the success of the term comes from the fact that it allows all the potential players to contribute to the debates. It can include formal procedures and rules as well as the more informal spaces typically studied by anthropologists. However defined, it is clear that the ascendancy of this term is part of a new focus on trying to understand the very important transformations in the state and state institutions that are now taking place.

Consistent with this approach, a growing number of scholars in the social science disciplines now state that they are interested in the law, courts, and legal institutions. Unfortunately, however, very few scholars actually inquire into the structural history of the creation and production of national legal practices. That is to say, there is very little effort to explain the "rules for the production of the rules." Instead, the discourses within the disciplines tend to proceed in a quasi-legalistic mode, describing what the rules should be. In Bourdieu's terms, what we find is "prescriptive discourse" or "description as prescription" (1981). By describing what can be as if it is possible, the discourse contributes to making the desired outcome possible and reasonable—ideally as a self-fulfilling prophecy.[7] As Annelise Riles observed at the conference, "whenever international law and global institutional structures are discussed," we always see the phenomenon of "description becoming justification." Within this kind of legal or quasi-legal discourse, as suggested above, we find very little effort to describe how the law is made. Those who push law reform typically seek to make the desired reform appear to be necessary and legitimate. In doing so, they are careful not to do anything that could destroy the credibility and symbolic value of law—including discussing what makes the credibility of law (see Bourdieu 1987).

This general phenomenon relates again to the division of labor of disciplines. Many of the social science disciplines were constructed at a time when the authority of the law was uncontested. Economics and sociology, for example, were constructed around the law in many parts of the world, challenging the law from outside. Marx could be seen from this perspective as one of many challengers arguing that it is necessary to take into account the social context of the economy and the sphere of production. Such challengers from outside, however, have rarely sought to understand why the law is what it is. Efforts to examine the law itself have instead tended to reproduce legal discourse. Sociological accounts, for example, which define (or challenge) the commitment of professions to the public good tend to reproduce professional stances (e.g., Talcott Parsons), while instrumental arguments that a certain law is "required" for a particular economic or political reason still leave aside the topic of the production and legitimation of law.

Within the countries that are the leading global producers of the rule of law, above all the United States, the prevailing hierarchy of professions and disciplines therefore plays a major role in warding off scrutiny of the production and legitimation of law itself. Social scientists, lured by the higher status and better pay within law schools, are co-opted into becoming law professors, making it that much easier to take for granted the taboos that are part of the construction of the credibility of law (Garth and Sterling 1998).

In sum, there are many reasons for the lack of attention to the topic of the social construction of rules—taking into account competitive processes and hierarchies of authority. For those who wish to break some of the taboos and begin to tell this complex story, another problem is that the analysis of the internal fabrication and refabrication of law remains largely at the level of "journalistic or academic gossip." Professional hierarchies and strategies are the subject of dinner conversations involving ambitious academics, but they are rarely the stuff of social scientific analysis. There are few acceptable social scientific tools inside or outside of the law that can be used to get around these taboos.

This book therefore comes at a time when, despite a truly remarkable convergence of disciplinary interest in governance, including law, there has been very little exploration of the black box that produces the law and more generally the rules of the game for governance. Indeed, from a sociological point of view, a better metaphor of the space that produces the law is that of a black hole. Few can get into this powerful core, and those who do are typically absorbed into that otherwise invisible space.

In this conclusion we try to sketch an approach to make sense of social constructions of rules at the national and transnational levels. We do not rely on the slippery idea of globalization, even though this book can be read as a discussion of efforts to "globalize" law as part of a universal prescription for the legitimate state. Instead we focus more precisely on actors who may use the slogan or concept of "globalization" in promoting their strategies. In particular, we focus our attention on international capital, international strategies, and national palace wars (see Dezalay and Garth 2002). International strategies allow actors to take advantage of the national value of international capital—degrees, expertises, and networks with international credibility—in order to build their own positions at home—their own local palace wars. Depending on their positions and local structures of power, the use of international strategies may lead to a reshaping and transformation of local institutions and governing rules.

What we characterize as *international capital*—including degrees, expertises, and relationships—does not exist apart from the struggles that take place in more local contexts. The relative values of the Harvard Law School versus the Kennedy School versus other expertises or other places in the United States, for example, are determined by local palace wars. Further, the competition for setting the relative values of international capital locally is structured by the historically determined—but always contested—hierarchy of states. In the period after World War II, in particular, it is easy to map a shift in the relative value of expertises made in the United States versus those made in Europe. We cannot talk of international institutions, rules, and capital, in other words, without at the same time examining the role of imperialist processes in producing them.

The essays in this book have served a double purpose. First, as we have noted, the topic of the construction of rules and its relationship to international transformations has gained increasing attention from social scientists and from legal scholars. The essays illustrate the variety of approaches that are emerging. In addition, as part of our own effort to exemplify a research approach that can help us understand these processes, we can draw on the other contributions to suggest how the scholarly approaches themselves may fit into the processes that we (and they) are studying. In using these essays for this purpose, we will undoubtedly simplify and distort the complexities of their argument. Nevertheless, we hope that our effort to push the analysis one level further will be helpful to an understanding of the processes of production, exportation, and importation that are the focus of this book. Academic work plays an essential part in determining what can and cannot gain credibility in the United States and elsewhere.

Four essays focus on a key point of entry into the academic literature, which might be considered a potential or emerging new orthodoxy about transnational processes for the production of rules. The potential new orthodoxy focuses on what has been called the "emancipatory pillar" by Boaventura de Sousa Santos (1995), which is also the world of NGOs and advocacy networks described by Kathryn Sikkink (see Keck and Sikkink 1998). The authors in this first part are leading scholars in seeing the potential of this new orthodoxy—with a greater focus on institutions, nonstate actors, and especially the rule of law. In somewhat simplified terms, we might describe the potential orthodoxy as one that sees the formation of new groups around issues such as human rights, violence against women, and the protection of the environment. Individuals from many countries form local NGOs and advocacy networks to promote their political agendas, attend conferences, use the Internet to exchange information, and mobilize on behalf of new rules that favor these progressive causes. If successful, they transform their concerns into legal rules that can be protected both through international mechanisms—new institutions and procedures—and through the sanction of publicity. In terms of the production of international law, as David Trubek summarized at the conference:

> There also appears to be an agreement that in the processes of global restructuring in economics and politics, in social arrangements in world society conceived in broad terms, that there is a multiplicity, a proliferation of actors. There may be disagreements about which actors are most important, but there can be no question of their multiplicity. States of course are there, but these states may not operate as unitary players, as some theory suggests. Anne-Marie Slaughter has disaggregated the state and suggested that pieces of the state might float out of and work with pieces of other

states, creating horizontal regulatory networks that may or may not be completely aligned with other parts of the state from which the fragment comes. There is also general agreement surrounding the proposition that states are changing, both internally and in their role in the world system.

The proliferating actors can produce a new law that brings new legal standards for the protection of the environment and for the promotion of human rights.

This learned approach to international law is prescriptive in the sense that it promotes the construction of a new international state along the lines favored by the analysis. The prescribed model, not surprisingly, fits well with the U.S. model of the production of law and rules, which also suggests that—if the model is successfully exported—lawyers from the most elite institutions will occupy the key leadership positions. We do not disagree with the proposition that the process of constructing this transnational state is moving quickly. It is also understandable and to some extent unavoidable for scholarship describing this process to help make the process natural and seemingly inevitable. Nevertheless, whether or not we believe that the goal of an international state modeled on the United States is politically desirable, it is important to distinguish that political goal from what can be learned through critical and self-critical scholarly approaches. Our own effort, as suggested above, is to try to find tools for that kind of analysis.

Our academic objective is therefore to produce a more "realist" reading and understanding of the production of the new international economic and political order. The first essays come from different disciplines and traditions, and indeed represent what can be seen as the avant garde in the study of the production and export of the rule of law. Nevertheless, the circumstances of the production of work on the export and import of the rule of law tend to leave out phenomena that also should be examined through systematic research—in particular, academic and international hierarchies that are almost never mentioned by scholars of these phenomena. From this perspective, the Slaughter and Sikkink essays can be seen as representations of prescriptive discourse close to that of traditional legal scholarship—even while opposing an earlier legal orthodoxy linked to particular understandings of the state and economy.

Learned producers operating in a particular social context may seek to build up a new orthodoxy to replace or modify what went before. Part of this process involves strong oppositional statements challenging the status quo both in terms of its substance and how we understand it. Such oppositional representations—typical of legal scholars—can be novel and enlightening, but the point for present purposes is that, even when they challenge the established order, the producers of these prescriptive discourses are careful not to dismantle the tools that the older establishment used to build its legitimacy. The aim is precisely to use the conventional tools to pursue objectives of different groups or generations.

The Slaughter essay, for example, argues for a rethinking of the framework for examining international law—one that moves nonstate actors to center stage. It challenges that prior orthodoxy of states as the key actors and subjects in international law. The essay is reflexive in the stance that it takes toward different contributions that can be made to international law from minority and women law professors. As the essay suggests, they cannot be expected to have the same agenda as the earlier WASP establishment or even the generation of Europeans who helped reproduce international law in the post–World War II period. What Slaughter ultimately arrives at, however, is a new representation of universals. She speaks of a desired "community of law" which—typical in international law generally—does not take into account tactical approaches, hierarchies, and power struggles. The fights that underlie "gentlemen's agreements," for example, are outside of the approach in her essay. The goal is a new consensus that produces newer and better norms.

The goal of legal discourse, here as elsewhere, is precisely to gain recognition as natural, legitimate, and taken for granted by the relevant community. From the point of view of preserving the legitimacy of the desired result, there is no reason to examine too carefully how success is obtained. It also goes without saying, even though it is relevant to the general process, that Slaughter, fortified with the status of the Harvard Law School, can speak with an authority that requires little explanation. The question of Harvard's role in the production of norms (and, more generally, of who has authority to speak in the name of the law) is not something that belongs in prescriptive discourse. Instead, Slaughter's discussion of globalization, the consequence of states losing power, and the new group of NGOs gaining power presents a "soft" transnational law that can be seen as the wave of the future—already nearly there and something that can be welcomed rather than feared.

The approach of Sikkink is similar but draws more on empirical research to support this potential new orthodoxy. The essay focuses on NGOs and their activities according to what they are and how they ought to operate in a manner consistent with their defined role. The essay develops categories that can be used to codify the immanent theory of NGOs. It does not concentrate on history, the battles that have gone into this construction, or what the costs might be of this new orthodoxy. In the manner of prescriptive discourse, the essay focuses more on what the NGOs should do than on what they actually do. Sikkink's analysis thus describes a desired evolution that will help contribute to making the evolution happen. The dilemmas raised by NGOs—and the power of law that has come with this strategy—are addressed at the end of the essay, but its purpose is not to highlight how the structure of the world of NGOs may systematically produce arguments and norms that both overrepresent powerful NGOs in the north and privilege a kind of argument that favors the discourses used and legitimated in the northern centers of power—places like Harvard Law School.

As with respect to Slaughter, however, the focus is very much on a description that also becomes a prescription. Indeed, Sikkink's essay complements Slaughter's by providing empirical research that adds legitimacy to what Slaughter portrays as the new legal orthodoxy—law produced by NGOs and epistemic communities. Examined together, the Sikkink and Slaughter essays help in fact to uncover some of the internal dynamics that produce and legitimate the law. As Bourdieu notes (e.g., 1987), a common social process is for professionals to speak for dominated groups by directing more or less harsh criticisms toward dominant groups. The speakers for the dominated can then use all the recipes of the dominant to seek to revise the agenda to take more account of the dominated—or more account of science, rationality, or morality. The result is a hierarchical division of work in producing and helping to legitimate a new discourse of domination. In this case, we cannot resist noting the complementarity between scientific and empirical literature from a political scientist in the Midwest and new discourse produced by a law professor at Harvard. Legal representation is combined with more scientific mechanisms to ensure its credibility.

The legal authority embedded in Harvard can draw on—and give credibility to—social science, which provides the analysis of the new pluralism and disaggregation of states, and the new strength of epistemic communities and issue networks.

The analyses of Slaughter and Sikkink may very well be the key to a new orthodoxy. As we have already suggested, their analyses naturally do not provide much detail about what it happening inside the production of such an orthodoxy. Most obviously, it is not clear that everyone is happily coexisting together in this effort to work together to produce new and emancipatory global norms. Rather, closer examination of details that are not generally studied would likely find battles between the old establishment and the new speakers for dominated groups. Again, power struggles within the world of NGOs and contestants about soft law are not generally discussed in academic literature. Annelise Riles at the conference made a similar observation about the fascination of academics with the idea of networks as builders of consensus and ultimately of law:

> The question to be asked is, why the appeal of network right now? I do not mean the appeal of nongovernmental actors or things beyond the state, I mean, why this particular form at this particular moment? We could have collective institutions, as we've had in the past, we could have clans as anthropologists often find, we could have families, we could have all kinds of things. Nothing, however, has quite gripped the public and the academic imagination as much as this word "network" has.

She suggested that academics who are quite comfortable with criticisms of law that "expose the reality of ambiguity and indeterminacy in the law," indeed "even seeing power relations at stake in the legitimization of law," tend not to apply their analyses to networks. For some reason,

> a critique of these networks does not seem so necessary. We are not struck by the fact that they are indeterminate and hegemonic and are pretending to be real things out there. Nevertheless, in the academic understanding, as in the self-understanding of networks, networks are a functional equivalent to, if not a precursor for law. So, why could not the same critiques be relevant?

Articles by practitioners have begun to focus in some detail on the divisions in the roles of NGOs, double games of criticism and co-optation, and the hierarchies and divisions within what is called the NGO community (see, e.g., Fox and Brown 1998; Hulme and Edwards 1997). Those immersed in the battles of practice are better able to see and report on the conflicts and compromises that do not fit well into the prescriptive discourses characteristic of legal scholarship. As Nancy Reichman stated at the conference in reference to her research on the implementation of the Montreal Protocol for the protection of the ozone layer, "The people who are constructing this community are very savvy institutional entrepreneurs. They know how to get people committed to their organization. And they know that ideas alone are not enough, interest alone is not enough, and so they systematically build social patterns."

Similarly, when NGOs and the networks that unite them are described in legal scholarship as below, beside, and around the state, they tend to be presented without an emphasis on the conflicts and strategies that build and legitimate this approach. Quite clearly the NGOs and networks are not only the product of a new kind of international law, they are also the product of well-designed strategies designed by leaders of the United States, transnational NGOs, and internationally active foundations. Similarly, we might characterize them as not against the state, but rather as part of a program to export a particular U.S.-based model of the state—taken for granted as a national and legitimate political organization. The shift to nonstate actors may reflect above all a shift from "universals" based on continental Europe—emphasizing the state—toward "universals" fitting the more open U.S. mode of governance.

William Carmichael, a former vice president of the Ford Foundation, highlighted the great importance of the Ford Foundation in helping to build the NGO community. In his words at our conference, "the Ford Foundation has indeed been a major actor in the development of a wide array of nongovernmental organizations promoting human rights and the rule of law." He also noted that "grantmaking with the intent of promoting human rights, the rule of law, and peaceful transitions to democracy in overseas settings is never an easy task." The accomplishments of the human rights movement have justifiably been celebrated, and the Ford Foundation's contribution was no doubt essential to that success as Carmichael suggested, but the process was much more complex than simply funding worthy causes. Accordingly, academic discourse should incorporate not only the successes of the movement in discrediting dictators but also the conflicts and hegemonic relationships that have accompanied this movement—and that tend not to be seen by those whose universals are in the first instance made in the U.S.A.

Twenty years ago, for example, the criticisms made by the law and development program gained acceptance almost as part of the official account. When we go deeper into today's descriptions and prescriptions of NGOs and the rule of law, we find the same unconscious attitudes within many of the idealist exporters. Many are so convinced that what they represent is universal that they do not consider it necessary to look behind the ideals. Naïveté is of course understandable, perhaps even admirable, but pure intentions not only can lead to privileging only one set of ideals, but also can blind actors to the embeddedness of the processes of exportation and importation in hierarchies of power.

The new drive to export the rule of law, as our essays have shown, may also come to results and assessments similar to what happened with law and development. It is not simply a question of success or failure of the processes that lead to the importation and exportation of particular approaches and expertises. The legacy of law and development, for example, is more ambiguous than the critics or proponents have recognized. The process was used locally by descendants of the traditional elite to build their positions in the field of state power—at the same time as they served to enhance U.S. power (and the position of those in the United States friendly to legal elites, e.g., in Latin America). As John Comaroff commented at the conference, "Even the best intentions in the world in coming to help government reform corruption or reform practice, create the possibility for other kinds of things, again engendering corruption and the very things that are the object of reform."

The concentration on national models of the state is evident in Robert Boyer's essay. The essay does not specifically suggest a particular road toward a new prescribed orthodoxy. Boyer's method toward the end of his essay, instead, is to produce a set of potential scenarios designed to show a number of possible futures. Writing from a French perspective, the possible futures do not all occupy the same level. Indeed, the suggestion is that a theory of the embeddedness and nestedness of complex institutions must be taken seriously in order to avoid a potential economic disaster. Market forces cannot be expected to produce the institutions necessary for the economies to operate effectively. The prescriptive aspect of the description uses the language of governance to highlight the importance of national and European models and the limits of models stressing U.S. approaches to regulating markets.

The essay by Elizabeth Heger Boyle and John Meyer also focuses squarely on the importance of institutions, including the law, and the authors also use their tools to map major changes internationally. Highlighting the processes of isomorphism following patterns designed in the West, they reject the common assumption that legal institutions are simply adaptations to economic changes. Instead, they argue, legal changes have their own independent momentum, continuing a long process of rationalization and secularization centered in the West. Their perspective evokes the literature in economics and anthropology that capitalism is built out of precapitalist forms. Weber's analysis of Protestantism and, more recently, discussions of Confucianism and Asian capitalism follow this line (e.g., Greenhalgh 1994; Wade 1990). Boyle and Meyer suggest that law gains power by moving in the forms of the church and religion. The insight is useful especially because it reminds us that the national credibility of law is essential for its success in providing the organizing rules and structures of legitimacy. It also makes clear the hierarchy of nations in this process.

Their emphasis on this point, however, moves so far in the other direction that it may make the process appear too easy—as if there is a ready-made credibility for the law. An understandable eagerness to discredit the sociological bottom-up approach—which suggests that laws and institutions can become essential sources of legitimacy only if they match local "needs"—may lead them paradoxically toward a more formal and quasi-legalistic approach. The approach emphasizes a grammar or codification rather than the battles that take place in the medium term. As Susan Silbey stated at the conference, "This story of law as a universal, rational, and natural good is too easy." It does not "acknowledge the pain, sacrifice, struggle with power, that comes with any normative order." Again, the description by Boyle and Meyer provides an essential criticism, but it also makes the process appear inevitable according to the cutting-edge social science.

The positions and conflicts that lead some actors to import laws and institutions in order to build their own positions at home are not part of the analysis. Further, we have few insights about how imported norms, approaches, and expertises can change local rules of the game and—at the same time—become part of long-standing local practices. Specifically, it is useful to mention here the importance of seeing the double games of lawyers who, as in the earlier period of law and development, use U.S. programs to build their own positions while helping to import U.S. law and therefore build U.S. influence. Boyle and Meyer's essay also makes the production of legitimacy and credibility appear too easy. As we shall suggest, it is important in a full account of the import and export of norms to see how lawyers can become the victims of their own rhetoric. That is to say, in order to produce and reproduce legitimacy, they must forgo some of the benefits that come with their successes (Dezalay and Garth 1996).

Jeremy Adelman and Miguel Centeno, in contrast to the other authors, take an explicitly historical approach. They examine the origins and development of a contradiction in Latin America that relates to the rule of law. In the nineteenth century, there was a particular contradiction between the rule of law in the sense of the protection of private property and the principle of broad participation in the government. Populist tendencies later, especially after the 1930s, came to clash with the protection of private property. At present, according to Adelman and Centeno, there are still unresolved questions about the legitimacy of the law. The authoritarian reactions to populism joined with neoliberal economics to promote private property, but they paid too little attention to the institutional framework necessary for the economy to thrive. Currently, they suggest, Latin America leaders still pay too little attention to the need for a broadly legitimate rule of law.

This reading of past centuries in Latin America provides insights into enduring tensions and also lost opportunities, bolstering the idea that these countries, while not doomed to be authoritarian, require much better legal institutions. The historical approach of Adelman and Centeno makes important points, but they do not examine the producers of the law or how social capital and the law relate to one another in the picture that they provide. It is therefore difficult to see from their account how lawyers came to occupy such a strong position in the state in Latin America, what led to the loss of some of that strength, and what mechanisms may be facilitating a kind of comeback. These are not, of course, their particular concerns. Their legal reading of history, however, can be see as a prescriptive approach characteristic of more traditional legal scholarship.

According to this reading, the essay uses history to join what appears to be a chorus in favor of a potential new orthodoxy united around the flexible idea of governance—which includes the rule of law. The authors make a strong case for what must be done in order to provide the legal legitimacy that will protect against the twin evils of populism and authoritarianism. By helping to generate scholarly momentum to invest in the strengthening of the rule of law, they also participate in facilitating that investment.

The essays in the beginning of this book, therefore, illustrate a variety of approaches to issues connected with governance and the rule of law. As we noted before, it is remarkable how they converge on the central and growing importance of law to their own work—whether as law professors or as scholars from other disciplines. The scholars can be seen as pioneers in these concerns—and also as academic leaders competing to create a potential new orthodoxy that will also serve to build their scholarly careers. While this new scholarship seeks to explain, it also can help to make possible an important social phenomenon, namely, the internationalization of a U.S.-style version of the rule of law. The authors make convincing cases that the law matters and that their colleagues need to invest more in understanding the role of law as an object of study and as a potential solution to social problems. But it is also important to provide a different and complementary social scientific perspective—directing social science tools in the unfamiliar direction of trying to understand more precisely the production of law and its legitimation in different settings.

The remaining essays contain some of the key ingredients that can be used to overcome the problems that come from disciplinary and professional blind spots. Rather than focusing on larger theoretical questions, these essays provide the kind of detail that can allow more attention to the processes of production and reproduction that are generally ignored. It can also provide more attention to the black hole where the law is produced and legitimated. The approach that is beginning to be developed in these essays is still quite new, and we will therefore make some suggestions for places for further research to explore. As with respect to our own reading of the other authors' essays, we may simplify or distort some of the texts in trying to highlight the strengths of our own sociological approach.

The essay by Larissa Adler Lomnitz and Rodrigo Salazar shows how law has been built out of relational and social capital in Mexico. The essay, therefore, provides a context for a key issue that concerns Slaughter—the role of state and nonstate actors in Mexican governance. We can see that international strategies are allowing nonstate actors to become more important in Mexican governance, but, because of Mexico's particular history, we also see that the main role of international strategies in law has been to begin to bridge a historical divide between the otherwise private world of business and the public world of the legal elite educated at the National University in Mexico City. The international thus feeds into the fabric of existing Mexican practices.

In terms relevant to the essay by Boyer, the levels of nestedness of governing institutions in Mexico exist in a more or less coherent fashion. Lomnitz and Salazar show that, in fact, people can play several cards—that of a "technopol," schooled in the latest U.S. expertise (economics, NGOs, trade law, the environment),[8] involvement in family enterprises, involvement in the state, or involvement in transnational activity. Drawing on Lomnitz and Salazar, we can suggest that the potentially catastrophic scenarios that Boyer suggests could happen from too much economic liberalism have not occurred in Mexico because the players who have promoted those policies can mobilize different resources on their behalf—including Wall Street and Washington, D.C., in addition to the more traditional domestic forms of social capital. There are certainly tensions, but the available strategies have helped to manage and contain them. The same point can be made in reference to the essay by Adelman and Centeno. The other sources of legitimacy in addition to the law have probably allowed Mexico so far to endure economic crises and rising inequality with relatively little actual improvement in legal institutions and their legitimacy. That is not to say that it will necessarily continue, but the key is to see why there has not been a major crisis yet.

Outside of the world of Mexican elites, the same complex interaction between national and international is found in struggles defined in terms of "indigenous rights." George Collier, on the basis of his own research in Mexico, described at our conference how the world of non-state actors and transnational NGOs is helping to transform politics in the Chiapas region—away from the domination by a patronage system under the guidance of the party that has dominated Mexican politics since the Revolution, the Partido Revolucionario Institucional (PRI). According to Collier:

> [One] example has to do with the emergence of autonomy in the indigenous rights discourses, which, of course, participate in the larger kinds of things that have happened throughout the Americas.

. . . However, in Chiapas that has also coupled itself with an interesting kind of exceptionalism, where indigenous communities within the framework of autonomy are, in a sense, shopping for the ways in which they want to relate to the national state. An interesting example is that the Zapatistas are pressuring the government to provide certain kinds of services—clinics, hospitals and so forth. . . . [T]here is an independent teacher's movement that has decided to buy out of the education system completely. They want to have their own system of alternative, bilingual education. They might like to have state or federal funds to fund it, but they want complete autonomy in deciding what that curriculum is going to be, and how they are going to teach it. Consequently, they are turning to NGOs to provide them with the curricular services and so forth. . . .

There is also a good deal of political shopping around. The Partido Revolucionario Institucional (PRI) used to be the only party in town. That was the only political group to whom indigenous people could turn to as clients. . . .

In addition, there is a considerable amount of church-shopping taking place. The advent of new evangelical groups has led to a proliferation of different kinds of churches. In the Chiapas landscape there used to be basically two principal players: The Catholic Church and the Presbyterians. Now there are more than half a dozen, and moving from Presbyterian to Evangelical to Seventh-Day Adventists is something that is occurring, this is again a response to the opportunities to "shop" in this changing global world.

There is a lot of foundation shopping; the Rockefeller Foundation, the World Bank is funding things in Mexico, the Inter-American Foundation, the MacArthur Foundation. There are emerging experts in how indigenous groups should format their applications to foundations so they can be sure to have the right kinds of structures, the language of accountability. All of these are things which the Foundation world seeks.

The potential for local groups and individuals to gain power and influence through the new opportunities to "shop" in the global marketplace illustrates how international strategies can play into and transform the local fields of state power in Mexico.

Setsuo Miyazawa and Hiroshi Otsuka's essay on Japan shows that law faculties teaching mainly traditional legal doctrine have been central in the reproduction of the power elite. This legal education thus provides a key to the legitimacy of the state, but that does not mean that Japanese leaders rely on the courts or the rule of law to legitimate their leadership positions. Miyazawa and Otsuka note that there is unequal access to the elite educational institutions because of the resources that are needed to prepare for the entrance examinations. In this sense family capital is important. As suggested in Lomnitz and Salazar's account of Mexico, it may be that social and family capital also work in other ways in Japan. It would be interesting, therefore, to see how family capital may help to build elite careers in the state and in the private sector in Japan. Miyazawa and Otsuka's essay also focuses on changes in Japan. From our perspective, it would also be useful to add more detail on how and whether international strategies play a role in the dramatic domestic transformations that are otherwise difficult to explain. From our own research in Korea, we can suggest that a graduate education in the United States can become another necessary ingredient in a "Confucian" competition to move to the top of the hierarchy—for example, Harvard as the completion of the education at the faculty of law in Tokyo University (or Seoul National in Korea). International strategies can also provide a means to blur the boundaries by short-circuiting traditional career strategies, for example, getting an elite U.S. degree without graduating from the law faculty at Tokyo or without passing the bar exam.

These two essays show that, while we tend to think of the rule of law as an international concept, law must also be produced at the national level to make national sense. The essays by Lomnitz and Salazar and by Miyazawa and Otsuka illustrate that process for Mexico and Japan, both of which—in very different ways—had law schools at the center of the reproduction of state power. More generally, these essays suggest that law is not simply a set of techniques, but rather must be understood as a point of entry into the core of the construction and reproduction of the field of state power. The production of law depends on the characteristics of the field of power. We cannot understand the processes of the internationalization of the rule of law, therefore, without also exploring key questions at the core of state power in different national settings. We must investigate how law is constructed out of various kinds of symbolic capital. Instead of seeing the rule of law as an abstraction or recipe, the essays on Mexico and Japan suggest that we can see "law" more generally as a changing crossroad where different actors and different sources of legitimacy can meet. As a crossroad, law draws on varying amounts and kinds of social capital.

Our own research perspective makes the process of constructing law from various forms of capital a key part of national stories. The law in this more general sense is also more or less essential in producing legitimacy and reproducing a particular kind of state. Law is a vital resource for dominant groups to legitimate their power and authority. To take an example from recent research in Korea, the rigidly meritocratic system for producing judges, prosecutors, and lawyers, which requires moving through a series of extremely difficult examinations every step of the way, seems absurd if looked at in isolation from the Korean state. The meritocratic process of legitimation, however, can be understood only if considered in relation to a division of role that excludes lawyers from actual power in the state or the economy. The legitimacy that law provides does not grant law any major role in governance.

Again drawing on our own research, we can contrast Korea to Brazil, where the legal elite is completely embedded in the national field of power. International strategies in Brazil have tended to challenge that domination on the basis of imported expertise and transnational networks of relationships. The potential imported expertises compete, as seen especially in the competition between European and U.S. approaches. In Korea, competition between other potential models for Korean governance not only includes the battles between Europe and the United States, as in Brazil, but also involves Japan. In all the countries that we have mentioned, international strategies in law are having an important impact. What that impact is, however, depends on the position of law in the field of state power. Thus, international strategies in Korea are bound to be quite different from Brazil's—even though Koreans and Brazilians are found together at conferences and may very well produce scholarship that states the very same thing (as recognized in the essays by Boyer and by Boyle and Meyer) about the need to end corruption, build legal institutions, and promote the rule of law. Within each country, however, such a strategy works in different ways. The national rules of the game will tend to shift toward U.S. approaches to governance—including a U.S.-style state with lawyer-led NGOs under, above, and around it—to the extent that the battles favor those who invest in U.S. law and promote the potential new orthodoxy.

Several comments at our conference provide further illustration of this kind of relationship between international strategies and the field of state power. William Alford, for example, noted that law in China looks very different from what might be celebrated as "the inexorable sweep of Western legality." Despite the great differences produced by the local Chinese context, however, Chinese actors are often ready to try to use foreign understandings of law to build their local positions:

> Foreign actors—the human beings and the norms—from the normative exporting country can be used and manipulated in the norm receiving country. From personal experience, for example, many people try to speak through me, not because it has anything to do with me, but coming out of the mouth of a Caucasian foreigner, they carry some import that they might not in the domestic debate.

Similarly, explaining the differences between Malaysia and Indonesia in terms of the position of law, Daniel Lev suggested that an interaction between international strategies and local state power struggles was crucial:

> I would like to suggest that the courts are strong because in a country like Malaysia the political elite had absolutely no choice but to fall back on a process of law in order to avoid widespread slaughter. Malaysia is essentially comprised of three ethnic groups. About 52 percent Malay, 37 percent Chinese and 10 percent Indian. The difficulty was that these groups are actually demographically separated in many ways, whereas the elite was not. The Malay elite, the Chinese elite and the Indian elite had all been trained by the English, with many of them going to Oxford, Cambridge or the University of London and the majority of whom learned the law (and something about good scotch). They returned knowing one another and understanding that the communities which they represented, to varying degrees, would be very hard, indeed, almost impossible, to weld together into a form of post-colonial society. Almost immediately, three political parties were formed, a Malay party, a Chinese party, an Indian party, and a few others, among them a socialist party, and a labor party that had no chance of gaining support at all.
>
> Recognizing that the party system itself was creating the preconditions for a wonderful war, the leadership of those three groups

got together immediately in 1952, before independence, and decided to create an alliance. This they did in much the same way, though without any historical connection, as the Dutch did in the sixteenth and seventeenth century, thus avoiding the terrible wars between Catholics and Protestants that occurred in the Thirty Years War.

The alliance understood perfectly well that the one idea on which they could base their own legitimacy and win support was the law, and they literally sat down together and agreed that they had to have very strong courts. They appointed their own people to them, and one of the reasons the Malaysian judiciary is so strong is that the judges are actually part of the political elite. If one looks at English and American history, much the same situation occurred.

These courts were also politically very useful precisely because they did what the political elite were inclined to do; they applied the laws advantageously. Notably drawing upon the English heritage of a sedition law, which was originally established in order to control Communists, which the Malaysian elite discovered could be used against anybody at all.

The essay by Catalina Smulovitz on the role of the judiciary in Argentina reveals how the judiciary suddenly found itself in an unexpected position after the debacle of the Malvinas/Falkland War. She shows how the unforeseen prominence and success of judicial remedies for major social issues placed new pressures on the judiciary whose role could not be translated into something new and more important. The opening was in fact only a false opening. Law—building on the relative influence of the international human rights movement, which helped bring Raul Alfonsín, the president, to the forefront—was unable to take advantage of the opening. Alfonsín defined his government as the restoration of the rule of law, but there was not any major change in the position of law and the courts. In contrast, the media thrived, using the new market opening to place pressures on judges and to use judges for their own purposes. Media processes were much more successful than legalization was. This institutional study again makes it clear that, while international events and influences can open up new possibilities, the consequences will not necessarily be consistent with what international norms seem to require. What Smulovitz does not explore, however, is the kind of historical background provided by Lomnitz and Salazar for

Mexico and by Miyazawa and Otsuka for Japan. To complete the picture of the role of the courts, we need to learn more about how the courts were produced historically in relation to larger issues of the law and the state in Argentina, and how international strategies are being played in the particular Argentine context. Courts today are now working in conjunction with media strategies in highly politicized fights, such as that between former minister of finance Domingo Cavallo and President Menem and his allies. The continuing lack of autonomy of the courts can be understood better in relation to their structural history, which also provides an essential starting point to see how various international strategies are affecting the field of state power in Argentina.

The essay by Heinz Klug again provides unique insights that could also be extended by a further inquiry into local structures and histories of the field of state power. It shows the complex way in which international factors played into local debates about the constitution in South Africa, providing resources and legitimacy of considerable importance. While the other essays at the end of the book tend not to highlight the role of transnational factors in shaping domestic agendas and possibilities, Klug provides rich detail about how that transnational dimension was perceived by those fighting to build a new South Africa. As we suggested for the Smulovitz essay, it would also be interesting to undertake a further detailed inquiry into the national positions of the players in the debates, the position of the judiciary and the actors who have moved into that domain, and how these groups relate specifically to their counterparts in the Western world. They have come together to produce the particular constraints and outcomes that Klug explores. We can see the processes of internationalization at work. Ideally, in addition, we would also be able to relate those outcomes to the position of law in the national field of state power.

This volume is a first effort to try to bring together scholars who have come to recognize the importance of the renewal of activity that once again could be characterized as law and development. This scholarly interest, including our own, helps to make possible what we all theorize and describe about transformations in the governing rules and in structures of governance. Recognizing that a description of legal developments as "the production, import, and export of a new legal orthodoxy" is also potential prescription, we have sought to situate the emerging scholarship better in the processes within which the scholars are embedded. We have therefore highlighted the production of rules and the means by which professional expertises and different kinds of capital compete in national and transnational palace wars. The major point is simple. If we wish to get beyond abstractions such as the "rule of law" and "globalization," it is crucial to examine the actors who produce these abstractions and use them in their own national and international strategies.

The new law and development, despite the failures of earlier efforts, is almost without critics today. Activists in and out of the academy see reforms in support of the rule of law through eyes that provide a form of tunnel vision. The academics disagree among themselves, but they tend to be united in their convictions of the virtue of their own universals and models of social change. The model of the state that they primarily draw on today—which is of course subject to challenge—accords a leading place to law, lawyers, and courts. Southern reformers may believe in the legitimacy of those universals, and they may also believe the pursuit of those universals can be useful in their careers or obtaining funds from the north. Whatever the ostensible motive, in short, there are incentives that produce the movement of ideas and institutions that we have seen in this book. The same is true for those who compete in national settings that lead to a net exportation of approaches and ideas.

This competition in the south and the north is central to the social production and legitimation of law and other potential orthodoxies. Most scholars, because of their own position in their own competitive hierarchies, tend to ignore the problems of the hierarchies of professional disciplines and also of states. They use what information they have about the production and legitimation of intellectual products, but they do not question what they use to advance themselves and their work. Without more academic study of these processes and how they operate in specific settings—in other words, without more transparency or realism about the production and exportation of transparency—idealists of the rule of law may be doomed to replicate, again and again, the failure of law and development. Each generation—fortified with academic research produced within a particular national field of power—will invest its idealism in exporting its own model of the state and be surprised by both the obvious failures and significant "successes" in building careers and producing local transformations of one kind or another.

NOTES

1. In Bourdieu's terms, "[The state] is embodied at the same time objectively in the form of structures and specific mechanisms and 'subjectively' . . . in the brains, in the form of mental structures, categories of perception and of thought. By realizing itself in social structures and in mental structures adapted to these structures, the instituted institution leads to forgetting that it is the result of a long series of acts of institutionalization that allows it to present itself with all the appearances of being *natural*" (1993:51). To understand this process, the most powerful instrument to break through natural appearances is "the reconstruction of the genesis: by bringing to the surface the conflicts and confrontations from the beginning and, at the same time, the possible variations, it reactualizes the possibility that it might have been (and that it might be) otherwise and, in addition to this practical utopia, places in question the possibility that, among all the others, was actually realized" (51).

2. This legal hegemony has of course been contested at various times, including in the New Deal, as Ronen Shamir has shown (1995).

3. Nor does it mean that actors in the United States have a consensus or fall in line automatically behind a particular model. Actors in the United States may even promote foreign models in their own scholarship and careers. The point is that their target is the field of power in the United States, and their actions abroad are shaped by their domestic struggles. At the conference, David Trubek thus criticizes the notion that "competition among national visions for the purpose of national economic agendas and perhaps cultural and political agendas [is] the central axis of competition and struggle in the processes of reconstructing the rules of the game." In Trubek's opinion, national actors must take national positions when it is a matter of struggles "structured with national actors, particularly if a vote at the United Nations, or the signing of a treaty, a directive from the European Union, and anything else that requires formal intergovernmental action," but otherwise it is important to pay "attention to the multilevels of governance, both in terms of multilevels of public governance, and in terms of multilevels in the sense of public and private governance being mixed. So the complexity blows apart the simple formation of conflict and competition along national lines." It is too simple to see particular positions as always "national," but his point is that the positions are produced nationally, which does have a strong impact on their shape and content.

4. And they urged Yale law students and alumni to focus on this missionary effort. This potential orthodoxy, described below, has already generated a counterattack. Those who argued earlier that the East Asian Miracle was a model for the United States are quite naturally suggesting different prescriptions (Wade 1996; Wade and Veneroso 1998; Rodrik 1998).

5. And leading Mexican opponents took their fight to Washington, D.C.

6. The Multilateral Agreement on Investment was supposed to be an agreement negotiated by the countries of the Organization for Economic Cooperation and Development to facilitate foreign investment. It was oriented toward the protection of investors in the initial drafts. According to an article by Stephen Kobrin (1998), antiglobalism NGOs, labor unions, and a variety of other groups mobilized their networks to derail the negotiations in the spring of 1998.

7. In Bourdieu's terms, "That is to say that science is devoted to exercise an effect as theory, but in a particular form: by showing in a coherent and empirically valid discourse what had been ignored, . . . the theory transforms the representation of the social world and, at the same time, the social world, to the extent that it renders possible practices conforming to this transformed representation" (1981: 72).

8. As noted by Hector Fix Fierra and Sergio López Ayllón at the conference, some "80 percent of actual federal legislation was produced between 1982 and 1996. Basically all economic regulation, including trade, bank, investments, intellectual property, and many other areas are involved because it is necessary for Mexico to change its legislation to go into the global market, and more particularly perhaps, the North American market." Further, "there is now a much more significant influence from international agreements and international institutions, and there has been the creation of new agencies [in Mexico] that deal with economic matters, such as antitrust, antidumping, energy, intellectual property, telecommunications."

REFERENCES

Bourdieu, Pierre. 1981. Décrire et précrire: Note sur les conditions de possibilité et des limites de l'efficacité politique. *Actes de la Recherche en Sciences Sociales* 38 (May): 69–73.
———. 1987. The force of law: Toward a sociology of the juridical field. *Hastings Law Journal* 38, no. 5: 814–53.
———. 1993. Esprits d'état: Genèse et structure du champ bureaucratique. *Actes de la Recherche en Sciences Sociales* 96–97 (March): 49–62.
Dezalay, Yves, and Bryant G. Garth. 1996. *Dealing in virtue: International commercial arbitration and the construction of an international legal order.* Chicago: University of Chicago Press.
———. 2002. *Global palace wars: Lawyers, economists, and the contest to transform Latin American States.* Chicago: University of Chicago Press.
Fox, Jonathan, and L. David Brown. 1998. *The struggle for accountability: The World Bank, NGOs, and grassroots movements.* Cambridge: MIT Press.
Garth, Bryant, and Joyce Sterling. 1998. From legal realism to law and society:

Reshaping law for the last stages of the social activist state. *Law and Society Review* 32, no. 2: 409–72.

Greenhalgh, Susan. 1994. De-orientalizing the Chinese family firm. *American Ethnologist* 21:766–67.

Hulme, David, and Michael Edwards. 1997. *NGOs, states, and donors: Too close for comfort.* London: Macmillan.

Keck, Margaret, and Kathryn Sikkink. 1998. *Activists beyond borders: Advocacy networks in international politics.* Ithaca: Cornell University Press.

Kobrin, Stephen. 1998. The MAI and the clash of globalizations. *Foreign Policy* 112:97–109.

Rodrik, Dani. 1998. The global economic crisis and how to stop it. *New Republic* (November 2): 17–19.

Santos, Boaventura de Sousa. 1995. *Toward a new common sense: Law, science and politics in the paradigmatic transition.* New York: Routledge.

Shamir, Ronen. 1995. *Managing legal uncertainty.* Durham, N.C.: Duke University Press.

Wade, Robert. 1990. *Governing the market.* Princeton: Princeton University Press.

———. 1996. Japan, the World Bank, and the art of paradigm maintenance: The East Asian miracle in political perspective. *New Left Review* 217:3–36.

Wade, Robert, and Frank Veneroso. 1998. The Asian crisis: The high debt model versus the Wall Street-Treasury-IMF complex. *New Left Review* 228:3–23.

Wallerstein, Immanuel. 1991. *Unthinking social science: The limits of nineteenth-century paradigms.* London: Blackwell.

CONTRIBUTORS

Jeremy Adelman is Professor of History at Princeton University and the director of Princeton's Program in Latin American Studies.

Robert Boyer is an economist affiliated with the Centre d'études prospectives d'économie mathématique appliqué à la planification (CEPREMAP) in Paris. He is also a professor at the École des Hautes Études en Sciences Sociales.

Elizabeth Heger Boyle is Assistant Professor of Sociology and Law at the University of Minnesota.

Miguel Angel Centeno is Professor of Sociology at Princeton University.

Yves Dezalay is Director of Research at the Centre National de Recherches Scientifiques (CNRS) located at the Centre de Sociologie Européene and attached to the Collége de France and the Maison des Sciences de l'Homme in Paris.

Bryant G. Garth is Director of the American Bar Foundation, Chicago, Illinois.

Heinz Klug is Associate Professor of Law at the University of Wisconsin-Madison.

Larissa Adler Lomnitz is Professor of Anthropology at the Instituto de Investigaciones en Matemáticas Aplicadas Sistemas y Servicios (IIMASS) at the Universidad Nacional Autonoma de Mexico (UNAM).

John W. Meyer is Professor of Sociology at Stanford University.

Setsuo Miyazawa is Professor of Law at the Waseda University School of Law, Tokyo.

Hiroshi Otsuka is a lecturer at Nara Women's University, Nara, Japan.

Rodrigo Salazar is Professor of Anthropology at the Instituto de Investigaciones en Matemáticas Aplicadas Sistemas y Servicios (IIMASS) at the Universidad Nacional Autonoma de Mexico (UNAM).

Kathryn Sikkink is Professor of Political Science at the University of Minnesota.

Anne-Marie Slaughter is the J. Sinclair Armstrong Professor of Law at Harvard Law School, Cambridge, Massachusetts.

Catalina Smulovitz is Professor of Political Science at the Universidad Torcuato Di Tella, Buenos Aires, Argentina.

Index

Note: Tables and figures are referred to with italic page numbers

Academic
  disciplines, restructuring of maps
    of, 311, 312
  hierarchies and legal and social
    scientific expertise, 306
  study of legal processes, need for,
    331
  tools for understanding rule of
    law, 3
Ackerman, Bruce, 278
Activists beyond borders (Keck and
  Sikkink), 57n. 1
Actors
  government networks, 18–19
  nongovernmental organizations
    (NGOs), 16
  nonstate, and interdependency
    with state, 26–27
  nonstate, and shift from European
    to U.S. mode of governance, 319
  proliferation of, in international
    system, 12–32, 314–15
  suprastate and substate, 17–18
  transnational corporations
    (TNCs), 16–17
Adelman, Jeremy, 6, 322–23, 324
Advocacy networks, transnational.
    See Transnational advocacy net-
    works
African National Congress (ANC),
    276
  and argument with government

regarding constitutional prop-
    erty clause, 290–91
  and Bill of Rights, 281–82, 283,
    287–88, 291, 292–93
  and "Economy and Land" section
    of Constitutional Guidelines,
    282–83
  Land Commission of, 283, 285,
    287–89, 299–300n. 9
  and Land Manifesto and demand
    for both restitution and reform,
    285
  and nationalization of existing
    landholdings, 282
  and pressure to grant recognition
    to property rights in May 1991,
    284
  and strategic commitment to
    international norms, 297–98
  See also South Africa, land reform,
    and constitution making
African National Congress Law
    Commission, 284–85
Alberdi, Juan Bautista, 145
Alfonsín, Raul, 251, 329
Alford, William, 328
Alien Tort Claims Act of 1786, 53
Allende, Salvador, 152
Allinson, Gary D., 180
Americas Watch, 52
Amnesty International, 48, 53–54
Apartheid, 283, 285, 298

Arbenz, Jacobo, 150
Argentina, 141, 147, 148, 149, 153
  and Alberdi, 145
  and Juan Perón, 150
  liberal economically and conserva-
    tive politically in 1800s, 147
Argentina and discovery of law, 8–9,
    249–73, 329
  and *aggiornamento* of judicial
    institutions, 259
  and appointment and removal of
    judges, 260, 261
  and Buenos Aires Federal Court of
    Appeal, 251
  and claims brought to regulatory
    commissions, 257, *258*, 264–65
  and confidence in judiciary, 250,
    251
  and Controladuría General Comu-
    nal, 257, *257*, 264–65, 272n. 11
  and courts as holder of hopes of
    democracy, 252
  and Defensoría del Pueblo de la
    Nación, 257, *257*, 264–65, 272n. 11
  and domestic reasons for politi-
    cization of judiciary, 266–67
  and Due Obedience Law, 261,
    273n. 19
  and "extraordinary decrees" con-
    trolling judiciary, 260, 261
  and fighting by all entities of state,
    249
  and future scenarios for judicial-
    ization, 267
  and human rights violations
    becoming prominent in early
    1980s, 250–51
  and international patterns of
    "judicialization of conflicts,"
    249, 266–67
  and judicialization breaking
    impasses but also preventing
    potentially collective social
    action, 260
  and judicialization giving appear-
    ance of handling issues but truly
    postponing their handling, 251
  and judicialization of conflicts,
    253, 257, 262, 272n. 10
  and judiciary as a matter of public
    debate, 249, 262
  and judiciary's appearance as
    activists, 253
  and liberalization after
    Malvinas/Falklands War, 250–51
  and necessity for rule of law for
    economic reform, 267–68
  and numbers of files received by
    courts, *254–56*
  and ombudsman agencies, 257
  and political interventions to con-
    trol courts, 259–60, 261–62
  and "politics of rights," 266
  and reasons for increased claims
    made by individual citizens,
    264–65
  and repeal of Law of Self-Amnesty,
    251
  and restricting of citizens' capacity
    to petition for rights, 259–60
  and Supreme Court, 260, 272–73n.
    18
  and trials of military junta, 249,
    251–52, 271n. 3
  and use of oral procedures creat-
    ing unusual efficiency, 252–53,
    271–72n. 9
  See also Citizenship; Media and
    courts in Argentina
Artigas, José, 144
Asian Development Bank, 1

Batista, Sergeant Fulgencio, 150
Beatty, David, 278

Bello, Andrés, 145
Binswanger, Hans, 289
Blanco, Guzmán, 146
Boli, John, 54
Bolívar, Simón, 145, 159n. 1
Bourdieu, Pierre, 307, 311, 317, 332n. 1, 333n. 7
Boutros-Ghali, Boutros, 40
Boyer, Robert, 4, 139, 320–21, 324
Boyle, Elizabeth Heger, 4, 5, 41, 321–22
Brazil, 5, 148, 149, 153, 155, 158
    and constitutional transformation, 150
    and government in 1800s, 146, 147
    and international legal strategies, 327
Britain, 126, 129, 157, 199
Budlender, Geoff, 287
Bull, Hedley, 15, 59n. 17

Calles, Plutarco, 149
Camp, Roderic, 228, 232
Campaign against Torture, 48
Cansino and Riva (law firm), 229
Capitalism
    as built on precapitalist forms, 105, 321
    and dependency on coordination mechanisms other than markets, 107
    See also Economic institutions
Cárdenas, Lázaro, 149, 150, 151–52
Carmichael, William, 319–20
Carothers, Thomas, 2, 10n. 2
Carter, James, 308
Castro, Fidel, 153
Catholic Church
    and Chiapas, 325
    and legal systems, 67–68, 69
Cavallo, Domingo, 330

Centeno, Miguel Angel, 6, 322–23, 324
Center for Constitutional Rights, 53
Center for Justice and International Law (CEJIL), 52
Central America, 148
Centre for Applied Legal Studies (CALS), 287
Ceremony, 80–81
Chaskalson, Matthew, 292
Chávez, Hugo, 141
Chiapas, Mexico, 324–25
Chiarotti, Susana, 44
Children's rights, 47
Chile, 5, 145, 147
China, 328
Christiansen, Robert, 289, 290
Citizenship
    as atomized and weakened from changes in representation and media, 270, 271
    and dedication of time to public activity, 269–70
    and mechanisms of legal claims and media resources, 269, 270
    necessary requirements for exercise of, 269
    and party identity losing significance, 268–69
    and representation, 268–69
Civic organizations, 24
Civil Servant Examination of 1929 (Japan), 204n. 3
Claassens, Aninka, 287
Cold war, 22–23, 156
Collier, George, 324–25
Colombia, 146, 149, 152, 153
Colonialism and diffusion of legal system, 67–68, 89n. 1
Comaroff, John, 320
Common law, 222–23, 280
"Community of law," 29, 32n. 15

Consistency, 86–87
Constitutional order, 113–14, 128
Constitutions
  global adoption of new, 278–79
  and use of international foreign
    legal sources, 296
  See also South Africa, land reform,
    and constitution making
Controladuría General Comunal,
  257, 272n. 11
Convention for the Elimination of
  All Forms of Discrimination
  against Women (CEDAW),
  43–44, 48–49, 50–51
Convention on the Rights of the
  Child, 47
Council of Foreign Relations, 310
Creoles, 143
Cross, Catherine, 287
Cuba, 149, 150, 153

"Declaration of the Rights of the
  Child," 47
Declaration on the Elimination of
  Violence against Women, 45,
  58n. 11
Defensoría del Pueblo de la Nación,
  257, 272n. 11
Dehousse, Renaud, 30n. 2
de Klerk, F. W., 282
Democracy
  and conditions for exercise of
    rights, 269
  need to create new theory of, 131
  unsuccessful attempts to build, in
    Latin America, 139
Dezalay, Yves, 58n. 14, 210, 211,
  299n. 2
  and relations between social net-
    work sectors, 213–14, 245, 246
Díaz, Porfirio, 147, 148
Diet of Japan, 163

Dolny, Helena, 282
Domination, 317
Dore, Ronald, 112
Drucker, Peter, 16
Dumbarton Oaks, 47–48

Economic institutions, 101
  and business associations at inter-
    national level, 121–22
  and constitutional order, 113–14,
    128
  and creation of new institutions,
    108, 110
  and crises vs. rational expecta-
    tions, 117
  development and selection of,
    115
  and embeddedness hypothesis and
    pre- or (non-)capitalist logics,
    105
  and future production of gover-
    nance modes, 125
  and historicity, 108
  and interaction of internal and
    external forces, 107–8, *109*
  levels of, and alternative institu-
    tional arrangements, *118*
  and market as selective device,
    101–4
  and model of government inter-
    vention and power, 108–10,
    112–13
  neoclassical field of research of,
    114–17, *116*
  and nestedness, 122–28
  and networks, 121
  and rationality principle, 101, 110
  and Régulation Theory, 115, 117
  required for flexible specialization
    or production, 105, *106*
  and requirement of monitoring by
    extramarket mechanism, 104

and self-building of institutions,
102, *103*, 104, 105
as social contracts, 107–10
and social embeddedness of relationships and trust, 110–12
and social transformation, 114, 115
and three visions of institutional
change, 110–17, *111*
and traditional institutions as
alternative to corrosive market,
107–10
See also International political
economy; Markets; Nestedness
Economy. *See* International political
economy
Enlightenment, the
and Latin America, 142–43
view of humanity, 66
Environment, protection of
international, 3
and isomorphism, 78
and new legal orthodoxy, 314, 315
and organizations, 40
Escuela Libre de Derecho, 242
European Bank of Reconstruction
and Development, 1
European Court of Human Rights, 75
European Monetary System, 118–19
European Union, 17, 120
and monetary and economic zones
scenario, 129
and nestedness of various levels of
regulation, 130–31
and supranational partnerships, 29

Family capital, 326
Female genital mutilation (FGM),
42–43, 45, 58nn. 8, 9, 77
Filartiga, Jose, and family, 52–53
Finnemore, Martha, 38
Fiske, Susan, 84
Ford, Henry, 104

Ford Foundation, 55, 299n. 1, 319–20
Fordism, 98–99, 117
"Framing," 42, 58n. 6
Franck, Thomas, 49
"Freedom of information" act in
Japan, 7, 202–4
French Ecole de la Régulation, 98
Fujimori, Alberto, 141, 158

GABRIELA, 56
Gaitán, Jorge Eliecer, 152
Gakureki shugi (education-based elit-
ism), 170
Garner, Maria, 16
Garth, Bryant G., 58n. 14, 210, 211,
299n. 2
and relations between social net-
work sectors, 213–14, 245, 246
GATT. *See* General Agreement on
Tariffs and Trade (GATT)
Geisel, Ernesto, 155
General Agreement on Tariffs and
Trade (GATT), 119, 129, 240
Genocide, 47, 58n. 13
Gerlach, Michael L., 188
Germany, 126, 286
Global constitutionalism, 278–79
Globalization
and competition in laws and
approaches to state and governance, 308, 319, 327
and construction of new rules,
277
and dialectical interaction between
global and local, 277–78
and five stages of life cycle of interaction with local, 277–78
as inexorable force, 13
and information technology revolution, 23
and judicialization and Argentina,
266–67

Globalization (*continued*)
  and opening of international mar-
    ket and Mexico, 241, 246
  and pressures for law to legitimate
    state and economy, 4–5
  of the rule of law, 277–78
  and society, 70
  and success of imports, 6
  and taking root of new legal ortho-
    doxy, 96–97
  and threat to Latin American rule
    of law, 6, 139–40, 142, 158–59
  and universalism and rationality,
    68
Gonzalez, Inés, 259
"Governance," 311, 330
Government intervention, 100, 108
Government networks, 18–19
Graham, Richard, 146
Green Cross, 189–90
Grindel, Merilee, 230–31
Guatemala, 148, 150, 155

Haiti, 144
Harvard Law School, 84
Heinz, John P., 223
Hoffman, Stanley, 21, 31n. 11
Honduras, 52
Hopkins, Ann, 84
Human rights, 4, 46–49
  and Argentina, 249
  and funding of NGOs by Ford
    Foundation, 55, 319–20
  international standards of, 297–98
  law, international, 3
  networks, and NGOs, 39, 40
  and new legal orthodoxy, 314,
    315
  and NGOs facilitating interna-
    tional litigation, 52–53
  protection of, by lawyers in Japan,
    170

and requiring U.S. to sanction
    states abusing, 53–54
  and UN Charter, 47–48
  universal declarations of, and
    modern state, 69
Humphrey, John, 48
Huntington, Samuel, 20, 31n. 8, 32n.
  13

IDEA Annual Seminar, 273n. 23
Ideals, 66
Imperialism, Western, 68
Imperial University. *See* University of
  Tokyo (Tokyo Imperial Univer-
  sity)
"Information politics," 45–46
Information technology revolution,
  23, 27
Institutions as social constructs,
  107–10
  See also Economic institutions
Instituto de Investigaciones Jurídicas,
  218
Inter-American Commission and
  Court, 52
Inter-American Convention on the
  Prevention, Punishment, and
  Eradication of Violence against
  Women, 45
Inter-American Development
  Bank, 1
International capital, 313
International law, 3, 12, 41
  compliance with, and transna-
    tional advocacy networks, 49–53
  and different policies based on dif-
    ferent actors, 13–14
  and economics-based rationalism,
    25
  and global economy, 66
  nation-state as sole source and
    subject of, 13

and neoclassical economic theory,
101, 102
and new actors, 3, 12–37, 316
and new generation of scholars in
1980s and 1990s, 23–24
numbers of NGOs dedicated to,
40–41
and public spending, 101
and social and economic justice, 25
socialization to, 50
and spatial distribution of social
systems of production, 100
systems of, and functional and
conflict perspectives, 66
International political economy, 5, 13,
96
and business associations, 121–22
and competing national systems of
production, 100
and crisis of previous institutional
arrangements, 99–101
and deregulation, 125
and difficulty of establishing institutional arrangements at supranational level, 120
and "Fordism," regulatory institutions embedded in nation-
states, 98–99, 117
and future scenarios, 123, 128–30
history of, 97–98
and institutions as social constructs, 107
and international trade agreements, 124–25
law as regulatory alternative to,
96
and levels of institutions and alternative institutional arrangements, 118
and markets, 97, 98, 100
and national-level coordination of
economic actors, 128

and nestedness of levels of regulation scenario, 129–30
and new theory of democracy for
governing institutions, 131
and Pax Americana after World
War II, 98, 99
and pluralistic coordination of
regimes scenario, 129
and public interventions and
regional rather than national
level, 119
and regional economies, 117, 119
and return to nationalism scenario, 128–29
and transplantation of U.S. model
to other countries, 96
and trends toward both supranationalism and regionalism,
117–22
See also Economic institutions;
Markets; Nestedness
International relations
and economics-based rationalism,
25–26
and new generation of scholars,
including women and minorities, in 1980s and 1990s, 23–24
and norms, 38, 41
International Standards Organization, 17
International trade agreements,
124–25
International Women's Rights
Action Watch (IWRAW), 49, 50
Islamic legal system, 75

Japan
and "alliance capitalism," 188–89
and dense localized networks, 126
and discrimination against women
in workplace, 51
and Liberal Democratic Party, 163

Japan (*continued*)
and resistance to reform, 7
Japan, legal education in, 6–7,
162–205, 325–26
and *amakudari* or "descent from
heaven," 189–90
and business corporations giving
highest positions to law graduates from Imperial Universities,
172–73
and business groups associated
with leading politicians, *191,* 199
and business leaders, 188–90
and "cram" schools, 196–97
and elite in ruling party, public
bureaucracy, and business community, 163, 169
and faculties of law, 162
and Freedom of Information Act,
7, 202–4
future of, 198–201
and graduate professional law
schools, 199–200, 203, 204
history of, and legal profession,
165–68
and improved prestige of legal
profession after World War II,
181
and Judicial Reform Council
(JRC), 202–4
and Judicial Research and Training Institute, 197, 201
and judiciary elite, 190–93
and Justice Ministry Law School,
164, 168
and lack of genuine legal education, 197–98
and large number of law-related
occupations, 199, *199,* 203
and law faculties as most competitive in nearly all universities, 186
and lawyers in opposition to government (*zaiya hoso*) vs. lawyers
in government (*zicho hoso*), 170
and legal academia, elite in,
193–95, *194*
and Legal Research and Training
Institute, 204
and monthly salaries at Mitui
Mining Company compared by
education, *173*
and National Bar Examination
reforms, 203
and National Law Examination,
192–93, *193*
and politics, 173–78
and private schools compared with
public, 164, 168, 169–70
and production of power elite
before World War II, 164–73
and protection of human rights,
170
recruitment of law graduates as
raw material not for legal education, 186, 196–97
and rule by law not rule of law, 186
and Rules of Civil Service Examination and Apprenticeship, 169
and stratification of Japanese society, 201–2
and suggested expansion into liberal arts education, 198–99
and Supreme Court and Justice
Department's control over professional training and examinations, 200
See also Japanese bureaucracy and
legal education; Japanese politics and legal education; Kyoto
Imperial University; University
of Tokyo (Tokyo Imperial University)
Japanese bureaucracy and legal education, 178–88

and background of members of
Diet, *179*
and civil service examination and
employment, 182–84, *183, 184*
and faster promotion of Tokyo
Imperial University graduates,
182, 185
and Finance Ministry, 183, 184–85,
204 5n. 8
and Health Ministry HIV infection
scandal, 185–86, 189–90
of high-ranked in postwar period,
181–82, *182*
and movement to politics or business upon retirement, 179–80
reproduced by legal education at
University of Tokyo, 186
and technical vs. clerical staffs,
185–86
See also University of Tokyo
(Tokyo Imperial University)
Japanese Federation of Bar Associations, 200
Japanese politics and legal education,
173–78
and cabinet ministers, 175, *176, 177*
and graduates from Tokyo Law
Faculty, 175
and members of Diet, 175, 177,
178
and prime minister and cabinet
ministers as key positions, 174
See also University of Tokyo
(Tokyo Imperial University)
Jebb, Eglantyne, 47
Jessup, Philip, 17, 19, 31nn. 5, 6
Johnson, Chalmers, 179
Johnson, Joseph, 31n. 5
Judicial reform, 5
Japanese resistance to, 7
late campaign for, and limitations
of projects promoting, 2–3

See also Argentina and discovery of
law
Judicial Research and Training Institute (Japan), 197, 201
Justice
law founded in, 67, 68
of system vs. personal outcomes,
85–86

Kaiser, Karl, 21–22
Keck, Margaret, 54, 55, 57n. 1
Keohane, Robert, 20–21, 23, 31n. 9,
31–32n. 12
Keynesian economics, 100
Khor, Martin, 289
Kindleberger, Charles, 14
Klug, Heinz, 9, 330
and formulation of World Bank's
rural restructuring program,
290
as member of ANC Land Commission, 283
and wealth tax, 285–86
and workshop on Land Question,
282
Kobe University, *187,* 188
Koizumi, Jun'ichiro, 203
Korea, 278, 326, 327
Kyoto Imperial University, 172
employers of graduates of law
schools of, *187,* 188
graduates from, in bureaucracy,
181, *182*
graduates from, in politics, 175
and judiciary elite, 191–92
and legal academia, elite in, *194,*
195

Labyrinths of Power (Smith), 227
Landi, Oscar, 259
Latin America. *See* Liberalism in
Latin America

Laumann, Edward O., 223
Law
    as bounded and unified profes-
        sion, 80
    and business law and transforming
        foreign institutions, 5
    and changes in, having own
        momentum, 321
    as key authority for legitimating
        state and economy, 4–5
    modern, 65–90
    natural, 68, 71
    need to go beyond institutions and
        reform to understand position
        of, 3
    and secularized versions of univer-
        sal principles, 69
    technical, 7
    transnational, 17, 19, 31nn. 5, 6
    and understanding why it is what
        it is, 312
Law and development movement
    criticisms of original taken almost
        as part of official account, 320
    and critiques of U.S. cultural
        imperialism, 279–80
    and cultural diffusion model and
        transporting legal systems, 279
    and efforts and money spent in
        early 1990s, 278–81, 299n. 1
    failure of, in 1960s and 1970s, 1–2
    and incorporation and hybridity
        in 1990s, 281
    and legal transfer's history, 280
    and liberalism in Latin America,
        139
    and local actors shaping reception
        of law, 280–81
    new, almost without critics today,
        331
    and use to empower local elites
        and U.S. influence, 320

Lawyers Committee for Human
    Rights, and limitations of
    projects promoting judicial
    review, 2
Legal orthodoxy, new, 96–97, 306–33
    and academic study of legal
        processes, 331
    and "description as prescription,"
        311–12
    and drawing on various kinds of
        social capital, 326–27
    fits U.S. model of production of
        law and rules, 315
    and formation of groups around
        issues such as human rights,
        violence against women, and
        environment, 314–15
    and globalization as competition
        in laws and approaches to state
        and governance, 308, 319, 327
    and "governance," 311, 322–23
    individuals involved in discussion
        relative to, 309–10
    and interest of social science disci-
        plines, 311
    and international capital, 313
    and international strategies and
        relationship with different fields
        of state power, 307, 327–29
    and law as setting key terms of
        legitimacy, 307
    and legitimating through aca-
        demic theories, 306
    and national credibility essential
        for providing legitimacy, 321
    and national rules central to inter-
        national rules, 307
    and need to examine actors, 331
    and reasons for lack of attention to
        social construction of rules, 312
    and rule of law as export of U.S.
        product, 306, 307–8, 327

and rules cannot be separated
   from circumstance of their creation, 307
and state power, 326–27
and uninspected belief in "universals" based in national histories,
   310–11
See also Rule of law; Rules, legal
Legal reforms, 1
Legal systems, modern
   arising concomitantly with nation-
      state, 68
   based on universalistic and ratio-
      nal principles, 66, 69, 71–72
   and ceremony, 80–81
   and citing of cases under different
      sovereignty, 75
   and consistency, search for, 86–87
   and contemporary sociological
      institutionalism, 67
   coordinating function of, 88
   decoupling from ordinary social
      reality, 81–83
   derived from Catholic Church,
      67–68
   and diffusion and expansion of
      universal principles, 72, 73,
      74–79
   as distinguished from mundane
      organization, 80–81
   and exchange of laws, rules, and
      legal discourse, 74–76
   and existence of integrated and
      rationalized cosmos, 74, 83–88
   and expanding jurisdiction of
      legalized rule systems, 78–79
   and expansion, drive to, 87–88
   and family issues, 77–78
   and isomorphism among different
      nations, 76–79
   and justice of system vs. personal
      outcomes, 85–86

and nation-state system, 69–71
and resource capacity, 72–73
rest on exogenous cultural
   assumptions, 68, 72
and restrictions on determining
   truth, 83
and ritualized enactment of law,
   74, 79–83
rooted in sovereignty of nation-
   state, 71
and scientific progress of the law,
   84
See also Organizations vs. legal
   system, modern; Universal
   principles and modern legal
   systems
Lemkin, Raphael, 47, 58n. 13
Lev, Daniel, 328–29
Liberal Democratic Party of Japan,
   163
Liberalism in Latin America, 139–59,
   322
   and agrarian reform in 1950s and
      1960s, 150–51
   and authoritarianism in 1950s and
      1960s and its legacy, 152–54,
      156–57
   and cold war, 155, 174–75
   and constitutional transformation
      in 1940s, 150
   and corruption and public scan-
      dal, 157–58
   and Creole rule, 143–45
   and deregulation and privatization
      and lack of legal rules, 157
   and economic and political crises
      of 1920s and 1930s, 149–50
   and economic debts and pressures
      to restructure, 156
   and 1800s, first half, and dilemma
      of guarantees of both freedom
      and stability, 144–46

Liberalism in Latin America
    (*continued*)
    and 1800s, mid, and calls for cen-
        tralized executive-dominated
        politics, 145
    and 1800s, second half, and aban-
        donment of freedom for stabil-
        ity and economic well-being,
        146–48
    and Enlightenment as panacea,
        142–43
    and internationalization of rule of
        law, 6, 139–41, 142, 150, 158–59
    and lack of liberal heritage, 142
    and legitimacy and law, 139, 140,
        158
    and neoliberalism, 141, 157
    and new democrats of 1980s, 156
    and peasant society mobilization
        to popular sovereignty, 144
    and populism, 150–54
    and property rights and citizen-
        ship, 140–41
    and public freedoms restrictions in
        early 1900s, 147, 148–49
    and public power suffocating pri-
        vate initiative and electoral
        democracy, 142
    and purely external factors to
        account for problems, 142
    and tutored exports of 1980s, 156
    and use of law in late 1900s to
        uphold private rights but deny
        freedom in public realm, 148
    and weakness of judiciary, 156
Life careers, 216–19
Lomnitz, Larissa Adler, 7–8, 323–24,
    326
    model of structure of relation-
        ships, 212–13
    and three-generational family
        group unit of solidarity, 232

López Ayllón, Sergio, 245, 333n. 8
López Pumarejo, Alfonso, 149
López Rega, José, 252, 271n. 4

Malaysia, 328–29
Malvinas/Falklands War, 250–51
Mandela, Nelson, 297–98
Manin, Bernard, 268
Markets, 4, 105, 107
    containment of, 97–98, 100
    flexibility of, 114
    usefulness as arbiter, 101–2, 120, 131
    See also Economic institutions
Marx, Karl, 312
Mass production, 105
Mathews, Jessica, 16, 27
Media and courts in Argentina, 249,
    252, 257, 259
    and continuous exposure, 270–71
    and creation of scandal, 263, 265
    and first appearance as effective
        means of access, 262–63
    and media "public sentences" or
        "media justice," 263–64, 265
    See also Argentina and discovery of
        law
Medievalism, new, 15, 17, 30n. 1
Méndez, Juan, 10n. 3
Menem, Carlos, 157–58, 330
Mexico, 8, 148, 153
    and Cárdenista legacy, 151–52
    and Chiapas region "shopping" in
        global market, 324–25
    and globalization opening interna-
        tional market, 241, 246
    and membership in GATT, 240
    and political system of 1800s, 146,
        147
    and rule of law, 141
Mexico, practice of law in, 209–47
    and academia, employment in, 230
    and *apertura económica* (economic

opening) of 1986 and growing importance of economists, 240, 241–42

basis in Napoleonic Code rather than Anglo-Saxon law, 222

basis in written constitution, 222, 223

and "the Chicago boys" networks, 210, 245

and consulting specialists, 236–37

and corruption, 237–39, 244

and employment in private sector, 228–29

and employment in public sector, 226–28, 234

and family firms working in international business, 229

and foreign firms contracting with Mexican firms for sake of contacts, 237

and foreign investment and exportation law, 240

as formalistic rather than pragmatic, 222

and international practice, 239–43

and international strategies, 323–24, 333n. 8

and isolation of Mexico up until 1975, 239–40

and legal training, 222–26

and Lomnitz model of structure of relationships, 212–13

and middle-class traditional sectors defending interests against technocratic elite, 246

and NAFTA, 241

and numbers and production of lawyers, 214–15

and personal relations vs. technical law, 209, 242

and postgraduate training in foreign universities, 243, 245

and private universities, 228, 235, 242

and professional ethics questions, 238–39

and ratification of conventions on private international law, 240

and recruitment into labor market, 232–35

and rise of economists in politics over lawyers, 228

and role of courts, 209

and rule of law vs. relational capital in Mexico, 210, 211, 244

and social networks, 8, 210, 212–14, 230–32, 233–34

and social relations in normal practice, 210, 235–37, 244

and state apparatus closing doors to middle-class professionals, 241, 246

and technocratic elite, new legal, 7, 209, 227, 241–42, 245

and three-generational family group, 232

and weathering of economic crises and rising inequality, 324

whether imported expertise will help or exacerbate divisions of, 210

See also National University of Mexico (UNAM)

Meyer, John, 4, 5, 41, 321–22

Military strategy, 78

Mills, C. Wright, 162–63, 169, 173–74, 178–79, 189, 190

Minc, Alain, 265

Miyazawa, Setsuo, 6, 325–26

Model Rules of International Arbitration and Model Law on International Arbitration, 309

Modern law and legal systems. See Legal systems, modern

Money, management of, 118–19
Montesinos, Vladimiro, 158
Morelos, Father, 144
Movsesian, Mark, 30n. 1
Mujeres por la Vida, 56
Multilateral Investment Agreement, 310, 333n. 6

Nadelmann, Ethan, 58
Napoleon, 143
National Conference on Affirmative Action, 285–86
National palace wars, 313
National Party of South Africa, 293
National Revolutionary Party (PNR)/Party of the Mexican Revolution (PRM), 151
National University of Mexico (UNAM), 8, 209, 215
  and academic life career, 216–17
  basic program of training, 223, 224, 244
  contrasted with private universities, 228
  and family income of students entering, 221
  and fieldwork experience or pasantía, 225
  increased demand for admission to, 222, 222
  and Institute of Juridical Studies, 219, 230
  and lack of training of technocratic elite or in transcultural arena, 235, 242, 243
  and life careers, 216–19
  multiple functions of, 215–16
  and occupational distribution of 1990 graduates, 235, 236
  and political life career, 217–18
  and professional life career, 217

  and professors also practicing professionals, 217
  and recent fading of prominence of graduates from in politics, 228
  social and status origins of students of, 220–22, 232–33
  social network building among students of, 218–19, 230
  and taking stand in public affairs, 217–18
  and training following postrevolutionary nationalistic ideology, 240
  as training ground for new state elites, 209, 215, 227–28
  and training of lawyers, 222–26
Nation-state
  and centrism debates of 1970s, 14
  conceptual framework of, 14–15
  as creator of law, 68
  and declarations of universal human rights, 69
  decline as basic organizing unit of domestic and international life, 13–14
  disaggregated, 3, 12, 15–16, 28, 30n. 2
  and dual weakening of supranationalism and regional economics, 119
  expansion of, 70
  global diffusion of form of, 4
  and governance by cultural assumptions derived from religious principles, 67
  and government networks, 18–19
  as interdependent with non-nation-state actors, 26–27
  and legal systems arising concomitantly, 68

as primary actor in international system, 27–28
and society, 69–70
and sovereignty, 69
and transnationalism, 21–22, 32n. 13
Natural law, 68, 71, 89–90n. 3
Nestedness, 122–28
and change from national toward spatial, 122, 123
and international and subnational levels, 124
more spatial of institutional arrangements, 124, 126, 127, 128
and national sources of competition more complex, 125–26
and no single authority able to regulate, 124
and parts of system more interdependent, 128
as scenario of future economic development, 130–31
Networks
dense localized, in Japan, 126
economic, 121
government, 18–19
human rights, and NGOs, 39, 40
social, as basis of relational capital, 211–12
See also Social networks; Transnational advocacy networks
Njobe, Bongiwe, 282
Nongovernmental organizations (NGOs), 2–3, 317
activities of, 42, 57nn. 4, 5
as actors in international system, 13
as based in developed world, 55
bringing greater diversity of viewpoints and information, 57
and building of legal norms, 42–49

and civic rather than corporate actors, 24
facilitating human rights litigation, 52–53
funding of, 55, 59n. 20
global expansion of, 70
and human rights, 40, 47–49
and international legal rules, 38
lack of internal democracy within, 55
and new legal orthodoxy, 314
as nonstate actors, 16
and persuasion, 45–46
role in United Nations, 40
and shift from European to U.S. mode of governance, 319
and transnational advocacy networks, 37, 39–41
See also Transnational advocacy networks
Noriega y Escobedo (law firm), 229
Norms in international relations, 38
definition of, 41
empowering and exclusionary effects of, 56
importing and exporting, 321–22
which are effective transnationally and cross-culturally, 54–55
North American Free Trade Agreement (NAFTA), 129, 241, 310
Nye, Joseph, 20–21, 23, 31n. 9, 31–32n. 12

Olsen, Douglas, 58–59n. 16
Organization of American States (OAS), 45
Organization of the Supreme Courts of the Americas, 18
Organizations vs. legal system, modern, 73
and association with universal principles, 73, 79

Organizations vs. legal system,
    modern (*continued*)
  and consistency, 87
  and employment of scientific
    methods, 84
  and linking to universalistic cul-
    tural accounts, 82
  as mundane compared to legal sys-
    tem, 80–81
  and rationality, 85
  See also Legal systems, modern
Otsuka, Hiroshi, 6, 325–26

Partido Revolucionario Institutional
    (PRI), 151, 325
Peña Irala, Américo, 52–53
Pérez-Lisaur, Marisol, 232
Perón, Juan, 150
Peru, 141, 158
Picciotto, Sol, 30n. 2
Pinochet, Augusto, 155
Polanyi, Karl, 97, 102, 131, 212, 244
Political science, 38
Populism in Latin America, 150–54
Portales, Diego, 145
Power
  asymmetries, hidden, 4
  and economic intervention, 112–13
Prescriptive discourse, 311
Private international law, 13
Public international law, 12, 13, 20
Punto Final Law, 252, 271n. 7
Putnam, Robert, 24

Rape laws, 75
Rationalism, 68, 69
  expanded and invented nature of,
    85
  and rationality principle and eco-
    nomic history, 101, 117
  See also Universal principles and
    modern legal systems

Reed, Steven R., 180
Reform. *See* Judicial reform
"Régulation Theory," 115, 117
Reichman, Nancy, 319
Religious principles and legal sys-
    tems, 4, 67–68, 70, 321
Richardson, Bradley, 174
Riles, Annelise, 311, 318
"Rise of World Constitutionalism,
    The" (Ackerman), 278
Risse-Kappen, Thomas, 23, 27
Roca, Julio A., 147
Rokumoto, Kahei, 195
Rosenau, James, 21, 30n. 1
Rubin, Robert, 309
Rule of law, 1, 2–3, 141
  and Argentine judiciary, 251, 329
  employment of, globally legiti-
    mated in constitutions, 296
  exportation of, to empower local
    elites and U.S. influence, 322
  and export of U.S. product, 5,
    307–9, 332n. 3
  globalization of, 277–78
  internationalization as threat to, in
    Latin America, 6, 139–40, 158–59
  in Japan, 186
  and justice, 67
  in Latin America, 6, 139–42, 150,
    158–59, 322–23
  and Malaysia, 328–29
  money spent on projects of, in
    1990s, 278
  as necessity for economic reform
    in Argentina, 267–68
  vs. relational capital in Mexico,
    210, 211, 244
  social construction of, 4
  and South African Constitution,
    281
  See also Law and development
    movement

Rules, legal
  cannot be separated from circumstances of their creation, 307
  and disaggregated states, 28–29
  flows of, across boundaries of nominal sovereignty, 75–76
  and human rights activism, 39
  nation central to production of international, 307
  social construction of, 39, 54–58, 311–13
  and social systems of production, 99
  transnationalism and enforcement of, 29
  transnational, require study of U.S. state power, 307
  and women's activism, 39
Russett, Bruce, 23

Sachs, Albie, 287
Sachs, Jeffrey, 309
Salazar, Rodrigo, 7–8, 323–24, 326
Salinas de Gortari, Carlos, 157
Santo Domingo, 144, 159n. 2
Santos, Boaventura de Sousa, 314
Save the Children Fund, 47
Scholars
  new generation of, including women and minorities, in late 1980s and 1990s, 23–24
  and overinvestment in scientific or moral authority, 320
  of this book as pioneers in governance and rule of law issues, 323
Schreuer, Christoph, 30n. 2
Schweitz, Martha, 42
Secularized version of wider culture, and nation-state, 69
Sikkink, Kathryn, 4, 5, 65, 153, 314
  and description that becomes prescription, 317

essay of, as prescriptive discourse close to traditional legal scholarship, 315
  and Slaughter, 317–18
Silbey, Susan, 321
Simon, Herbert, 101–2
Slaughter, Anne-Marie, 3, 4–5, 37, 95, 316–17, 323
  and disaggregating state, 314–15
  essay of, as prescriptive discourse close to traditional legal scholarship, 315
  and new orthodoxy, 318
  and new representation of universals, 316
  and Sikkink, 317–18
Smith, Peter, 227, 230, 232
Smulovitz, Catalina, 8–9, 329–30
Snow, David, 58n. 6
Social
  capital, 326–27
  construction, 38–39
  science disciplines and interest in law, 311
Socialization to international law, 50
Social networks
  as basis of relational capital, 211–12
  in Mexico, 8, 210, 212–14, 230–32, 233–34
  and relations between sectors, 213–14, 245, 246
Society, 70
Sociology
  and institutionalism, 67
  of law, 72
  and social networks, 211–12
Somoza, Anastasio, 154
Sorimachi, Masao, 196–97
South Africa, land reform, and constitution making, 9, 276–77, 281–301

South Africa, land reform, and con-
    stitution making (*continued*)
and Advisory Commission on
    Land Allocation, 283
and argument between govern-
    ment and ANC over constitu-
    tional property clause in 1993,
    290–91
and Bill of Rights, 281–82, 283,
    287–88, 291, 292–93
and CALS conference on possible
    effect of right to property, 287
and Constitutional Court and
    decision regarding 1996 Consti-
    tution property clause, 294–95
and Constitution of 1993, interim,
    292
and Constitution of 1996, 292–97
and Democratic Party right to
    property proposal, 285
and "Economy and Land" section
    of Constitutional Guidelines,
    282–83
and framing of property question
    by international options, 276,
    295
and Freedom Charter of 1955,
    282
and hybridity, conditions that
    allowed, 297–98
and hybridized outcomes, 277, 295,
    296
and international norms, 297–98
and keeping alive alternative possi-
    bilities while employing globally
    legitimate "rules," 296
and Land and Agricultural Policy
    Centre (LAPC), 289
and Lands Act of 1913, 286
and Lands Claims Commissions
    and Land Claims Court, 287,
    288, 292, 293

and mass protests at constitutional
    negotiations, 291, 301n. 19
and negotiation and serendipity,
    298
and participation in international
    "community" of jurisprudence
    not solving local problems,
    276–77
and politics of constitution mak-
    ing bounded on both sides,
    295
and property clause of 1996 Con-
    stitution, 293–95
and protection of wealth of
    apartheid's beneficiaries, 298
and restitution of property taken
    under apartheid, 285, 290, 298
and rural restructuring program
    devised by World Bank, 290
and Swaziland seminar, 289
and Urban Foundation (UF)
    engagement, 288, 289
and wealth tax to fund land redis-
    tribution, 285–86
and Workshop on Land Rights
    and the Constitution, 293
and World Bank's engagement
    over land reform, 288–90, 301n.
    17
See also African National Congress
    (ANC)
South African Agricultural Union,
    293
South African Law Commission,
    284–85
Sovereignty, 65, 69
Sovereignty at Bay (Vernon), 24
State. See Nation-state
Steiner, Henry, 19, 31n. 6
Sunstein, Cass, 41
Supreme courts, 3, 12, 29
Suzuki, Zenko, 190

Tate, Neal, 266
Technical law, 7
Technocrats (*técnicos*), 7, 209, 227,
    241–42, 245, 246
Third-World Network, 289
Thomas, George M., 54
Tokyo Imperial University, 6–7
Torture, 48, 49, 51–52
Torture Convention, 48
Trachtman, Joel, 17, 31n. 3
Tradition, as outcome of yesterday's
    interactions, 112
Transgovernmental interactions,
    20–21
Transnational advocacy networks, 4,
    5, 16, 37–59
  appeal of, 318
  as communicative structures and
    political spaces, 55–56, 59n. 22
  and compliance with international
    law, 49–53
  and convincing actors to impose
    sanctions to enforce interna-
    tional law, 53–54
  and creation of issues and aware-
    ness, 43–44
  definition of, 38
  divisions and imperfections
    within, 55
  and drafting legal rules, 46–49
  environmental, and multilateral
    banks, 54
  and facilitating international liti-
    gation, 52–53
  and "framing," 42–43, 55, 58n. 6
  and means of building legal
    norms, 42–49
  and new international norms,
    41
  and new legal orthodoxy, 314
  and north/south framing, 55
  and persuasion through providing

  information and testimony,
    45–46
  and publicizing existence of inter-
    national legal norms, 50–51
  and publicizing rule-breaking
    behavior, 51–52
  and social construction of legal
    rules, 37–59
  and strategic social construction,
    38–39
Transnational corporations (TNCs)
  and dependency on strong state, 27
  and generation of their own law, 17
  as nonstate actors, 16–17
  as part of international system, 13
Transnationalism
  as cyclical process, 19, 26
  defined via actors or nature of
    activity, 20
  and external factors for its resur-
    gence in 1990s, 22–24
  and information technology revo-
    lution, 23, 27
  and internal factors for its resur-
    gence in 1990s, 24–26
  and major powers politics, 22–23
  and peace and liberal democracy,
    23
  and restructuring and reinventing
    government, 23–24
  role of "substate" or governmental
    actors in, 20–21
  round of, from 1950s to 1970s,
    19–22
  and shared communities, 26, 27, 29
  society of, 22
  and transgovernmental interac-
    tions, 20–21
  as trend rather than cyclical
    process, 26
  See also Globalization
Transnational law, 17, 19, 31nn. 5, 6

*Transnational Relations and World
    Politics* (Keohane and Nye),
    20–21
Trubek, David, 314–15, 332n. 3
Trust, 112

Umlas, Elizabeth, 59n. 22
UN Charter
    Art. 2(4) on refraining from use of
        force, 13
    and human rights declarations,
        47–48
United Nations, 23–24, 40
United Nations Commission for
    International Trade Law
    (UNCITRAL), 309
United States
    and diffusions of mass production
        and consumption to Europe
        and Japan, 99
    and establishment of Pax Ameri-
        cana after World War II, 98, 99
    export from, to other countries, 5,
        96, 307–9, 322, 332n. 3
    and faculties of law developing
        new legal technologies oriented
        to U.S., 5
    federal courts and adjudication of
        human rights abuse cases, 52–53
    law and orientation toward, of for-
        eign faculties of law, 5
    law as pragmatic with common
        law being developed constantly,
        222–23
    and modeling of Latin American
        law system, 139
    model of market forces, 4
    rules of, key to understanding
        transnational rules, 307
    and sanctions against states com-
        mitting human rights abuses,
        43–44

and suffrage development in
    1800s, 147
university degree and career in
    south, 2, 326
Universal Declaration of Human
    Rights, 48, 58–59n. 16
Universal principles and modern
    legal systems, 68, 69, 72
    diffusion and expansion of, 73,
        74–79
    and exchange of laws, rules, and
        legal discourse, 74–76
    and existence of integrated and
        rationalized cosmos, 74, 83–88
    and national laws, 4
    and organizations, 73
    and penetration of many levels of
        society, 73
    and ritualized enactment of law,
        74, 79–83
University of Tokyo (Tokyo Imperial
    University), 6, 7, 164–73,
    211
    and absorption of Ministry Law
        School, 168
    becomes Imperial University in
        1886, 168
    and business positions, 188–90
    "Decree on," and purpose to train
        students for government agen-
        cies, 168–69
    employers of graduates of law fac-
        ulty of, 186–88, *187*
    employment of its graduates,
        169–70
    establishment of, 164
    faster promotion of graduates of,
        182
    and founding of Kyoto Imperial
        University, 172
    and *gakureki shugi* or education-
        based elitism, 170

graduates of, in bureaucracy,
178–88, *182*, *183*
graduates of, in politics and slowly
declining influence, 174–78
and judiciary positions, 190–93
and legal academia positions,
193–95, *194*
and prestige of legal profession
after World War II, 181
reproduction of bureaucratic elite
by legal education at, 186
requirements to enter, 168
and stratification of Japanese society, 201–2
and student ranking of possible
career paths, 180–81
and subjects taught by Faculty of
Law, 1974–75, *171–72*
and subjects taught in Department
of Law in 1893, 170, *171–72*, 172
summary conclusions of dominance of, 195–96
as superior national university, 188
and supervision of private schools,
169
See also Kyoto Imperial University

Vagts, Detlev, 19, 31n. 6
Vallinder, Torbjorn, 272n. 10
Vargas, Getulio, 150
Venezuela, 141, 153
Vernon, Raymond, 24, 32n. 14
Violence against women, 4, 37, 43–45
and development of issues in local
action, 56
in India, 51–52

Wallerstein, Immanuel, 311
Waltz, Kenneth, 50
Werner, Jacques, 308–9
Westphalian state system of 1648, 26

Witches, 85–86
Women
and female genital mutilation,
42–43, 45, 58nn. 8, 9
and gender discrimination lawsuit
of Ann Hopkins, 84
isomorphism regarding role of,
78
networks of, and legal rules, 39
violence against (*see* Violence
against women)
Women's rights
and international law and privileging lawyers, 56
and NGOs, 40, 48–49
publicizing norms of, 50–51
World Bank
and criticism of judicial reform
programs, 3
and criticisms and procedural
changes, 2
and engagement with South Africa
over land reform, 288–90, 301n.
17
and environmental advocacy networks, 54
and Inspection Panels, 2
and models of new state orthodoxy, 139
and necessity of relevant and
efficient state, 131
and programs to strengthen rule of
law, 1, 11
World Trade Organization, 2

Yaguchi, Koichi, 192
Yrigoyen, President, 149

Zaibatsu, 188
Zoku, 163
Zolo, Danilo, 269